COMPLETE SECONDARY CHORAL MUSIC GUIDE

Donald W. Roach

Professor of Music Education
Western Illinois University
Macomb, Illinois

PARKER PUBLISHING COMPANY
West Nyack, New York 10995

Library of Congress Cataloging-in-Publication Data

Roach, Donald W.
  Complete secondary choral music guide / Donald W. Roach.
    p. cm.

  Includes bibliographical references.
  ISBN 0-13-162538-1
  1. Choirs (Music) 2. Choral singing—Juvenile—Instruction and
study. 3. Conducting, Choral. I. Title.
MT88.R68 1989
782.5—dc20   89–48386
                                                          CIP
                                                          MN

ISBN 0-13-162538-1

PARKER PUBLISHING COMPANY
BUSINESS & PROFESSIONAL DIVISION
A division of Simon & Schuster
West Nyack, New York 10995

PRINTED IN THE UNITED STATES OF AMERICA

Acknowledgments

A book like *Complete Secondary Choral Music Guide* evolves from a lifetime of choral music singing and teaching. I extend my sincere appreciation to my high school choral director and my church choir director, both of whom inspired me to pursue a career in music. I also wish to thank all my school and university students who have broadened my experience in the choral field. I also appreciate all the encouragement for this project from my professional colleagues at Western Illinois University and in the American Choral Directors Association. Lastly, I express my gratitude to my wife, Netta, for her patience and encouragement during the writing of this book. Hopefully, many directors and aspiring choral directors will benefit from this endeavor.

About the Author

Donald W. Roach, Ed. D., is Professor of Music Education at Western Illinois University, Macomb. He has taught school, church, university, and community choruses over a period of twenty-five years in Pennsylvania, Florida, and Illinois. Dr. Roach has presented sessions at national, division, and state conventions of the American Choral Directors Association and Music Educators National Conference. He has served on the Executive Board of the Illinois ACDA for the past six years. He has numerous choral compositions published and has served as guest conductor and adjudicator at choral festivals and contests.

Dr. Roach is the compiler-editor of *Music for Children's Choirs: A Selective and Graded Listing,* published in 1977 by the Music Educators National Conference, Reston, Virginia. In 1987 Choristers Guild of Garland, Texas, published his *Handbook for Children's and Youth Choir Directors* which is oriented toward church choir directors.

Among his other writings are articles on choral music, general music, and research that have appeared in *The Choral Journal, Choristers Guild Letters, American Music Teacher, Music Educators Journal, Journal of Research in Music Education,* and the *Bulletin for the Council for Research in Music Education.* He has also reviewed books and dissertations for some of these journals.

Currently Dr. Roach teaches Choral Literature and Methods, Elementary and Secondary Methods courses, and supervises the music student teaching program at Western Illinois University.

Preface

The purpose of the *Complete Secondary Choral Music Guide* is to help choral teachers and directors meet the stimulating challenges of training junior and senior high school choruses today. The choral movement has grown steadily over the years as more and more young people enter into the choral experience in schools. Curricular and social changes are requiring that choral directors train their young singers effectively in school settings so that they will possess training in an artistic medium of expression that will continue to serve them throughout their adult lives.

The school choral program really begins in the elementary school where early interest and singing skills are developed. This book is directed particularly to new and experienced inservice choral directors and those training to become teachers of choral music in junior and senior high schools. Practicality and comprehensiveness were important factors motivating its development.

For easy use, the *Guide* is organized into four major parts. Part I, "Administration of Junior and Senior High School Choruses," covers the administrative aspects of organizing and directing secondary choruses. Philosophy, curriculum, director qualifications, facilities, equipment, budget, apparel, student officers, accompanists, copyright law, teacher relations, and planning social events are considered. The junior high singer is realistically presented with regard to psychological problems, boy changing voice, voice testing and seating, scheduling, and performances. Senior high recruitment techniques are presented as well as auditions, ranges, seating, scheduling small and large ensembles, and voice classes.

Part II, "The Conductor and the Choral Score," provides the director with basic information to be an effective interpreter and conductor of choral music. The five traditional style periods (Renaissance, Baroque, Classic, Romantic, Twentieth Century) are presented in depth with major choral composers represented with titles of representative choral literature. Chapter 6 provides useful criteria for selection of choral repertoire for junior and senior high. Balance and variety of repertoire is suggested along with an approach to building a reference file. Effective ways to study the choral score in terms of its form, melody, rhythm, harmony, texture, dynamics, and text are presented.

Part III, "Developing Choral Musicianship in Students," encompasses the technical aspects of vocal techniques, English and Latin choral diction, and various sight-reading techniques which a choral director may employ with choruses. Additional sources are suggested for developing these choral musicianship skills. The voice mechanism, posture, breathing, intonation, balance, dynamics, and voice resonance are discussed.

Part IV, "Planning Rehearsals and Performances," explores many practical and proven means for organizing effective rehearsals with junior and senior high school choruses. Introducing a new choral work, meaningful repetition in rehearsals, rehearsing with instruments, and preparing extended choral works are discussed. Two sample rehearsal plans are provided, one for junior high level, and one for senior high. The closing chapter focuses on performing at concerts, festivals, and contests. Program-building, preconcert planning, staging, concert manners, and a concert checklist are presented. The strengths and weaknesses of contests and festivals are discussed. Attention is also given to the value of working under guest choral conductors, commissioning a choral work, exchange concerts and tours, and singing at professional meetings.

The Appendixes include selected lists of music for Two- and Three-Part Treble Chorus, Junior High Mixed Chorus, Senior High Mixed Chorus, Male Chorus, Show Choir, and Junior High and Senior High Choral Collections and Extended Choral Works. Vocal techniques and sight singing sources are presented, as well as music theater resources. Choral equipment and instrument sources include choir robes, risers, chairs, storage cabinets, folios, handbell manufacturers, Orff instruments sources, recorders, guitars, autoharps, percussion instruments, and choir pins and certificates. Professional choral organizations and journals are also listed as well as a current directory of choral publishers.

The Bibliography includes many resources to further assist the junior and senior high school choral director. Included are sources on choir organization and administration, vocal training and music teaching, the boy's changing voice, conducting techniques, and choral music repertoire and interpretation.

It is my hope that this book will provide significant help to both inservice choral teachers and those about to enter the choral teaching field. Much of the information provided will also prove valuable to directors of university, church, and community choirs.

Donald W. Roach
July 1989

Table of Contents

PART III

DEVELOPING CHORAL MUSICIANSHIP IN STUDENTS

PART ONE

ADMINISTRATION OF JUNIOR AND SENIOR HIGH SCHOOL CHORUSES

Chapter One

Managing Junior and Senior High School Choruses

Choral programs today occupy a significant position in the curricula of typical junior and senior high schools. This growth of interest in the choral art provides a challenge and stimulus to school choral directors. Curricular and social changes require choral directors to train their young singers effectively in school settings.

A PHILOSOPHIC BASIS FOR THE CHORAL PROGRAM

Choral singing is one of the oldest forms of music. It has its roots in the Middle Ages as church music evolved from mere chanting of texts to singing in parts. From the Renaissance to the present, a rich heritage of both sacred and secular choral literature has evolved.

The values of choral music study and performance in the junior and senior high schools are many.

1. First, choral participation provides for the development of aesthetic sensitivity and the expressive values of music. Students' lives may be enriched and refined by contact, study, and performance of choral music. Developing the sense for beauty in the arts is a major task of choral music education.

2. Since music is an integral and significant part of man's culture, it is the school's responsibility to assist young people to become more intelligent consumers of music. Through participation in the choral program, students' individual tastes may be promoted and our cultural heritage transmitted.

3. Choral music has significant content to be mastered academically. In addition to vocal and sight singing skills, knowledge of styles, composers, theory, and general musicianship are stressed.

4. Choral singing also contributes to physical well being. Correct posture and proper breathing techniques must be emphasized to develop a well-trained chorus.

5. Choral singing also serves as a wholesome outlet and expression of individual emotions. Singing, unlike communicative speaking, is a unique artistic means for individuals to express themselves. Music thus serves as an emotional outlet for self-expression and can help to release tension and frustration so common in today's society.

6. Choral participation can help develop a sense of discipline and responsibility in students. Effective choral singing requires cooperation to achieve a common end.

7. Choral organizations provide a social vehicle whereby students may fulfill their need to belong to a group. Adolescents' natural desire to belong to a group results in satisfaction and acceptance by peers. Through cooperative group endeavor the chorus provides opportunity for democratic attitudes and wholesome channeling of interests toward members of the opposite sex. Students in chorus take great pride in being identified with an outstanding music organization and often make many social adjustments through close association with their peers.

8. Choral participation may well promote a vocational or avocational interest in music. A small percentage of school choral singers will elect music as a career area in performing, teaching, or related fields. After high school graduation, many singers will continue to participate in choral singing through the mediums of church choirs, college choirs, community choirs, and professional choruses.

DEVELOPING THE CHORAL CURRICULUM

Most subject areas in the schools have developed a curriculum for each grade-level course from junior high school through senior high school. Such guidelines are frequently missing for choral groups and classes. The choral curriculum is usually designed to meet the needs of students of a particular school, type of community, and the size of the student body. A choral curriculum implies (1) structuring of large and small choral ensembles and other vocal classes, (2) scheduling patterns for each group, (3) selecting the choral literature to be studied and performed, (4) developing vocal technique as it pertains to choral singing, (5) developing vocal sight singing skills, (6) scheduling public performances, and (7) evaluating both the students and the choral program.

At the junior high school level, large and small choral ensembles usually consist of

1. one or two mixed-voice choral groups. These may be scheduled daily or no less than three times a week.
2. one girl's chorus meeting three to five times a week.
3. one boy's chorus meeting three to five times a week.
4. several small mixed, girl's, and boy's ensembles meeting at least once or twice weekly, preferably during school time with the music instructor. The large ensembles in the junior high school should present three to five performances each year for parents, peers, and the community. The small ensembles may perform at these concerts and other less formal community and school events. In some schools small ensembles do not regularly meet the entire year, but are organized six or eight weeks prior to music contests in order to participate in the small ensemble and solo events.

At the senior high school level, large and small choral ensembles usually consist of

1. one or two mixed voice groups meeting daily. One of these choral groups may be a training chorus made up of students from grades nine and ten and newly recruited upper-class singers. The other chorus will be the more select concert choir with more experienced singers. Both choral groups should meet daily because of increased performance demands at the senior high school level.
2. one girl's chorus which meets daily. There are frequently more girls than boys readily available to sing and a treble group makes a welcome addition to the total choral program.
3. one boy's chorus which meets daily. This may be made up of boys from both mixed chorus groups, as well as other boys who desire a male chorus singing experience.
4. smaller groups which may be scheduled twice weekly or one double period after school. These typically include madrigal or chamber singers, jazz/show choir, girls' sextet, boys' octet, etc. These small ensembles should be available by audition to students.
5. A voice class may be available in some senior high schools for those choral students who can benefit from class voice instruction. This class may meet two or three times a week. In some schools a number of students are studying voice privately.

In the senior high school, academic credit should be awarded for music study on the same basis as for comparable courses. Grades earned in music courses should be considered in determining grade-point averages and class rankings of students on the same basis as grades in comparable courses. Many chorus directors make membership in a larger choral ensemble mandatory to belonging to a small ensemble such as madrigal group or jazz/show choir. It is in the large ensemble that students receive the vocal and sight singing training, as well as exposure to a comprehensive choral repertoire.

At both the junior and senior high school levels a systematic choral curriculum must be developed for each choral group to provide for growth in vocal skills, sight singing skills, and knowledge of all types and styles of choral literature.

The literature may include

1. choral masterpieces by composers of the Renaissance, Baroque, Classic, Romantic, and Twentieth-Century style periods of both a sacred and secular type
2. folk song, carol, and spiritual arrangements
3. madrigal music and chamber choir literature
4. broadway musical tunes and medleys (possibly a performance of an entire musical some years)
5. lighter pop arrangements suitable for large ensembles and jazz/show choir
6. choral suites and extended works such as cantatas, gloria's, requiem's, masses, and operatic choral pieces.

At the senior high school-level courses in theory or musicianship, music appreciation, guitar, and related arts may be offered along with the instrumental music offerings of band and orchestra.

Choral directors at both junior and senior high school levels may be confronted with flexible modular scheduling and with a six-, seven-, or eight-period day. With increased emphasis on the academic subjects, an extended school day with eight periods may be required for students to be able to elect one or two music groups. The attitude of the administration is very pertinent to successful scheduling of choral groups. Choral groups cut across grade levels. If courses with only one section are scheduled against the chorus period, some students who need the other course will not be able to schedule chorus. The choral director must be knowledgeable with the rest of the schedule and be willing to discuss all possibilities with administrators. Figure 1–1 illustrates an ideal high school choral teaching schedule.

It is wise to work for curricular acceptance of the choral program. Where it is outside the schedule, work to have it placed in the school day schedule. Strive to have

8:30	Free Period (clerical, solos, duets, trios, etc.)
9:30	Girl's Chorus
10:30	Concert Choir
11:30	Boy's Chorus
12:30	Lunch
1:00	Mixed Chorus (Training Chorus)
2:00	Voice Class (T–Th); Theory/Music Appreciation (M–W–F alternate years)
3:00	(After school) Madrigal, Jazz/Show Choir, Small Ensembles, Contest Small Groups

Figure 1–1 Ideal Senior High School Schedule

each large choral group meet daily and to be fully credited in order to stimulate a curricular, rather than extracurricular, image. Most administrators desire to have a strong choral program in the curriculum, one that can bring credit to the school. Chorus performances, as well as instrumental and sports events, are very much in the public eye. When the choral groups are well trained and present an inspiring concert, the administrator's, choral director's, and school's image are greatly enhanced.

How well the choral director is able to organize and implement the various activities of a choral program will determine the success of the program. Administrators who feel less than qualified to judge the choral director's musical competencies do feel competent to judge the choral director's organizational abilities. Careful long- and short-range planning is required. All performances must be scheduled on the school calendar, as free of conflicts as possible, prior to the start of the school year. Budgets and purchases must be submitted punctually. The two times for bargaining with administrators with regard to changes in scheduling of groups, director's salary, and choral budget are (1) when accepting a new position, and (2) when the choral department has become more successful.

The choral director will also need to evaluate the progress of students in the choral ensembles and classes. Individual attendance and punctuality at all rehearsals and performances is a major factor contributing to the success of each choral group and should weigh heavily in grading students. Attitude is another factor that is important to the group's functioning. Directors must develop an *esprit de corps*. Some students may have to be graded somewhat lower if attitudes are poor. The director may also evaluate students in choral groups by calling upon individual students to perform their parts at certain points in rehearsal. Also, written tests on music theory, vocal technique, diction, composers, and style periods may be administered to measure what students have learned.

The choral director, in evaluating the total choral curriculum, will need to periodically determine the effectiveness of the school's choral program. Questions that need to be answered include:

1. Are the numbers of students enrolled in the various choral groups satisfactory? Why or why not? Is expansion of offerings possible?
2. Are recruitment procedures adequate to maintain the continuity of the choral program? Is there a strong liaison between music teachers in elementary, junior high, and senior high?
3. Is the choral program providing for varying abilities of students through both large and small ensemble offerings?
4. Are the scheduling patterns for each choral group satisfactory?
5. Are existing facilities, equipment, and materials adequate?
6. Is the choral budget sufficient or must fund raising be conducted?
7. Does the choral program provide for contest participation by large groups, small groups, and solo events?
8. Does the program provide for festival participation of selected students and possibly an entire ensemble?

9. Are the number of performances scheduled yearly for each choral ensemble, about right, too little, or too excessive?
10. Are students receiving exposure and study of a wide variety of choral literature each year?
11. Are grading procedures adequate?
12. Does the choral program have strong support from administration, other teachers, students, and parents?

QUALIFICATIONS OF THE CHORAL DIRECTOR

The effectiveness of the school choral program lies almost totally upon the choral director. The desirable qualifications of the successful school choral director include:

1. a sound music training in vocal music and choral performance, conducting, music theory, and music history
2. a strong commitment to assist young people to grow both musically and socially
3. fundamental skill at the piano to vocalize students and to accompany the choral literature, as well as play individual parts singly and collectively. However, the director should not be tied to the piano keyboard and a student or adult accompanist should be utilized frequently.
4. extensive choral singing and chorus directing experience in high school, church, university, or community choral groups
5. a strong organizational and planning ability sufficient to administer the choral program
6. a working knowledge of psychological processes of working with junior and senior high school-level students in large groups and individually. This includes motivation and maintaining interest.
7. a thorough understanding of classroom management procedures to promote effective learning
8. a basic knowledge of choral literature appropriate to junior and senior high school level.

Not every musician can conduct school choruses. The director must be willing to approach students at their level of interest and skill. The director must seek the cooperation of principal, guidance counselor, parents, and the students themselves in developing a successful program. A choral curriculum must then be implemented which allows for systematic growth of the singers.

FACILITIES AND EQUIPMENT

The choral facilities for junior and senior high schools should contain a choral rehearsal room separate from the instrumental rehearsal room. The choral rehearsal room should contain 1800 square feet of floor space, with a ceiling at least 16 feet high and a double entry door. Each school should also have at least one ensemble rehearsal room of at least 350 square feet. The school should also contain several practice rooms for students enrolled in performing groups. Office space of at least 55 square feet and a telephone should be available for each music teacher. Such space should be adjacent to the rehearsal facility or instructural area so that the choral director may supervise the area.

In the junior high school a room should be available for teaching general music. This room is large enough to accommodate a class size of 25 to 30 students. It should have ample space for physical movement and storage space for texts and recorded materials, classroom instruments, and audio-visual equipment. In the senior high school, a similar room should be available for nonperformance classes such as theory/musician-ship, music appreciation/history, and related arts.

Both rehearsal rooms and class teaching rooms should be acoustically treated to provide appropriate sound dispersion and reverberation. Each room is acoustically isolated from the rest of the school and the vocal and instrumental areas are separated by an acoustical barrier or wall with a Sound Transmission Classification (STC) of 50 or more. Noise Criterion (NC) levels of lighting and ventilating systems should not exceed NC20 for the auditorium, NC25 for music classrooms and rehearsal rooms, and NC30 for studios and practice rooms. Each music classroom and rehearsal room should contain at least 32 square feet of chalkboard with permanent music staff lines and 24 square feet of corkboard for bulletin board display.

The music facilities (suite) should be immediately accessible to the auditorium stage. The stage is large and open and is adaptable to the varying needs of the per-forming arts. The auditorium is designed as a music performance space with good, ad-justable acoustics for music and speech requirements, stage lighting of at least 70 foot-candles, and adequate ventilation and lighting systems not to exceed a Noise Criterion of NC20.

The required equipment and materials for an effective choral program at junior and senior high school level includes the following:

1. a grand piano or quality upright at least 44 inches high for each choral class-room and rehearsal room (tuned at least twice yearly)
2. a grand piano for the stage-auditorium (tuned at least twice yearly)
3. a quality sound reproduction system, including reel to reel tape recorder and microphones, a stereo record player with high-quality amplifier and speakers, six pairs of headphones and a listening station, two cassette recorders, and a compact disc player
4. a library of music books, periodicals, recordings, filmstrips, films, and videotapes
5. a set of portable choral risers and acoustical shells
6. a library of choral music of at least 50 to 75 titles for each type of choral group, with at least 10 new titles for each group added each year
7. two or three choral collections for each large performing ensemble and each small ensemble in sufficient copies to allow one copy for each student

8. the library of choral music is sufficient size to provide a folder of music for each student in all choral groups

9. a complement of 80 or more choral robes and stoles for the major choral organizations in junior and senior high school. Blazers or tuxedos may substitute for robes.

10. filing cabinets or shelving to house the choral library in 8½ by 11 in. and filing boxes

11. folder cabinet for each major choral group. Each folder is numbered according to the shelf area and assigned to students accordingly.

12. choral music filing cards (available commercially)

13. Ten or more music stands for conductor and accompanying instrumentalists.[1]

It may well require six years or more to secure equipment and materials for all large and small choral ensembles. Justifying needs to administration is an on-going task and requires careful budgeting of school allotments, as well as additional fund-raising projects. Some of the previous budget items are one-time purchases, where others are purchased annually.

STORING AND FILING CHORAL MUSIC

There are several ways to organize school choral libraries. Some large school districts maintain a central choral (and instrumental) library of all the choral music owned by the district. Choral directors must then check out for a period of time those pieces they may wish to utilize. The strengths are that the music coordinator, who collects titles from directors and orders new music each year, can be efficient in preventing duplication of titles. The library grows rapidly since it serves a number of junior and senior high schools. This administrative system of choral music is often used by city school systems.

More common is the practice of directors procuring their own music and adding to a choral library housed in the individual school. It is best if music for all large and small ensembles be stored just adjacent to the choral room, perhaps in a separate facility. Regular choral octavos may be stored in commercially made storage boxes, either on shelves or in metal filing cabinets. Some directors prefer filing envelopes or file folders for individual octavos; however, large choruses, requiring 80 or more copies will almost necessitate the use of a box. (Available in several sizes from J. W. Pepper and Son and other companies, see Appendix P.) Larger choral works and collections will need to be stored on shelves.

Retrieving choral pieces and adding to the choral library requires some type of filing system. Some directors like to file music alphabetically by composer/arranger, and others file alphabetically by title. Some prefer to classify the music under such

---

[1]*The School Music Program: Description and Standards*, 2d ed. (Reston, Va.: Music Educators National Conference, 1986), 32–52.

categories as Mixed Chorus (SATB and divisi), Girls Chorus (SA, SSA, SSAA), and Boys Chorus (TB, TTB, TBB, TTBB). Some directors like to further divide the music into classifications as General, Christmas, Sacred, Secular, Folk/Spiritual, Madrigal/ Chamber Chorus, Jazz/Show Choir, and so on. As the school library grows, it is difficult to recommend any of these filing approaches since they require constant shifting of pieces in drawers or on shelves to place newly acquired octavos in their proper alphabetical order.

A more expedient manner to file choral music is to number each octavo from number one to the most recent octavo purchased. Thus, no shifting of pieces is required. However, this system, similar to current computer filing systems, requires making a card index file for the entire choral library. Each piece is alphabetized by (1) title, (2) composer/arranger, and (3) classification. There will be only one title and composer/arranger card; however, there may be two or more classification cards for the choral piece (SATB, Sacred, Christmas, Solos, Instruments, Accompanied or a Cappella). Choral octavos and larger works may thus be located by title, composer/arranger, and by several classifications. Doug Skerritt[2] and Bob Dingley[3] have outlined how to utilize computer programs for Commodore, Apple, and IBM Personal Computers to store and retrieve choral music. These articles in *The Choral Journal* provide excellent assistance to directors interested in computer filing of choral music. (See Fig. 1–2.)

As pieces are utilized and returned to storage files, the number of copies available should be noted on each filing box or filing cards. It is also wise to keep an accurate record of any music loaned on separate cards. A librarian should be selected from each choral group to repair any damaged music before it is returned to storage. The filing cards are available from Southern Music Company in Texas, and from other choral distributors. (See Appendix P.)

ASSIGNING FOLIOS AND MUSIC

Rehearsal time is too short to waste distributing music to choirs. A choral folio for *each singer* in *each choir* is an indispensable aid to efficient use of rehearsal time as well as better organization and discipline. If funds are minimal, envelopes (8½ by 11 in.) may be substituted for choral folios. Directors will find it efficient to have choir librarians fill individual folios with the choral music to be rehearsed. Vocalises and sight reading materials may also be placed in the folios. The folios should be numbered consecutively and each singer in the chorus assigned a number. The same number can be used to assign choir robes or other choral apparel. The folios should be stored in a cabinet located in a convenient place in the rehearsal room along with a master list of names/folio numbers beside it. Each choir should have a separate folio cabinet. Wenger Corp. is

---

[2]Doug Skerritt, "Choral Library for Computer File," *The Choral Journal* 27 (Sept. 1986):21–27.

---

[3]Bob Dingley, "Choral Music Library Computer Filer for IBM & Compatible PC Version," *The Choral Journal* 27 (May 1987):33–37.

FORM 4			TITLE CARD												

NAME OF COMPOSITION   **COMPOSER**

☐ SACRED   ☐ SECULAR   **CLASSIFICATION**   **8VO. NO.**

In Lib.	Voice Arr.	Arranger	Pub.	Text & Eng.	A Cap.	With Acc.	With Solo	With Band	With Orch.	Grade	Per. Time	No. Copies	Lib. No.
	UNISON												
	SA												
	SSA												
	SSAA												
	SAB												
	SATB												
	TB												
	TTB												
	TBB												
	TTBB												
	BOYS												

REMARKS _____

® Musi-Dex Filing System   **SOUTHERN MUSIC COMPANY**
© Copyright 1941   1100 BROADWAY • P. O. BOX 329 • SAN ANTONIO, TEXAS 78292

Figure 1–2 Musi-Dex Title Card, Southern Music Co., San Antonio Texas. Used by permission

a main supplier of folio cabinets and the new choir "posture chair." (See Appendix P.)

New pieces may be added to the folios periodically by the librarians or director. Some directors find it efficient to collect an octavo(s) performed by calling out the title(s) and having the choir members pass the copies to the end of the choir rows; however, this task can be handled by librarians by using a sorting table to separate the octavos from individual folios. The librarians should also repair any damaged octavos before they are returned to storage.

In addition to numbering the folios, many directors also number each copy of a particular octavo title when purchased so that each singer's choral folio and octavo numbers match. This may be helpful in making students responsible for their own copies and easier to collect compensation for replacement copies of lost octavos. Most directors find that permitting singers to take choral folios home for special practice is unworkable in junior and senior high schools. It is frustrating to try to rehearse when students have left their folios of music at home or elsewhere. Occasionally, a small ensemble such as a madrigal group, may profit from outside rehearsal.

DEVELOPING LONG- AND SHORT-RANGE BUDGETS

Most schools have a choral budget as for every other curricular area. Very large school systems have a music supervisor who is responsible for disbursement of funds.

Smaller school systems may designate a certain sum of money yearly to the choral director to spend as that person sees fit. Directors may also establish special "choral funds" within the school organization in a special bank account. Through fund raising activities such as car washes, candy and card selling, special concerts, and so on, additional monies may be raised to augment the regular school budget. This may be necessary for large purchases and for extended choir trips.

The typical items in an annual choral budget will include:

1. music for each large and small ensemble (one copy per singer)
2. cleaning of choir robes and other choir apparel
3. tuning and maintenance of all pianos and possibly, organ
4. attendance at professional conferences and workshops by director
5. monies for refreshments for choir social events
6. transportation monies for contest and festival attendance
7. contest and festival enrollment fees
8. sight reading and vocal techniques materials

Other budget items that will need consideration on a long-term basis include:

1. music filing cabinets and supplies
2. choral folios and storage cabinets
3. music risers, chairs, stands, chalkboard, acoustical shell, bulletin board
4. choir robes and other choral apparel
5. piano purchases or repairing
6. record player and tape recorder for the rehearsal room (disc, cassette, compact disc)
7. video tape camera and VCR recorder/playback with TV monitor
8. auxiliary instruments (recorders, small percussion, Orff instruments, guitars, handbells)

(See Appendix P. Equipment and Instrument Sources.)

Directors should submit school choral budgets promptly to the school administration on the official school budget forms. Additional information about the items may be included separately to justify the need of certain budget items. Some school administrations request directors to list items in priority order.

When buying choral risers, those with casters, carpeted treads, and those with a shell that can be attached are recommended. If the choral rehearsal room has a flat floor, the director may wish to consider purchase of rehearsal risers to accommodate chairs on several levels.

CONCERT APPAREL

The concert attire of choral ensembles has undergone change over the years. Where it was once the norm to have all choirs perform in robes, the robe is now only one of several concert attires. Since robes are widely associated with churches, they are ideal for the singing of sacred literature in schools. Today, however, tuxedos, formals, blazers, and jazz/show choir attire are also utilized. Many ensembles dress according to the type of choral group and the singing occasion.

Robes and stoles give the choir a more uniform appearance and eliminate personal features that would be apparent in other attire. They can be used by several ensembles and may be purchased in many colors (often, the school colors). The robe eliminates the necessity of purchasing accessories such as shirts, ties, blouses, matching skirts or slacks. Robes and stoles are a ten- to fifteen-year investment.

Tuxedos and formals may be used for both a sacred and secular atmosphere. The color of tux accessories and gowns can easily be changed, and the formal dress may be made from patterns by the girls and their parents. However, tuxedos and formals cannot be used as easily from year to year. Poor fits are obvious.

The blazer is a good choice for young junior and senior high chorus singers. They are not as workable for both sacred and secular literature, and again, size differences are noticeable.

Self-designed costumes are often used by small ensembles such as madrigal groups and jazz-show choirs. For show choirs, a nonwrinkling material which allows flexibility of movement is required.

Some large choral ensembles have for years utilized white shirts and dark ties and slacks for boys and white blouses and small dark ties and dark skirts for girls. This is a simple, but effective decor suitable for performance of all types of choral literature.

For staged musicals, a specialized wardrobe is required for the solo roles as well as supporting chorus and dancers. Scenery, lighting, and makeup will also be necessary.

Each special choral attire (robes, blazers, tuxedos, formals, etc.) should be numbered and assigned to singers accordingly. The numbers should be readily visible on the hanger top and placed in numerical order in storage closets.

STUDENT OFFICERS

Directors can help junior and senior high youth grow as responsible leaders by having each school chorus elect officers: president, vice-president, secretary-treasurer, and librarian. These officers can assist the director in formulating policy, assigning apparel, decorating for concerts, planning parties, organizing tours, raising funds, and maintaining the choral library. Each large ensemble needs to elect responsible officers to represent the group.

Directors should consult with the choir officers frequently and solicit their advice and suggestions on many matters. A short meeting during rehearsal time should be held at least bi-monthly and each of the officers should have specific duties assigned which need to be fulfilled.

Some directors like to assign section leaders to assist in section rehearsals (soprano, alto, tenor, bass). These should be the most musical and experienced singers who read music well and perhaps play the piano. They may be able to rehearse their section, take attendance at rehearsals and performances, and give the director input for grading purposes. Directors must not abdicate the leadership role, however. The role of section leaders needs to be clearly defined to the choir and the leaders.

SELECTING STUDENT ACCOMPANISTS

A good choral accompanist is frequently hard to secure. Although the director may play for rehearsals occasionally, it is best to have a student or adult accompanist for each choral group. An accompanist can make or break the choir. Some students, even though they have studied piano for many years and play in piano recitals, do not adjust well to accompanying a chorus. Playing for rehearsals requires not only playing choral accompaniments, but playing individual choral parts in solo, duet, trio, or quartet fashion. It is true score reading. The ability of the accompanist to follow the verbal or conducting directions in quick fashion keeps the rehearsal moving. Some directors like to vocalize the choirs themselves, but many accompanists can also learn to assist. The key to accompanying is having the music well enough in advance to practice it and to lead the chorus in rehearsal. This implies that the director supplies the accompanist well ahead of rehearsal dates in order that the *vocal lines* as well as the *accompaniment* may be practiced.

Some schools are able financially to provide an adult accompanist, often a chorus member's parent, to assist the director. This is a tremendous asset where available. Sometimes another music teacher may provide accompaniment. Regardless of whether a student or adult accompanist is available, the director should spend some time with the accompanist, specifying what is required. Such things as tempo, phrasing, and dynamics should be discussed and demonstrated. Sometimes a recording of an octavo will assist the overall interpretation.

Directors should not lock themselves to the piano keyboard, since they will not have the best control of the chorus. Director eye contact is important and conducting the chorus provides the necessary leadership for precise and artistic choral singing. The director is also in a better position to hear mistakes and to correct them when standing before the chorus. The accompanying should complement the directing.

PURCHASING MUSIC

When purchasing music over the school year, directors must be careful to follow the procedures of the business office and see that every purchase goes through that office; otherwise, the director may find the bill charged to his or her own name! When ordering choral music, state clearly the title, composer or arranger, the publisher, publisher's octavo number, voicing (SATB, SSA, TTBB, SACB, and so on), number of copies desired and how you want the copies delivered—united parcel, first class mail, fourth class mail, etc. If quick delivery is required, it is best to specify private carrier or first class, otherwise the order will probably be sent by slower fourth class mail. Realize that postage will increase the cost of the total order. Directors often order about five percent more copies to allow for growth and loss of copies.

Orders for choral music may be placed with local dealers or with larger choral distributors such as Carl Fischer Music Stores, Malecki Music, J. W. Pepper, Wingert–Jones, and others. (See Appendix P.) Some dealers still give as much as 20 percent discount for schools and churches. In some cases, choral music may be purchased directly from the publisher. (See Appendix R, Directory of Publishers.)

THE COPYRIGHT LAW

A major revision of the Copyright Law took effect January 1, 1978. United States Copyrights are designed to protect the time and creative effort of the composer/arranger, the investment of time and money by the publisher, and the music retailer who supplies the director's musical needs. The following practices are prohibited:

1. copying to avoid purchase
2. copying music for any kind of performance (See emergency exception, number 1, which follows)
3. copying without including copyright notice
4. copying to create anthologies or compilations
5. reproducing material designed to be consumable such as workbooks, standardized tests, and answer sheets
6. charging students beyond the actual cost involved in making copies as permitted

The following practices are permissible without prior permission:

1. Emergency copying to replace purchased copies which for any reason are not available for an imminent performance provided purchased replacement copies shall be substituted in due course.
2. For academic purposes other than performance, multiple copies of excerpts of works may be made, provided that the excerpts do not compromise a part of the whole which would constitute a performable unit such as a section, movement, or aria but in no case more than 10 percent of the whole work. The number of copies shall not exceed one copy per pupil.
3. Printed copies which have been purchased may be edited *or* simplified provided that the fundamental character of the work is not distorted or the lyrics, if any, altered or lyrics added if none exist.
4. A single copy of recordings of performance by students may be made for evaluation or rehearsal purposes and may be returned by the educational institution or individual teacher.

5. A single copy of a sound recording (such as a tape, disc, or cassette) of copyrighted music may be made from sound recordings owned by an educational institution or an individual teacher for the purpose of constructing aural exercises or examinations and may be retained by the educational institution or individual teacher. (This pertains only to the copyright of the music itself and not to any copyright which may exist in the sound recording.) The penalities for violating the current Copyright Law range from $250 to $50,000 and/or two years imprisonment or both.[4]

RELATIONS WITH STUDENTS, ADMINISTRATORS, PARENTS, AND TEACHERS

Junior and senior high choral directors must be many things to many people. The choral director can provide students with a model of a responsible, caring adult. Through a common interest with the fine art of choral singing, students and director can share many exciting and aesthetically fulfilling experiences together. Students respect those directors who demand much musically of them. It is important that directors provide strong motivation and leadership to the school choral program. They should nourish the singers' musical tastes with a balanced diet of choral music and should work for the best rendition of the music possible.

Although directors work with large choral groups, they must make the effort to know each student individually. Students like personal attention and the director should take note of each singer's individual interests. A sense of humor goes a long way with young adolescents. At the same time, the director must demand strong discipline in each choral ensemble for musical growth and satisfaction to evolve. Limits to student behavior must be set, and the director must be consistent in his expectations of students each day. Junior and senior high choruses need calm, energetic directors who understand the developmental characteristics of this age and can provide responsible models of adulthood, as well as good singing. To enable choirs to sing their best, directors need to know when to smile, when to joke, and when to crack down hard. Adolescents appreciate and respect directors who are firm, consistent, and fair in their discipline. They take pride in belonging to organizations that have a worthwhile purpose and are successful in carrying that out. Chorus membership should not be easy, but a challenge and when high standards are set for a group it becomes an honor to belong.

Prompt attendance and disciplined participation in rehearsals and performances should be mandatory, not a matter of choice. Minor disturbances can often be resolved by a discussion between student and director. Other situations require a two- or three-way discussion with parents and student. If this does not help, the student should be denied the privilege of participating in the choral ensemble.

---

[4]*The United States Copyright Law: A Practical Outline.* New York: Music Publishers Association. See also *The United States Copyright Law: A Guide for Music Educators.* Reston, VA: MENC; or write: The Copyright Office, Library of Congress, Washington, D.C. 20559.

Well-planned rehearsals will usually take care of most discipline problems. Directors must keep the pace moving and provide as much variety as needed to sustain interest. Frequent performances provide considerable motivation for singers to master the music, since embarrassment before an audience is not rewarding and does damage to the reputation of the chorus.

Directors should reward good work, both through positive comments in rehearsals and following performances, but also through grades and award systems. Each director must formulate a set of criteria for student evaluation. These are sometimes organized around a point system, with so many points for each criterion. Students earning higher points may be rewarded at year's end by choir lapel pins; service certificates; jewelry; patches for robes, jackets, or stoles; decals; and so on. Special recognition and appreciation may also be shown through a school choir sponsored breakfast or dinner, a special outing, or other such events.

In any award system, accurate records must be kept. Unfair practices by directors can cause hard feelings and betray the trust established.

The school administrator must be treated fairly with respect by choral directors. The principal wants to see the choral program succeed and directors should provide the necessary information and expertise for wise administrative choices to be made. Many principals desire input about musical matters. Directors can supply expertise information regarding organization of the choral curriculum, successful scheduling patterns for each choral ensemble, budget matters, the performance schedule of ensembles for the year, a workable rehearsal discipline, and other information. Administrators enjoy working with well-organized choral directors who bring honor and recognition to the school. Directors should recognize the many problems of the school administrator and respect his or her expertise in school management. Administrators must deal not only with teachers, but students and parents as well. The choral director can greatly assist the principal in establishing positive school–community relations.

Choral directors must also work cooperatively with parents to make the school choral program function. Some directors like to organize a "parent choir council" to provide outside support to the program. Parents appreciate receiving in the mail a schedule of all major performances over the school year. This lets parents see the demands that will be expected of chorus members and greatly reduces the possibility of absences at required performances. Parents may better plan a special event if they know about a performance well in advance. Similarly, many senior high students work on evenings and weekends and an advance performance schedule is mandatory to avoid conflicts.

One way directors communicate with parents is through the written grade report. This is only one type of interaction and directors frequently need to talk to parents about the musical progress of individual singers. Parents enjoy knowing how their children are progressing musically. The director should also be able to provide counselor-type assistance with regard to private study in voice, piano, or other instruments. Parents often seek advice about which music schools and degree programs are possible for students seeking a career in music.

Parents are quick to recognize a strong choral program. The director must establish the choral program as a strong, worthwhile undertaking. The public image of the choral department can be an effective tool in requesting more funding for expansion and improvement of the program. Other people in the community with whom the choral director should become acquainted are directors of local radio and television stations, editors of newspapers, officers of music and service clubs, and other music teachers/directors. News releases about choral events and pictures of ensembles provide recognition to the school choral program.

Working with other colleagues in the school teaching profession can broaden the choral director's overall vision of the total school mission. It is to the choral director's benefit to make many friends in the schools. Three people of significant worth, in addition to the principal, are the instrumental music teacher, the physical education teacher, and the school custodian. Cooperation and respect is required between the choral and instrumental teachers in junior and senior high schools. Joint planning of schedules and performances are necessary for smooth functioning. Ways should be examined that permit students to elect both band/orchestra and chorus. A happy relationship between choral director and the coach is important. Coaches can often convince boys of the worth of music and guide them into choral ensembles. Students should not be placed in the situation of choosing whether a choral performance should take precedence over a basketball or football game. Schedules need to be resolved early for students to participate in a wide range of school events. Also, a choral director will need the kind and repeated assistance of the school custodian to provide for logistical problems at concerts and assemblies. Risers, acoustical shells, pianos, stands, seating, and other essentials must be provided through the cooperation of the school custodian.

Directors should also try as much as possible to convince professional colleagues that school music deserves a time in the school curriculum, just as reading, history, English, math, science, and other subjects. This helps to reduce the common feeling that music is an extracurricular subject. All major choral groups should meet during the school day and only small ensembles should meet outside the regular school day.

Choral directors should show interest in other subject areas and serve on school committees. Sometimes the typical academic teacher does not receive the high degree of community visibility that music teachers and coaches do. Directors should give credit as much as possible to others for the success of a concert. These people can be publicly thanked in the printed program, at the concert, and in newspaper accounts. If the art department contributed backdrops, the teacher and students should be recognized. Being respectful of others promotes strong personal relationships and high degree of professionalism.

PLANNING SOCIAL EVENTS FOR THE SINGERS

During the school year, chorus members enjoy sharing in opportunities for extra-musical enrichment at parties, picnics, overnight camp-outs, and attending concerts or films together. A Halloween party or after-caroling party at Christmas are possibilities. Taking the chorus to hear a fine university or professional ensemble pays musical dividends. Seeing a musical together is also appealing. Sometimes the director or several parents may sponsor a party at school, a restaurant, or at a home where students may gather to listen to a tape of a recent performance, and enjoy refreshments and social interaction.

Directors need to organize some of these events into the choral program schedule each year. Sometimes an event such as this may provide the opportunity to recognize students through choir awards. A Parent Choir Council can be an excellent vehicle for organizing such events.

Chapter Two

The Junior High School Choral Program

Teaching in today's junior high schools (grades seven, eight, and nine) or middle schools (six, seven, and eight, usually) requires a music teacher with a high degree of motivation, perseverance, and dedication to students. The junior high youngster can be a real challenge to choral directors since this is a period of great physical, emotional, social, and intellectual growth. Music is the common denominator that can provide the vehicle for enthusiastic participation.

PSYCHOLOGICAL CONSIDERATIONS

Junior high school students in the early adolescent stage generally possess the following personality characteristics:

1. Desire status as individuals. They need much encouragement and social acceptance through belonging to a group such as a chorus.
2. Fluctuate from childish to adult behavior. The teacher should reward positive adult behavior and discourage childish actions.
3. Like excitement, adventure, and variety. The junior high student needs to participate actively in chorus through a fast paced and varied rehearsal plan.

21

4. Exhibit sharp changes in attitudes and interests. Students seek understanding from the teacher as they fluctuate from excitement to depression.

5. Exhibit the need for immediate gratification. Junior high youngsters desire learning experiences to be relevant and wish to be "modern" and "current." These are normal and often short-lived limitations and suggest that teachers must widen horizons for students to sense the long-range goals. Helping students develop standards and values to make wise judgements is necessary.

Junior high chorus students have the capacity for great enthusiasm in a rehearsal situation which provides stimulation, variety, and a conducive atmosphere for learning. Lacking these provisions, however, the same students will often react with varying amounts of indifference, belligerence, and rudeness.

There is a difference between attitudes of girls from boys toward chorus participation. Girls generally are more positive to music than boys. Also, girls' voices are more settled, changing only in quality and strength of tone. Boys, however, undergo the voice change during the junior high years, making pitch matching and singing a part difficult. The change is also embarrassing to boys. Then too, the attitude often prevails among young adolescent boys that singing is a "sissy" thing. Recruiting the boys into the choral program requires considerable tact and convincing by the choral director and parents. Letting boys hear a good male ensemble like a barbershop quartet in the community will work wonders. There is also the young male pop music idol which is motivating to boys.

Many girls have studied piano and are much more amenable to choral participation. Fathers frequently desire their sons to participate in athletics, sometimes to the exclusion of music. Being manly is the "in" thing. Both the junior high girl and boy are very emotional, but boys tend to hide this. Although the girls will usually enter into the rehearsal activities willingly, the boys often must be won into active participation and will often question the music chosen for singing.

Junior high youngsters are very peer oriented and usually conform to the crowd. They do not want to be seen with their parents. They will tend to conform to their peer group, and only rarely dare to be different. They require coaxing to accept the "adult" way. There is also a new junior high school environment with which to contend. The sixth grade student in elementary school is "king of the walk," cocky, and sure of self. Seventh grade students are confronted with a new school environment, new type of class schedule, and a variety of teacher personalities. They are "low on the totem pole" and made to feel they know next to nothing about life and school by their upper grade peers.

Closely intertwined with psychological development is the high degree of physical development that is taking place. Physically, students entering the adolescent period exhibit the following characteristics:

1. Awkwardness and lack of detailed coordination resulting from rapid muscle and bone growth.

2. Changes in vocal quality and range in boys resulting from lengthening and thickening of vocal chords.

3. Restlessness, nervousness, and headaches resulting from glandular changes and adjustments.
4. Sensitivity and shyness about physical appearance whether from body size (small to large) or skin disorders. The greatest physical growth in boys is age 13.8 and 11.5 for girls. One of the distinguishing characteristics of a junior high mixed chorus is the enormous differences in physical maturation present.

The junior high chorus (mixed, treble, or male) can provide a stimulating vehicle for musical growth and wholesome social interaction. The enthusiasm of junior high choruses can be overwhelming as these students seek to prove their worth. Often they tend to sing "sharp" and race the tempo of a piece in their excitement. Under a good, caring director they are loyal to the highest degree.

THE GENERAL MUSIC CLASS

The importance of a strong elementary music curriculum cannot be overemphasized enough. It is there that initial interest and participation in music in a formal school setting transpires. Most elementary students participate in the general music program from kindergarten through grade six, whether under a music specialist or specialist-classroom teacher instructional mode. The general music class should develop singing, instrumental, sight reading, listening, movement, and creative skills and knowledges. Students should have developed concepts of rhythm, melody, harmony, tone color, dynamics, and form in music.

Some children in elementary school will begin instruction on band and orchestra instruments, as well as piano, guitar, and others. Many elementary schools develop an elementary chorus for upper grade children to promote choral singing abilities through attention to vocal production, sight singing, and part singing. The junior high choral director should develop a strong working relationship with the elementary music teachers. They can assist immeasureably in recruiting elementary children into the junior high school choral groups. It is also wise to become acquainted with the private music teachers in the community and the chorus members who are studying privately.

In the junior high school, general music should be required of all students through grade eight, regardless of whether the students are enrolled in chorus, band, or orchestra. The general music class can broaden the student's depth of music knowledge beyond the skill development usually associated with performing groups. The two can enhance the student's music education. Indeed, choral participation should grow from the junior high general music experience. The activities of singing, instrument playing, music reading, listening, moving, and creating should continue on a more sophisticated level. Use of guitars, recorders, Orff instruments, small percussion, and possibly handbells should be encouraged in junior high general music classes. Listening and analyzing may help students with voice and instrument recognition and identification of music forms. Movement may help to clarify many music concepts (Dalcroze) and add a dance dimension to instruction. Junior high students may also create melodies to poems, descants and ostinatos, chordal accompaniments, and small percussion accompaniments.

In the contemporary vein, students may create tape pieces, synthesizer compositions, sound pieces using vocal-body-environmental-nontraditional instrument sounds.

Singing should not be neglected in junior high school general music classes and students should have the opportunity to sing in part harmony through rounds and canons, descants, ostinati, partner songs, harmonic vocalises, and chordal two-, three-, and four-part harmony. Opportunities to sight read need to be structured. In short, a strong junior high general music curriculum through the eighth grade will provide for both the general student who will experience music throughout life, as well as for the student who desires to become a better performer of music through choral participation and education.

THE CHALLENGE OF THE BOYS' CHANGING VOICES

The voice change in the boys usually occurs somewhere between the ages of twelve and fifteen. Although a few boys enter the first stage of voice change in grade five, the largest number of voices change in grades seven and eight. This can be a slow process for some and a faster process for others depending upon the individual speed of physical maturation. Although girls' voices may change in quality and power, they do not undergo the pitch change of the boy's voice. The boy's vocal cords actually double in length and thicken, giving the voice an octave lower pitch.

By asking each singer to read a sentence, the director can immediately discover which voices are still treble in pitch, and which are in a state of change or lowering of pitch. The physical characteristics that indicate possible voice change include:

1. physical maturation in terms of body size
2. protruding larynx (Adam's apple)
3. prominent nose and jaw
4. facial hair indicating the beginnings of a beard
5. prominent wrist and anklebones
6. audible differences in speaking voice

Sometimes the young man's voice will fluctuate and break occasionally between higher and lower pitches as vocal cord development takes place. As boys' voices change, they may move from being able to sing soprano or alto to the cambiata first phase change or possibly move downward further to the baritone range. Some new baritones may eventually become tenors later. This means that boys undergoing voice change cannot sing a mature tenor and bass choral part in junior high school. The cambiata term which means "changing" was applied to the first phase of a boy's voice change by Irvin Cooper who conducted extensive research into the boy's changing voice and published texts and choral materials for this age. Don Collins, a student of Cooper while attending Florida State University, has continued Cooper's work through publications of the Cambiata Press in Conway, Arkansas. John Cooksey has also researched the boy's voice change and published articles in *The Choral Journal*. (See Bibliography C.)

Cooper has found no true alto girls in junior high school and prefers to label this section Soprano II. All junior high girls' voices tend to be thin and breathy sounding, but gradually change in color and strength. Usually girls require more stimulation and motivation than junior high boys to realize their full potential. The cambiata (alto-tenor) voice has a deep alto quality and is rich and sometimes strident when forced. The cambiata section of the chorus often gives the illusion of sounding an octave lower. The junior high baritone voice is the second change and the lower range is rather light. It is not until about the sophomore year in high school (tenth grade) that young men can sing the standard ranges of mature tenors and basses.

ASSISTING UNCERTAIN SINGERS

A junior high student who cannot sing certain pitches does not indicate tone deafness. Very often boys who have sung well in elementary school find pitch-matching difficult during the voice change process. Some girls and boys may have had limited home and school singing experiences. Very often those junior high students with pitch-matching problems will be discovered in the voice classification process.

Many of the devices used in elementary school are useful in working with junior high school uncertain singers.

1. Have the students move their voices by imitating environmental sounds such as sirens, the wind, trombones, boat horns, and animal voices.

2. Play tone-matching exercises, using one or several pitches which the student must emulate. The falling minor third (sol-mi) is most natural.

3. Use visual and physical hand movements to a song melody, moving the hand up, down, or the same for the melody contour. The entire scale may be done physically from low to high full body movement. Following dashes or music notation at the chalkboard is useful in indicating pitch direction. Some directors, trained in the Zoltan Kodály approach, use Curwen handsigns to show scale degrees to develop music reading skills.

4. Have junior high students repeat song fragments that the director sings or plays on bells, xylophone, piano, or recorder. Sometimes instruments provide a clear model of pitches to match.

5. Have students speak the text of a song phrase, then immediately sing it in an acceptable range and key.

6. Seat any uncertain singers in chorus beside a strong singer for positive tone reinforcement.

7. If a student can sing a song like *America* in a given key, start there, and work the voice up or down by half-step key changes. As the song is pitched in higher keys the student will realize more effort and breath support is needed.

Unlike the early elementary school years, junior high choral directors will need to work with any uncertain singers on an individual basis. This may be done informally with a student before or after school or during a free period. Junior high students are shy and do not want to have their singing problems exposed in front of peers. Some large group vocalises, however, are useful in pitch matching and extending range upward and downward. With some effort most uncertain singers will improve. Another vital prerequisite to successful singing in junior high chorus is placement of each singer to the proper voice part. Some directors, such as Frederick Swanson, have advocated separating the boys and girls during some rehearsals to work on vocal production problems.

JUNIOR HIGH VOCAL RANGES AND VOICINGS

Directors can count on having some girl sopranos and altos (but not true altos) at the junior high school level, and there may be some unchanged boy voices who can sing these parts as well. Boys should be assigned to the part they can actually sing at a given time. They need to know that singing soprano or alto is not "sissy" and that their voices will soon begin to drop in pitch. Directors should retest voices every two months or so to discover changes in the boys' voices. Also, boys may be encouraged to speak to the director when they feel they no longer can sing the part they are assigned to, whether it be soprano, alto (S II), cambiata, or baritone. More mature boys, probably in eighth or ninth grade will be able to sing a baritone line. Figure 2–1 shows the typical junior high voice ranges.

If all singers are properly assigned to the correct voice parts, singing dissatisfaction will be minimized. Telling boys to "sing an octave lower" does not work. A boy will "jump octaves" as the need arises. When this occurs directors can be sure the boy is not singing the proper part.

Although the above ranges are possible, the tessitura or most comfortable singing ranges lie toward the middle of each part range. Extremes of range may not be a problem in a choral piece; however, if the extremes of range (such as sustaining very high and low pitches for numerous counts) will present unsolvable vocal problems, the piece is best avoided.

Junior high directors should be aware that unison singing is almost impossible in junior high school. The lowest pitch, the treble singers (male and female), and baritones can sing comfortably when singing in octaves is "D" (above middle C for soprano, alto, and cambiata, third line bass clef for baritone). The highest pitch the cambiata can sing comfortably is A, second space of the treble clef. Therefore, for unison/octave

Figure 2–1 Junior High Mixed Choir Ranges

Figure 2-2 Common Unison/Octave Range

singing, the range can only encompass that of a perfect fifth of "D to A," too narrow for most songs. (See Fig. 2–2.)

This suggests the need for directors to fit the music to the chorus and not the chorus to the music. If all the boys in a junior high/middle school chorus are still using treble voices, use SA and SSA voicings. If the chorus has boys in the first change (cambiata), use SC, SSC, SAC, and SAT, and possibly some SSA with a low alto part for the cambiata singers. If there are young baritone voices (usually eighth and ninth grades), directors should choose SB (two-part mixed), SAB, SSCB, SACB, or limited range SATB music. Although some octavos today are labeled "three part," with the lowest part usually written on the bass staff, they may not really be SAB pieces. The lowest part is on the high side to accommodate the cambiata voices, and forces young baritones to sing in their upper ranges. A four-part chorus is ideal (SSCB) in providing proper ranges for all singers this age. Directors must decide which voicing is best for their particular groups and which provides the most acceptable part balance. Cambiata Press, Hope Publishing, Heritage Music Press, Carl Fischer, Kjos Music, Jenson Publications, Pro-Art Publications, Hal Leonard, Augsburg, Belwin–Mills, Coronet, G.I.A., and Choristers Guild are major publishers of music for changing junior high voices. (See Appendix R.)

TESTING VOICES AND RECORDING DATA

Irvin Cooper developed and demonstrated to junior high choral directors a large group voice test for junior high choruses, as well as for general music classes. Although an individual voice test is also desirable, the large group test is useful in classifying singers quickly. It can be accomplished in less than fifteen minutes and can identify the four junior high voice types: Soprano I, Soprano II (Alto), Cambiata, and Baritone. The group test is as follows:

1. The chorus sings the first stanza of *America* (My Country 'Tis of Thee) in the key of G major. The keys in the test apply only when *America* is used as the voice-test song. The teacher plays the melody in octaves.

2. The chorus sings the first phrase (range of a fifth).

3. Choose a small group (8 to 10 singers) to sing the first phrase while the teacher listens to the group closely checking the octave chosen by each singer.

4. The boys who sing an octave lower in G major key are temporarily assigned to a changing voice category and asked to move to one side of the room. These boys will be rechecked later in the test to determine which are cambiata and which are baritone.

5. With the remainder of the voices who sang the upper octave in the G major key, repeat the first phrase in B-flat major. Those who sing the upper octave in this

new key are designated soprano. The remaining voices are assigned as altos (Soprano II).

6. Continue the above procedure (8 to 10 singers at a time) until the entire chorus has been tested and assigned to either the soprano, alto, or changing voice category.

7. Then proceed to test the changing voices at the side of the room to determine which are cambiata and which are baritone. Have this group of boys sing the first phrase of *America* in the key of C major, giving starting pitches in octaves. Those who choose to sing the upper octave are assigned to the cambiata part, and those who sing the lower octave, to the baritone part.

See that students understand the purpose of voice testing and discuss the interesting changes taking place in their voices. Early in the year an individual voice test may be administered. Students should be encouraged to request a voice check when their assigned parts feel out of range. When conducting individual voice tests, a variety of information will be required to function over the school year. Utilizing a Personal Data Card provides much information at the director's fingertips. (See Fig. 2–3.)

The individual schedules of singers is important information to have on file. Extracurricular clubs and activities, as well as part-time employment of singers (usually, senior high) may affect rehearsal scheduling. It is also important to be able to communicate with the parents, and to know the musical background of each singer. The director will fill in the music information from the voice test and students may complete the remainder of the information.

Often it is wise to avoid the word "test" and "audition" which can be frightening to timid singers. Keep the atmosphere informal, explaining that it is important to hear the voices of all the singers, new and old, to learn how they are developing. Individual auditions should be limited to five or seven minutes.

The range of each voice may be discovered by singing up and down the first five notes of the scale (do-re-mi-fa-sol for finding upper range limits and sol-fa-mi-re-do to find lower range limits) in as high and low a key as the singer can negotiate. Note this range on the staff on the card.

Use a simple four-phrase folk tune or *America* to ascertain *vocal quality* (tone color, resonance, volume) and to find out how well the singer can sing in tune (intonation).

As an ear pitch-rhythm retention test, devise four or five melody-rhythm examples to be played on the piano for the student to sing back on "lah." This will help to determine the singer's degree of pitch and rhythm accuracy. Figure 2–4 illustrates an example that may be scored on the Personal Data Card.

In addition to the Pitch-Rhythm Retention Test, directors of junior and senior high choruses should have each singer sight sing his or her choral part of a patriotic tune, hymn, or a contrived sight singing example. See Fig. 2–5 for two examples of sight singing.

The ability of the singer to sight sing the music should be recorded. Some singers will have considerable experience with reading music notation, while others may be somewhat limited. The tune used may be sung on "lah" or "loo."

PERSONAL DATA CARD

<u>General Information</u> (to be filled in by singer)

Name of Chorister _____

Birthdate _____ Age _____

Address _____

Telephone _____ Grade in School _____

Parents' Names _____

Current Date _____

Previous Choir Experience (church and school) _____

Music Instruments You Play and Years _____

Voice Training and Years _____

<u>Music Information</u> (to be filled in by choir director)

Range:

Vocal Quality _____

Intonation _____

Pitch/Rhythm Accuracy ___ 1   2   3   4   5   (4 pts. ea.) Total ___

Sight Singing _____

Part Assigned _____

Comments _____

Figure 2–3(a) Personal Data Card

Schedule

Period	Class	Teacher	Room Number
1.			
2.			
3.			
4.			
5.			
6.			
7.			
8.			

Clubs/Activities _____ Mtg. Time _____

Clubs/Activities _____ Mtg. Time _____

Part-time Employment _____ Wrk. Hrs. _____

Height: _____ Weight: _____ Chest Meas.: _____

Robe/Blazer/Tuxedo/Other Apparel Assigned: No. _____

Figure 2–3(b) Reverse Side-Personal Data Card

Figure 2–4 Pitch-Rhythm Retention Test

Figure 2–5 Sight Singing Examples

WAYS TO DEVELOP PART SINGING

Many junior high school students have experienced singing in harmony in elementary general music classes, elementary choruses, or possibly in church or community children's choirs. At the beginning of seventh grade, choral directors may find the following approaches helpful to developing an ear for part singing.

Ostinati, rounds, and canons. An ostinato is a repeated chant sung against a melody. Ostinati may be performed on pitch instruments such as bells, recorders, flutes, or Orff-type mallet instruments and applied to pentatonic, major, and minor songs. They may be pitch patterns extracted from a song melody. Pentatonic songs, and songs harmonized by I (tonic) and V (dominant) chords are easiest to harmonize with a pitch ostinato. (See Fig. 2–6.)

An ostinato also makes an interesting introduction to a song, or a coda at its conclusion. Several ostinati may be sung or played simultaneously.

A canon is a single melody imitated by different voices or instruments at different times. When each group's melody is identical, the piece is called a "strict" canon or a "round." If the melody has been altered or placed at a different pitch entrance level, it is termed an "imitative canon." All voices in a round imitate at the unison or octave interval. This type of singing provides practice with polyphonic music.

Some guidelines for singing rounds are as follows:

1. have the chorus sing the round well in unison first
2. let the chorus "hear" the harmony by singing the second entrance yourself to their unison. Then divide the chorus and sing both parts.
3. after two-part harmony has been established, gradually divide the chorus into three or more parts as the round allows. Direct each section entrance.
4. maintain a strict, steady tempo so the polyphonic structure will not collapse
5. work for balance of parts. Rounds are not a contest to see which part sings loudest.
6. Indicate before beginning the round how many times it is to be sung. End the round by having each part drop out after a specific number of repetitions or have all the parts stop simultaneously at the end of phrases for a chordal effect.

When Jesus Wept

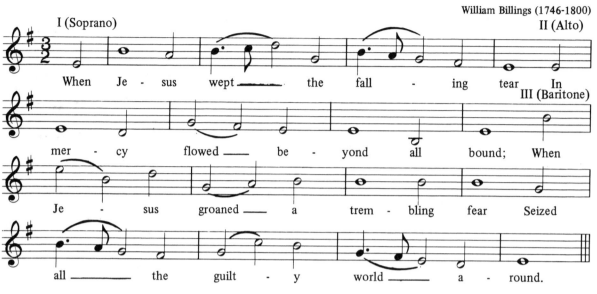

Figure 2–6 Ostinato and Round Example

Descants and counter melodies. A descant is a counter melody that is usually, but not always, sung above the song melody. Contrapuntal singing is somewhat easier than singing vertical chord harmony in thirds and sixths. Descants are readily available in junior high music series texts as well as in some octavo choral music.

Partner songs. These are two or more tunes that can be combined effectively in harmony because their harmonic chord structures are identical. The texts of the tunes sometimes conflict, but singing them together helps singers develop skill in part singing. Some partner songs include:

> *All Night, All Day* and *Swing Low Sweet Chariot*
> *When the Saints Go Marching In* and *Swing Low, Sweet Chariot* (refrain)
> *He's Got the Whole World in His Hands* and *Rocka My Soul*

Sometimes the stanza and refrain sections of a tune may be sung together. This is true of *Battle Hymn of the Republic* and *Rocka My Soul*. Directors should examine the following collections of partner songs:

Beckman, Frederick. *Partner Songs.* Ginn

Beckman, Frederick. *More Partner Songs.* Ginn

Jenkins, David and Visocchi, Mark. *Mix 'n' Match: Instant Part Singing for Juniors.* Universal Ed

Perinchief, Robert. *Honor Your Partner.* Perry Publications

Harmonic vocalises. Directors can help junior high students develop good intonation through various types of harmonic vocalises and chord progressions. These may be two-, three-, or four-part harmony vocalises, depending upon the voicing of the junior high chorus. Many are illustrated in Chap. 7, Vocal Techniques for the Chorus.

O SANCTISSIMA
(SSC)

Sicilian Hymn

Figure 2–7 Three-Part Hymn

Figure 2–8 Four-Part Carol (SSCB)

Two- three- and four-part songs. After junior high students have experimented with chordal vocalizing, easy part songs may be attempted. Hymn tunes or chorales are often useful. (See Figs. 2–7 and 2–8.) These may be followed by more extensive octavo literature.

EFFECTIVE SEATING PLANS FOR MIXED, TREBLE, AND MALE CHORUSES

Seating plans for the junior high/middle school mixed chorus are given in Fig. 2–9. Notice that the boys (cambiata and baritone) are placed in front of the girl-boy sopranos and altos so the director can pay close attention to the boys' voices.

If an SAB seating plan is used due to lack of cambiata voices, the baritones may be placed in the center between the sopranos and altos; however, it is best to aim for a four-voice chorus, since the boys will be singing on more comfortable parts (SSCB). Boys may easily be moved from one part to another in both the three-voice and four-voice seating plans.

Three-Voice Chorus

Girl-Boy Sopranos	Girl-Boy Altos
Cambiata	

Four-Voice Chorus

Girl-Boy Sopranos	Girl-Boy Altos
Baritones	Cambiata

or

Girl-Boy Sopranos	Baritones	Girl-Boy Altos
	Cambiata	

Figure 2–9 Seating Plans for Junior High Mixed Chorus

Some junior high choruses may contain no cambiata or baritone voices. If this is the case the chorus may be organized and seated to sing SA and SSA voicings. The second soprano in the center may be divided to sing either soprano or alto when performing only SA music. (See Fig. 2–10.)

Two-Voice Chorus

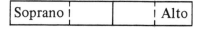

Three-Voice Chorus

Soprano I   Soprano II   Alto

Figure 2–10 Girls' Chorus and Unchanged Voice Chorus Seating Plans and Ranges

Cambiata I	Cambiata II	Baritone I	Baritone II

Baritone II	Baritone I
Cambiata I	Cambiata II

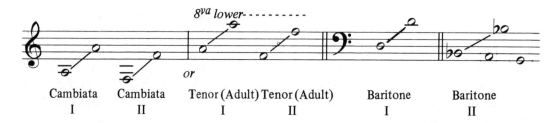

Figure 2–11 Junior High Male Chorus Seating Plans and Ranges

At the junior high level, the all-male chorus is becoming popular again. Boys this age enjoy having their own glee club, and music is now available for this young male chorus. (See Appendix E, Junior and Senior High Male Chorus Octavos and Appendix M, Male Chorus Collections.) Some publishers utilize CCBB voicings or CB, CCB, CBB with the cambiata parts for the young tenor and the lower parts for the junior high baritones. Directors must be careful when utilizing adult TTBB octavos to restrict the choices to those within the cambiata and baritone ranges. The first seating plan is useful when the sections are strong and balanced. (See Fig. 2–11.) The second plan allows for a smaller number of cambiata voices by placing them in front of the baritones to be better heard.

SCHEDULING JUNIOR HIGH CHORAL GROUPS

The typical junior high music teacher may teach some required general music classes and several choruses or instrumental groups. Sometimes the choruses may be scheduled by grade level—seventh, eighth, and ninth grade separate choruses. Directors should realize that a seventh grade chorus may be able to sing SSC or SSA choral voicings. Most baritone voices will be found in grades eight and nine. Therefore, some directors prefer to have perhaps two mixed choruses which cut across all three grade levels. This retains a nucleus of two grade levels from year to year; however, it is often difficult for administrators to clear a common rehearsal time in the schedule for all three grade levels. Directors must weigh the benefits of each organizational plan. Perhaps an eighth and ninth grade common rehearsal time can be found. Depending upon the size of the junior high school, the following model may be desirable:

1. one or two mixed-voice choral groups or one at each grade level (7, 8, and 9). These should be scheduled daily or no less than three times a week during the school day. No large ensemble should meet before or after school.
2. one girl's chorus (glee club) meeting at least three times a week during the school day
3. one boy's chorus (glee club) meeting at least two or three times a week during the school day
4. several small mixed, girls', and boys' ensembles meeting at least once or twice weekly either during school hours or on an extracurricular basis. In some schools the small ensembles do not meet regularly the entire year, but organize six or eight weeks prior to music contests in order to participate in the small ensemble and solo contest events.

Scheduling is a major problem for choral directors. Schedules affect all teachers, and therefore, the choral director should work closely with the principal and other teachers in establishing a functional schedule. Sometimes, a less than ideal schedule may be the only alternative. The choral and instrumental directors should work together to achieve the best workable schedule for the most students. Some parents want their sons and daughters to sing and play both. This may require sharing the students involved between the choral and instrumental ensembles. A word of caution is in order regarding the practice of calling additional rehearsals prior to performances. This is very upsetting to the other teachers at the school if the rehearsal cuts into class teaching/testing time. An evening dress rehearsal may also present problems for some students. The best practice is to avoid scheduling extra rehearsals outside the regular rehearsal time. The wise director plans well.

PERFORMANCES: HOW MANY?

The large ensembles should present three or four performances yearly for parents, peers, and the community. Typically there will be a "Christmas" or winter concert and a spring concert. One or two other performances over the year will promote higher motivation to master the music quickly, since singing before an audience tends to bring out the best efforts of the ensembles. The repertoire sung should be varied and include folk, spiritual, traditional choral literature (Renaissance through Contemporary), patriotic, carol, hymn, musical show tunes, and lighter pop music. School assemblies should be scheduled where not only the choruses perform, but group singing by the audience is done. A brass choir may lead the audience in singing of carols at Christmas.

The small ensembles may perform at the same concerts and other less formal school and community events. Taking a large or small ensemble to the elementary school is a good way to advertise the junior high choral program and recruit new singers for next year. Also, some solos, duets, and so on may be included on programs.

The large and small ensembles will typically participate in music contests. Directors will often need to prepare soloists for these contests and provide for piano accompanists.

Directors should be careful not to exploit the choral groups for personal gratification by having them perform excessively. The chorus exists for its members. Fewer performances of higher quality are preferable to frequent weak performances. Junior high students become demoralized if a performance goes badly. Excellent performances, on the other hand, build morale and support for the school choral program.

Chapter Three

The Senior High School Choral Program

The main difficulty for senior high school students, as with junior high students, is making the transition from childhood to adulthood. Older adolescents often adopt contradictory views, rejecting and accepting the adult world at the same time. Students see themselves as part of the youth culture that is committed to nonadult values and distrustful of the adult world.

UNDERSTANDING TEENAGERS

Teenagers frequently depend on their peers more than their parents and teachers because of the tensions and uncertainties of their in-between status. The need to conform to one's peers is strong during the senior high years as exemplified by fads in dress, grooming, and behavior. Joining a club or gang affords a sense of security for the adolescent. Parents often feel helpless to exercise guidance when confronted with "everybody's doing it." Teenagers do not want to be singled out, since it separates them from the security of their peers. It partly explains why teenagers do not like students who try too hard to win a teacher's approval. It also suggests that teachers will be more successful with discipline problems on a one to one basis rather than trying to discipline in front of the entire group.

Adolescents are in the process of developing a self-image. They are sensitive about appearance and capabilities. Emotional turmoil is often present, including restlessness, nail biting, frequent physical complaints, daydreaming, withdrawal, anxiety over mistakes, lack of concentration, uncontrolled laughing or crying, bragging, resenting authority, and being generally destructive. There is also the emergence of sexual desires and feelings during adolescence. Unfortunately, adolescence in our complex society lasts far longer than in simpler societies. Where the child assumes adult responsibilities quickly in simpler societies, young persons in our American society require a high level of education for widely different and complex jobs. Senior high students and often college students must live for years in a state of dependency on their parents and society. This is upsetting to both adolescents and adults. Delaying adult responsibilities also postpones marriage for many years after the development of sexual powers and frustrates life.

Another factor complicating adolescent growth is the change in male and female roles in American society. Where the woman's role was more confined to the home and child rearing in the past, the young woman may choose today from a variety of roles. The man's role as breadwinner is also undergoing change, since he not only pursues his career, but often assists with child rearing and home activities. In many instances both the father and mother must work to meet living expenses of the family. These changing roles of parents can put strain upon relations between parents and adolescents.

The adolescent is also confronted by changing mores in sex and marriage, drug use, drinking and smoking, religious practices, economic well-being, unemployment, racial tension, international conflict, and problems of the disadvantaged in our society. Some adolescents mistake such practices as drinking, smoking, drug use, or sexual encounters as a quick way to attain adult status. They frequently are not able to act and respond to such pressures in a *mature* adult way and should be guided by parents and teachers to make the best choices.

The junior high problem of the changing voice in boys is no longer a problem to choral directors in senior high school. The more adult ranges and sound are possible at this level. Excessive demands on senior high voices should be avoided.

Choral directors should be honest, fair, and understanding to their students. The teacher should retain adult status and not attempt to be "one of the gang" in trying to be popular and liked by their students. Teachers must lead, guide, and live the adult model. Adolescents realize they need adult parents and teachers as well as their teenage friends. In fact, adolescents need and desire order and routine in their lives, both at home and school. Limits to acceptable behavior must be set by both parents and teachers. Organization and routine are important ingredients to successful living. Too much freedom of choice and action can confuse not only adolescents, but adults, as well.

Another factor which choral directors must remember is that the students, even though they have elected chorus membership, are probably much less interested in music than the director. The music teacher is a highly trained individual in society, and it is sometimes difficult to meet the musical level and needs of the amateur singer. Showing off musical abilities in front of choral groups, talking over the students' heads, or constant negative criticism will undermine the relationship between director and chorus. Using too advanced choral literature which frustrates the chorus will not work either. The musical level inherent in the singers must be appraised and dealt with in a practical way. Through hard work the musical standard may be gradually raised.

Praising the chorus for good work is desirable. Success breeds success. A strong *esprit de corps* helps motivate the group. A choral group, more than a class, can develop strong group cooperation and feeling of achievement. The success of an individual in a class mostly depends upon the individual. The success of the chorus requires the sincere cooperation of every individual in the group. Teachers should appeal to adolescents' desires for group success. Teenagers do not want the less motivated students to detract from the group's efforts. Successful rehearsals and performances will propel the chorus forward to greater accomplishments and assist in recruiting new members. The applause and verbal responses of the audience are important to singers.

A director with a pleasant, optimistic outlook will encourage cooperation. Students want a director who will make them work hard, make them laugh, and allows them to relax and feel comfortable in rehearsal. Firmness and consistency to behavior limits from day to day must be enforced by the director, however. The director's attitude can build security and confidence in the chorus members. Students should be encouraged to "talk up" the chorus to friends and not make negative remarks about the group. The director should be willing to receive constructive criticism from students, colleagues, principal, and parents.

Group motivation may be enhanced by

1. giving service awards to chorus members (pins and certificates)
2. using a common group apparel such as robes which provide identity to the chorus
3. having singers invest in the chorus by buying a stole with school letters on it. Bars may be added for each year of service to the choir.
4. giving recognition to the singers by including all names in the printed program and announcing special assistance at concerts
5. involving as many of the chorus members as possible in the operation of the chorus—robe committee, choral library committee, concert set-up committee, student officers, and so on.
6. making a recording of the choral group, which may be bought by chorus members and friends
7. inviting graduates of the chorus to come back and participate in a spring concert on a well-known piece
8. planning a parents' night where a potluck dinner is served and students perform for parents. A mini-rehearsal, complete with vocalises and sight singing, may be informative to parents. Too often parents see only the finished product. Directors and selected singers may orient parents to how the chorus functions.
9. inviting a guest conductor to spend the day rehearsing choral groups for an evening concert
10. commissioning an original choral composition by a community composer or a composer colleague of the director. This can be performed under the direction of the composer at a concert.

RECRUITING TECHNIQUES

Many times, upon taking a choral position, a new teacher is confronted with low enrollments, especially males, in the school choral groups. Since chorus membership is elective, sufficient students need to be recruited and retained to make the chorus a worthwhile music experience for all. The most successful way to obtain new students is to have a successful organization. Prospective singers will want to know how present members feel about the choral program, what kind of music is sung, and what the choral director is like. Directors should realize that parents also are able to influence their sons and daughters to join chorus.

If the choral director finds only a small enrollment in the choral groups from last spring the following suggestions might be helpful:

1. Do as much as possible over the summer months to identify possible new singers, or those who have sung at one time or another.
2. Schedule a meeting with the principal or head counselor to seek approval for schedule changes for students who may wish to enroll in chorus. Check to see which students are in a study hall during chorus period. Also, some students may be placed in another section of the same class.
3. Talk personally to those students who are able to enroll, either in person or by telephone. Sometimes a talk to parents will provide additional momentum to join chorus.
4. When the choruses meet in the fall ask all present members for leads to prospective singers, and ideas about recruiting them. Each chorus member may be assigned one name to contact and report back to the director. An audition should then be scheduled for interested students.
5. Make the first rehearsals of the chorus a successful and pleasant experience, and utilize a variety of literature to stimulate interest. Show considerable leadership and set acceptable limits to student behavior. Work the students hard and compliment them on their cooperation and good work.

To recruit junior high singers into the senior high chorus the following year, a large or small ensemble may perform at a junior high assembly or in the junior high rehearsal room. Junior high students enjoy hearing from their more advanced peers, and a fine performance can win many students to enrolling in senior high choral groups. The brief program of selections must be chosen carefully for variety and strong, positive effect upon the junior high students. Lively pieces such as spirituals, patriotic tunes, and some pop tunes will stir interest. The senior high director should develop a strong working relationship with the directors of junior high "feeder" schools. Names of junior high chorus members should be presented in the previous spring to the senior high director so that students may be scheduled into the beginning senior high choral groups.

Recruiting boys into senior high chorus or male glee club requires tact. Although some boys feel that music is not too manly, this attitude has lessened over the past two decades. Inviting a male quartet to a rehearsal or an assembly at the school will help bolster the notion that many men like to sing. Some boys in senior high also feel they cannot sing well, and need technical assistance with the voice. An all male chorus which sings with a strong, rich tone can entrance an audience. The choral director should encourage athletes on the football and basketball team to sing in chorus. Their belonging to the group gives music a stamp of approval. Even though some conflicts will occur because of athletic and music events falling on similar dates, it is wise to solicit recruitment help from the coaches at the school.

When talking to boys, they enjoy direct "manly" comments from the director. Instead of a polite, "Boys, that sounds fine," an "Alright men, that balance is great!" will be more appropriate and enjoyed by males. Boys enjoy humor and attention from the director.

THE VOICE AUDITION

At the senior high level, the director will need to hear all voices on an individual basis to best assess potential, voice quality and range, and sight singing ability. The Personal Data Card presented in Chap. 2 can serve as a model for gathering information at the audition. Since some senior high choruses will sing in eight parts, the director needs to pay close attention to the best singing tessitura of each voice as well as total ranges. The range and quality of the senior high voice may be determined by singing the following five-note scale passages in Fig. 3–1. The first exercise will determine the upper range limit at which excessive strain occurs, and where the quality begins to change. Start the exercises in the middle range of each singer and progress up or down by half steps.

Directors should record the *tone quality* of the voice by having each person sing a short folk or hymn melody known to most singers. The *intonation* of each singer may also be recorded on the Personal Data Card. The Pitch-Rhythm Retention Test may then be administered and scored to determine the degree of each singer's ability to reproduce *pitch-rhythm* patterns. This should be followed by a sight reading exercise, or the singer may be asked to sight sing his or her part to a choral piece.

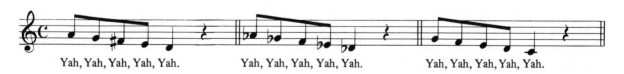

Figure 3–1 Senior High Vocal Range Test

The entire voice audition should not last more than seven minutes. Scheduling students at ten- or fifteen-minute intervals is workable. The director will discover some weak signals in the auditions who may be placed in the "training choir" to improve musicianship if the schedule permits. Decisions about accepting a student into an advanced, select choir should be posted on a bulletin board beside the choral rehearsal room. The director should not try to make the decision at the audition. It is wise to audition all students who desire to sing in an advanced chorus, even though some have sung in the group previously. Equal and fair treatment is respected by students.

SENIOR HIGH VOCAL RANGES AND TESSITURA

When testing higher and lower ranges, the outer limits (when strain or voice quality changes) should be recorded on the music staff on the Personal Data Card. The following ranges are characteristic to senior high school untrained voices. (See Fig. 3–2.)

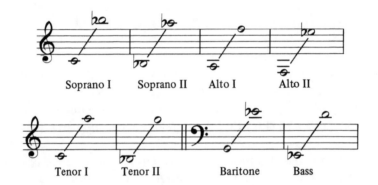

Figure 3–2 Senior High School Mixed Chorus Ranges

First sopranos' voices are light, with a lyric quality, where second sopranos' voices have a fuller, more dramatic quality. The first alto is similar in quality to the second soprano, but with a more developed lower range. The second alto is a heavier, deeper voice in the lower range and more developed than the first alto.

The senior high first tenor has a light, lyric quality, where the second tenor has a fuller, more dramatic voice quality. The baritone voice, similar to second tenor, has a more developed middle and lower range. Some baritones may move upward to sing a tenor part eventually. The bass singer has a heavier, darker quality in the middle and lower ranges of the voice.

Directors should realize that the ranges in Fig. 3–2 are the widest possible, and that the best tessitura of each part lies toward the middle of the range. Vocalizing will help to expand the ranges to the upper and lower limits. Vocalises for senior high choruses are given in Chap. 7. When selecting octavos and extended works for senior high chorus, it is best to avoid the extremes of each range. Although adults with training can sustain long, high pitches numerous counts, this technical skill may be lacking except in a few senior high students who are studying voice privately.

Soprano I	Soprano II	Alto II	Alto I
	Bass	Baritone	
	Tenor II	Tenor I	

Figure 3–3 SSAATTBB Seating Plan (Small Male Sections)

SEATING MIXED, TREBLE, AND MALE CHORUSES

The senior high mixed chorus is capable of singing more quality choral literature in as many as eight parts if sufficient vocal talent is available. The type of seating arrangement selected depends upon (1) the size of each part, (2) the voice qualities of the members, and (3) the musical experience of the singers.

The seating plan in Fig. 3–3 allows for an eight-part chorus with small male sections. The tenors are to the front and middle with the baritones and basses behind them. Some second altos may join the first tenors if necessary. The soprano and bass are fairly close for good chord stability. A few girls behind the boys can develop a better blend since all voices can hear the other parts.

If the parts are balanced, the seating plan in Fig. 3–4 is preferable. The first soprano and second bass (outer parts) in close proximity aids intonation in homophonic choral singing. The baritone and second tenor may be shifted back and forth. Low tenor parts may be bolstered by baritones, who, in turn, can be helped with high baritone passages by the second tenors. First alto and second alto parts may shift, also. Second altos are also seated beside first tenors and may help first tenors with high parts or when there is a scarcity of first tenors.

For smaller choruses which sing only SATB music, the seating plans in Fig. 3–5 are more workable. The smaller tenor and bass sections are placed in the center. These seating arrangements are also useful for SAB singing. The soprano and alto sections are larger and placed on either side (and possibly to the front and back) of the tenors and basses.

Bass II	Baritone	Tenor II	Tenor I
Soprano I	Soprano II	Alto I	Alto II

Figure 3–4 SSAATTBB Seating Plan (Balanced Parts)

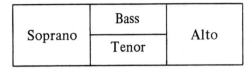

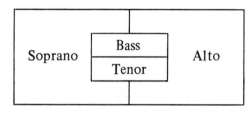

Figure 3–5 Small SATB Chorus Seating Plans

The quartet arrangement often produces a homogeneous sound, better balance, and better intonation. It requires excellent singers who can hold their own part independently and is useful for singing homophonic chordal-type music. It is not as effective for contrapuntal singing since a good section tone is desired for the independent vocal lines. Directors cannot lead the sections as well in the quartet seating plan. Young, inexperienced choruses will not benefit from this type of quartet seating plan. (See Fig. 3–6.)

B	A	T	S	B	A	T	S	B	A	T	S	B	A	T	S
S	T	A	B	S	T	A	B	S	T	A	B	S	T	A	B
B	A	T	S	B	A	T	S	B	A	T	S	B	A	T	S
S	T	A	B	S	T	A	B	S	T	A	B	S	T	A	B

Figure 3–6 Quartet Seating Plan

It is important to have good leaders in each section. These will frequently be those who have studied piano or some other instrument, or who may be studying voice privately. Leaders will become known in the voice audition and sight reading test. Strong singers may be placed beside weaker singers. After a week or two of rehearsals the director may alter the seating plan for better choral effect.

The treble chorus (SA, SSA, SSAA) may be seated as shown in Figs. 3–7 and 3–8.

By placing the sopranos to the left and altos to the right for SA singing, it is possible to take singers from the middle ends of each section to form a soprano II part. Voices placed on soprano II must be seated carefully for range, since some may need to sing soprano and others alto in SA voicings. See the previously given voice ranges for SSAA choral singing.

Two male chorus seating plans are presented in Fig. 3–9. The first is best when there is a definite lack of tenor voices, since the tenors are placed forward to be heard. The second plan is preferred when the male parts are fairly well balanced.

Figure 3–7 Treble Chorus Seating Plan (SA/SSA)

Soprano I	Soprano II	Alto I	Alto II

Figure 3–8 Treble Chorus Seating Plan (SSAA)

Bass	Baritone
Tenor I	Tenor II

Tenor I	Tenor II	Baritone	Bass

Figure 3–9 Male Chorus Seating Plans (TTBB)

SCHEDULING LARGE CHORUSES

At the high school level (grades 9, 10, 11, 12 or 10, 11, 12), one or two mixed choruses should be scheduled daily. One group may be a "training chorus" made up of students in grades nine and ten, and perhaps newly recruited, but inexperienced singers in grades eleven and twelve. The other ensemble will be the high school concert choir and will be much more select in membership. Both choruses should rehearse daily because of time for skill and knowledge development and the increased performance demands at the senior high school level. A very small high school will be able to organize only one mixed chorus, whereas, very large high schools may need three or four choruses. The mixed chorus may range in size from fifty to eighty voices. For some performances, two or more of the choruses may be "massed" for festival-type pieces with instrument accompaniment.

A girl's chorus and boy's chorus (glee clubs) should also be formed. These are also large ensembles which should be scheduled during the school day. They provide specialized experiences with treble and male chorus literature. Frequently there are too many girls who wish to sing to balance the number of boys in the mixed choruses. A girl's chorus provides a satisfying vehicle for girls and the literature is abundant and excellent in quality. Boys enjoy having their own singing group, and the director will be able to assist individual voices better in the all-male chorus. Frequently the male chorus is made up of boys from both mixed choral groups in high school. If a daily meeting time is not available for the treble and male chorus, they may meet at a certain hour in the school day, with girl's chorus on Monday, Wednesday, and Friday and boy's chorus on Tuesday and Thursday.

A model schedule for all ensembles is given in Chap. 1. (See Fig. 1–1.) Many directors prefer to schedule the select concert choir in mid-morning before lunch, since voices are flexible by this time, and the singers are not yet fatigued as they may be later in the afternoon.

ORGANIZING SMALL VOCAL ENSEMBLES

Many talented students need to sing in a smaller choral ensemble to develop their music abilities to the fullest. These include mixed ensembles such as madrigal groups or chamber ensembles, jazz/show choirs, girls sextet (triple trio), boy's octet (or quartet). These small groups should be select auditioned ensembles with the membership coming from the concert choir. It is wise to require membership in concert choir as a prerequisite to auditioning for any of these specialized small ensembles. Choral technique is best developed in the large ensemble with adequate rehearsal time. The small ensembles are usually scheduled on an extracurricular basis before or after school. There are frequently students who desire to sing in a jazz/show choir because of the popular type of music sung, the flashy choreography performed, and the overall "showy" character of this group. Solid choral training is also required for this type of group, making participation in concert choir mandatory.

As contests arrive during the spring season, these small ensembles may compete along with the large ensembles. The director may also rehearse solos, duets, and trios for these events for interested and talented students. The small ensembles may sing for community organizations and churches over the year. They may be utilized for recruitment by singing for "feeder" junior high schools. The small ensembles provide advanced choral experiences for the talented student. Rehearsal time is often minimal. Singing in a madrigal group with only one or two voices to a part requires a high degree of musical independence. The small ensembles, as well as solos, duets, trios, and quartets, provide stimulating challenges to the talented singer in senior high school.

THE SENIOR HIGH SCHOOL VOICE CLASS

The voice class is a specialized class for student soloists in the advanced concert choir. Membership should be selective and limited to those students with a fairly high degree of music ability and vocal proficiency and who display exceptional interest in solo singing. Although some students in late senior high school may study voice privately, the voice class may serve a number of students who find lessons financially prohibitive. Taught by the choral director, usually, the class approach to voice training allows singers to observe each other and discuss common vocal difficulties. The voice class allows time for preparation of solos, duets, trios, and quartets for music contests, as well as for school concerts and community events.

The voice class will focus on such things as diaphragmatic breathing; resonating cavities of larynx, pharynx, mouth, nose, and sinuses; consistent vocal quality; extension of range, and other topics. Much group and individual vocalization will be done. Songs will be learned and sung in group fashion as well as in solo renditions. Recordings of vocal artists may be presented for study of style, interpretation, technique, tone, and repertoire. Some basic vocal exercises may stress sustained tones, scale passages, arpeggios, or combinations of these. Diction will need to be stressed, just as in chorus, through work with vowels, diphthongs, triphthongs, and voiced and unvoiced consonants. The international phonetic alphabet may be utilized to demonstrate all vocal sounds in the English language. Some students in voice class may sing foreign texts, and Latin, Italian, German, and French pronounciation may be studied.

Some vocal technique and sight singing materials are listed in Appendix N and in Bibliography B, Vocal Training and Choral Teaching. Texts for class voice instruction are available, also. A valuable source of graded materials for all solo voice classifications, as well as choral listings of music, is *1985 Selective Music Lists: Vocal Solos and Ensembles*. Reston, Virginia: Music Educators National Conference, 1985. Vocal techniques and English and Latin choral diction are discussed in Chaps. 7 and 8.

PART
TWO

THE CONDUCTOR AND THE CHORAL SCORE

Chapter Four

Basic Conducting Principles and Techniques

The conductor's primary role is to interpret the music for the singers. This leader must be more than a mere time beater. The conductor's musical knowledge and interpretive wishes should be conveyed through an effective conducting technique. Thus, the conductor endeavors to instill life and vitality into the music so that the end result will be a truly thrilling and aesthetically satisfying experience for both the singers and the listening audience.

THE CONDUCTOR AS INTERPRETER AND COMMUNICATOR

The choral conductor is a leader who must inspire, sensitize, and control the choral ensemble. Relationships with the choir depend upon the morale, *esprit de corps*, and teamwork of the choir as a whole. The conductor must be able to communicate the music's power to both the choir and accompanist. The face and the body are employed, along with the arms, to convey subtle meanings and impulses to the choir. The conductor must also possess a significant knowledge of vocal technique, diction skills, music theory, and music history to be able to interpret the traditional choral styles.

There are other qualities that will enhance the choral conductor's effectiveness. These include a high degree of organization and administrative ability, a sense of humor, a cheerful businesslike manner, and a strong desire to assist others to learn to sing well in a choir. The ability to plan and direct consistently effective rehearsals is mandatory. The choral conductor must also know how to select literature and plan choral concerts.

POISE, POSTURE, AND THE BATON

Conducting involves physical coordination of the entire body. A clear understanding of the basic conducting patterns is necessary before one can expand them into a personal conducting style. Some conductors never are able to achieve a sense of poise at the podium. Their gestures are awkward, excessive, or uncoordinated. They bury their heads in the music as though the choir did not exist. They do not anticipate the entrances of individual parts and appear to be following the singers, rather than leading them. The ability to conduct the typical beat patterns is easily within the grasp of the average person with normal coordination. Interpretation of the music, however, lies far beyond mere beating of time. A good conducting technique is of value only to those who study and understand the musical score, who establish a good rapport with the choral ensemble, and who are able to transmit the ultimate beauty of music with sensitivity.

Use of the videotape allows student conductors to review their conducting as they actually conducted. Seeing is believing and the videotape teaching aid is well worth the time and effort.

Posture transmits the positiveness, strength, and self-confidence of the conductor to the choir. The stance on the podium should appear solid, but not forced or rigidly locked into position. The element of dynamic tension that is important to the bouyancy of singing applies to conductors, also.

The feet of the conductor should be eight to ten inches apart, with one foot slightly ahead of the other for balance. The knees should be flexible, not stiff. The chest should be held high, with shoulders slightly back. The head should remain in vertical alignment with the body. A hunched position should be avoided. When the body is in proper position, the hands are ready to begin communicating. The arms must be in a position to operate freely, raised high enough to be seen clearly by the ensemble. A larger ensemble will require the arms to be higher, while a small ensemble will function well using a smaller conducting plane. The average conducting plane will normally be just below the height of the shoulder. Rarely should any beats go below the waist. Very few beats will rise above the head, except the last beat of a measure, occasionally.

The size of the beat will be determined by the style and tempo of each piece of music. Fast tempi demand smaller gestures as do most soft passages. Loud passages require larger and more dramatic gestures, as do slow tempi. A large festival chorus of five hundred singers will demand broader gestures than a choir of forty or fifty singers.

As the arms are raised into conducting position, the elbows should be forward, not cramped against the body. This is much like a hand-shaking position. Conducting the beat is done with the right hand. The forearm should be parallel to the ground and the palm turned down in a rounded position. If a baton is not used, the fingers should be rounded slightly, but not held closely together or spread too far apart. The thumb of the conductor's right hand should be in a moderate position, neither sticking out, nor held too tight to the hand. The little finger should join the gentle curve of the rest of the fingers. The conductor may practice the conducting plane and arm and hand position in front of a mirror until these look comfortable. Tension in the arm and wrist should be avoided. The body, hand, arm, and wrist must appear natural. The conductor will wear either a business suit or tuxedo in most cases (occasionally, tails). The jacket should be buttoned and body motions kept to a minimum.

Although many choral conductors prefer to conduct without a baton, every conductor should learn to conduct with a baton whether one is used in all performances or not. A 12 to 14 in. baton is desirable for most situations. For large festival choruses, or performances by chorus and orchestra, a longer baton may be warranted. The regular use of a baton will force the conductor into better conducting habits, since unnecessary gestures made with the hands are impossible with the baton. There are times when the choral conductor will find it necessary to use the hands only in conducting in order to be more expressive and to accurately execute attacks and releases with the fingers. Release of final consonants is such a situation.

The baton is an extension of the arm. The palm of the hand should be down with the baton held between thumb and forefinger. It should lie across the first joint of the forefinger with the ball of the baton resting comfortably in the palm of the hand. The baton should not be held so tight that the wrist becomes tense and movement is restricted. A too loosely held baton, however, results in loss of control and precision.

PREPARATORY BEATS, ATTACKS, AND RELEASES

The conductor must think the tempo, the mood, and dynamics of the first entrance before the start of a choral piece. One should raise the hands to a point slightly lower than the shoulders. When the music begins on a beat of the measure, the preparatory beat will usually be one beat in advance of the first sounded note. On rare occasions, the conductor will use two preparatory beats to clearly establish the tempo for the choir and to avoid ragged entrances. This situation occurs when the choir begins the piece between beats.

The preparatory beat must be in the same tempo, mood, dynamics, and style of the first phrase of the music. This first gesture of the conductor conveys the opening of the piece and is of vital importance. The conductor's motions should convey the character of the music to the choir. If a piece is to begin *fortissimo*, and at a slow tempo, the preparatory beat and downbeat must convey that information to the choir. The various preparatory beats in 4/4 meter are shown in Fig. 4–1.

If the music begins on beat one, the last beat of the 4/4 pattern will be used as the preparatory beat. If the music begins on beat two of the measure, beat one will become the preparatory beat. Similarly, beat two will be the preparatory beat if the music starts on beat three. If the music starts on beat four of the 4/4 measure, beat three becomes the preparatory beat. With practice the conductor can develop a clear preparatory beat in any meter (duple, triple, quadruple, irregular meters, and compound). The basic principle of the preparatory beat is the same.

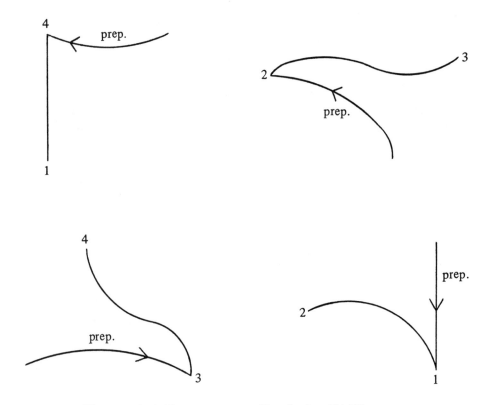

Figure 4–1 Preparatory Beats in 4/4 Measure

Music that starts on a fraction of a beat causes difficulty for the conductor. This may occur at the beginning of the piece or later after a pause, meter change, or after a fermata. If a piece begins on the second half of beat one in 4/4 meter, it would seem wise to give beat four and one as preparatory beats to effectively set the tempo and allow a smooth entrance. Figure 4–2 is such a piece. It is strongly recommended that the conductor mentally "conduct" several measures of each piece before beginning it. This establishes the tempo and reviews the rhythm of the opening phrase.

For attacks and releases to be effective, precision is required. A clear preparatory beat will improve the attacks; however, an alert physical stance and appropriate facial expression helps to improve the readiness of the singers. Many conductors breathe with the ensemble during the preparatory movement, and "mouth" the words of the first measure or so of the text.

Just as the size of the preparatory beat is determined by the mood and dynamics of the music, the size of the release will also vary. Sometimes the entire choir will be

F.J. Haydn

Figure 4–2 Starting on a Fraction of the Beat

Left Hand   Right Hand

Figure 4–3 A Large Two-Hand Fortissimo Release

given a precise release, often including the fingers if a consonant is involved. If the release is soft, the palm of the hand may be turned down and closed to stop the tone. If a forceful *forte* release is demanded, the hand gesture will need to be a longer upward and a longer and deeper downstroke to be effective. This circular type release for both hands is illustrated in Fig. 4–3.

FUNDAMENTAL BEAT PATTERNS

Of all the beats, the downbeat is slightly more important than others. If singers lose their part, they will look for the conductor's downbeat which is made at the center of the conducting plane. As the music becomes rhythmically more complex, the conducting beat should become clearer and simpler, without extraneous gestures and motions. The beat pattern is at the core of any conductor's style.

The *ictus* is the exact moment when the conducting gesture indicates the rhythmic pulse. A slight rebound following the *ictus* helps the ensemble determine the precise pulse beat. In fast tempi the rebound will be short and quick, whereas, in slower tempi, it may be higher and slower. Figure 4–4 illustrates the most common beat patterns. They are performed with the right hand, while the left hand is reserved for gestures other than beating time. The left-handed person should use the right hand to conduct. Each pattern should be practiced until it feels natural. The two-beat pattern can be used with 2/4, 2/2, alla breve, and fast 6/8 meters. When the tempo is fast in the two-beat pattern the hand movement will be down, up. When a slower two is conducted the arm will rebound slightly to the right to allow a longer beat one.

The three-beat pattern may be utilized with 3/4, 3/2, and fast 9/8 meters. The third beat, which is often rushed by amateur conductors, is an inward and upward direction in order to stretch the third beat prior to the next downbeat. Rushing the third beat will cause rhythm and tempo problems.

The four-beat pattern may be used with 4/4, 4/2, and fast 12/8 meters. Beat two goes to the left, with the beats two and three slightly higher than the downbeat.

There are two six-beat patterns often used by conductors. The first example of the

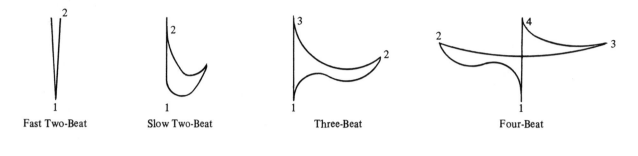

Fast Two-Beat   Slow Two-Beat   Three-Beat   Four-Beat

German Six-Beat   French Six-Beat

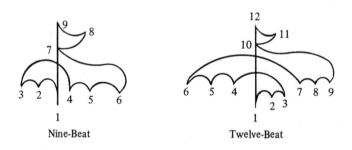

Nine-Beat   Twelve-Beat

Figure 4–4 Fundamental Beat Patterns

six-beat in Fig. 4–4 is referred to as the German six pattern, whereas, the second six-beat pattern is labeled the French six pattern. This French six is useful when the conductor alternates between six and two beats in a measure. The six-beat pattern may be used for slow 6/8, 6/4, and 6/2 meters.

The nine-beat pattern is a subdivision of a three pattern. It is used for slow 9/8 and 9/4 meters mainly. If the tempo becomes faster it is easy to modify the nine-beat pattern into a three-beat pattern.

The twelve-beat pattern is useful for slow 12/8 and 12/4 meters. For faster tempos, the beat pattern can be modified to a four-beat pattern.

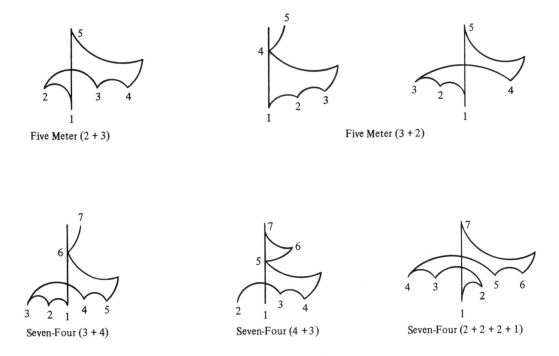

Five Meter (2 + 3)   Five Meter (3 + 2)

Seven-Four (3 + 4)   Seven-Four (4 + 3)   Seven-Four (2 + 2 + 2 + 1)

Figure 4–5 Irregular Conducting Patterns

IRREGULAR METERS, CHANGING METERS, AND FREE RHYTHM

Irregular meters (asymmetrical) often occur as a result of word stress, particularly in more contemporary compositions. Irregular beat patterns require modification to the fundamental beat patterns. The most common irregular beat patterns are 5/4 meter (2 + 3 or 3 + 2) and 7/4 meter (3 + 4, 4 + 3, or 2 + 2 + 2 + 1). There are some other combinations of irregular meters, but Fig. 4–5 illustrates the ones that appear most often.

The conductor will frequently find choral pieces that change meters within the composition. The first examples appeared in Baroque pieces as the hemiola effect where a three meter was temporarily changed to the feel of two meter for several measures. The hemiola ties notes over the barline as in Fig. 4–6.

In Fig. 4–7 the choral example, *I Will Greatly Rejoice* by Knut Nystedt, the meters alternate from 5/4, 2/2, 4/2, and 3/2. Careful examination of the piece indicates that the half note is the "beat" note. This piece requires careful study to successfully beat the time. Directors may wish to put the counts in each measure above the music for the eye to follow.

Figure 4–6 Hemiola Effect (Three to Two Meter Feel)

I WILL GREATLY·REJOICE!

for Mixed Voices, S.A.T.B., a cappella

Isaiah 61:10-11

KNUT NYSTEDT

Figure 4–7 Conducting Changing Meters

Figure 4–8 Free Rhythm

Sometimes the composer uses no meter signature, leaving the music in free rhythm. (See Fig. 4–8.) This happens in unison chant and chordal harmonic passages. The conductor should not divide the passage into arbitrary measures in order to beat some type of meter. The stress (downbeat) will be determined by the text. The most important words will receive more weight. The conductor should sing the words until the conducting feels comfortable and musical.

MARCATO AND LEGATO CONDUCTING

Some choral pieces call for a forceful beat with the arm. This is often the case with very declamatory texts. In this marcato type of conducting, the beat gives a strength to the choral tone. Singers are required to give more stress to the text with greater separation of words and syllables. Syncopated pieces often require a marcato conducting style.

On the other hand, a smooth legato style piece requires a gentle placement of the beat pattern. This pattern requires a flexible wrist and resembles painting a wall in the air. The arm and wrist movement attempts to connect the notes into long phrases to make the singers stretch the tone from note to note with no break of tone. This legato style demands gentle articulation of word consonants.

Occasionally, a short, staccato type of conducting beat may be required. This will require the singers to separate the sounds as they move from note to note. The hand should make short, detached type of beat patterns. This style is not used as much in choral singing as are the marcato and legato styles.

FERMATAS

Typically a fermata indicates a moment when the rhythmic motion of the choral piece ceases. Usually fermatas are prepared by a slight ritard as the fermata is ap-

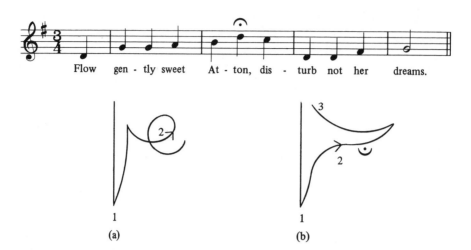

Flow   gen - tly sweet   At - ton, dis - turb not her   dreams.

(a)   (b)

Figure 4–9 Two Types of Fermata Releases: (a) Complete Release, and (b) Carrying Over

proached. The conductor's beats enlarge to gain the choir's attention. If the fermata is released at a *forte* level, the hands may rise slightly before the release to maintain the singer's breath. The release of the fermata may be accomplished in two ways. One procedure is to cut off completely the tone being held. The alternative is to carry over the tone to the succeeding phrase without a break in the flow of breath. The conducting patterns for both procedures are illustrated in Fig. 4–9.

Sometimes the conductor will need to "hold" one part on a fermata, while other parts are still moving rhythmically. The fermata may be executed with the left hand in this case while the right hand continues beating time for the other choral parts. Often all the parts will be released from the fermata simultaneously using both hands.

CONDUCTING FAST, VERY SLOW, AND CHANGING TEMPI

Fast tempos will often modify the standard conducting patterns. A fast two will become simply a one beat per measure. In a fast three, the second and third beats may be implied by a rounded gesture after the downbeat. A very fast three will be conducted one beat per measure. Fast tempos in four will be conducted in two usually, as will a fast 6/8 meter.

Fast irregular meters of 5/4 or 5/8 will be conducted in a modified two pattern with either beat extended to include the extra quarter or eighth note. Also, fast 7/4 or 7/8 meters will be conducted in a modified three pattern.

When the tempo of a piece is quite slow, the normal beat patterns will not seem sufficient to control the rhythm and singers will lose the slow beat. Instead of the slow beat pattern, the normal beats need to be divided. Figure 4–10 shows the standard divisions of the beats in duple, triple, and quadruple meters. These are the meters that most necessitate the divided beat; however, other beat patterns may be divided. Pieces such as the Bach "Crucifixus" from the *B Minor Mass* and Handel's "Surely He Hath Bourne Our Griefs" from *Messiah* require the divided three and four beat, respectively.

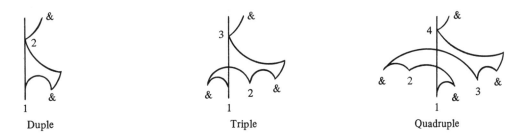

Figure 4–10 Divided Beat Patterns in Duple, Triple, and Quadruple Meters

Another occasion for the conductor to divide the beat is to indicate a slowing of tempo, such as when approaching a final cadence. The ensemble will respond with more precision to the divided beat. There are other times when the music calls for an accelerando. In this situation the conductor must gradually increase the speed of the beat, sometimes giving emphasis to the change with the left hand, also. If there is an abrupt tempo change, such as beginning a new section, the preparatory beat should set this new tempo, along with the appropriate facial and body gestures to establish the mood change.

DETERMINING THE TEMPO

The tempo or speed of the beat for a choral composition will be determined by a number of factors. There is no one tempo for each piece; however, there is a norm that should not be violated. Very often the composer will place markings on the music to guide the conductor. These include such terms as largo, langsam, andante, allegro, lively, and so on, in various languages. Ritards and accelerandos may be written on the music, also. A thorough knowledge of music performance styles and practices will assist in determining tempo. (See Chap. 5.)

Pieces prior to the invention of the Maelzel Metronome during Beethoven's day used no metronome marks. Many editions of Renaissance, Baroque, and Classic works contain metronome marks which have been added by an editor. These may or may not be useful. Directors should not diligently adhere to these numbers, i. e., ♩ = 116, but should arrive at an acceptable tempo based upon music theory and style period practices.

Other factors that contribute to tempo selection include: (1) the text, (2) the music style period, (3) the smallest rhythmic unit, (4) the harmonic complexity, (5) the rhythmic complexity, and (6) the overall character of the choral piece.

Texts vary greatly in mood. A gentle text should not be sung fast out of character. If the piece contains many words, a moderate or slower tempo may be necessary. A piece with fewer words to articulate might be performed at a faster tempo.

Knowing the date of the composition and performance practices of that time will assist in making proper tempo decisions. Tempi were fairly strict in the Baroque period, but fluctuate more in the Romantic and Twentieth Century.

Each conductor should examine both the shortest and longest rhythmic unit in the piece. If the shortest rhythmic unit, i. e., sixteenth notes, cannot be musically performed, the tempo may be too fast. If, on the other hand, too slow a tempo is set, the longest notes will become difficult to sustain. The conductor must mentally "feel" the subdivision of the beat before starting to beat time.

The more harmonically complex a work is, the more difficult to perform at a faster tempo. Pieces that have a slow harmonic rhythm may be moved faster. Chromatics are harder at fast tempi. Similarly, complex rhythm features will necessitate a slower tempo to negotiate the rhythm patterns.

The conductor will want to ask if the overall character of the piece is being conveyed to the singers and audience by the tempo chosen. A technically correct piece is still unmusical if a poor tempo is chosen.

There are such factors as size of the choir, music capabilities of the singers, and acoustical features of the auditorium that can affect the choice of tempo. Large choirs are difficult to "move" at fast tempi. Better trained singers will be able to handle pieces at faster tempi and extremely slow tempi. The vocal technique helps the performance. Certainly, the acoustics of the auditorium can affect tempo choice. A large, live hall, in which sound decay is longer, may necessitate a slower tempo. A dry, dead hall may require a faster tempo. The conductor needs to know the auditorium where the ensemble is to sing.

THE LEFT HAND ROLE

When the left hand is not in use it should be held in front of the body at waist level. Here it is both out of sight of the audience and in a readiness position. The left hand is usually not utilized for beating time and is therefore free for other purposes. It may be used for (1) cueing entrances of various sections of the choir, (2) indicating style and dynamics, (3) assisting in starting and stopping the ensemble, (4) controlling changes of tempo, (5) controlling balance among the choir parts, and (6) occasionally assisting with the beat pattern.

Cueing refers to the many times a conductor needs to indicate important entrances throughout the piece, or parts that need emphasis. Since cues often come in rapid succession, a nod of the head or a glance from the conductor will supplement the cues of the left hand. The left hand cue is best given one beat before the entrance with the gesture made directly at the section or individual performer involved. Left hand cues with eye contact are most effective; however, eye contact is not always possible. The two hands must learn to operate independently of each other. Directors often overstress their cues with amatuer choirs, to be sure the singers will not miss the entrances. Missed entrances by an entire section will be very harmful to the rendition of the choral piece. Therefore, well-defined cues can promote successful performances.

The left hand can also indicate the style and expressive dynamics of the choral literature. The mood of the composition can be conveyed by the left hand frequently. Although the right hand beat pattern can show legato, marcato, or staccato styles and indicate dynamics by the size of the beat, the left hand can assist in this process. An upward motion of the left hand with palm up indicates an increase in volume and a downward motion with palm down will show a decrease in dynamic level. These gestures must be made gradually; otherwise the choir will respond too sudden and the crescendo or diminuendo will be ineffective. This is especially true for the diminuendo signal since most choirs move too quickly to a soft level, leaving no space for a further volume decrease. The singers tend to relax breath support of the tone when the diminuendo signal is given.

As the crescendo signal is given, the arm rises with the palm up. The diminuendo signal is given with palm down and a lowering of the arm. *Subito* dynamic changes can be given with the left hand, along with the change of size of the right hand beat pattern.

Very often the left hand will assist in starting and stopping the ensemble. This ensures precision and emphasis. Whether the piece starts or ends *forte* or *piano*, the left hand can indicate this type of entrance or release.

When the tempo of a piece changes, it is critical to catch the attention of the entire ensemble. The left hand can help make clearer the change of tempo. The left hand is used, however, only until the new tempo is clearly established, and then it returns to its position of rest in front of the body.

Balance of parts within the choir is also controlled by the conductor's left hand. The gesture is similar to those that indicate dynamics, except the signal to become louder or softer is directed only to one section. Much of the balance problem will be achieved in rehearsal and the conductor will not need to signal as much in performance. However, there are occasions when the hall acoustics, illness of one or two key singers, or performance excitement can create balance problems. In the performance itself, these gestures must be cautious and controlled so the singers do not overreact.

The left hand should not mirror the beat pattern of the right hand. The left hand can assist with the beat pattern when the conductor wishes to make the beat clear to the left side of the ensemble at some critical point. When the music is broadening, reaching a climax, or simply changing tempo, the left hand can help to emphasize these to the ensemble. The left hand gesture will be most helpful with larger ensembles. If the left hand is used to beat time, it should be only for a limited time, since the windmill appearance of two-hand conducting is less than pleasing to the audience. Often it is wise to place the piano to the right of the conductor so the accompanist can see the right hand beat pattern clearly.

EXEMPLARY REPERTOIRE TO IMPROVE CONDUCTING TECHNIQUES

Conducting is not learned by reading about it. It is an art that must be learned through practice to achieve poise on the podium. There are several anthologies of choral music which contain music in varied meters and tempi, various style periods, as well as many specific conducting problems. These collections include:

Adler, Samuel. *Choral Conducting: An Anthology*. Schirmer Books
Bach, J. S.–Goetschius, P. *Sixty Chorales*. Oliver Ditson/Presser
Clough–Leighter. *The A Cappella Singer* (Renaissance). E. C. Schirmer
Hartshorn, W. *Five Centuries of Choral Music*. G. Schirmer
Kirk, Theron. *Choral Music for Mixed Voices*. General Words and Music/Kjos

Kjelson, Lee and McCray, James. *The Conductor's Manual of Choral Music Literature*. Belwin/Columbia

Robinson, Ray. *Choral Music: An Anthology*. W. W. Norton

Schott, Sally, et al. *Sing* (Text and Literature). Hinshaw Music Co

G. Schirmer. *Something to Sing About, Vols. 1, 2, 3*. G. Schirmer

Specific titles of choral literature which exemplify certain choral conducting problems follow:

Two Beat

Berger. "Alleluia" from *Brazilian Psalm*

Des Prez. *The Cricket*

Dowland. *Now, O Now I Needs Must Part*

Hindemith, "Since All is Passing" from *Six Chansons*

Morley. *My Bonnie Lass*

Palestrina. "Kyrie" from *Missa Iste Confessor*

Three Beat

Berlioz. "The Shepherd's Farewell" from *L'Enfance du Christ*

Billings. *When Jesus Wept*

Brahms. "How Lovely Is Thy Dwelling Place" from *German Requiem*

Holst. *Psalm 148*

Persichetti, *Proverb*

Four Beat

Bach. *Two Chorales: Jesu, Priceless Treasure and Break Forth, O Beauteous, Heavenly Light*

Brahms. *Wondrous Cool, Thou Woodland Quiet*

Handel. "Hallelujah, Amen" from *Judas Maccabeus*

Haydn. "Gloria in Excelsis" from *Harmoniemesse*

Morley. *April Is In My Mistress' Face*

Mozart. *Ave Verum*

Victoria. *Ave Maria*

Vivaldi. "Propter Magnam Gloriam" from *Gloria*

Five Beat

Brahms. *Nächtens*

Copland. *Lark*

Kodály. *Wainamoinen Makes Music*
Piston, "Psalm" from *Psalm and Prayer*

Six Beat

Diamond. *Chorale*
Drink to Me Only with Thine Eyes (Folksong)
Greensleeves (Folksong)
Lekberg. *Gladly for Aye We Adore Him*
Menotti. "Sixth Madrigal" from *The Unicorn*

Seven Beat

Britten. "Dies Irae" from *War Requiem*
Hanson. *The Cherubic Hymn* (Excerpt)

One Beat

Bach. "Behold, My Savior Now Is Taken" from *St. Matthew Passion*
Brahms. *Liebeslieder Walzer*
Dello Joio. *A Jubilant Song*
Donati. *Alleluia, Haec Dies*
Morley. *Sing We and Chant It*
Pfautsch. "Jack der Spratt" from *Songs Mein Grossmama Sang*
Schuman, W. *Holiday Song*

Changing Meter

Barber. *Sure on This Shining Night*
Bartholomew, arr. *Shenandoah*
Berger. *It Is Good to Be Merry*
Bernstein. "America" from *West Side Story*
Britten. *Festival Te Deum*
Britten. "Let Nimrod the Might Hunter" from *Rejoice in the Lamb*
Diemer. *A Fancy*
Faure. "Libera Me" from *Requiem*
Heisinger. *O Praise the Lord*
Hennagin. *Walking on the Green Grass*
Holst. *Lullay My Liking*
Nystedt. *I Will Greatly Rejoice*
Poulenc. "Kyrie" from *Mass in G Major*

Praetorius. *In Dulci Jubilo*
Victoria. *O Magnum Mysterium*

Free Rhythm

Britten. "Hodie" from *Ceremony of Carols*
Gretchaninoff. *Our Father*
Ives. *Psalm 67*
Ives. *Psalm 90*
Willan. *Magnificat and Nunc Dimittis*

Fermata

Bach–Goetschius. *Sixty Chorales*
Britten. *A Boy Was Born*
Haydn, F. J. *Evensong*
Ippolitov–Ivanoff. *Bless the Lord*
Ives. *Psalm 90*
Schutz. *Psalm 150*

Divided Beats

Bach. "Crucifixus" from *B Minor Mass*
Handel. "Surely He Hath Bourne Our Griefs" from *Messiah*
Mozart. "Agnus Dei" from *Missa Brevis in F*
Mozart. "Kyrie" from *Coronation Mass*

Ritardando, Accelerando, and Tempo Change

Handel. "And the Glory of the Lord" from *Messiah*
Page. "Your Countenance" from *Six for Song*
Thompson, R. *Alleluia*

Nontraditional Notation

McCray. *Haiku*
McElheran, *Patterns in Sound*
Nystedt. *Psalm 77*
Pinkham. *In the Beginning* (tape)
Toch. *Geographical Fugue*

Cueing Entrances

Brahms. "How Lovely Is Thy Dwelling Place" from *German Requiem*

Handel. "Hallelujah" from Judas *Maccabeus*

Mendelssohn. "He Watching Over Israel" from *Elijah*

Mozart. "Kyrie" from *Requiem*

Praetorius. *Psallite*

Schutz. *Cantate Domino*

Chapter Five

Interpreting the Traditional Choral Literature

Selecting appropriate choral repertoire for junior and senior high school choruses is a major responsibility of the director. If music is to be studied and sung, it is important that quality and worthwhile choral literature representing a wide spectrum of styles be chosen. Young people need to be exposed to the choral music of master composers of the Renaissance, Baroque, Classic, Romantic, and Contemporary periods. This literature, along with folk, spirituals, carols, patriotic pieces, broadway show tunes, jazz-show choir pieces, madrigals, as well as longer choral works, should make up a sizeable portion of the school choral repertoire. School directors need to be aware of stylistic considerations and performance practices of the various style periods. It is always satisfying to hear choirs make a good Baroque closing cadence, to hear Renaissance choral music sung with some dynamic restraint (non-Romantic), and to hear a convincing interpretation of a contemporary choral work.

RENAISSANCE STYLE PERIOD (1400-1600)

Although music existed in the ancient civilizations of Greece and Rome, Western music really began to evolve in the late Middle Ages and Renaissance. The church kept alive the chants in various modes. Polyphonic music, which began in the Middle Ages, was cultivated in the period of the Renaissance. During this period of "rebirth" of the humanistic Greek ideal, man began to express himself in very artistic ways. Florence, Italy, was the center of artistic growth, but Germany, France, Netherlands, Spain, England, and others experienced artistic growth in the arts of music, painting, sculpture, drama, architecture, and dance. Although sacred music dominated the Renaissance period with the mass compositions and motets, secular madrigals, chansons, lied, and other forms developed simultaneously. Renaissance choral composers composed in both the sacred and secular vein.

Although the Catholic Church had dominated the Middle Ages, the Renaissance saw the birth of the Protestant Reformation under Martin Luther and others. The anthem and the hymn were thus born. Sometimes the Renaissance is regarded as the golden period of beautiful a cappella singing. Much of the literature is designed to be sung unaccompanied, particularly the polyphonic motets and anthems and the madrigals. However, some instruments existed, such as organ, cornettes, trombones, recorders, crumhorns, lutes, viols, and harpsichords. These instruments simply doubled the vocal parts. It was not until the Baroque that instrumental accompaniments, complete with introductions, interludes, and codas, evolved as a new style.

Two types of masses were sung in the Catholic Church, the Ordinary and the Proper. The Ordinary of the Mass followed a set pattern of movements of Kyrie, Gloria, Credo, Sanctus, Benedictus, and Agnus Dei. However, the Proper of the Mass consisted of movements of varying texts in Latin which changed according to the day of the church year. The multimovement mass form has continued up to the present time. The single movement forms of motet, anthem, hymn, madrigal, chanson, lied, catches, ballads, street cries, quodlibets, and roundelays also dominated the Renaissance period.

Major Characteristics

The characteristics associated with the Renaissance are mostly applied to the music written between 1450 and 1550. Some of the Baroque qualities are found before 1600, including the homophonic treatment of both madrigals and sacred literature. Also, some characteristics of the Renaissance may be found much later than 1600. The older techniques of writing chant, and choral pieces based on a cantus firmus were relaxed as polyphonic writing came into favor. The Renaissance composers were part of an intellectual community which began to be as concerned with life on earth as well as life after death. They began to view themselves as artists and their music as something more than a utilitarian service to the Church. The major characteristics of Renaissance music include

1. polyphonic texture with equal voice lines (linear)
2. overlapping points of imitation and overlapping cadences (continuous sound)
3. text of mass and motets which greatly influenced the form of the piece
4. music that was unmetered, without barlines and accent. Stress and flow is determined by the text.
5. suspension device generously applied as dissonance (2nd) and resolution
6. melody moves conjunctly (steps), with only small leaps

7. melody of early compositions that were influenced by plainsong (unison chant)
8. Major and minor tonality that evolved as the church modes began to break down.

Tempo should not vary, and accents and ritards, generally avoided. The Renaissance composer built in ritards at cadence points by using longer note values. Any instruments used doubled the voice parts. A light, flowing tone is required for singing Renaissance music, with dynamics achieved through text meaning and the rise and fall of the many vocal lines. The major Renaissance composers were:

John Dunstable (c. 1385–1453)	Orlando di Lasso (c. 1532–1594)
Gilles Binchois (c. 1400–1560)	William Byrd (c. 1543–1623)
Guillaume Dufay (c. 1400–1474)	Tomas Luis de Victoria (c. 1549–1611)
Johannes Okeghem (c. 1420–1495)	Jacobus Gallus (c. 1550–1611)
Jacob Obrecht (c. 1453–1505)	Orazio Vecchi (c. 1550–1605)
Heinrich Isaac (c. 1450–1517)	Luca Marenzio (c. 1553–1599)
Josquin des Pres (c. 1450–1521)	Thomas Morley (c. 1557–1603)
Jean Mouton (c. 1470–1522)	Carlo Gesualdo (c. 1560–1613)
Thomas Tallis (c. 1505–1585)	John Dowland (c. 1562–1626)
Jacob Arcadelt (c. 1510–1567)	Hans Leo Hassler (c. 1564–1612)
Andrea Gabrieli (c. 1510–1586)	John Wilbye (c. 1574–1638)
G. P. Palestrina (c. 1525–1594)	Thomas Weelkes (c. 1575–1638)
Richard Farrant (c. 1530–1580)	Orlando Gibbons (c. 1583–1625)

Representative Junior/Senior High Choral Literature

Senior High Mixed Voices (SATB and Divisi)*

Anerio, G./Stephens. *Cantate Domino* (SATB). G. Schirmer 11273

Byrd, W. *Ave Verum Corpus* (SATB). Stainer & Bell 4833

Byrd, W. *I Thought That Love Had Been a Boy* (SSATB). E. C. Schirmer 653

Certon, P./Randall. *La, La, La, Je Ne L'ose Dire* (SATB). McAfee/Belwin DMC 1202

Croce, G./McCray. *Two Motets*. Shawnee A1731

De Rore, C./Echols. *Musica Dulci Sono* (SATB). McAfee/Belwin DMC1237

De Rore, C./Malin. *En Vos, Adieux, Dames* (SATB). Belwin 2321

De Sermisy, C./Greyson. *Hail, Hail, Play and Sing!* (SATB) Bourne ES126

---

*Many limited range SATB are workable in Junior High School Mixed Choruses.

Dering, R. *Quem Vidistis Pastores* (SSATTB). Church Music Review

Di Lasso, O. *Echo Song* (Double Choir). J. Fischer 7518

Di Lasso, O. *Good Day My Dear* (SATB). Bourne ES49

Di Lasso, O. *Matona, Lovely Maiden* (SATB). C. Fischer 4637

Di Lasso, O. *My Heart Doth Beg You'll Not Forget* (SATB). E. C. Schirmer 1145

Di Lasso, O. *We Adore Thee Lord Jesus* (SATB). Elkan/Vogel 362-03245

Di Lasso, O. *When Home from Work My Husband Comes* (SATB). Mark Foster 306

Dowland, J. *Come Again, Sweet Love* (SATB). E. C. Schirmer 420

Dowland, J./McCray. *Say, Love* (SATB). Shawnee A1452

Farmer, J. *Fair Phyllis I Saw* (SATB). Stainer & Bell M8-15

Farmer, J. *A Little Pretty Bonny Lass* (SATB). Hoffman/Alexandria H-5002

Farrant, R. *Call to Remembrance* (SATB). Novello 1751

Ford, T. *Since First I Saw Your Face* (SATB). Somerset SP703

Franck, M./Stone. *Du bist aller Dinge schön* (SSATB). Associated NYMP18

Frederici, D./Fisher. *For Music* (SSATB). Shawnee A1448

Gallus, J. *Alleluia, Sing a New Song* (Three Choirs). Augsburg PS613

Gastoldi, G./Schmidt. *Six Balletti* (SSATB). C. F. Peters Set I 6877a, Set II 6877b

Gesualdo, D. C. *Madrigale* (Collection in Five Voices). Peters 4363

Gibbons, O. *Almighty and Everlasting God* (SATB). Oxford Press 36

Gibbons, O. *The Silver Swan* (SATBB). G. Schirmer 7789

Hassler, H./Greyson. *Cantate Domino* (SATB). Bourne ES74

Hassler, H. *Come, Let Us Start a Joyful Song* (SATB). Bourne ES74

Hassler, H./Ehret. *Love Brings All People Riches Untold* (SATB). Lawson-Gould 51658

Jannequin, C./Hall. *Je Ne Fus Jamois Si Aise* (SATB). National CMS 117

Le Jeune, C./Randall. *Revecy Venir Du Printans* (SSATB). McAfee-Belwin DMC 1203

Marenzio, L./Haberlen. *Veggo Dolce Mio Bene* (SATB). Kjos 5949

Monteverdi, C./Malin. *Anima Del Cor Mio* (SSATB). Belwin 2423

Monteverdi, C./Malin. *Ch' Ami La Vita Mia* (SSATB). Belwin 2425

Monteverdi, C./Malin. *Quel Augellin Che Canta* (SSATB). Belwin 2426

Morley, T. *April Is in My Mistress' Face* (SATB). E. C. Schirmer 1612

Morley, T. *Now Is the Month of Maying* (SATB). G. Schirmer 2267

Morley, T. *Sing We and Chant It* (SSATB). E. C. Schirmer 573

Palestrina, G. *Adoramus Te* (SATB). G. Schirmer 6091

Palestrina, G. *Adoramus Te Christe* (SATB). Oliver Ditson 332-0369

Palestrina, G. *O Bone Jesu* (SATB). G. Schirmer 10022

Pilkington, F. *O Softly Singing Lute* (SSAATB). Oxford Press 65

Praetorius, M. *Sing We All Now with One Accord* (SATB). G. Schirmer 7543

Vecchi, O./Field. *My Sweetest Love I'm Grieving* (SATB). T. Presser 312-4093C

Victoria, T. *O Magnum Mysterium* (SATB). G. Schirmer 35752

Weelkes, T./Hall. *All At Once Well Met Fair Ladies* (SSATB). National CMS106

Weelkes, T./Richardson. *Early Will I Seek Thee* (SATB). Word C5316

Weelkes, T./Lang. *Now Every Tree Renews* (SATB). Chor Pub 30045

Weelkes, T. *On the Plains* (SSATB). Oliver Ditson 14964

Weelkes, T./Hall. *We Shepherds Sing* (SSATB). National CMS 111

Willaert, A./Hall. *Madonn' Io Non Lo So* (SATB). National CMS 107

Junior High Mixed Voices (SB, SAC, SAT, SCB, SAB, SSCB, SACB)

Bateson/Weelkes/East/McKinney. *Madrigals, Set I* (SAB). J. Fischer 9455

Byrd W./Collins. *Ave Verum Corpus* (SSCB). Cambiata Press D978121

Byrd, W./Weck. *Non Nobis Domine* (Three-Part Mixed). Somerset Press SP749

Certon, P./Haberlen. *The Joy of Dancing* (SAB). Elkan-Vogel 362-03261

Costantini, A./Kirk. *Confitemini Domino* (Three-Part SAC). Pro Art CH3002

Croft, W./Young. *Ye Servants of God* (SB). Kjos 5277

Cruger/Bach/Collins. *Jesu, Priceless Treasure* (SSCB). Cambiata Press M982170

Da Viadana, L./Razey. *Rejoice in the Lord* (SAB). C. Fischer CM8083

Des Pres, J./Coggin. *Thou, Lord, the Refuge of the Meek* (SAB). J. Fischer 10085

East, M./Freed. *See Amaryllis Shamed* (SAB). Sam Fox EA7

Este, M./Razey. *How Merrily We Live* (SAB). Plymouth PCS 409

Ford, T./Proulx. *Almighty God Who Hast Me Brought* (SAB). G.I.A. Pub. G2353

Franck, M./Pardue. *Da Pacem Domine* (SSACB). Cambiata Press M979126

Gabrieli, Andrea/McCray. *Agnus Dei* (SACB). Cambiata Press M97682

Grancini, M./Proulx. *Lord of Life King of Glory* (SB). G.I.A. Pub. G2357

Hassler, H./Greyson. *Dancing and Springing* (SAB). Bourne ES8B

Hassler, H./Wilhelm. *God Now Dwells Among Us* (SAB or TBB). Mark Foster 129

Hassler, H./Hopson. *O Sing Unto the Lord* (SAB). C. Fischer CM8200

Ingegneri, M./Collins. *Tenebrae Factae Sunt* (SSCB). Cambiata Press D981155

Morley, T./Proulx. *Sound Forth the Trumpet in Zion* (SAB). G.I.A. Pub. G1867

Obrecht, J./Proulx. *O Vos Omnes* (SAB). G.I.A. Pub. G2289

Palestrina, G./Ehret. *O Jesus Christ, Lord Most Holy* (SAB). Skidmore 5026

Tallis, T./Hopson. *All People That on Earth Do Dwell* (SAB). C. Fischer CM8204

Tallis, T./Proulx. *If Ye Love Me* (SAB). G.I.A. Pub. G2290

Weelkes, T./Carl. *Since Robin Hood* (SAB). National NMP107

Treble Chorus (SA, SSA, SSAA)

Anerio, G./Harris. *Cantate Domino* (SSA). Plymouth SC208

Attwood, T. *Teach Me, O Lord* (SA). E. C. Schirmer 1576

Beobide, J./Davis. *God Our Father, Lord of Heaven* (SA). E. C. Schirmer 1558

Corsi, G./Scott. *Adoramus Te, Christe* (SSA). Choral Art R117

Decius, N./Davis. *To God on High Be Thanks and Praise* (SA). E. C. Schirmer 1577

Des Pres, J./Payson. *The Cricket* (SSA). Frank Music 2101

Di Lasso, O. *My Heart Is Offered Still to You* (SSA). Lawson-Gould 51071

Di Lasso, O. *Serve Bone* (SA). Mark Foster MF801

Di Lasso, O./Cramer. *O Lord of Heaven* (SSA). Marks MCH51

Di Lasso, O./Williams. *We Adore Thee, O Christ* (SSA). E. C. Schirmer 1284

Farrant, R./Whitford. *Lord, For Thy Tender Mercies' Sake* (SSA). E. C. Schirmer 1232

Gabrieli, A./Kingsbury. *Ave Maria* (SSA). A. Broude 999

Hilton, J./Stoufer. *My Mistress Frowns* (SSA). National CMS 123

Monteverdi, C. *Ah, Must We Part* (SSA). Roger Dean CA 109

Morley, T. *Now Is the Month of Maying* (SSA). Bourne B237008-353

Morley, T./Weelkes/Harris. *Three Renaissance Pieces* (SSA). Shawnee B407

Palestrina, G./Malin. *Benedictus* (SSA). Belwin 2428

Palestrina, G./Greyson. *Gloria Patri* (SSA). Bourne ES 46A

Passereau, P. *He Is Good and Handsome* (SSAA). Bourne ES 9A

Praetorius, M./Ades. *Three Chorale Settings by Michael Praetorius* (SSA). Shawnee B349

Tallis, T./Harris. *All Praise to Thee, My God, This Night* (SSA). Plymouth PCS 222

Tallis, T./Harris. *Purge Me, O Lord* (SSA). Plymouth PCS 213

Victoria, T. *O Magnum Mysterium* (SSAA). T. Presser 312-40737

Male Chorus (CB, CCB, CCBB, TB, TTB, TTBB)

Azzaiolo, F./Malin. *My Dear Heart, Your Departing* (TTBB). Belwin 2329

Este, M./Clough-Leighter. *How Merrily We Live* (TTB). E. C. Schirmer 540

Hassler, H. *Gratias Agimus Tibi* (TTBB). Lawson-Gould 782

Victoria, T. *Ave Maria.* (TTBB). E. C. Schirmer 2515

BAROQUE STYLE PERIOD (1600-1750)

Although many choral pieces of the late 1500s anticipated the Baroque period, 1600 is a convenient date to mark the beginning of a new style of writing. An overall grandness pervades the music of the Baroque. Kings and queens ruled supreme in Europe, and colonization of the New World began. It was a time of dramatic expression, and of a vigorus and ornamented music. The Protestant Reformation continued and the multimovement cantata evolved alongside the older mass form. The grand oratorio form using biblical text, soloists, choruses, and orchestra accompaniment found favor. The oratorio's secular counterpart, opera, also developed into a popular form. Solo song, recitatives, and arias evolved in these larger multimovement works. The most common single-movement forms were the motet, anthem, chorale or hymn, and the madrigal. Baroque differs from Renaissance music in that instrumental accompaniments, complete with introductions, interludes, and codas, dominated. Sometimes a hymn tune was used much as the old cantus firmus as the basis for a composition. The difference between the Renaissance and Baroque styles is sometimes referred to as Stile Antico and Stile Moderno. *Stile antico* was similar to the old polyphonic style of the sixteenth century, whereas *stile moderno* represented the newer Baroque homophonic style. Church music, chamber music, and theatrical music existed and flourished during this time.

Instrumental music developed rapidly during the Baroque and the suite, solo concerto, fugue, concerto grosso, sonata, theme and variations, and orchestral overture were born. Two types of overtures were utilized, the Italian and French. Both were in ternary form, with the Italian overture following a fast-slow-fast organization, and the French overture utilizing a slow-fast-slow format. These overtures were found at the beginning of operas, oratorios, and cantatas and were sometimes labeled sinfonia. The free, independent vocal lines of the Renaissance were replaced by metered music with bar lines and regular accents. There is a driving rhythmic pulse to the music. The hemiola device was used to change the feel from three meter to two meter occasionally during a composition.

Use of dynamics during the Baroque was generally restricted to forte or piano in a terraced dynamics effect. Neither the crescendo or diminuendo were practiced at this time. The keyboard players of the Baroque frequently played from a figured bass, realizing the harmonies to a melodic line. The soprano and bass lines dominated in this homophonic style of writing. However, contrapuntal writing took on more of a fugal style, utilizing subjects and countersubjects. Although some Baroque composers utilized strict fugue writing, others would utilize the stretto device as entrances were made before the entire fugue subject was finished. Bach and Handel, respectively, represent these two types of fugal writing. The Baroque composers also understood the importance of emotion contained in the texts utilized. The Doctrine of Affections was thus born, whereby the music conveyed the meaning of the text. Such words as "resurrection" or "heaven" were given rising melodic lines, where descending melodic lines were used to denote "earth" and "depths of hell." Joviality was achieved by both rapid tempo and fast moving text.

Major Characteristics

The major characteristics of Baroque music include

1. vertical chords rather than linear polyphonic structure (*stile moderno* style)

2. use of figured bass (outer polarity of soprano and bass)
3. exclusive use of major-minor tonality, except in a few *stile antico* pieces
4. fugal counterpoint subordinate to the harmonic structure
5. accompanied (conertate) style with introductions, interludes, and codas
6. terraced dynamics (loud to soft sections, with no crescendo or diminuendo)
7. text painting and use of emotion (Doctrine of Affections)
8. form less influenced by the choral text than previously
9. steady pulsating rhythms that pervade with the use of barlines and meter signatures. The half note pulse of the Renaissance is replaced by the quarter note pulse in the Baroque.
10. virtuosity and improvisation dominated with much ornamentation by performers.

Tempo in the Baroque is strict and fairly moderate. Rallentandos should be reserved for final cadences over the last several beats. Dotted notes were frequently lengthened beyond the normal values, and the short note following was made even shorter. The major Baroque composers include:

Giovanni Gabrieli (c. 1557-1612)   Giuseppe Pitoni (1657-1743)
Jacopo Peri (1561-1633)   Henry Purcell (1659-1695)
Claudio Monteverdi (1567-1643)   Alessandro Scarlatti (1659-1725)
Michael Praetorius (c. 1571-1621)   Antonio Lotti (1667-1740)
Heinrich Schütz (1585-1672)   Antonio Vivaldi (c. 1678-1741)
Johann Schein (1586-1630)   Georg Philipp Telemann (1681-1767)
Samuel Scheidt (1587-1684)   Johann Sebastian Bach (1685-1750)
Giacomo Carissimi (1605-1674)   Domenico Scarlatti (1685-1757)
Jean-Baptiste Lully (1632-1687)   George Friedrich Handel (1685-1759)
Dietrich Buxtehude (c. 1637-1705)   Giovanni Pergolesi (1710-1736)

Representative Junior/Senior High Choral Literature

Senior High Mixed Voices (SATB and Divisi)*

Bach, J. S. *Blessing, Glory and Wisdom and Thanks* (SATB). Kjos 5140
Bach, J. S. *Break Forth O Beauteous Heavenly Light* (SATB). G. Schirmer 7929
Bach, J. S. *Grant Me True Courage, Lord* (SATB). E. C. Schirmer 313
Bach, J. S. *Jesus, Joy of Man's Desiring* (SATB). C. Fischer CM6211
Bach, J. S. *Now Let Every Tongue Adore Thee* (SATB). E. C. Schirmer 354

---

*Many limited range SATB are workable in Junior High School Mixed Choruses.

Bach, J. S. *O Rejoice Ye Christians, Loudly* (SATB). E. C. Schirmer 367

Bach, J. S. *Sheep May Safely Graze* (SATB). Galaxy 1278

Bach, J. S. *Rejoice and Sing* (SATB). Kjos 20

Bach, J. S./Hirt. *Alleluia! Sing Praise* (Cantata 142) (SATB). C. Fischer CM7140

Bach, J. S./Malin. *We Pledge You Forever* (SATB). Belwin 2406

Bach, J. S./McKelvy. *Come Sweet Death* (SATB). Mark Foster 241

Hammerschmidt, A. *How Lovely Is Thine Own Dwelling Place* (SSATB). Belwin 2536

Handel, G. F. *And the Glory of the Lord* (SATB). G. Schirmer 3829

Handel, G. F. *Coronation Festival* (SATB). Kjos 5407

Handel, G. F. *Hallelujah, Amen* (Judas Maccabaeus) (SATB). G. Schirmer 9835

Handel, G. F. *Hallelujah Chorus* (Messiah) (SATB). Presser 332-11700

Handel, G. F. *Let Their Celestial Concerts All Unite* (SATB). Hal Leonard 08681444

Handel, G. F. *Verdant Meadows* (Alcina) (SATB). Schmitt 1061

Handel, G. F./Carlton. *Great Lord God Thy Kingdom Shall Endure* (SATB). Presser 312-41125

Handel, G. F./Clough-Leighter. *Then Round About the Starry Throne* (SATB). E. C. Schirmer 305

Handel, G. F./Malin. *Glory and Worship Are Before Him* (Chandos #8 SATB). Belwin 2435

Handel, G. F./McKelvy. *And I Will Exalt Him* (SATB). Mark Foster 252

Lotti, A. *Gloria In Excelsis* (SATB). Coronet CP353

Lotti, A. *Lord Have Mercy On Us* (SATB). Coronet CP379

Marcello, B. *Psalm Nineteen* (SATB). Agape HH3912

Monteverdi, C. *If I Should Part from You* (SSATB). Presser 312-40939

Pachelbel, J. *Canon in D* (SATB). Flammer A5833

Pachelbel, J. *Magnificat* (Double chorus). C. F. Peters 6087

Pachelbel, J. *Nun Danket Alle Gott* (SATB). Robert King 604

Pergolesi, G. *Glory to God in the Highest* (SATB). B. F. Wood 44-239

Pitoni, G. *Praise Ye the Lord of Heaven* (SATB). A. Broude 1044

Pitoni, G./Greyson. *Cantate Domino* (SATB). Bourne ES5

Praetorius, M. *En Natus Est Emanuel* (SATB). E. C. Schirmer 2298

Praetorius, M. *In Natali Domini* (SATB). Kjos 2007

Praetorius, M. *Lo, How a Rose E'er Blooming* (SATB). G. Schirmer 2484

Praetorius, M. *Psallite* (SATB). Bourne ES21

Purcell, H. *In These Delightful Pleasant Groves* (SATB). M. Witmark 19273

Purcell, H. *Thou Knowest Lord the Secrets of Our Hearts* (SATB). B. F. Wood 209

Purcell, H./Davison. *O Sing Unto the Lord* (SATB). E. C. Schirmer 1103

Purcell, H./Hilton. *O Worship the Lord* (SATB). Mercury MC396

Purcell, H./Roberts. *Consider and Hear Me* (SATB). G. Schirmer 2484

Scarlatti, A./Brandvik. *O Magnum Mysterium* (SATB). Schmitt 1439

Scarlatti, A./Ehret. *O Thou Most High* (SSATB). Lawson-Gould 52105

Schein, H. *Christmas Chorale* (SSATB). Mercury DCS7

Schütz, H. *Blessed Are the Faithful* (SSATTB). G. Schirmer 10314

Schütz, H. *A Child To Us Is Born* (SATB). G. Schirmer 10829

Schütz, H. *Herr, Auf Dich Traue Ich* (SSATB). Walton WW1008

Schütz, H. *Moses and Saint Luke Passion* (SATB). Presser 312-41468

Schütz, H./Ehret. *Be Thou Exalted, Lord My God* (SATB). Flammer A5632

Sweelinck, J. *We Have Heard the Words* (SATB). Mercury 86

Tallis, T. *O Lord, Give Thy Holy Spirit* (SATB). Concordia 98-2249

Telleman, G. *Psalm Settings* (SATB & violins). Concordia 97-4838

Victoria, T. *Ave Maria* (SATB). A. Broude AB719-5

Vivaldi, A. *Gloria in Excelsis Deo* (Gloria) (SATB). Walton

Vivaldi, A./Kjelson. *Et Misericordia* (SATB). Belwin 2236

Vivaldi, A./Martens. *Et in Terra Pax* (SATB). Walton 2044

Vivaldi, A./McEwen. *In Memoria Aeterna* (SATB). Hinshaw HMC179

Junior High Mixed Voices (SB, SAC, SAT, SCB, SAB, SSCB, SACB)

Bach, J. S./Coggin. *Jesus, Source of My Salvation* (SAB). Flammer D5226

Bach, J. S./Ehret. *Blessing, Glory and Wisdom* (SAB). Elkan-Vogel 362-03118

Bach, J. S./Preston. *Holy, Holy, Holy* (SAB). Flammer D5243

Bach, J. S./Wagner. *Prepare Thyself, Zion* (SAB). Flammer P5252

Bach, J. S./Weck. *Two Chorales from Christmas Oratorio* (SAT). Somerset SP774

Caldara, A./Hines. *Lord, Have Mercy on Me* (SAB). Lawson-Gould 51981

Handel, G. F./Beal. *Behold the Lamb of God* (SACB). Cambiata Press M17427

Handel, G. F./Causey. *O Worship the Lord* (SB). Coronet CP277

Handel, G. F./Edwards. *Come, Lord, Quickly Come* (Two-Part Mixed). Coronet 277

Handel, G. F./Hines. *Let the Whole Earth Stand in Awe* (SAB). Concordia 98-2473

Handel, G. F./Hopson. *Blest Are They Whose Spirits Long* (SB). Chor. Guild CGA183

Handel, G. F./Hopson. *Praise the Lord* (SAB). Flammer D5225

Handel, G. F./Hopson. *Shout the Glad Tidings* (SAB). Flammer D5337

Handel, G. F./Kirby. *Deck Thyself, My Soul, with Gladness* (SAB). Flammer D5237

Handel, G. F./Kirby. *Now Let Us Sing the Christian Joy* (SAB). Flammer D52355

Handel, G. F./Proulx. *Keep Me Faithfully in Thy Paths* (SB). G.I.A. Pub. G2355

Handel, G. F./Richison. *Hallelujah* (Messiah). Cambiata Press M97317

Handel, G. F./Sherman. *Give Thanks to the Lord* (SAB). Flammer D5349

Handel, G. F./Taylor. *Hallelujah, Amen* (SSCB). Cambiata Press M17312

Lotti, A./Farrell. *Joy Fills the Morning* (SACB). Cambiata Press M983177

Lotti, A./Foote. *Mighty Lord, Thy Faithfulness Abideth Ever* (SAB). E. C. Schirmer 1716

Monteverdi, C./Contino. *Damigella Tutta Bella* (SAB or TTB). Roger Dean HCC101

Pachelbel, J./Petker. *Sing Songs of Jubilation* (SAB). Gentry JG474

Pergolesi, G./Collins. *Glory to God in the Highest* (SCB). Cambiata Press D983175

Pergolesi, G./Hopson. *O, My God, Bestow Thy Tender Mercy* (2-part Mixed). C. Fischer CM7974

Pergolesi, G./McCray. *Agnus Dei* (SAB). Mark Foster 220

Praetorius, M./Greyson. *Psallite* (SAB). Bourne ES21B

Vivaldi, A./Collins. *Gloria* (SSCB). Cambiata Press M117207

Treble Chorus (SA, SSA, SSAA)

Bach, J. S./Aufdemberge. *Comfort Ye, My People* (SSA). Flammer B5032

Bach, J. S./Clough-Leighter. *Grant Me True Courage, Lord* (SSA). E. C. Schirmer 800

Bach, J. S./Craig. *The Lord Is Merciful* (SSA). Plymouth DC204

Bach, J. S./Davis. *Jesu, Lead My Footsteps* (SSA). E. C. Schirmer 1836

Bach, J. S./Davis. *O Jesu So Sweet* (SA). E. C. Schirmer 1570

Bach, J. S./Davis. *O Rejoice, Ye Christians, Loudly* (SSA). E. C. Schirmer 1872

Bach, J. S./Fargo. *Jesu, Be Thou Here Beside Us* (SA). Kendor 4319

Bach, J. S./Holler. *Now Thank We All Our God* (SA). Gray 1206

Bach, J. S./Kjelson. *Alleluia! Sing Praise to the Lord* (SA). Belwin 2020

Bach, J. S./Kjelson. *O Death, None Could Conquer Thee* (SA). Belwin 2131

Bach, J. S./Kochanek. *Den Tod* (Cantata # 4) (SA). Heritage Music Press HV117

Bach, J. S./Malmin. *O Joyous Easter Morning* (SSA). Augsburg 1235

Bach, J. S./Warren. *Beside Thy Cradle* (SA). E. C. Schirmer 1938

Couperin, F./Jewell. *Be Joyful in the Lord* (SA). Concordia 98-1734

Graun, C./Coggin. *O Lord, My God, I Bow Before Thee* (SSA). Kjos 6161

Handel, G. F./Clough-Leighter. *O Lovely Peace* (SA). E. C. Schirmer 1978

Handel, G. F./Glaser. *O Lovely Peace* (SSA). E. C. Schirmer 1978

Handel, G. F./Hines. *Make a Joyful Noise Unto God* (SSA). Lawson-Gould 51395

Handel, G. F./Lefebvre. *Thanks Be to Thee* (SSA). Galaxy 1.1288.1

Handel, G. F./Pisano. *Lord of Our Being* (SSA). Plymouth PCS-202

Handel, G. F./Spicker. *Trust in the Lord* (SSA). G. Schirmer 4423

Handel, G. F./Warren. *Daughter Zion, Now Rejoice* (SA). E. C. Schirmer 1956

Handel, G. F./Whitford. *Hallelujah, Amen* (SSA). E. C. Schirmer 1915

Handel, G. F./Wiley. *Come Holy Light, Guide Divine* (SA). Pro Art 2990

Lotti, A./Harris. *Holy, Holy, Holy* (SSA). Plymouth SC207

Lotti, A./Hunter. *Surely He Hath Bourne Our Griefs* (SSA). Marks 4457

Marcello, B. *O Lord, Our Governor* (Unison). Concordia 98-1045

Martini, G. *Come, Sing This Round with Me* (SA). Bourne B236844-351

Pachelbel, J./Petker. *Sing Songs of Jubilation* (SSA). Gentry/Hinshaw G460

Pergolesi, G. *Stabat Mater* (SA). G. Schirmer 498

Pitoni, G./Greyson. *Cantate Domino* (SA). Bourne B237115-352

Praetorius, M. *Lo, How a Rose E'er Blooming* (SS). G. Schirmer 10216

Purcell, H./Henry-Moffat. *Sound the Trumpet* (SA). E. C. Schirmer 487

Schein, J./Stone. *Christ Lag in Todesbanden* (SSA). A. Broude 225-10

Schütz, H. *Give Ear, O Lord* (SA). E. C. Schirmer 2789

Vivaldi, A./Martens. *Laudamus Te* (Gloria) (SA). Walton W5014

Male Chorus (CB, CCB, CCBB, TB, TTB, TTBB)

Bach, J. S. *Good Fellows Be Merry* (Peasant Cantata) (TTBB). Boston 12065

Bach, J. S. *Jesu, Joy of Man's Desiring* (CBB). Cambiata Press M97687

Bach, J. S./Davison. *My Spirit, Be Joyful* (TB). E. C. Schirmer 938

Bach, J. S./Ehret. *Unto His Holy Name Sing Praises* (TTBB). Marks MC4266

Cruger, J./Cain. *Now Thank We All Our God* (TTB). Flammer CS028

Schutz, H./Biester. *Wir Danken Dir, Herr Gott* (TTBB). Lawson-Gould 51780

CLASSIC STYLE PERIOD (1750-1820)

The link between the Baroque and Classic periods was marked by music of Rococo characteristic of superficial, gallant, and expressive style as opposed to the grandiose style of the Baroque. Much of this music was designed for the aristocratic salons in France and Germany. Short pieces with graceful lines and sometimes elaborate ornamentation dominated the gallant style. In Germany, the expressive *Empfindsamer stil* was rather plain with less freedom in applying ornaments in performance. Couperin, Telemann, and Bach's sons wrote Rococo style music.

Music of the Classic period flourished under the patronage of the aristocracy in Europe. The Viennese composers, Haydn, Mozart, and Beethoven (transitional) dominate the period. Classic music adheres to the Greek characteristics of clarity, balance, objectivity, simplicity, formalism, dignity, and symmetry. This was the time of the French Revolution, the American Revolution, and the Napoleonic Wars. German literary writers evolved who began to display toward the end of the Classic period a rebellion toward formalism and an emphasis on the individual which led to the Romantic period style features. Although the music of the Classic period is refined in the *stile galant* style, there are moments of power in the music. A light beat and restrained gestures are appropriate when conducting this music. The terms andante, allegro, adagio, and so on refer now to tempo and not just to the character of the music as they applied in the Baroque. Tempi are moderate with some tempo rubato, accelerando, and rallentando used with restraint. Terraced dynamics were replaced with crescendo and decrescendo. These are not excessive changes of volume, however. Often when identical phrases occur, the first is performed forte, and the repetition, usually, piano. Good form, stressing unity and variety is a dominate feature of classic music. Ternary form, sonata-allegro, rondo, and theme and variation dominated the instrumental forms. Symphonies evolved in four movements as well as concertos written for solo instrument and orchestra.

The opera dominated the vocal forms, with a better balance between the drama achieved. Mozart dominated this field by writing in all three forms of opera seria, opera buffa, and Singspiel with some spoken dialogue. The operas contained choruses, as did the many oratorios written. Sacred vocal music was composed for the court by Haydn and Mozart and others in the form of Mass, Te Deum, Magnificat, Stabat Mater, and smaller works such as offertories and motets. Although homophonic style continued to dominate during the classic, the choruses featured both polyphonic and homophonic textures. During this time improvisation declined as composers wrote into the music the embellishments they desired in a finalized form. Toward the end of the Classic period the harpsichord gave way to the invention of the piano, with its capability of being played forte, piano, and gradations in between. Beethoven was among the first to use Maelzel's metronome markings to indicate the beat of the tempo desired.

Conducting as we know it today was often performed at the harpsichord and later by the first chair violinist in the classic orchestra. The ruling aristocracy surrounded itself with all the arts, and the artist created for his patron. The size of the average eighteenth-century orchestra was 18 to 20 string players, 4 winds, and kettledrums. Choruses were of moderate size and choral music performances took place largely at the court or in the churches.

Major Characteristics

The major characteristics of music from the Classic period include

1. form of music that is important, with unity, variety, and balance stressed
2. Orchestra that grows in size and accompanies opera and large choral works. Instrumental music achieves an independence from vocal music with text.
3. Dynamic levels that increased and moderate crescendos and diminuendos were used
4. major-minor tonality that is exploited and used exclusively

5. improvisation and ornamentation that is restricted by writing in finalized form
6. vertical homophonic structure that prevails along with counterpoint

It should be noted that in America, the "singing school" movement produced a number of early American hymn writers, the most famous of whom was William Billings. He was especially known for his contrapuntal pieces known as "fuging tunes." Other contemporary American hymn composers included Daniel Read, Timothy Swan, Jeremiah Ingalls, and others. Although their music was somewhat unorthodox by European standards, they stimulated an interest in singing in the churches which eventually led to the introduction of vocal music into the public schools of America. The Moravians, who settled in Pennsylvania in 1741 in Bethlehem, also composed music for choirs and instruments and were trained in the fine musical tradition of central Europe. The major composers of the Classic period are:

Christoph Willibald Gluck (1714–1787)

Franz Joseph Haydn (1732–1809)

Michael Haydn (1737–1806)

William Billings (1746–1800)

Wolfgang Amadeus Mozart (1756–1791)

Luigi Cherubini (1760–1842)

Ludwig van Beethoven (1770–1827)

Representative Junior/Senior High Choral Literature

Senior High Mixed Voices (SATB and Divisi)*

Beethoven, L. van. *Hallelujah* (Mount of Olives) (SATB). Boosey & Hawkes 5180

Beethoven, L. van. *The Heavens Declare the Glory of God* (SATB). Flammer 84802

Beethoven, L. van. *O God, Thy Goodness Reacheth Far* (Prayer) (SA). E. C. Schirmer 1569

Billings, W. *David's Lamentation* (SATB). C. Fischer CM6572

Billings, W. *A Virgin Unspotted* (SATB). Mercury MP64

Billings, W. *When Jesus Wept* (SATB Fuging Tune). G. Schirmer 11145

Billings, W. *Ye Tribes of Adam* (SATB). Concordia 98-3187

Gasparini, Q. *Adoramus Te, Christe* (SATB). Brele DM

Haydn, F. *Awake the Harp* (The Creation) (SATB). G. Schirmer 51982

Haydn, F. *The Heavens Are Telling* (The Creation) (SATB). G. Schirmer 3521

---

*Many limited range SATB are workable in Junior High School Mixed Choruses.

Haydn, M. *Sanctus* (SATB). Mercury 352-00469

Haydn, F./Ehret. *Sing to the Lord with Joy and Gladness* (SATB). Richler GP-R1420

Haydn, F./Hopson. *O Praise the Lord with Heart and Voice* (SATB). Flammer A5832

Ingalls, J./Bennett. *Three Fuging-Tunes* (SATB). Broude Bro. WW2

Mozart, W. *Ave Verum Corpus* (SATB). G. Schirmer 5471

Mozart, W. *Gloria* (Twelfth Mass) (SATB). Summy-Birchard 386

Mozart, W. *Gloria in Excelsis* (Missa Brevis in C) (SATB). Marks 4553

Mozart, W. *Lord, We Pray to Thee* (SATB). Pro Art 1849

Mozart, W. *Sanctus* (Missa Brevis in C) (SATB). Marks 4555

Junior High Mixed Chorus (SB, SAC, SAT, SCB, SAB, SSCB, SACB)

Beethoven, L. van/Gillam. *We Bring Our Eager Souls to Thee* (SAB). Plymouth AS403

Boyce, W./Wagner. *Praise the Lord, Alleluia* (3-Part). Coronet CP326

Cherubini, L./Wagner. *Alleluia, Praise!* (SAB). Hope MW1223

Cherubini, L./Wagner. *Like As a Father* (3-Part Canon). Chor. Guild CGA156

Gluck, C. W./Payne. *Give Unto the Lord* (SAB). Hoffman/Hinshaw R-2003

Gluck, C. W./Taylor. *O Saviour, Hear Me* (SACB). Cambiata Press M17672

Haydn, F./Suchoff. *In Thee, O Lord* (SAB). Sam Fox PS162

Haydn, F./Wagner. *The Heavens Are Telling* (SAB). Coronet Press 318

Haydn, F./Brahms, J./Hopson. *Sound the Trumpet! Praise Him!* (SAB, Brass). Coronet 242

Mozart, W./Carl. *Due Pupille Amabili* (SAB). National CMS103

Mozart, W./Carl. *Piu Non Si Trovano* (SAB, Clarinets). National CMS101

Mozart, W./Coggin. *Praise Him! Declare His Glory* (SAB). Flammer D-S227

Mozart, W./Collins. *Gloria in Excelsis Deo* (SSCB). Cambiata Press M97437

Mozart, W./Ehret. *Alleluia* (SAC). Cambiata Press M979124

Mozart, W./Ehret. *Praise the Lord, Our God, Forever* (SAB). Alex. House B-60464

Mozart, W./Lyle. *Ave Verum* (SSCB). Cambiata Press M17552

Mozart, W./Martin. *Jesu, Son of God* (SAB). Schmitt 5502

Mozart, W./Wagner. *Bless Us with Your Love* (SAB). Somerset MW1224

Telemann, G. *Dies ist der Tag den dir Herr macht* (SAB). Mark Foster HV 39.010

Telemann, G./Ehret. *Hallelujah* (SAB). Flammer D5215

Telemann, G./Hoagland. *Amen, Praise and Honor* (SAB). Mark Foster 180

Treble Chorus (SA, SSA, SSAA)

Billings, W. *Wake Every Breath* (SA). Choristers Guild R-20

Cherubini, L./Ehret. *Come, O Jesus, Come to Me* (SA). Plymouth SC501

Gregor, C./Trussler. *Hosanna* (SS). Plymouth TR-106

Haydn, F. *Gloria in Excelsis* (SSA). Joseph Boonin 146

Haydn, F. *Sanctus* (Imperial Mass) (SSA). Plymouth SC-202

Haydn, F./Davis. *The Spacious Firmament* (SSA). E. C. Schirmer 1877

Haydn, F./Suchoff. *Gloria from Heiligmesse* (SSA). Walton 5025

Haydn, F./Suchoff. *In Thee, O Lord* (SSA). Sam Fox PS163

Mozart, W. *Wiegenlied Lullaby* (SSA). Kjos 6140

Mozart, W./Davis. *Laudate Dominum* (SSA). Warner R3350

Mozart, W./Ehret. *Gloria in Excelsis* (SSA). Sam Fox PS77

Mozart, W./Hardwicke. *Holy, Holy, Holy* (SSA). Plymouth SC205

Mozart, W./Hardwicke. *O Praise the Lord* (SSA). Plymouth SC206

Mozart, W./Page. *Jesu, Word of God Incarnate* (SSA). Ditson 332-11796

Mozart, W./Quinn. *Ave Verum* (SSAA). Plymouth NBC-204

Mozart, W./Riegger. *Alleluia* (SA). Flammer 86046

Mozart, W./Riegger. *Alleluia* (SSA). Flammer B-5002

Mozart, W./Track. *Spring* (SSA). Elkan-Vogel-Presser 362-03269

Telemann, G. *Wach set in der Gnade* (SA or SAB). Mark Foster HV 39.003

Male Chorus (CB, CCB, CCBB, TB, TTB, TTBB)

Boyce, W./Kirk. *Alleluia* (TTBB). Pro Art 2383

Cherubini, L./Hines. *Sanctus* (TTBB). Lawson-Gould 51307

ROMANTIC STYLE PERIOD (1820-1900)

The nineteenth century is usually described as the Romantic period in the arts. The Romantic spirit was one of change, individuality, and subjectivity. The music is intensely emotional, deriving its strength from massive vocal and instrumental forces. The composer, no longer supported by the aristocracy after the European democratic revolutions, was more on his own to write music. The aristocratic salons were replaced by large concert halls and opera houses. Literary endeavors reached a peak, and composers utilized many texts for operas, art songs, and choral works. Programatic music, with its extra-musical associations reached a peak in Richard Strauss and Richard Wagner. Yet, the older forms of music continued under such composers as Mendelssohn and Brahms. The orchestra expanded to over one hundred pieces, and the piano became the dominant keyboard instrument. Conducting techniques improved and the conductor achieved a notability second only to the composer. Music criticism in written form was born.

Although program music utilized such devices as idee fixe, leitmotiv, and themes to depict characters and ideas, absolute music utilized the forms of the mass, oratorio, concerto, symphony, theme and variations, rondo, ternary, and binary forms. Suites, ballets, sonatas, and small chamber pieces continued to be composed. Opera flourished under the Italian and German composers of the nineteenth century. The solo art song reached a peak under Schubert, Schumann, Brahms, and Hugo Wolf. Song cycles appeared and composers also used cyclic form borrowing the same thematic material in several movements of a large work. In the choral area multimovement masses, oratorio, and cantatas continued to be composed. Many beautiful Requiems appeared during the century. Also, short part songs, usually secular in nature, were written for choruses of mixed, male, and female voices.

Tempi ranged from very slow to very fast, with rapid changes within a piece. Use of syncopation and accent were employed, although changing meter rarely occured. Tempo rubato was used extensively and dynamics became excessive ranging from *pppp* to *ffff*. Crescendo and diminuendo were frequent to enhance the mood and text. There was personal freedom to express for the composer.

Major Characteristics

The major characteristics of Romantic music include

1. less emphasis on form and more on texture and color
2. a greater romantic subjectivity in composer and performer
3. much chromaticism, with limits of the major-minor systems exploited
4. wide contrasts in dynamics and tempi
5. program music (literary story) was composed
6. vertical homophonic structure that dominates with less polyphonic writing
7. large forces of voices and instruments are utilized.

The major Romantic composers include:

Karl Maria von Weber (1786–1826)	Antonin Dvorak (1841–1904)
Gioacchino Rossini (1792–1868)	Gabriel Faure (1845–1904)
Franz Schubert (1797–1828)	Leos Janacek (1854–1928)
Hector Berlioz (1803–1869)	Edward Elgar (1857–1934)
M. I. Glinka (1804–1857)	Anton Bruckner (1824–1896)
Felix Mendelssohn (1809–1847)	Johannes Brahms (1833–1897)
Robert Schumann (1810–1865)	Camille Saint-Saens (1835–1921)
Franz Lizst (1811–1886)	Theodore Dubois (1837–1924)
Richard Wagner (1813–1883)	John Stainer (1840–1901)

Giuseppe Verdi (1813–1901)

Mikhail Ippolitov-Ivanoff (1859–1935)

Robert Franz (1815–1892)

Hugo Wolf (1860–1903)

Charles F. Gounod (1818–1893)

Sergei Rachmaninoff (1873–1943)

Cesar Franck (1822–1890)

Paul Tschesnokov (1877–1944)

Representative Junior/Senior High Choral Literature

Senior High Mixed Voices (SATB and Divisi)*

Arkhangelsky, A. *Incline Thine Ear* (SATB). M. Witmark 5–W2689

Arkhangelsky, A./Tellep. *To Thee We Sing* (SATB). Schmitt 857

Arkhangelsky, A./Walker. *Light Divine* (SATB). Hal Leonard 086811500

Berlioz, H. *Thou Must Leave Thy Lowly Dwelling* (SATB). Gray CMR1898

Bortniansky, D. *Cherubim Song No. 7* (SATB). Gray 687

Brahms, J. *All of My Heart's Desiring* (SAATTBB). Summy–Birchard 5406

Brahms, J. *Create in Me, O God* (SATBB). G. Schirmer 7504

Brahms, J. *How Lovely Is Thy Dwelling Place* (Requiem)(SATB). F. Colombo 1515

Brahms, J. *Let Nothing Ever Grieve Thee* (SATB). Peters 6093

Brahms, J. *Mary's Pilgrimage* (Songs of Mary)(SATB). Choral Art

Brahms, J. *Six Folk Songs* (SATB). Marks 9

Brahms, J. *Wondrous Cool, Thou Woodland Quiet* (SATB). G. Schirmer 9335

Brahms, J./Fettke. *All Sing Loudly* (SATB). Flammer A5717

Brahms, J./Freed. *The Farewell* (SATB). Sam Fox RC2

Brahms, J./Freed. *The Joys of Marriage* (SATB). Sam Fox RC8

Brahms, J./Greyson. *O Lovely May* (SATB). Bourne R14

Brahms, J./Klein. *Es Geht Ein Wehen Durch Den Wald* (SATB). G. Schirmer 12564

Bruckner, A. *Ave Maria* (SATB, SATB). Marks 47

Bruckner, A. *Christus Factus Est* (SATB). Summy–Birchard 5249

Bruckner, A. *Let Us Celebrate God's Name* (SATB). Augsburg PS626

Bruckner, A. *O How Blessed* (SATB). Choral Art R154

De Pearsall, R./Opheim. *Sing We* (SATB). Schmitt 1212

De Pearsall, R. *When Allen-A-Dale-Went-A-Hunting* (SATB). Summy Birchard 2214

Dvorak, A. *Blessed Jesu* (Stabat Mater)(SATB). G. Schirmer 4490

---

*Many limited range SATB are workable in Junior High School Mixed Choruses.

Elgar, E. *As Torrents in Summer* (King Olaf)(SATB). Belwin 1356

Faure, G. *Cantique de Jean Racine* (SATB). Broude Bros. 801

Franck, C. *Psalm 150* (SATB). J. Fischer 5670

Glinka, M. *Cherubim Song* (SATB). G. Schirmer 5216

Gretchaninoff, A. *The Cherubic Hymn* (SSAATTBB). Kjos 7015

Gounod, C. *Sanctus and Benedictus* (St. Cecilia Mass)(SATB). G. Schirmer 3768

Gretchaninoff, A. *Hail, Thou Gladening Light* (SATB).

Gretchaninoff, A. *Our Father* (SATB). Ditson 332–13000

Ippolitoff-Ivanoff, M. *Bless the Lord* (SATB). B. F. Wood 445

Kalinnikof, V. *Agnus Dei* (SATB). Belwin 848

Kopylow, A./Wilhousky. *Heavenly Light* (SATB). C. Fischer CM497

Mendelssohn, F. *He, Watching Over Israel* (Elijah)(SATB). Ditson 332–00827

Mendelssohn, F. *How Lovely Are the Messengers* (St. Paul)(SATB). Jack Spratt 509

Mendelssohn, F. *Judge Me, O God* (SATB). Walton 2157

Mendelssohn, F. *The Lord Is a Mighty God* (SATB). Flammer 5393

Mendelssohn, F. *See What Love* (St. Paul)(SATB). Belwin 2173

Mendelssohn, F. *Then Shall a Star Come Out of Jacob* (Christus)(SATB). Schmitt 1903

Rachmaninoff, S. *Glorious Forever* (SATB). Boston 1080

Saint-Saens, C. *Praise Ye the Lord of Hosts* (Christmas Oratorio). Belwin 60597

Schubert, F. *Der Tanz* (SATB). Hinshaw HMC247

Schubert, F. *Holy Father* (SATB). Shawnee A1203

Schubert, F. *Stabat Mater* (SATB). Belwin 2164

Schumann, R. *Kyrie from Mass in C Minor* (SATB). Chor Pub. 30049

Schubert, F./Frank. *Hail, Beauteous Night* (SATB). Sam Fox MM21

Tschesnokov, P. *Let Thy Blessed Spirit* (SATB). J. Fischer 4497

Tschesnokov, P. *Salvation is Created* (SATTBB). J. Fischer 4129

Junior High Mixed Voices (SB, SAC, SAT, SCB, SAB, SSCB, SACB)

Bortniansky, D./Collins. *Cherubim Song No. 7* (SSCB). Cambiata Press D978119

Dubois, T./Richison. *Adoramus Te Christe* (SSCB). Cambiata Press M17797

Faure, G./Kicklighter. *Introit and Kyrie from Requiem* (SSCB). Cambiata Press M117692

Kopyloff, A./Ehret. *Christ Indeed Is Risen Today* (SAB). Flammer D5218

Mendelssohn, F./Edwards. *The Passion Chorale* (SAB). Coronet Press Z34

Mendelssohn, F./Ehret. *I Will Sing of Thy Great Mercies* (SAB). Roger Dean MRD115

Mendelssohn, F./Farrell. *Cast Thy Burden Upon the Lord* (SSCB). Cambiata Press M980143

Mendelssohn, F./Hopson. *The Lord Is a Mighty God* (2–Part Mixed). Hope A540

Saint-Saens, C./Eilers. *Praise Ye the Lord of Hosts* (3–Part Mixed). Jenson 402–16020

Schubert, F./Ehret. *Kyrie* (Mass in G)(SAB). Marks 4520

Schubert, F./Harris. *Sound the Trumpet* (SAB). SC405

Schubert, F./Weck. *Sanctus* (SAT). Somerset SP767

Tchaikowski, P./Ehret. *Praise Ye the Lord* (SAB). Hope A411

Treble Chorus (SA, SSA, SSAA)

Berlioz, H./Zipper. *Veni, Creator Spiritus* (SSA). Ed. Marks 13

Bortniansky, D./Davis. *Lo, A Voice to Heaven Sounding* (SSA). E. C. Schirmer 1079

Bortniansky, D./Ehret. *Cherubim Song No. 7* (SA). Pro Art 1537

Brahms, J. *Four Songs for Treble Voices* (SSAA). Shawnee B243

Brahms, J./Carroll. *As the Clouds with Longing Wander* (SSA). G. Schirmer 12282

Brahms, J./Pooler. *Serenade in Vain* (SSA). Schmitt 2129

Brahms, J./Track. *Psalm 13* (SSA or TTB). Elkan-Vogel 362–03275

Dvorak, A. *Dyby Byla Kosa Nabrosena* (SA). National Music

Dvorak, A./Jewell, K. *I Will Sing New Songs of Gladness* (SA). World Library ESA1718–2

Elgar, E. *As Torrents in Summer* (King Olaf)(SSA) Gray 8

Faure, G. *Holy, Holy, Holy* (Requiem)(SA). H. T. FitzSimons 5017

Faure, G. *Il Est Ne Le Divin Enfant* (SA). A. Broude 1034

Faure, G. *Messe Basse* (SSA). A. Broude 1041

Faure, G./Sisson. *Tantum Ergo* (SSA). A. Broude 950

Franck, Cesar/Kjelson. *O Lord Most Holy* (SA). Belwin 1971

Humperdinck, E. *Prayer* (Hansel and Gretel)(SSA). G. Schirmer 8599

Ivovsky, A./Hardwicke. *Hospodi Pomilui* (SSA). Alfred 9

Mendelssohn, F. *A Greeting* (SSA). Schmitt 2582

Mendelssohn, F. *Lift Thine Eyes* (Elijah)(SSA). G. Schirmer 26

Mendelssohn, F. *Ye Sons of Israel* (SSA). E. C. Schirmer 1839

Mendelssohn, F./Craig. *Cast Thy Burden Upon the Lord* (SSA). Plymouth DC203

Mendelssohn, F./Coggin. *The Earth Is Hushed in Silence* (SSA). Plymouth PCS210

Mendelssohn, F./Hardwicke. *Grant Us Thy Peace* (SSA). Alfred 6205

Mendelssohn, F./Riegger. *How Lovely Are the Messengers* (SA). Flammer 86068

Mendelssohn, F./Stone. *Veni, Domine* (SSA). A. Broude 166–10

Mendelssohn, F./Strickling. *Blessed Redeemer, At Thy Word* (SSA). Plymouth PCS–207

Rachmaninoff, S. *Lilacs* (SA). Mark Foster 856

Rossini, G. *Duetto Buffa Di Due Gatti* (SA). National WHC–52

Saint-Saens, C./Fargo. *Praise Ye the Lord of Hosts* (SA). Kendor 4317

Schumann, R. *The Lotus Flower* (SSA). Willis 4289

Schumann, R. *Were I a Tiny Bird* (SA). National WHC–80

Stainer, J./Manten. *God So Loved the World* (SSA). Choral Art R109

Schubert, F./Craig. *Gloria* (SSA). Plymouth DC205

Schubert, F./Craig. *Sanctus* (SSA). Plymouth CD201

Schubert, F./Ehret. *Agnus Dei* (SSA). Marks Music 4598

Schubert, F./Ehret. *Holy, Holy, Holy* (SA). Marks Music MC4127

Schubert, F./Trusler. *The Radiant Morn* (SSA). Plymouth TR201

Sibelius, J. *Onward, Ye Peoples* (SSA). Galaxy 952–7

Tschesnokov, P./Ehret. *Let Thy Holy Presence* (SSA). Pro Art 1687

Verdi, G./Davis. *Ave Maria* (SSA). Galaxy 1897

Male Chorus (CB, CCB, CCBB, TB, TTB, TTBB)

Brahms, J. *Two Liebeslieder Waltzer*, Op. 52 (TB). E. C. Schirmer 2329

Dvorak/Schumann/Beethoven. *Songs of the Masters* (TTBB). Jenson 436–19011

Grieg, E. *Brothers, Sing On* (TTBB). J. Fischer 6927

Janacek, L. *Veni Sancte Spiritus* (TTBB). Universal 1678NJ

Schubert, F./Rodby. *O Be Joyful* (TTBB). Somerset MM9002

Schumann, R./Pfautsch. *The Minnesingers* (TTBB). Lawson–Gould 52091

TWENTIETH CENTURY STYLE PERIOD (1900-   )

Twentieth-century music is representative of many styles and schools extending from the conservative neo-romantic to more radical music of an electronic or aleatory (indeterminate) type. Whether one places the Impressionist composers, such as Debussy and Ravel, in the Romantic or twentieth century is a matter of choice. Impressionism utilized many Romantic techniques, as well as dreamy innovative chords, during its brief existence from 1880–1920. Its goal of having the listener hear impressions (or complete visual impressions as in the coexisting art movement) and complete missing links was an attempt to free music from the slavish emotionalism of the nineteenth century, and prepared the way for the more liberating compositional devices of the twentieth century.

Devices such as the whole-tone scale, pentatonic and other unusual scales found favor with composers. Nontertian chords, parallel harmonic motion, and extended dissonances came to dominate the new music. Some composers developed an expressionism style with dissonant harmonies, massive timbres, thick textures, and other replacements to impressionist composition. Schoenberg and Berg fall into this group. Stravinsky, Prokofiev, and Orff utilized the percussive possibilities and irregular rhythms in a new primitivism. Some composers chose to write in a neo-classicist style, reverting back to eighteenth century ideals of balance and clarity and utilization of diatonic melodies and regular, simple rhythms. Prokofiev, Hindemith, and Piston contributed to this style.

Another technique exploited by Schoenberg and Webern was the tone row or serial technique called dodecaphonism. All twelve tones of the chromatic scale are used in a set that is inverted, performed in retrograde or retrograde inversion. Bartok, Kodály, Copland, Vaughan Williams, and Britten exhibited an interest in nationalism and native folk music materials as a basis for composition. With the birth of jazz in the United States, Milhaud, Gershwin, Copland, Hindemith, and Stravinsky utilized jazz features in their compositions. Syncopation and a new interest in improvisation evolved. Aleatory or chance music developed and has been successfully used by choral composers as a separate form and as a combining of traditional note composition with chance effects. Electronic tape pieces evolved and synthesizer music was also employed by many composers. Since the period is still evolving, it is difficult at this point to know which pieces and styles will prove to be of lasting quality and interest.

Major Characteristics

Some of the major characteristics of twentieth century music include

1. extension beyond major-minor tonality to bi-tonal, poly-tonal, atonal, and twelve-tone row
2. numerous changes of meter signatures within a composition
3. increased dissonance caused by the new tonal systems employed
4. use of nonsinging sounds as in aleatory (chance) music
5. use of new music notation systems to express the new sounds
6. complex scores and increased vocal demands on performers.

When Romanticism reached its peak at the end of the nineteenth century, composers turned to new compositional devices. Intricate rhythms, accent groupings and changing meters, and extremes in tempo are found. Many textures prevail from vertical homophonic texture to horizontal-type texture of twelve-tone music. Electronic tape and synthesizer are used with choral compositions. Dynamics are wide and some unusual tone qualities are sometimes required of both instrumentalists and singers. The major contemporary composers include:

Claude Debussy (1862–1918)	Roy Harris (1898–)
Frederick Delius (1862–1934)	Francis Poulenc (1899–1963)
Ralph Vaughan Williams (1872–1958)	Randall Thompson (1899–)

Gustav von Holst (1874–1934)
Charles Ives (1874–1954)
Martin Shaw (1875–1958)
Ernest Bloch (1880–1959)
Healey Willan (1880–1969)
Bela Bartok (1881–1945)
Zoltan Kodaly (1882–1967)
Igor Stravinsky (1882–1971)
Heitor Villa–Lobos (1887–1959)
Arthur Honegger (1892–1955)
Darius Milhaud (1892–   )
Paul Hindemith (1895–1963)
Leo Sowerby (1895–1968)
Carl Orff (1895–1983)
Howard Hanson (1896–   )

Sven Lekberg (1899–   )
Aaron Copland (1900–   )
Jean Berger (1901–   )
William Walton (1902–1983)
Normand Lockwood (1906–   )
Samuel Barber (1910–   )
William Schuman (1910–   )
Benjamin Britten (1913–1976)
Norman Dello Joio (1913–   )
Irving Fine (1914–1962)
Knut Nystedt (1915–   )
Vincent Persichetti (1915–1987)
Leslie Bassett (1923–   )
Daniel Pinkham (1923–   )
John Rutter (1946–   )

Representative Junior/Senior High Choral Literature

Senior High Mixed Chorus (SATB and Divisi)*

Bartok, B. *Four Slovak Folk Songs* (SATB). Boosey & Hawkes 17658
Bartok, B. *Three Hungarian Folk Songs* (SATB). Boosey & Hawkes 5326
Beadell, R. *Holly Sonnet* (SATB). Shawnee A1353
Beadell, R. *Out of the Depths* (SATB Tone Row). Belwin
Beck, J. N. *Canticle of Praise* (SATB). Presser 312–40588
Beck, J. N. *Every Valley* (SATB). Beckenhorst 1040
Beck, J. N. *The Quiet Heart* (SSATB). Beckenhorst 1120
Berger, J. *The Eyes of All Wait Upon Thee* (SATB). Augsburg U–1264
Berger, J. *Five Canzonets* (SATB). A. Broude 111
Berger, J. *It Is Good to Be Merry* (SSAATTBB). Kjos 5293
Berger, J. *Life Again* (SATB). A. Broude 405
Berger, J. *The Poor Have Little* (SATB). Kjos 5943
Berger, J. *A Rose Touched By the Sun's Warm Rays* (SATB). Augsburg 11–0953
Berger, J. *Waiting in the Night* (SATB, Perc.) C. Fischer CM7867
Bernstein, L. *Sanctus from Mass* (SATB). G. Schirmer 11973
Binkerd, G. *Two Browning Choruses* (SATB). Boosey & Hawkes 5945

---

*Many limited range SATB are workable in Junior High School Mixed Chorus.

Bloch, E. *America* (SATB). Summy Birchard 808

Britten, B. *Choral Dances from Gloriana* (SATB). Boosey & Hawkes 17411

Britten, B. *Concord* (SATB). Boosey & Hawkes 5014

Britten, B. *Old Abram Brown* (SATB). Boosey & Hawkes 1786

Brubeck, D. *Gloria from Fiesta de la Posada* (SATB). Shawnee A1365

Butler, E. *Give Ear, O Lord* (SATB). C. Fischer CM7836

Butler, E. *Glory to the Son* (Tpts., Timp., SATB). Hope A520

Butler, E. *How Excellent Is Thy Name* (SATB). Bourne 837

Butler, E. *In Commendation of Music* (SATB). Hinshaw 486

Clokey, J. *If I But Knew* (SATB). J. Fischer 6148

Clokey, J. *Night Song* (SATB). Summy Birchard B1001

Clokey, J. *A Snow Legend* (SATB). Summy–Birchard B120

Copland, A. *Sing Ye Praises to Our King* (SATB). Boosey & Hawkes 6021

Copland, A., arr. *Ching-a-Ring-Chaw* (SATB). Boosey & Hawkes 6021

Copland, A. *That's the Idea of Freedom* (SATB). Summy–Birchard B751

Delius, F./Suchoff. *Appalachia* (SATB). Sam Fox PS170

Dello Joio, N. *A Jubilant Song* (SATB). G. Schirmer 9580

Diemer, Emma Lou. *A Babe Is Born* (SATB). Sacred Music Press S61

Diemer, Emma Lou. *A Fancy* (SATB). C. Fischer CM8011

Diemer, Emma Lou. *I Will Sing of Mercy and Judgment* (SATB). C. Fischer CM7804

Diemer, Emma Lou. *Madrigals Three* (SATB). C. Fischer CM7799

Felciano, R. *Three Madrigals from Wm. Shakespeare* (SATB). E. C. Schirmer 2917

Fissinger, E. *Thoughts on Nature* (SATB). Jenson 411–20034

Frackenpohl, A. *Three Limericks in Canon Form* (SATB). Marks Music 112

Frackenpohl, A. *Three Recent Rulings* (SATB). G. Schirmer 12305

Harris, R. *Red Bird in a Green Tree* (SATB). Belwin 64428

Heisinger, B. *O Praise the Lord* (SATB). Belwin 2165

Hindemith, P. *Drink Up! from Twelve Madrigals* (SSATB). Schott/Belwin AP47

Hindemith, P. *Six Chansons* (SATB). Associated Music Pub.: *The Doe* A–504; *A Swan* A–505; *Since All Is Passing* A–506; *Springtime* A–507; *In Winter* A–508; *Orchard* A–509

Holst, G. *Christmas Day* (SATB & Solos). Novello 983

Holst, G. *Turn Back, O Man* (SATB). Galaxy 1.5001.1

Ives, C. *Psalm 90* (SATB). Presser 342–40021

Lamb, G. *Aleatory Psalm* (SATB). World Library of Sacred Music CA4003–8

McCray, J. *Haiku* (SATB). Belwin 2250

McElheran, B. *Patterns in Sound* (Unison Mixed). Oxford Press

Menotti, G. *The Shepherd's Chorus* (Amahl)(SATB). G. Schirmer 10801

Nystedt, K. *All the Ways of a Man.* Augsburg

Nystedt, K. *Hosanna* (SATB). Hinshaw 518

Nystedt, K. *I Will Greatly Rejoice!* Hinshaw 226

Parker, A. *Three Circles* (SATB). C. Fischer CM7805

Persichetti, V. *I Celebrate Myself* (Celebrations)(SATB). Elkan-Vogel 362-03342

Persichetti, V. *Jimmie's Got a Goil* (SATB 2–Part). G. Schirmer 9860

Persichetti, V. *Sam Was a Man* (SATB 2–Part). G. Schirmer 9791

Pfautsch, L. *Go and Tell John* (SATB). Hope C73334

Pfautsch, L. *O Be Joyful in the Lord* (SATB & Brass). Hinshaw HMC445

Pfautsch, L. *Prelude and Dance for Voices and Hands* (SATB). C. Fischer 7803

Pfautsch, L. *Songs Mein Grossmama Sang* (SATB). Lawson–Gould 562

Pierce, B. *Gloria In Excelsis Deo* (SATB). Plymouth BP503

Pinkham, D. *In the Beginning* (SATB & Tape). E. C. Schirmer 1902; Tape 2241

Pooler, R. and Pierce, B. *The Rising Sun* (SATB Aleatory). Somerset CE4328

Poulenc, F. *O Magnum Mysterium* (SATB). Salabert

Roberton, H. *O Lovely Heart* (SATB). G. Schirmer 8595

Rorem, N. *In Time of Pestilence* (SATB). Boosey & Hawkes 5888

Rutter, J. *It Was a Lover and His Lass* (SATBB). Oxford X255

Rutter, J. *For the Beauty of the Earth* (SATB). Hinshaw 550

Rutter, J. *Riddle Song* (SATB). Oxford X230

Rutter, J. *Soldier Boy* (SATB). Hinshaw 813

Rutter, J. *Two Songs from Five Childhood Lyrics* (SATB). Oxford 53.108

Schuman, W. *Carols of Death* (SATB). G. Schirmer

Sowerby, L., arr. *The Snow Lay on the Ground* (SATB). Gray

Thompson, R. *Alleluia* (SATB). E. C. Schirmer 1786

Vaughan Williams, R. *The Turtle Dove* (SATB). Curwen/G. Schirmer 45489

Wilder, Alec. *Lullabies and Nightsongs, Set I* (SATB). Boosey & Hawkes 6089

Junior High Mixed Voices (SB, SAC, SAT, SCB, SAB, SSCB, SACB)

Burt, A. *The Alfred Burt Carols* (SAB). Flammer (Set I D–113, Set II D–114, Set III D–115)

Butler, E. *Advent Song* (SAB). Coronet 285

Butler, E. *Blessed Is the Man* (SACB). Cambiata Press S97203

Butler, E. *Sanctus* (3–Part Mixed). C. Fischer CM8156

Butler, E. *Sing Aloud to God Our Strength* (SAB). Galaxy 1.2373.1

Butler, E. *Sing to His Name for He Is Gracious* (SACB). Cambiata Press C17429

Kirk, T. *Praise the Lord All Ye Nations* (SSCB & Brass). Cambiata Press C117694

Kirk, T. *Sing a Song to the Lord* (SSCB). Cambiata Press C978107

Kodály, Z. *Veni, Veni, Emmanuel* (SAB). Boosey & Hawkes 5564

Leontovich, M./Knight. *Carol of the Bells* (SSCB). Cambiata Press U983176

Pfautsch, Lloyd. *Lovers Love the Spring* (SSCB). General/Kjos GC69

Vaughan Williams, R./Cooper. *For All the Saints* (SCB). Cambiata Press I1978103

Vaughan Williams, R./Elrich. *Festival Piece on Sine Nomine* (SAB). Flammer D5323

Treble Chorus (SA, SSA, SSAA)

Bartok, B. *Breadbaking* (Six Children's Songs)(SA). Boosey & Hawkes 1669

Bartok, B. *Only Tell Me* (SSA). Boosey & Hawkes 1570

Bartok, B. *Teasing Song* (Six Children's Songs)(SSA). Boosey & Hawkes 1672

Berger, J. *Facts* (Three Equal Voices). Presser 312–40632

Berger, J. *A Set of Songs* (SA). Summy–Birchard 5885

Berkowitz, S. *Don't Ask Me* (SA). Lawson–Gould 52056

Bernstein, L. *Gloria Tibi from Mass* (SA & Tenor). G. Schirmer 11964

Binkerd, G. *An Evening Falls* (SA). Boosey & Hawkes 5989

Binkerd, G. *The Christ-Child* (SA). Boosey & Hawkes 5987

Bright, H. *Sacred Songs for the Night* (SSA). Shawnee B190

Britten, B. *Corpus Christi Carol* (A Boy Was Born)(Unison). Oxford E94

Britten, B. *Psalm 150* (SSAA). Boosey & Hawkes 5584

Butler, E. *How Excellent Is Thy Name* (SSA). Bourne 205765–354

Butler, E. *I Never Saw a Moor* (SSA). Richmond F–33

Butler, E. *Sing to the Lord a Marvelous Song* (SSA). A483

Carpenter, J. A. *The Sleep That Flits on Baby's Eyes* (SSA). G. Schirmer 8639

Casals, P. *Nigra Sum* (SSA). A. Broude 120

Copland, A./Swift. *Younger Generation* (SA). Boosey & Hawkes 5506

Davis, K. *Thou Who Wast God* (SSA). Galaxy 1.2185.1

Dello Joio, N. *The Holy Infant's Lullaby* (SSA). Marks 4392

Diemer, E. L. *Alleluia* (SSA). C. Fischer CF7289

Diemer, E. L. *The Magnificat* (SA). Piedmont Music 99

Diemer, E. L. *The Shepherd to His Love* (SSA). Piedmont/Marks 121

Felciano, R. *Sic Transit* (SSA & Tape) E. C. Schirmer 2807; Tape 2243

Fissinger, E. *Night* (SSA). Lawson–Gould 850

Floyd, C. *Long, Long Ago* (SA). Boosey & Hawkes 5648

Frackenpohl, A. *Odd Owls* (SSA). Piedmont/Marks 4381

Frackenpohl, A. *Roll Call* (SA). Plymouth PCS–528

Frackenpohl, A. *Three Limericks in Canon Form* (SA). Marks 90

Goemanne, N. *Sanctus from Missa Hosanna* (SSAA). Mark Foster 907

Hagemann, P. *A Madrigal of Travel* (SA). Presser 312–40923

Harris, R. *Freedom's Land* (SSA). Belwin 64423

Jothen, M. *Sing Hosanna* (SSA). Beckenhorst BP1045

Kodály, Z. *The Angels and the Shepherds* (SA). Universal 10755NJ

Kodály, Z. *Christmas Dance of the Shepherds* (SA). Universal 10878NJ

Kodály, Z. *Ladybird* (SSA). Boosey & Hawkes 5674

Kodály, Z. *Psalm 150* (SA). Oxford Press 83.072

Kodály, Z. *See the Gipsies* (SSAA). Oxford W38

Krenek, E. *Leviathan* from Three Motets (SSA). Rongwen Music 3506

Nelhybel, V. *Gift of Love* (SSA). E. C. Kerby 4674–324

Parker, Alice. *Gabriel's Message* (SSA). E. C. Schirmer 2832

Persichetti, V. *Hist Whist* (SA). C. Fischer CM6651

Pfautsch, L. *Beautiful Yet Truthful* (SSA). Lawson–Gould 549

Pierce, B. *Come and Follow Me* (SA). Plymouth BP–501

Pinkham, D. *Ave Maria* (SA). Associated A–367

Pinkham, D. *Five Canzonets* (SA). Associated A–329

Pinkham, D. *Listen to Me* (Five Motets)(SA). E. C. Schirmer ECS2581

Quilter, R. *Non Nobis, Domine* (Unison). Boosey & Hawkes 69

Rutter, J. *All Things Bright and Beautiful* (SA). Hinshaw HMC663

Rutter, J. *Donkey Carol* (SA). Oxford T111

Rutter, J. *For the Beauty of the Earth* (SA). Hinshaw HMC663

Rutter, J. *Three Carols* (SA, SSA, SSA). Oxford 44.085

Schuman, W. *Five Rounds on Famous Words* (SSA).

Schuman, W. *Orpheus with His Lute* (SSA). G. Schirmer 11787

Spencer, W. *In Excelsis Gloria* (SSA). Associated A–673

Sowerby, L., arr. *The Snow Lay on the Ground* (SA). Gray 2238

Thompson, R. *The Pelican* (SSAA). E. C. Schirmer 2801

Thompson, R. *The Place of the Blest* (SSA). E. C. Schirmer 2599

Thompson, R. *Velvet Shoes* (SA). E. C. Schirmer 2526

Tomas, Henri. *Messe de la Nativite* (SA). Alphonse Leduc

Walters, E. *Babe of Bethlehem* (SA). Boosey & Hawkes 5996

Willan, Healey. *Come Jesus, Holy Child* (SA). Concordia 98–1645

Male Chorus (CB, CCB, CCBB, TB, TTB, TTBB)

Butler, E. *Blessed Is the Man* (CCBB). Cambiata Press C97564

Butler, E. *There Be None of Beauty's Daughters* (TTBB). Byron Douglas 2357

Diemer, E. L. *O Come, Let Us Sing Unto the Lord* (TTBB). C. Fischer CM8014

Holst, G. *Before Sleep* (TB). Boosey & Hawkes 5928

Holst, G. *Drinking Song* (TTBB). Boosey & Hawkes 5927

Holst, G. *How Mighty Are the Sabbaths* (TTBB). Boosey & Hawkes 5925

Holst, G. *A Love Song* (TB). Boosey & Hawkes 5926

Persichetti, V. *Song of Peace* (TTBB). Elkan-Vogel 362–00130

Pooler, F. *Gird Yourself with Lamentations* (TTBB). Somerset MM9009

Vaughan Williams, R./Kauffman. *Silent Noon* (TTBB). Elkan-Vogel 362–03322

The study of choral compositions by composers from all style periods is a life-long quest. This brief study of composers, style period characteristics, and suggested literature, hopefully will provide stimulation and a basis for further enlightment. There is more to a good choral performance than simply technical mastery. Choice of literature is a paramount concern and interpretation of that literature determines the true musicianship of the conductor–teacher. School directors must spend the necessary time in selecting and studying the literature to be performed over the year. Singers and conductor can then grow musically together.

Chapter Six

Selecting and Studying Choral Literature

Directors are responsible for choosing music for each school choral ensemble. This task is worth the time and effort invested in it, even though it is demanding and time-consuming for the choral director. A conductor's musicianship is reflected in the repertoire chosen. Each concert presented is fairly representative of the depth of the conductor's knowledge and the choir's musical capabilities.

CRITERIA FOR SELECTION OF CHORAL REPERTOIRE

Several considerations for selection of appropriate choral literature include: (1) aesthetic worth of the music and text, (2) difficulty level of the pieces, (3) the ranges and tessitura of each part, (4) school and community nonmusical influences, (5) educational purpose of the choral literature, (6) balance of accompanied and a cappella repertory, and (7) a balance and variety of quality choral literature.

Aesthetic Worth of Music and Text

The quality of the repertoire chosen over each school year for all choral ensembles is of critical importance. While voice training may be achieved in the performance of inferior music, the student will not profit aesthetically from the experience. Too often quality is equated with difficulty, yet there are many excellent examples of choral literature of easy to medium difficulty. These include pieces from Renaissance through the Contemporary, as well as many fine arrangements of spirituals and folk tunes.

Will the music be aesthetically satisfying to the singers and the intended audience? Is there a good blend of text and music? Does the text fit the junior and senior high age or is it too childish or too mature? If an arrangement, such as a spiritual, retains original style features, or does it appear to be contrived or overdone? Will the music wear well over rehearsals and sensitize the choir to the beauty of the piece? Will it be worth performing five or ten years from now?

Difficulty Level of Pieces

Is the degree of difficulty of the piece suitable to the choir that will sing it? Will there be enough rehearsal time to learn the piece? It will not be possible to successfully perform an entire program of difficult choral repertoire. Ideally, a conductor will want to select one or two difficult pieces and one or two easier works. The remainder of the concert program will probably be repertoire in the medium difficulty category. Although difficulty is relative depending upon the conductor, the choir, and the particular situation, the bulk of literature chosen should be toward the medium category for a particular choir.

Some of the factors that make a piece more difficult are complex meter and rhythm patterns, extremely fast or slow tempi, many chromatics, key change or lack of tonality, dissonant harmonic structure, awkward interval leaps, complex polyphonic texture that can expose weak sections of the choir, and texts difficult to execute. The size of the choir and the general musicianship level of the singers are important. Sometimes a translated text proves unsingable and the piece will need to be sung in the original foreign language. Do the overall characteristics indicate that the piece is within the performance capability of your choir? Is it technically within the grasp of your singers? Can the choir achieve the choral sonority necessary for a truly musical and aesthetically satisfying performance of the work? Can the work be memorized?

Ranges and Tessitura of Each Part

Most composers write for mature adult voices. However, there are many choral masterpieces within the ranges of junior and senior high school singers. In addition, there are many editors today who specialize in arranging for the junior and senior high singer. The junior high ranges were presented in Chap. 2 and senior high voice ranges, in Chap. 3. Be aware that young choirs sound best when the outer limits of the range for each part are avoided. This comfortable tessitura will permit the voice to sound satisfying and will not make extreme vocal demands upon the singers. Although an occasional high note or passage is acceptable and within mastery, a succession of long, sustained high tones in any part may indicate the piece is intended for mature voices only. Which vowel is being sung on high pitches needs careful examination. The *ee* and *oo* vowels are difficult at higher pitch levels, whereas, the *ah* and *oh* vowels are easier. Also, what is the dynamic level at the extreme range. If pianissimo, the result could be disastrous. Be careful to avoid high tessitura in the senior high tenor part and low tessitura in the alto part. Can other voices be added to the part to achieve the correct sonority? Sing each part yourself to determine how difficult each really is and circle the questionable intervals, range problems, and rhythm problems. If you as a director experience difficulty singing the part, the singers will likewise experience similar problems.

School and Community Influences

It is often difficult for the new choral director to get the feel of what is expected in the choral position. What kind of choral director was there previously and what type of music was sung? Was the program high powered or mostly a pop choir type of program? Is the position in a rural, suburban, or urban community? What is the socioeconomic level of the community? What is the religious makeup of the community? Are there minority group concerns? What do the parents expect from the choral program? Is the community a musical one? Are there community concert events available? Does a college or university serve the area?

A new director will need to "take the pulse" of the students, parents, principal, and other teachers of the community. Student loyalties may still lie with the prior director and a smooth working relationship may require time. There is no substitute for the conductor's musicianship; however, choral directors will need to know how to deal effectively with those with whom they work.

Educational Considerations in Repertoire Selection

Junior and senior high school choir directors must realize that they are working with immature voices and largely untrained musicians. Vocal technique, choral singing skills, sight-reading skills, music history-style-theory knowledge must be taught. A few senior high singers may be studying voice privately. A number of both junior and senior high singers may play piano, guitar, and the common band/orchestra instruments. However, the bulk of teaching and training the choir singers will fall upon the choral conductor. A few of the singers will be participating in church choir programs.

Directors will need to select pieces with a particular purpose in mind. Perhaps a particular piece will assist the choir's ability to sing polyphonic lines. Another piece will have rhythm/textual mastery problems. Still another may be excellent for improving major/minor intonation and part balance. Some pieces are fine for sight-reading purposes unassisted at the piano. A contemporary piece may be selected for the atonal treatment of the harmony. The form may be featured in an A-B-A Ternary type madrigal piece. In short, literature may be selected with a specific educational purpose. If the choir has not sung in a foreign language, a Latin motet may be chosen for study and performance. It is the director's educational responsibility to assist his students to grow musically. The audience may also learn something from performance of a piece.

Holidays, seasons, festivals, and contests also place demands upon the director's choice of literature. Contest literature requires pieces of quality that show off the choir's abilities. What is to be avoided is selection of music with no thought to each choir's musical growth. If music is selected to get through the next performance, the director then is an entertainer, not worthy of the title music educator.

Accompanied and A Cappella Literature

The human voice is the most personal of all musical instruments. Unlike orchestral instruments, the voice can produce not only musical tone, but also a text simultaneously. Some of the earliest music of the church was unison chant which led to the marvelous a cappella literature of the Renaissance.

It is important for directors to include both unaccompanied and accompanied choral literature in the school choral program. Students need to learn to sing the a cappella style unassisted by piano, organ, or other instruments. As instruments appeared in the Baroque choral compositions, they served as an accompaniment vehicle. Many Bach choral compositions are nothing more than chorales accompanied by introductions, interludes, and codas for instrument.

Many choral compositions have been composed with obbligato for flute, violin, trumpet, and so on, as well as for small ensembles of brass, string, woodwind, and percussion instruments. A brass choir greatly enriches the choral sonority and adds brillance to the piece. It is best if the instruments do not simply duplicate the voices, but have independent lines to truly decorate the voices. Also, it is not too interesting to listen to an a cappella piece with the piano duplicating the voice parts. This accompaniment is for rehearsal only and tends to cover up the beauty of unaccompanied singing.

Some beautiful unaccompanied choral literature abounds, including the Renaissance masterpieces, the late nineteenth century choral music of the Russian Orthodox Church, and the folk tune arrangements of Brahms. Randall Thompson has exploited this form in the twentieth century. A good balance needs to be struck in choral ensembles between the a cappella and accompanied choral literature.

Balance and Variety in Choices

Obviously, school choral groups will not be content to sing only Palestrina, Bach, Mozart, Mendelssohn, and Stravinsky. Although this literature represents the highest standard of compositional excellence, young people need a better mix of literature to sustain their interests. The director and the community is the key to how much? However, the masterpieces of choral literature need complemented by other choral compositional idioms.

Traditional choral repertoire. This repertoire is representative of choral composers from Renaissance, Baroque, Classic, Romantic, and Contemporary music style periods of our Western culture. It is music composed for choirs, not arrangements of folk tunes, spirituals, or popular songs. Today many SATB master choral compositions have been set for female and male voices, as well as SAB and SACB voicings; however, the mixed voice choir still dominates in both the church and school. It is important that at least *half* of the choral literature learned and performed in junior and senior high schools come from this mainstream of our Western choral culture. The best of our culture must be transmitted to present and future generations of young singers. The pop mediums of television and recordings have come to dominate the youth of today, creating a youth cult. This is a temporary phenomenon in the growth cycle of youth, and many youth already suspect there must be music of better quality in addition to the pop instantaneous gratification type. It is the director's responsibility to open these young singers to the broader conception of choral singing. Yes, Gibbons, Di Lasso, Schubert, Brahms, and Vaughan Williams have something to say to all of us, young or old, and need to be included in the choral repertoire of the schools.

Folk and spiritual arrangements. Folksongs and spirituals are expressions of the common people and are usually not composed. Arrangers have set many German, French, English, Italian, Spanish, Mexican, Jewish, and American folksongs for choirs of mixed, male, and treble voices. These are well worth including in the choral repertoire of junior and senior high school choral programs. The spirituals express underlying feelings of our multicultural society. The folk and spiritual repertoire on a concert adds a high degree of interest and variety. Folk accompaniments of guitar, harmonica, banjo, recorders, and percussion are effective.

Broadway and pop tune arrangements. The light opera goes back to Gilbert and Sullivan in England and Victor Herbert in the United States. Others such as Gershwin, Kern, Berlin, Rodgers and Hammerstein, Bernstein, and Webber have developed the Broadway Musical over the years. Students enjoy singing renditions of the show tunes in choir. Small jazz/show choirs utilize this literature also, along with lighter pop tunes. A number of pop styles of singing have developed including folk, jazz, country western, gospel, rock, and others. Some of these are popularized on television and recordings. Directors may include a limited number of Broadway and pop tunes to the choral repertoire of large ensembles; however, much of this literature can be taught effectively in a smaller jazz/show choir ensemble. The goal of the school choral program is largely to educate, not to entertain. Directors must be careful that pop groups do not dominate the choral program, and that the number of performances of this type group be kept in limits. There are many high school choral groups that perform a Broadway musical yearly or every other year. Directors must walk a fine line in balancing the vocal music experiences of young people. The music selected will represent the director's and the community's overall musical tastes.

Extended choral works. There are times when choirs in junior and senior high school should experience the singing of a larger extended choral work. This includes masses, cantatas, oratorios, and short suites of choral music. The music of Bach and Handel abounds in short works. The Bach cantata, *For Us a Child Is Born*, is appropriate. Some solo singing is possible in this work, or guest soloists may be invited to participate with the high school chorus. John Rutter's *Gloria* and *Requiem* have been performed successfully by high school singers, as well as Schubert's *Mass in G*, Britten's *Ceremony of Carols*, Vivaldi's *Gloria* , Saint Saen's *Christmas Oratorio*, and the Faure *Requiem*. Most high school choirs can perform several major choruses from such works as Mendelssohn's *Elijah* and Handel's *Messiah*.

If the high school has an orchestra, they may accompany a larger work. Some literature, such as the Pinkham *Christmas Cantata* and Rutter *Gloria* require smaller orchestral forces. If no instrumentalists are available, a piano or organ accompaniment may suffice. A longer work for SSA chorus is Faure's *Messe Basse* (low mass). For junior high mixed choirs, the Schubert *Mass in F* (SACB, Cambiata Press) is worthwhile performing.

BUILDING A REFERENCE FILE

All junior and senior high school choral directors need to develop a reference file of music deemed useable. The search for new choral literature is time consuming, but necessary. Many suggested octavos for use with all types of choirs in junior and senior high school are included in the Appendixes of this book. Collections, larger works, and choral materials and equipment sources are also listed.

Membership in professional organizations is helpful since they publish journals with news of choral events, reviews of choral music, and choral publisher's advertisements of new releases. Conferences, workshops, clinics, and choral reading seminars sponsored by these organizations provide excellent opportunities for discovering new repertoire and sharing ideas with colleagues. These sessions provide exposure to a more select choral literature, rather than to unsolicited repertoire of little or dubious quality. Lists are also useful in that they provide titles which may be examined through local music distributors. The American Choral Directors Association (ACDA) conventions and the Music Educators National Conference (MENC) conventions provide directors with an opportunity to hear new literature performed by outstanding groups.

In addition, ACDA and MENC have published selected lists of choral literature. (See Appendixes A through M.) Other auxiliary materials and equipment are listed in Appendixes N through P. Appendix Q lists the professional organizations and journals, and Appendix R is a Directory of Publishers. Other useful sources are included in Bibliography E, Choral Music Repertoire and Interpretation. Publishers are also happy to place your name on their mailing list to receive newly published music and current catalogs.

Since you will be receiving an enormous quantity of new choral publications yearly, it is wise to sort these out as they arrive and make a file card (as presented in Chap. 1) of those pieces you deem worthwhile to your choral needs. The cards may be filed either by title or composer, although filing by composer provides a chronological order. In addition to title, composer/arranger, voicing, order number, and difficulty level indications, add enough comments to remind you of the features of each particular piece. This system for evaluating newly received music will assist the director to find and order music to be studied and eventually performed.

STUDYING THE CHORAL SCORE

After selecting the music for each choir, the director's next task is to prepare for rehearsals. It is important to appraise the musical content of each choral work in terms of its form, melody, rhythm, harmony, texture, dynamics, and text features. In a short work, the form is fairly easy to discern. When examining a longer work, each movement must be examined as to structure and how it contributes to the entire scope of the work.

For each composition it is necessary for the director to sing each part, practice the accompaniment, and mark the score where trouble spots are likely to occur during rehearsal. Details about the music's features may be noted on the music for recall and possible transmission to the choir.

Discerning the Form of the Piece

Form is the underlying organizational plan for the choral piece of larger choral work. It allows for unity and variety, a key ingredient of fine music. Some choral music will be *strophic* in design, having the same music for all stanzas, such as a hymn or chorale. Other pieces will be *binary* (AB), with two contrasting sections, each of which may be repeated. Still others will follow a *ternary* (ABA) design, having a contrasting middle section between two similar sections. Other pieces are *through-composed* on the text, with the music difference throughout to enhance the words. Some contemporary *aleatory* music allows for the singers to improvise on texts or vocal sounds, so no two renditions are ever quite the same. Other devices that unify a piece are repeated rhythmic figures, repeated melodic figures, and harmonic progressions.

Melody Characteristics

The tune or melody of a piece may be in major, minor, or modal *tonality*. Its *phrases* may be short or arch-like. It may or may not have many *sequential patterns*. Some melodies are mainly *conjunct* (moving by step), some *disjunct* (moving by skip), and others are both. Some medodies outline tonic and dominant triads. Some are *diatonic* and others are *chromatic*. Some are sung *legato*, others *marcato*. Directors need to ask: Are there difficult *intervals* in any part? What is the most important part of each phrase? Of the entire melody?

Rhythm Features

Directors need to identify the proper *tempo* of a piece. *Metronome marks* may be helpful, but they may not be authentic. Metronomes did not come into use until the time of Beethoven. Marks on earlier works indicate additions by an editor. The best way to decide on a proper tempo is to look at the longest and shortest note values in a piece. If singers cannot articulate the shortest note values clearly, the tempo may be too fast. If they have difficulty sustaining the longest notes, the tempo may be too slow.

The rhythmic characteristics of each piece needs to be identified. Are *augmentation* and *diminution* (lengthening and shortening of note values) used? Are there *ritards* and *accelerandos*? How should the *fermata* be handled? What is the *meter signature*? If it changes in the piece, what is the reason? How will the piece be conducted? If the tempo is slow, a divided beat may be required for clarity.

Harmony and Texture

Directors should decide if the piece has a key center, if it is pentatonic or modal in tonality, and if it modulates from key to key. They should look at the chordal movement of the piece. Is it fast or slow? Is *suspension* (resolved dissonance) used? Is the harmony mainly chordal or are there *dissonant* harmonies? How is *unison* used? Where are the ends of sections and what kind of *cadences* are there? Is *pedal point* used? Is the piece based on the 12-tone row? Is the piece bi-tonal, polytonal, or atonal?

Music usually falls into one of three types of textures.

1. *Monophonic*—a single melody line, as in chant.
2. *Polyphonic*—many independent vocal lines, sometimes imitating as in a fugue (contrapuntal).
3. *Homophonic*—chordal or hymn-like, with all voices moving together. An accompanied melody is also considered homophonic. Homophonic music is sometimes called "familiar style."

Sometimes voices imitate at the octave and at the interval of the fifth. A *stretto* is a free imitation which deviates from the complete fugue statement, using only the "head" of the fugue. Modern choral compositions may use *tape backgrounds* (synthesizer), as well as voices, for an interesting texture.

Observing Dynamics

Dynamic markings (forte, piano, crescendo, diminuendo, accents, and so on) add color and expression to the composition and help enhance the text. They were nonexistent in the Renaissance period, and largely soft (p) and loud (f) in terraced fashion in the Baroque. Music from the Romantic and Contemporary periods sometimes requires abrupt changes in dynamics.

The Importance of the Text

Directors should be alert to devices a composer may have used to enhance the text of a piece. Handel uses *text* painting in *Messiah* by pitching "peace" on a heavenly high, and "on earth" on a worldly low. Determine whether the text is syllabic (one syllable per note) or melismatic (one syllable for two or more notes). Melismatic texts are sometimes difficult for young voices to sing. Is the text repetitive for stress purposes? Is the text fragmented in some voice lines? Is the next set in strophic form? Does it present diction problems of articulation? If the text is in a foreign language, can it be performed with correct pronounciation? If a translation is sung, does it fit the music well or should the original language be retained?

The text is important to successful performance of the piece. The audience wishes to understand the words of the piece. This is the major difference between instrumental and vocal music. The text must be projected musically.

PART
THREE

DEVELOPING CHORAL
MUSICIANSHIP IN
STUDENTS

Chapter Seven

Vocal Techniques for the Chorus

The underlying characteristics of a good solo tone are also desirable in producing a good choral tone. Although it is not possible to teach a voice lesson in a choral rehearsal, it is possible to incorporate basic vocal techniques in these rehearsals. A pleasing and properly produced choral sound is required.

THE HUMAN VOICE MECHANISM

The human voice is an amazing instrument. It consists of four main components: (1) the respiratory or breathing muscles, or sound generator, (2) the vocal cords, or vibrator, (3) the pharynx, mouth, and nasal cavity which serves as the resonator to amplify the sound, and (4) the tongue, lips, teeth, palate, and lower jaw, which serve as the articulator of the sound. Figure 7–1 shows (a) the breathing mechanism, and (b) the vocal chords, resonating cavities, and articulators.

The principal muscles used in breathing are the diaphragm, the abdominal muscles, and the intercostal muscles. The diaphragm is a large domed-shaped muscle which divides the chest cavity from the abdominal cavity. During inhalation of breath, the diaphragm contracts and pushes downward, while the contraction of the intercostal muscles raises the rib cage. This action enlarges the thorax, allowing the lungs to fill with air. In singing a long sustained note or phrase, the abdominal muscles gradually contract while the diaphragm slowly relaxes, with the intercostal muscles maintaining enough tension to prevent bulging in the intercostsal spaces. When one set of muscles contracts, the other set relaxes somewhat. During inhalation, the abdominal muscles will move outward. At exhalation, while a tone(s) is produced, the abdominal muscles will move inward as indicated in Fig. 7–1.

The larynx, a hard area that can be seen and felt, is found in the throat at the top of the trachea or windpipe. It protects the respiratory tract. Inside the larynx are two narrow, elastic, fibrous vocal cords that are enclosed in folds of mucous membrane. The vocal cords, which are about the size of a small paper clip, run from the front to the back of the lower throat. The front ends, which do not move, are attached to the inside of the thyroid cartilage, known as the "Adam's apple." The other ends are joined to two pieces of cartilage, which can move in and out, backward and forward, by action of the muscles. The opening between the vocal cords is called the glottis. The vocal cords are brought together by muscles controlling the position of the artenoid cartilage, and are set vibrating by the flow of breath pressure during exhalation. See Fig. 7–2 for a visualization of how the larynx and vocal cords function. When breathing normally the glottis assumes a V-shape position, but during deep breathing, it assumes a rounder shape. When a sound is produced (phonation), the vocal cords come very close together.

The highness or lowness of pitch produced depends upon the length, tension, and thickness of the cords. The male vocal cords are thicker and thus produce a lower pitch overall. To sing a high pitch, the vocal cords become shorter, more tense, thinner, and closer together. When singing a lower pitch, the cords become thicker, less tense, and longer. If the pressure or breath support is inadequate, the laryngeal muscles will function improperly in attempting to obtain the correct pitch. This can produce fatigue and strain on the voice.

For a pitch to have intensity and quality, the sound waves, made by the vibration of the vocal cords, must be made stronger in the resonators. These vocal resonators are the mouth, the sinuses, and the laryngeal, oral, and nasal pharynx areas. The nasal cavity is fixed, whereas, the pharynx and mouth may alter the resonance of the tone. On each side and above the vocal cords are cavities that amplify the vibration of the vocal cords and increase their intensity as they are projected from the larynx. These cavities are fully used as resonating chambers only when the throat is relaxed and kept open. Also, the mouth acts best as a resonating cavity when all the muscles, including the tongue, are relaxed and the mouth cavity is enlarged, allowing for an increased size in the resonance chamber. The nasopharynx and nasal cavities produce greater resonance to the tone when a small opening between the oropharynx is maintained. This allows the vibrating air to enter further for greater resonance and amplication of the tone.

If the singing mechanism is to function in choral singing, the articulating organs—lips, teeth, tongue, and soft palate (velum)—must be flexible. They permit good attack and release of tone by forming the vowels and consonants necessary for clear diction. The singing voice must be conditioned to withstand the demands on the voice which are greater than those of normal speech. Singing requires more support from the body and greater discipline than ordinary speech.

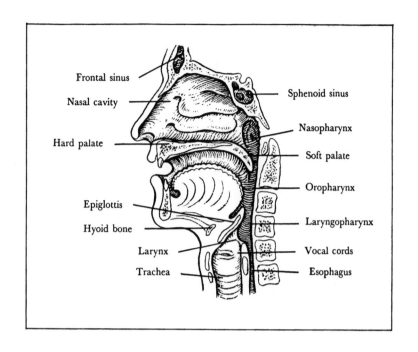

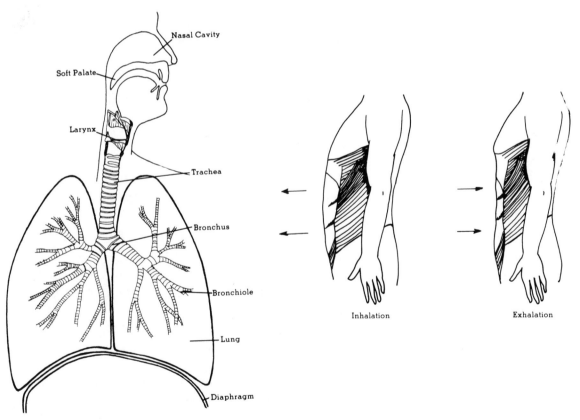

Figure 7-1 The Vocal Mechanism

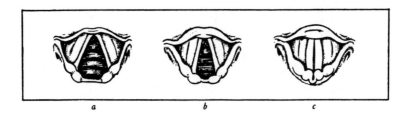

Figure 7–2 Action of the Vocal Cords: (a) Deep Breath, (b) Normal Breath, and (c) Sound Produced

POSTURE, BREATHING, AND PHRASING

Proper posture and breath support are important to the developing of good singing tone. Students must learn to exhale slowly when singing a phrase. Without proper support, phrases will sag. Junior and senior high school singers need frequent reminders about singing postures. In rehearsal and performance, posture rules need to be enforced.

Sitting

1. Students should not slouch, but sit erect with backs away from the backs of their chairs. The chests should be high to permit free breathing, and their chins should be down.
2. They should place their feet flat on the floor, and keep their legs uncrossed.
3. They should hold their music high enough to see the director, but not bury their heads in it.

Standing

1. Students should hold their spines straight and their chests high. Having them place their hands in the hollow of their backs sometimes helps them attain the desired position.
2. Their feet should be slightly apart, with one foot a few inches ahead of the other and the balance of their body weight slightly forward.
3. When singing without a score, their arms should be released and held comfortably at their sides. When music is used, it should be held at about chest height.

The shoulders should be relaxed and in a natural position, and the neck should be relaxed and aligned with the spine. The jaw should be loose and low, and the head free to turn from side to side. The body should be strong, relaxed, and flexible so that movements are free from tension. Correct posture aids muscular coordination and keeps the body from tiring. The Wenger Company's "posture chair" is useful for maintaining a good sitting posture in rehearsal. Two exercises for achieving good posture follow:

1. Raise the arms above the head and stretch upward. Join thumbs and pull light-

ly. Then, lower the arms slowly keeping them straight and extended. Maintain this "up" feel.

2. Stand against a wall allowing the small of the back to touch the wall with the head aligned above. Move the hips in and slightly forward. Step away from the wall, keeping this posture without feeling stiff or tense.

Good posture places the lungs and rib cage in the proper position for a big breath. Breathe in through the nose and mouth without making a sound. The rib cage will expand in front, back, and on the sides. When the breath is taken, the diaphragm muscle moves downward. Exhaling the air will start the vocal cords vibrating. The exhaling process requires the controlled contraction of the muscles controlling the diaphragm. The diaphragm pushes against the lungs, causing a stream of air to flow up the windpipe to the larynx which houses the vocal cords. The process is called phonation, or attack. Several breathing experiences follow:

1. To begin the attack and experience the action of the abdominal muscles, sound the following consonants in a long rhythmic succession: f, f, f; ch, ch, ch; sh, sh, sh.

2. To feel the action of the muscles during phonation, tell the students to pant like an animal for a few seconds. As they do so place one hand on the abdomen, just below the rib cage. Gradually slow the panting down to one inhalation and exhalation per second.

3. Exhale by pushing all the air out until the abdominal muscles are hard. Hold this position as long as possible, then release the muscles, allowing air to fill the lungs again.

4. Chant the alphabet or a text of a song on one pitch, singing as much as possible on one breath.

5. Have the students bend over at the waist with hands at the bottom of the rib cage, fingers apart. Have the students inhale deeply. They will be forced to breathe from the diaphragm, since that is the only possible way to breathe in that position. Then, stand erect, hands on the rib cage, and blow the air out in a steady stream on an "f" or hissing sound. The ribs should come in slowly. The "f" or hiss can then be changed to a singing vowel sound.

6. A more difficult exercise to bounce the abdominal muscles is to sing staccato a succession of quarter, eighth, triplets, and then sixteenth-note patterns using an "h" in front of each note. This develops clear articulation.

DEVELOPING GOOD INTONATION

Closely related to proper breath support in singing is the problem of singing "in tune." Intonation means singing in perfect unison with others within a section, and the sections singing the right intervals in relation to the intervals sung by the other sections. When singing goes "out of tune," the tone spreads, waivers, or "beats." The note may be slightly flat or sharp and tone quality and blend will suffer. The following guidelines will help:

1. Students need to think the tone before they sing it. They should sing the "center" of every pitch. The brain needs to tune the vocal cords for the vibrations to come.
2. Make sure everyone in the section is singing in unison.
3. Keep enough breath to support the pitch through the phrase.
4. Energize or support any soft singing even more than strong passages.
5. Listen carefully to sing ascending steps high enough, and descending steps small enough. Often ascending steps become too small and descending steps too large.
6. Keep the vowel uniform to avoid an "off pitch" effect.
7. Sing the third (mi or 3) and seventh (ti or 7) degrees of the major scale tones slightly higher than normal. These tones often tend to be low and can cause flatting. The same is true of half-step intervals in minor scales.

Figure 7–3 illustrates some vocalises to improve the intonation of junior and senior high school choral groups.

Faulty intonation may be caused by shallow breathing, poor posture, high tessitura, repeated tones, descending scale lines, difficult upward interval leaps, and sustaining of long tones. Sometimes the piano is too weak to be heard to maintain accurate tonality. Students need to understand the terms "flat" and "sharp" and to visualize whole and half steps on a paper keyboard as they sing them.

ACHIEVING BALANCE AND BLEND

Balance is the proportion of sound between two or more voice parts. Directors need to decide if there is an appropriate balance between parts, taking into consideration the number and quality of singers on each part. Typically, the melody line needs to be heard above the harmony parts (in homophonic music), and those singing harmony may need to be instructed to lighten their tone to achieve balance. Dynamic level of a section affects balance. Within a section, an ideal balance is achieved when all voices sing at about an equal dynamic level, although some voices are more timid than others who have stronger voices. Voice placement within a choir or section can improve balance, as well as blend. Very strong singers should be placed within the ensemble, rather than on the ends or in the front row. Singing in quartet arrangement in a SATB choir is one of the best ways to achieve both good blend and balance. This requires independent singers, however. Some solo voices may need to give up some individuality of sound to develop a good choral sound.

Blend is the degree of fusion of individual voices. A good blend is dependent upon each singer's listening habits, production of uniform vowels, and a shared concept of what constitutes a good singing tone. Directors should aim to mold their singers into "one large voice," rather than try to show off individual voices. They must listen to the section sound. Having one singer sing the first phrase of a piece, with others in

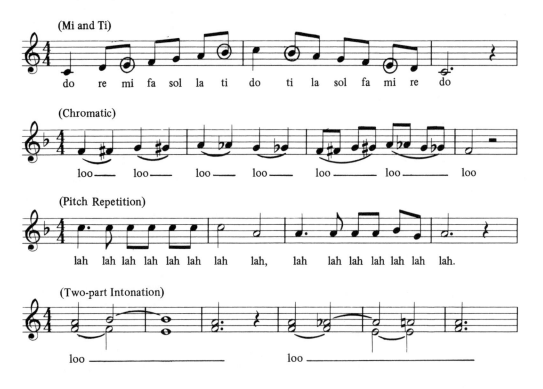

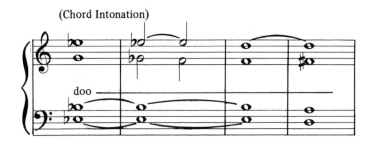

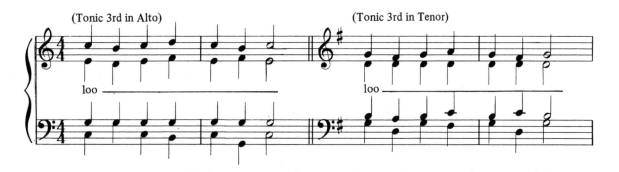

Figure 7–3 Intonation Exercises

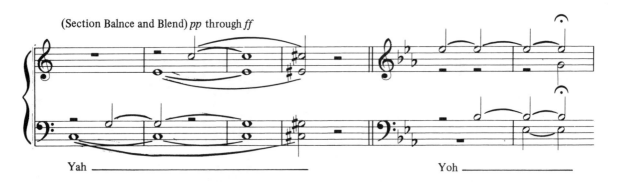

Figure 7–4 Blend and Balance Exercises

the section joining in one after the other, is one way to work at achieving a good blend. A so-called "white tone," completely devoid of any vibrato in the voice is not the desired tone, although this tone can be effective in a cappella Renaissance pieces. A natural, rich tone from all the singers that blends well is desirable. Figure 7–4 illustrates the blend and balance vocalises that will assist the listening process.

IMPROVING VOCAL RESONANCE

The director should work for a choral tone that has a singing resonance and a deep, rich warm sound. Some voices have this quality in part of their singing range, but constant voice training will help develop this quality throughout the singing range. Choirs need to focus the tone forward behind the nose. Some refer to this tone placement area as the mask. Singers will feel a buzz or ring when they perform the following exercises. Hold the "m" or "ng" before moving to the "ee" or other vowel sound. Maintain the buzz or ringing quality into the vowel. Move up and down by half steps. (See Fig. 7–5.)

Sometimes, have the singers place the back of their hands on their mouths and hum a pitch, and then move the hand away while moving to an "ah" or "oh." Keep the humming or buzzing quality in every tone. All sounds are focused just below the

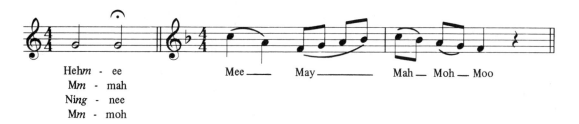

Figure 7–5 Resonance Vocalises

upper front teeth to achieve maximum resonance. The tone often loses focus as different vowels are sounded. A continuous "line" of focused sound is required in singing to achieve uniform quality throughout the range.

In order for the sound to be full and rich, as much resonating space as possible must be used. This means "dropping the jaw" to increase the size of the resonating cavity. Two holes are felt when the jaw is dropped, one just in front of the top of the ear lobe, and the other at the hinge of the jaw bone. When the tip of the index finger fits these depressions, the jaw is down, and the throat is open. The tongue must be flat in the bottom of the mouth, with the tip of the tongue touching the lower front teeth. The jaw must be kept loose and flexible, free of tension. Have the singers "yawn" several times to relieve tension in the jaw and to open the throat.

DEVELOPING EXPRESSIVE DYNAMICS

Singers need to be taught how to expand the intensity of the tone without strain. A good, warm, lyric tone is needed. Students must learn to stretch the tones, making the sound grow in intensity. A unison tone may be practiced first on a single vowel such as "mee" or "mah," stretching the tone over eight to twelve counts. The unison "nee, nay, nah, no, noo" and chordal version in Fig. 7–5 will assist this process.

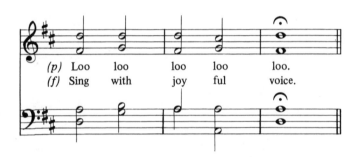

Figure 7–6 Dynamic Vocalises

Choirs also need to be trained to sing at various dynamic levels. Singers need to be taught how to get the last ounce of intensity out of a tone by sustaining final chords, and letting the sound continue to grow to the cut-off. Avoid harsh, raucous tones, and insist on strong diaphragm support. Do not allow the chins to stretch upward, but do keep full body support to the tone. Singing from the neck upward will cause strain, due to the shallow breath support.

A more difficult problem is learning how to sing softly with support under the tone. Often insufficient air is taken in to support a long, soft phrase, and the result is breathiness and fuzziness of the tone. One of the most dangerous signals a director can give a choir is the diminuendo, since the choir is inclined to relax the tone support. Choirs have difficulty making a long, four-measure diminuendo. Because the conductor's hand is turned over and facing down, there is no visual sign for lift or support of the tone. With amateur choirs, the director will need to work on both gradual crescendi and diminuendi to achieve proper support and evenness of effect. Expressive singing requires control of dynamics. The four-part vocalise in Fig. 7–5 may be practiced at varied dynamic levels throughout (ppp to fff). Or a crescendo may be made through the vocalise, as well as the reverse, the diminuendo. Next try a crescendo through the vowel "nah" and a diminuendo over "noh and noo," sustaining the "noo" at a pp level for eight beats. Exhalation of the air must be gradual and controlled. Figure 7–6 illustrates several vocalises to sing at various dynamic levels.

VOCALIZING JUNIOR HIGH MIXED VOICES
(SSC, SAB, SACB, LIMITED RANGE SATB)

Junior high voices need to develop flexibility for singing fast passages and passages with many notes per syllable (melisma). Sing the following exercises in Fig. 7–7 up and down by half steps.

Extending the range of singing voices can be accomplished through vocalization. A feeling of expansion as one goes higher in pitch is required. The tone still needs a good ringing and forward resonance. When producing the pitches in the lower range, the resonance chambers need to be opened as much as possible and the jaw dropped.

Figure 7–7 Flexibility Exercises

Figure 7–8 Range Exercises

Figure 7–8 illustrates some vocalises to expand singing ranges upward and downward by half steps.

The sixth and seventh grade mixed chorus often contains no baritone singers and voicings are often designated SSC, SAC, or SAT. Some choirs can sing SSA music. The lowest part is the boy alto-tenor or cambiata singer. His range may extend from fourth line F on the bass staff through third space C on the treble staff. Figure 7–9 illustrates good chordal intonation vocalises for this three-part choir.

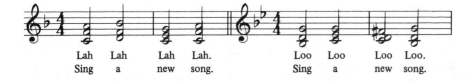

Figure 7–9 SSC Intonation Vocalises

Figure 7–10 Two SAB Chord Vocalises

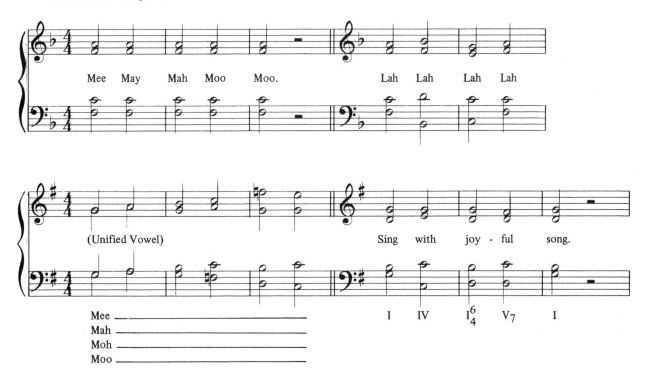

Figure 7–11 SSCB (SACB) or Limited Range SATB Chord Vocalises

The junior high baritone voice may go down to B♭ on the bass clef quite comfortably. Two chordal vocalises for SAB voicing are illustrated in Fig. 7–10.

Figure 7–11 illustrates vocalises for the SACB (SSCB) or limited range SATB choir. See Chap. 2 for a full discussion of junior high voice ranges.

VOCALIZING JUNIOR HIGH MALE VOICES
(CBB, CCBB, Limited Range TTBB)

The ranges of junior high male voices are illustrated in Figure 7–12.

The voicings which may appear for junior high boys in both separate octavos and collections of pieces are CB, CCB, CBB, CCBB, and limited range TTBB. Directors must

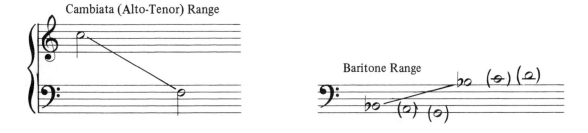

Figure 7–12 Junior High Male Voice Ranges

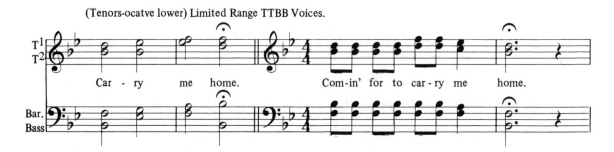

Figure 7–13 Junior High Male Chorus Vocalises

be careful when selecting music for junior high boys' chorus. Figure 7–13 illustrates some chord vocalises for junior high male chorus. Move up and down by half steps as far as range permits.

VOCALIZING JUNIOR/SENIOR HIGH TREBLE VOICES (SA, SSA, SSAA)

The sound of treble voices is appealing in both junior and senior high school. In junior high, the girls' chorus usually sings in unison, SA, and SSA voicings. In senior high, the girls' chorus may sing some fine SSAA choral literature. The junior high girls' voices tend to be light and breathy and the tone needs to be supported by deep breathing. In senior high, the voices are stronger and more developed. The director should not permit the alto voices to sing with a harsh quality, as so often happens. They should lighten their voices on the lower pitches. The following chord vocalises in Fig. 7–14 will help develop good intonation.

Figure 7–14 Junior/Senior High Girls' Chorus Chord Vocalises

Figure 7–15 Unison Vocalises for Mixed Chorus

1. Chromatics

Loo   loo   loo   loo   loo   loo   loo   loo   loo.

2.

Major   Minor   Diminished

Lah   lah   lah   lah   lah   *(etc.)*

Major   Augmented   Major

3.

Loo   loo   loo   loo   loo   loo   loo.

Maj.   Min.   Dim.   Min.   Maj.   Aug.   Maj.

4. Major Chord Progression

Lah   lah   lah   lah   lah   lah   lah   lah   lah.

5. Minor Chord Progression

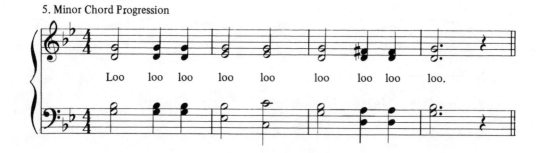

Loo   loo   loo   loo   loo   loo   loo   loo   loo.

Figure 7–16 Mixed Chorus Intonation Vocalises

6. SSAATTBB Vocalise *(pp-ff)*

Loo   loo   loo   Lah   lah,   Loo   loo   loo   lah.

VOCALIZING SENIOR HIGH MIXED VOICES (SATB, SSAATTBB)

The senior high school mixed chorus (SATB) provides great satisfaction to teen-age singers. The repertoire is plentiful for this medium as well as divisi of parts for SSAATTBB singing. Sing the following unison vocalises in Fig. 7–15 to develop a supported choral tone, clear diction, and pleasing choral tone. Move up and down by half steps.

Achieving good intonation with a mixed chorus may be accomplished through numerous chordal vocalises. Be careful of whole and half steps, and see that the third and seventh scale degrees are high enough. Utilize major, minor, diminished, augmented, and cluster chords for tune-up's. (See Fig. 7–16.)

VOCALIZING SENIOR HIGH MALE VOICES (TB, TBB, TTB)

The senior high school boys' chorus can be a rich sounding ensemble. Figure 7–17 illustrates some chord vocalises to tune the intonation of the male chorus.

Additional vocalises may be found in Chaps. 9 and 10. A vocalise should not become routine to the choir. It should serve a particular purpose. Directors should determine if a certain vocalise would be effective prior to rehearsing a specific piece, rather than just "tuning up" or "warming up" at the beginning of each rehearsal. Passages should be extracted from the literature for vocal work. The aim of vocalises is to produce excellent choral singing.

Figure 7–17 Senior High Male Chorus Vocalises

Chapter Eight

English and Latin Choral Diction

Singing is a means of communication. Diction is important if the textual message of the choral piece is to be conveyed to the audience. Uniform vowel sounds create a beautiful tone and consonants give the words intensity, clarity, and vitality. The obvious difference between vocal and instrumental music is the text. Unlike spoken words, the words of a choral piece are attached to rhythm-note values, and sung with the mouth and throat in a more open position to permit greater air flow and resonance. Diction in singing will be more exaggerated than in speaking if the words are to be understood. Consonants must be clear and vowels uniformly shaped to increase blend and precision. Since Latin is utilized frequently in motets and masses, it will be discussed in this chapter in addition to English diction.

ENGLISH DICTION AND THE INTERNATIONAL PHONETIC ALPHABET

The choir director must always work on diction in rehearsal to improve tone, clarity, and precision of attacks and releases. Most people speak English poorly in ordinary conversation, swallowing words and not articulating consonants properly. Singing requires more precision and is an excellent way to improve speaking. Having the choir pronounce the choral text phrase by phrase after the director gives the correct model, leads toward a uniformity in text pronunciation. Regional and dialects are not workable in the choir, unless the piece calls for such diction. Although we all come from various regions of the country, singing diction is standardized and nonregional.

Figure 8–1 lists the International Phonetic Alphabet (IPA) for single vowel sounds, diphthongs, triphthongs, and consonants. Single vowels have only one sound for the duration of the word or syllable. Diphthongs are two consecutive vowel sounds which glide from the first vowel to the second. Triphthongs are three consecutive vowel sounds. Vowels, diphthongs, and triphthongs provide for beautiful sustained sounds in singing. These sounds would be meaningless, however, without clearly articulated consonants. Consonants need to be articulated quickly, making way for the next vowel sound. Consonants usually need to be exaggerated more in singing than in normal speech.

Letter	Word Example	IPA Symbol
a	lap, master	|æ|
a	date, plate	|eɪ|
a	father	|ɑ|
e	met, better	|ɛ|
e	meet, heat	|i|
e	here, dear	|ɪə|
er	never	|ə|
i	mist, hymn	|ɪ|
i	night, mine	|ɑɪ|
ir	fire, inspire	|ɑɪə|
o	go, blow	|oʊ|
o	obey, token	|o|
o	top, talk	|ɑ|
o	for, Lord	|ɔ|
o	lose, zoo	|u|
oo	took, foot	|ʊ|
oo	boot, tomb	|u|
ou	our, tower	|ɑʊə|
oy	boy, toy	|ɔɪ|
ow	now, town	|ɑʊ|
u	up	|ʌ|
u	use, youth	|ju|
u	burn	|ɛ|
b	bat, best	|b|
c	precede, succeed	|s|
c	cat, cow	|k|

Figure 8–1 International Phonetic Alphabet Sounds Found in English Pronounciation

Figure 8–1 (cont'd.)

Letter	Word Example	IPA Symbol
d	date, diction	|d|
f	full, flute	|f|
g	George	|dʒ|
g	get, bag	|g|
h	home, hill	|h|
j	judge, jury	|dʒ|
k	king, kiss	|k|
l	love, all	|l|
m	marry, gem	|m|
n	no, unto	|n|
p	people, escape	|p|
q	queen, queer	|kw|
r	ride, glory	|r|
s	sing, blessing	|s|
s	easy, bays	|z|
t	top, posture	|t|
v	very, every	|v|
w	want, waltz	|w|
x	apex	|ks|
x	exert	|gz|
y	you, young	|j|
z	zone, zero	|z|
ch	church, rich	|tʃ|
ng	bring, anger	|ŋ|
sh	wish, shall	|ʃ|
th	there, this	|ð|
th	thing, breath	|θ|
zh	azure, vision	|ʒ|

It is often upsetting for singers to find that they have been pronouncing words incorrectly over the years. Before any vowels can be pronounced correctly they must be correctly identified. Examine the IPA sounds and practice speaking the various vowels, diphthongs, and triphthongs in the English word examples.

Vowels

Vowels provide the vehicle for singing a tone. A single unified vowel sound is the key to good tone, intonation, and blend. Diction work should begin with the five primary vowel sounds: EE, AY, AH, OH, OO. Please note that the AY sound is really a diphthong, or two sounds (AY + ee). When forming vowels it is important to have a relaxed tongue and jaw, and proper room in the mouth.

EE (as in me, we, thee), the brightest vowel, is formed very forward behind the front teeth. If the sound becomes pinched, have the singer add a little "oo" into the vowel to darken it. There should be enough room between the teeth to insert one finger.

AY (as in may, weigh, taste) will cause the jaw and tongue to come up slightly, but the tip of the tongue should remain behind the lower front teeth. The corners of the mouth will extend outward slightly. Sustain the AY sound as long as possible before moving to the ee of this diphthong.

AH (as in father, star, hot) lowers the jaw to its lowest and most open position. The fleshy soft palate will be arched and the throat very open. The tongue will be low in the mouth with its tip touching the back of the lower front teeth. Young singers are usually afraid to open their mouths. Vocalizing on AH will help them achieve a fuller, more resonant choral tone.

OH (as in obey, proceed, show) can be formed with the same open jaw as for AH except that the lips should be gently rounded away from the teeth. Be careful that singers do not curl the tongue back, but keep it behind the front teeth.

OO (as in soon, too, who) is a darker-sounding vowel, created by shaping the mouth as for AH or OH. However, there is a round, open feeling inside the mouth as the lips form a narrow, rounded opening. The lips should extend away from the teeth, but the sound should never be pinched. The tip of the tongue remains behind the lower front teeth.

Practice speaking these primary vowel sounds and other single vowel sounds in Fig. 8–1. Other vowels to be learned include:

a as in lap	uh as in cup
ih as in mist	uh as in turn
o as in Lord	uh as in around

Diphthongs and Triphthongs

Most diphthongs receive stress on the first vowel sound; however, in such words as music, new, and few, the second vowel receives the stress. Try pronouncing the following diphthongs at a slow speed:

go	(OH + oo)
way	(EH + ee)
why	(AH + ee)
now	(AH + oo)
joy	(AH + ee)
few	(ee + OO)

When singing diphthongs, the stress vowel should be sustained and the weak vowel sounded quickly. When a note is sustained for several counts, diphthongs can be troublesome to singers unless they follow this rule. For example, the word night (AH + ee) should have the AH sound sustained until an instant before the final "t." The vanishing "ee" should be sounded quickly between the sustained AH and "t" consonant.

Triphthongs contain three vowel sounds. Again, the first sound of the three is the sustaining sound, with the other two executed quickly. Slowly pronounce the following triphthongs:

fire	(AH + eh + uhr)
royal	(AW + ih + uh)
roar	(OH + oo + uhr)

Consonants

Choirs should avoid scooping into initial consonants, and perform all consonants quickly and uniformly. *Voiced* consonants are pitched so a vibration is felt in the throat. They must occur before the next vowel is sounded. *Unvoiced* consonants have no pitch. They are percussive, merely explosive mouth sounds.

Voiced		**Unvoiced**	
b	boy	p	prepare
d	day	t	night
g	great	k	king
z	zone	s	soon
v	voice	f	fight
j	jury	ch	church
th	with	th	thin
w	want	wh	when (aspirate)
s	easy	sh	shake

Consonants need exaggeration when singing to project the text to the audience. Initial and closing attacks need choral precision. Often the choral conductor must open or close his fingers and thumb to show the exact moment of attack of a consonant and release of a consonant. This is different from instrumental conducting, and one reason choral conductors often prefer to conduct without a baton.

BRIGHTENING AND DARKENING VOWELS

Very often the vowels may be modified or colored for special effects. Sometimes the highness or lowness of a pitch may require brightening or darkening the vowel. Often the "ee" vowel is too bright and piercing. More room in the mouth, by shaping for "oo" will tend to darken this "ee" vowel. The singers must think the "oo" but sing the "ee." Another vowel which may need darkened is the "ih" vowel. Putting some of the "oo" sound with it will make it more pleasant. To darken vowels, more room is needed in the mouth and the tone placed further back. To brighten the vowel, bring it further forward behind the front teeth.

The director may experiment with brightening and darkening the following vowels: ah, ee, ih, ae, ay, oh, aw. These are the most troublesome for choirs. Care should be exercised, however, not to distort the text so that it cannot be understood.

MARCATO AND LEGATO DICTION

Marcato diction employs explosive consonants and accented vowels. Very forceful, declamatory texts require marcato diction. To achieve this effect, some separation must occur between the vowel and the next consonant, with the consonant receiving strong stress.

Legato diction attempts to link together the consonant and vowel. Each pitch needs connected to the next with no space between them. The vowels need to stretch into the next note. Often the consonants "m" and "n" may be elongated some on a hum slightly before the consonant is sounded, as in "endureth."

There are a few occasions when a light staccato diction will be required. Quick, detached articulation of the text is necessary in this case.

COMMON ENGLISH DICTION PROBLEMS

Most diction problems are a result of: (1) failure to sing the correct vowel, or extend the correct vowel of a diphthong, (2) weak articulation of initial and final consonants, (3) improper word pronunciation, and (4) improper textual stress.

The conductor must examine each choral text carefully to locate the important words and how these are treated by the composer. All words are not of equal importance. The conductor must find the climax(es) of the entire piece and within each phrase or period of music. The text will come alive in the hands of a master choral conductor.

Sometimes words need to be separated to be clear. The words "repenteth him of the evil" contains two "ee" sounds "the evil," pronounced "thee evil." The two "ee's," need to be separated for the two words to project. Sometimes word pronunciation blurs the textual intent. "Round yon Virgin" may become "Round John Virgin." Some separation between "Round" and "yon" will clarify the text.

The consonants s, r, m, n, ng, p, t, d, and l, and prefixes re, de, and be can cause singing problems. The sibilant "s" can be very explosive when performed by a choir and should thus be minimized. The "r" as in "water," needs minimal attention and can be pronounced "watuh---r." Beginning "r's" as in "rejoice," can be flipped slightly for rhythmic clarity, but should not be overdone.

Sometimes incorrect substitutions are made: the unvoiced "p" for a voiced "b," and the unvoiced "t" for the voiced "d." The "l," as in "will," is often reached too quickly, thus destroying the "ih" vowel. Final "ls" need brief execution.

The prefixes "re," "de," and "be" should be pronounced "ih," not as long "ee" sounds.

Incorrect	Correct
Ree – deemer	Rih – deem – uh--r
Bee – hold	Bih – hold
Dee – liver	Dih – liv – uh--r
Dee – vine	Dih – vah + een

Other troublesome sounds include:

Incorrect	Correct
spiruht	spiriht
comin	coming
gum	come
liddle	little
priddy	prihtee
wen	when
noo	new (njee + OO)
beauteeful	beautihful
an	and

The article "the" is sung "thee" when it precedes a word beginning with a vowel, and "thuh" when it precedes a consonant. For example:

    "thee" evening   "thuh" morning

LITURGICAL LATIN PRONUNCIATION

Some of the finest choral masterworks have Latin texts. The mass and motet are sung in concert hall and church. Singers thus need to know the correct Liturgical pronunciation for Latin. Some high school students who have taken a year or two of academic Latin will question the director's pronunciation of Latin choral texts. The student needs to be informed that there is a difference between academic and the Italian or Liturgical Latin pronunciation, and that Litrugical pronunciation is the correct model for choral singing. Some useful books which are listed in Bibliography B, Vocal Training and Choral Techniques, include:

Hall, William D. *Latin Pronunciation According to Roman Usage*
May, William and Tolin, Craig. *Pronunciation Guide for Choral Literature*
Moriarty, John. *Diction: Italian, Latin, French, German*
Trusler, Ivan. *The Choral Conductor's Latin*

Vowels

The Latin language utilizes only the five fundamental vowel sounds. No diphthongs are used. The singing of Latin requires singing the pure vowel.

Latin Vowel	Example
A	father
E (OE, AE)	red
I and Y	see
O	swarm, for
U	noon

Consonants

The consonants in Latin may receive more than one pronunciation depending upon their use. The following lists the consonant pronunciation possibilities:

Latin Consonant	Example
b	benedictus
c (before e, i, y, ae, oe)	pacem, ecce (as in church)
c (hard k sound)	archangeli
d	dona
f	fili
g (soft before e, i, ae, oe)	angeli
g (hard)	gloria
h (silent, usually)	hodie, homine
h (hard k)	mihi, nihl
j (like y in yes)	Jesu
k (hard)	Kaeso, Kalendae
l	laetantur
m	miserere
n	natus
gn (ny)	Agnus
p	peccata
ph (f)	prophetas
q (k)	qui
r (slightly flipped)	virgo, adoremus
s (as in song)	miserere
sc (before e, i, u, ae = sh)	ascendit, suscipe

sc (other uses = sk)	obscurum
t (as in trust)	tibi, terra
th (as t, h is mute)	Sabaoth
v (as in victor)	vidi, exultavit
ex (egs, followed by vowel)	exultate
ex (eks, hard k)	excelsis
z (dz)	Lazurus
ti (tsee)	gratia

TYPICAL LATIN CHORAL TEXTS

A number of the most sung Latin texts are reproduced along with a phonetic pronunciation of each text. These need to be spoken phrase by phrase and repeated by the chorus before singing the text. If the pronunciation is followed consistently, the choral tone in a Latin work will improve.

The director can find other sources for pronunciation of Italian, French, German, Russian, and Hebrew. Most voice majors in university degree programs receive training in several of these languages, particularly, the pronunciation aspect of the languages. Students often sing easier in a foreign language, than in their native English. There are already too many incorrect speaking habits built up in the English language which need modified by proper English pronunciation. Students in high school should sing many Latin texts, as well as several other foreign language repertoire.

ADESTE FIDELES

Adeste fideles, laeti, triumphantes: Venite, venite in Bethlehem: Natum videte Regem Angelorum: Venite adoremus, venite adoremus, venite adoremus Dominum.

AVE MARIA

Ave Maria! gratia plena, Dominus tecum, Benedicta tu in mulieribus, et benedictus fructus ventris tui.

Ave Maria! Mater Dei,
Ora pro nobis peccatoribus,
nunc et in hora mortis nostrae.

AVE VERUM

Ave verum Corpus natum de Maria Virgine: Vere passum immolatum in cruce pro homine. Cujus latus perforatum fluxit aqua et sanguine: Esto nobis praegustatum mortis in examine. O Jesu dulcis! O Jesu pie! O Jesu fili Mariae.

CANTATE DOMINO
(from Psalm 149)

Cantate Domino canticum novum, laus ejus in Ecclesia Sanctorum. Laetetur Israel in eo, qui fecit eum, et filii Sion exultent in rege suo.

ADESTE FIDELES

Ah-DEH-steh fee-DEH-lehs, LEH-tee, tree-oom-FAHN-tehs: Veh-NEE-teh, veh-NEE-teh een *Beht-leh-ehm: NAH-toom vee-DEH-teh REH-jehm Ahn-jeh-LAW-room: Veh-NEE-teh ah-daw-REH-moos, veh-NEE-teh Ah-daw-REH-moos, veh-NEE-teh ah-daw-REH-moos DAW-mee-noom.
*or, if given Anglican pronunciation, "Behth-leh-hehm"

AVE MARIA

Ah-veh Mah-REE-ah! GRAH-tsee-ah PLEH-nah, DAW-mee-noos TEH-koom Beh-neh-DEEk-tah too een moo-lee-EH-ree-boos, eht beh-neh-DEEK-toos FROOK-toos VEHN-trees TOO-ee.

Ah-veh Mah-REE-ah! MAH-tehr DEH-ee,
AW-rah praw NAW-bees peh-kah-TAW-ree-boos,
noonk eht een AW-rah MAWR-tees NAW-streh.

AVE VERUM

Ah-veh VEH-room KAWR-poos NAH-toom deh Mah-REE-ah VEER-jee-neh: Veh-reh PAHS-soom, eem-maw-LAH-toom een KROO-cheh praw AW-mee-neh. KOO-yoos LAH-toos pehr-faw-RAH-toom FLOOK-seet AH-kooah eht SAHN-gooee-neh: Eh-staw NAW-bees preh-goo-STAH-toom MAWR-tees een ehg-SAH-mee-neh. Aw YEH-soo DOOL-chess! Aw YEH-soo PEE-eh! Aw YEH-soo FEE-lee Mah-REE-eh.

CANTATE DOMINO
(from Psalm 149)

Kahn-TAH-teh DAW-mee-naw KAHN-tee-koom NAW-voom, lah-oos EH-yoos een Eh-KLEH-see-ah Sahnk-TAW-room. Leh-TEH-toor EES-rah-ehl een EH-aw, kooee FEH-cheet EH-oom, eht FEE-lee-ee SEE-awn ehg-SOOL-tehnt een REH-jeh SOO-aw.

VENI CREATOR SPIRITUS

Veni Creator Spiritus, Mentes tuorum visita:
Imple superna gratia Quae tu creasti pectora.

Qui diceris Paraclitus, Altissimi domum Dei,
Fons vivus, ignis, caritas, Et spiritalis unctio.

Tu septiformis munere, Digitus paternae dexterae,
Tu rite promissum Patris, Sermone ditans guttura.

Accende lumen sensibus, Infunde amorem cordibus,
Infirma nostri corporis Virtute firmans perpeti.

Hostem repellas longius, Pacemque dones protinus:
Ductore sic te praevio, Vitemus omne noxium.

Per te sciamus da Patrem, Noscamus atque Filium,
Teque utriusque Spiritum Credamus omni tempore.

Deo Patri sit gloria, Et Filio, qui a mortuis
Surrexit, ac Paraclito, In saeculorum saecula.
Amen.

HODIE CHRISTUS NATUS EST

Hodie christus natus est
Hodie salvator apparuit
Hodie in terra
canunt angeli
Laetantur archangeli
Hodie exultant
justi dicentes
Gloria, in excelsis deo
Alleluia

VENI CREATOR SPIRITUS

VEH-nee Kreh-AH-tawr SPEE-ree-toos, MEHN-tehs too-AW-room VEE-see-tah:
Eem-pleh soo-PEHR-nah GRAH-tsee-ah Kooeh too kreh-AH-stee PEHK-taw-rah.

Kooee DEE-cheh-rees Pah-RAH-klee-toos, Ahl-TEES-see-mee DAW-moom DEH-ee,
Fawns VEE-voos, EE-nyees, KAH-ree-tahs, Eht spee-ree-TAH-lees OONK-tsee-aw.

Too sehp-tee-FAWR-mees MOO-neh-reh, DEE-jee-toos pah-TEHR-neh
DEHKS-teh-reh,
Too ree-teh praw-MEES-soom PAH-trees, Sehr-MAW-neh DEE-tahns GOO-too-rah.

Ah-CHEHN-deh LOO-mehn SEHN-see-boos, Een-FOON-deh ah-MAW-rehm
KAWR-dee-boos,
Een-FEER-mah NAW-stree KAWR-paw-rees Veer-TOO-teh FEER-mahns
PEHR-peh-tee.

AW-stehm reh-PEHL-lahs LAWN-jee-oos, Pah-CHEHM-kooeh DAW-nehs
PRAW-tee-noos:
Dook-TAW-reh seek teh PREH-vee-aw, Vee-TEH-moos AWM-neh NAWKS-ee-oom.

Pehr teh shee-AH-moos dah PAH-trehm, Naws-KAH-moos aht-kooeh FEE-lee-oom,
TEH-kooeh oo-tree-OOS-kooeh SPEE-ree-toom Kreh-DAH-moos AWM-nee
TEHM-paw-reh.

DEH-aw PAH-tree seet GLAW-ree-ah, Eht FEE-lee-aw, kooee ah MAWR-too-ees.
Soo-REHK-seet, ahk Pah-RAH-klee-taw, Een seh-koo-LAW-room SEH-koo-lah.
Ah-mehn.

HODIE CHRISTUS NATUS EST

Aw-dee-eh kree-stoos nah-toos ehst
Aw-dee-eh sahl-vah-tawr ah-pah-roo-eet
Aw-dee-eh een teh-rah
kah-noont ahn-jeh-lee
Leh-tahn-toor ahrk-ahn-jeh-lee
Aw-dee-eh eg-zool-tahnt
yoo-stee dee-chehn-tehs
Glaw-ree-ah een ek-shehl-sees deh-aw
Ah-leh-loo-yah.

PANGE LINGUA

Pange lingua gloriosi Corporis mysterium,
Sanguinisque pretiosi, Quem in mundi pretium
Fructus ventris generosi Rex effudit gentium.

Nobis datus, nobis natus Ex intacta Virgine,
Et in mundo conversatus, Sparso verbi semine,
Sui moras incolatus Miro clausit ordine.

In supremae nocte coenae, Recumbens cum fratribus,
Observata lege plene Cibis in legalibus,
Cibum turbae duodenae Se dat suis manibus.

Verbum caro, panem verum Verbo carnem efficit:
Fitque sanguis Christi merum, Et si sensus deficit,
Ad firmandum cor sincerum Sola fides sufficit.

Tantum ergo Sacramentum Veneremur cernui:
Et antiquum documentum Novo cedat ritui:
Praestet fides supplementum Sensuum defectui.

Genitori, Genitoque Laus et jubilatio,
Salus, honor, virtus quoque Sit et benedictio:
Procedenti ab utroque Compar sit laudatio.
Amen.

TE DEUM LAUDAMUS

Te Deum laudamus: te Dominum confitemur.
Te aeternum Patrem omnis terra veneratur.
Tibi omnes Angeli, tibi caeli et
universae Potestates:

PANGE LINGUA

PAHN-jeh LEEN-gooah glaw-ree-AW-see KAWR-paw-rees mee-STEH-ree-oom,
Sahn-gooee-NEES-kooeh preh-tsee-AW-see, Kooehm een MOON-dee PREH-tsee-oom
FROOK-toos VEHN-trees jeh-neh-RAW-see Rehks ehf-FOO-deet JEHN-tsee-oom.

NAW-bees DAH-toos, NAW-bees NAH-toos Ehks een-TAHK-tah VEER-jee-neh,
Eht een MOON-daw kawn-vehr-SAH-toos, SPAHR-saw VEHR-bee SEH-mee-neh,
SOO-ee MAW-rahs een-kaw-LAH-toos MEE-raw KLAHoo-seet AWR-dee-neh.

Een soo-PREH-meh NAWK-teh CHEH-neh, Reh-KOOM-behns koom
FRAH-tree-boos,
awb-sehr-VAH-tah LEH-jeh pleh-neh CHEE-bees een leh-GAH-lee-boos,
CHEE-boom TOOR-beh doo-aw-DEH-neh Seh daht SOO-ees MAH-nee-boos.

VEHR-boom KAH-raw, PAH-nehm VEH-room VEHR-baw KAHR-nehm
EHF-fee-cheet:
FEET-kooeh SAHN-gooees KREES-tee MEH-room, Eht see SEHN-soos
DEH-fee-cheet
Ahd feer-MAHN-doom kawr seen-CHEH-room SAW-lah FEE-dehs SOOF-fee-cheet.

TAHN-toom ehr-gaw Sah-krah-MEHN-toom Veh-neh-REH-moor CHEHR-noo-ee:
Eht ahn-TEE-koo-oom daw-koo-MEHN-toom NAW-vaw CHEH-daht REE-too-ee.
PREH-steht FEE-dehs soo-pleh-MEHN-toom SEHN-soo-oom deh-FEHK-too-ee.

Jeh-nee-TAW-ree, Jeh-nee-TAW-kooeh Lah-oos eht yoo-bee-LAH-tsee-aw,
SAH-loos, AW-nawr, VEER-toos Kooaw-kooeh Seet eht beh-neh-DEEK-tsee-aw:
Praw-cheh-DEHN-tee ahb oo-TRAW-kooeh KAWM-pahr seet lahoo-DAH-tsee-aw.
Ah-mehn.

TE DEUM LAUDAMUS

Teh DEH-oom lahoo-DAH-moos: teh DAW-mee-noom kawn-fee-TEH-moor.
Teh eh-TEHR-noom PAH-trehm AWM-nees TEHR-rah veh-neh-RAH-toor.
TEE-bee AWM-nehs Ahn-jeh-lee, TEE-bee CHEH-lee eht oo-nee-VEHR-seh
Paw-tehs-TAH-tehs:

Tibi Cherubim et Seraphim incessabili
voce proclamant:
Sanctus: Sanctus: Sanctus Dominus Deus Sabaoth.
Pleni sunt caeli et terra, majestatis
gloriae tuae.
Te gloriosus Apostolorum chorus:
Te prophetarum laudabilis numerus:
Te martyrum candidatus laudat exercitus.
Te per orbem terrarum sancta confitetur Ecclesia:
Patrem immensae majestatis: Venerandum tuum,
verum et unicum Filium:
Sanctum quoque Paraclitum Spiritum.
Tu Rex Gloriae, Christe.
Tu Patris sempiternus es Filius.
Tu ad liberandum suscepturus hominem,
non horruisti Virginis uterum.
Tu devicto mortis aculeo, aperuisti
credentibus regna caelorum.
Tu ad dexteram Dei sedes, in gloria Patris.
Judex crederis esse venturus.
Te ergo quaesumus, tuis famulis subveni,
quos pretioso sanguine redemisti.
Aeterna fac cum sanctis tuis in gloria numerari.
Salvum fac populum tuum Domine,
et benedic hereditati tuae.
Et rege eos, et extolle illos usque
in aeternum.
Per singulos dies, bendicimus te.
Et laudamus nomen tuum in saeculum,
et in saeculum saeculi.
Dignare Domine die isto sine peccato
nos custodire.
Miserere nostri Domine, miserere nostri.
Fiat misericordia tua Domine super nos,
quemadmodum speravimus in te.
In te Domine speravi:
non confundar in aeternum.

TEE-bee KEH-roo-beem eht SEH-rah-feem een-chehs-SAH-bee-lee
VAW-cheh praw-KLAH-mahnt:
SAHNK-toos: SAHNK-toos: SAHNK-toos DAW-mee-noos DEH-oos SAH-bah-awt.
PLEH-nee soont CHEH-lee eht TEHR-rah, mah-yeh-STAH-tees
GLAW-ree-eh TOO-eh.
Teh glaw-ree-AW-soos Ah-paw-staw-LAW-room KAW-roos:
Teh praw-feh-TAH-room lahoo-DAH-bee-lees NOO-meh-roos
Teh MAHR-tee-room kahm-dee-DAH-toos LAHoo-daht ehg-SEHR-chee-toos.
Teh pehr AWR-behm tehr-RAH-room SAHNK-tah kawn-fee-TEH-toor
Eh-KLEH-see-ah:
PAH-trehm eem-MEHN-seh mah-yeh-STAH-tees: Veh-neh-RAHN-doom TOO-oom.
VEH-room eht OO-nee-koom FEE-lee-oom:
SAHNK-toom kooaw-kooeh Pah-RAH-klee-toom SPEE-ree-toom.
Too Rehks GLAW-ree-eh, KREE-steh.
Too PAH-trees sehm-pee-TEHR-noos ehs FEE-lee-oos.
Too ahd lee-beh-RAHN-doom soo-shehp-TOO-roos AW-mee-nehm,
nawn aw-roo-EE-stee VEER-jee-nees OO-teh-room.
Too deh-VEEK-taw MAWR-tees ah-KOO-leh-aw, ah-peh-roo-EE-stee
kreh-DEHN-tee-boos REH-nyah cheh-LAW-room.
Too ahd DEHKS-teh-rahm DEH-ee SEH-dehs, een GLAW-ree-ah PAH-trees.
YOO-dehks KREH-deh-rees EHS-seh vehn-TOO-roos.
Teh ehr-gaw KooEH-soo-moos, TOO-ees FAH-moo-lees SOOB-veh-nee,
Kooaws preh-tsee-AW-saw SAHN-gooee-neh reh-deh-MEE-stee.
Eh-TEHR-nah fahk koom SAHNK-tees TOO-ees een GLAW-ree-ah noo-meh-RAH-ree.
SAHL-voom fahk PAW-poo-loom TOO-oom DAW-mee-neh,
eht BEH-neh-deek eh-reh-dee-TAH-tee TOO-eh.
Eht REH-jeh EH-aws, eht ehks-TAWL-leh EEL-laws oos-kooeh
een eh-TEHR-noom.
Pehr SEEN-goo-laws DEE-ehs, beh-neh-DEE-chee-moos teh.
Eht lahoo-DAH-moos NAW-mehn TOO-oom een SEH-koo-loom,
eht een SEH-koo-loom SEH-koo-lee.
Dee NYAH-reh DAW-mee-neh DEE-eh EE-staw see-neh Peh-KAH-taw
naws koo-staw-DEE-reh.
Mee-seh-REH-reh NAW-stree DAW-mee-neh, mee-seh-REH-reh NAW-stree.
FEE-aht mee-seh-ree-KAWR-dee-ah TOO-ah DAW-mee-neh soo-pehr naws,
kooeh-MAHD-maw-doom speh-RAH-vee-moos een teh.
Een teh DAW-mee-neh speh-RAH-vee:
nawn kawn-FOON-dahr een eh-TEHR-noom.

JESU DULCIS MEMORIA

YEH-soo DOOL-chees meh-MAW-ree-ah, Dahns VEH-rah KAWR-dees
   GAHoo-dee-ah:
Sehd soo-pehr mehl eht AWM-nee-ah, Eh-yoos DOOL-chees preh-SEHN-tsee-ah.
Neel KAH-nee-toor sooAH-vee-oos, Neel ahoo-DEE-toor yoo-KOON-dee-oos,
Neel kaw-jee-TAH-toor DOOL-chee-oos, Kooahm YEH-soos DEH-ee FEE-lee-oos.

YEH-soo spehs peh-nee-TEHN-tee-boos, Kooahm PEE-oos ehs
   peh-TEHN-tee-boos!
Kooahm BAW-noos teh Kooeh-REHN-tee-boos! Sehd kooeed
   een-veh-nee-EHN-tee-boos?
Nehk LEEN-gooah VAH-leht DEE-cheh-reh, Nehk LEE-teh-rah
   ehks-PREE-meh-reh:
Ehks-PEHR-toos PAW-tehst KREH-deh-reh, Kooeed seet YEH-soom
   dee-LEE-jeh-reh.

Sees YEH-soo NAW-stroom GAHoo-dee-oom, Kooee ehs foo-TOO-roos
   PREH-mee-oom:
Seet NAW-strah een teh GLAW-ree-ah, Pehr KOONK-tah sehm-pehr
   SEH-koo-lah.
Ah-mehn.

PSALM 150

Lahoo-DAH-teh DAW-mee-noom een SAHNK-tees EH-yoos:
lahoo-DAH-teh EH-oom een feer-mah-MEHN-taw veer-TOO-tees EH-yoos.
Lahoo-DAH-teh EH-oom een veer-TOO-tee-boos EH-yoos:
lahoo-DAH-teh EH-oom seh-KOON-doom mool-tee-TOO-dee-nehm mah-nyee
   TOO-dee-nees EH-yoos.
Lahoo-DAH-teh EH-oom een SAW-naw TOO-beh:
lahoo-DAH-teh EH-oom een sahl-TEH-ree-aw eht CHEE-tah-rah.
Lahoo-DAH-teh EH-oom een TEEM-pah-naw eht KAW-raw:
lahoo-DAH-teh EH-oom een KAWR-dees eht AWR-gah-naw.
Lahoo-DAH-teh EH-oom een CHEEM-bah-lees beh-neh-sawn-AHN-tee-boos:
lahoo-DAH-teh EH-oom een CHEEM-bah-lees yoo-bee-lah-tsee-AW-nees:
AWM-nees SPEE-ree-toos LAHoo-deht DAW-mee-noom.
Ahl-leh-LOO-eeah.

Latin

JESU DULCIS MEMORIA

Jesu dulcis memoria, Dans vera cordis gaudia:
Sed super mel et omnia, Ejus dulcis praesentia.
Nil canitur suavius, Nil auditur jucundius,
Nil cogitatur dulcius, Quam Jesus Dei Filius.

Jesu spes paenitentibus, Quam pius es petentibus!
Quam bonus te quaerentibus! Sed quid invenientibus?
Nec lingua valet dicere, Nec littera exprimere:
Expertus potest credere, Quid sit Jesum diligere.

Sis Jesu nostrum gaudium, Qui es futurus praemium:
Sit nostra in te gloria, Per cuncta semper saecula.
Amen.

PSALM 150

Laudate Dominum in sanctis ejus:
laudate eum in firmamento virtutis ejus.
Laudate eum in virtutibus ejus:
laudate eum secundum multitudinem magnitudinis ejus.
Laudate eum in sono tubae:
laudate eum in psalterio et cithara.
Laudate eum in tympano et choro:
laudate eum in chordis et organo.
Laudate eum in cymbalis benesonantibus:
laudate eum in cymbalis jubilationis:
omnis spiritus laudet Dominum.
Alleluia

Latin

THE MAGNIFICAT

Verse 1. Magnificat anima mea Dominum.

2. Et exultavit spiritus meus in Deo salutari meo.

3. Quia respexit humilitatem ancillae suae: ecce enim ex hoc beatam me dicent omnes generationes.

4. Quia fecit mihi magna qui potens est: et sanctum nomen ejus.

5. Et misericordia ejus a progenie in progenies: timentibus eum.

6. Fecit potentiam in brachio suo: dispersit superbos mente cordis sui.

7. Deposuit potentes de sede, et exaltavit humiles.

8. Esurientes implevit bonis: et divites dimisit inanes.

9. Suscepit Israel puerum suum, recordatus misericordiae suae.

10. Sicut locutus est ad patres nostros, Abraham et semini ejus in saecula.

11. Gloria Patri, et Filio, et Spiritui Sancto.

12. Sicut erat in principio, et nunc, et semper, et in saecula saeculorum.

Amen.

141

Pronunciation

THE MAGNIFICAT

Verse 1. Mah-NYEE-fee-kaht AH-nee-mah MEH-ah DAW-mee-noom.

2. Eht ehg-sool-TAH-veet SPEE-ree-toos MEH-oos een DEH-aw sah-loo-TAH-ree MEH-aw.

3. Kooee-ah reh-SPEHK-seet oo-mee-lee-TAH-tehm ahn-CHEEL-leh SOO-eh: eh-cheh eh-neem ehks awk beh-AH-tahm meh DEE-chehnt AWM-nehs jeh-neh-rah-tsee-AW-nehs.

4. Kooee-ah FEH-cheet MEE-kee MAH-nyah kooee PAW-tehns ehst: eht SAHNK-toom NAW-mehn EH-yoos.

5. Eht mee-seh-ree-KAWR-dee-ah EH-yoos ah praw-JEH-nee-eh een praw-JEH-nee-ehs: Tee-MEHN-tee-boos EH-oom.

6. FEH-cheet paw-TEHN-tsee-ahm een BRAH-kee-aw SOO-aw: dee-SPEHR-seet soo-PEHR-baws MEHN-teh KAWR-dees SOO-ee.

7. Deh-PAW-soo-eet paw-TEHN-tehs deh SEH-deh, eht ehg-sahl-TAH-veet OO-mee-lehs.

8. Eh-soo-ree-EHN-tehs eem-PLEH-veet BAW-nees: eht DEE-vee-tehs dee-MEE-seet een-AH-nehs.

9. Soo-SHEH-peet Ees-rah-ehl POO-eh-room SOO-oom, reh-kawr-DAH-toos mee-seh-ree-KAWR-dee-eh SOO-eh.

10. See-koot law-KOO-toos ehst ahd PAH-trehs NAW-straws, AH-brah-ahm eht SEH-mee-nee EH-yoos een SEH-koo-lah.

11. GLAW-ree-ah PAH-tree, eht FEE-lee-aw, eht Spee-REE-too-ee SAHNK-taw.

12. See-koot EH-raht een preen-CHEE-pee-aw, eht noonk, eht SEHM-pehr, eht een SEH-koo-lah seh-koo-LAW-room. Ah-mehn.

Latin

THE REQUIEM MASS
1. Requiem (Introit) and Kyrie

Requiem aeternam dona eis Domine:
et lux perpetua luceat eis. Te decet hymnus Deus in Sion, et
tibi reddetur votum in Jerusalem: exaudi orationem meam,
ad te omnis caro veniet. Requiem aeternam dona eis Domine:
et lux perpetua luceat eis.

Kyrie eleison. Christe eleison
Kyrie eleison.

2. *Dies Irae (Sequence)*

Dies irae, dies illa, Solvet saeclum
in favilla: Teste David cum Sibylla.

Quantus tremor est futurus, Quando
judex est venturus, Cuncta stricte
discussurus!

Tuba mirum spargens sonum Per se-
pulcra regionum, Coget omnes ante thronum.
Mors stupebit et natura, Cum resurget
creatura, Judicanti responsura.

Liber scriptus proferetur, In quo to-
tum continetur, Unde mundus judicetur.

Judex ergo cum sedebit, Quidquid la-
tet apparebit: Nil inultum remanebit.

Quid sum miser tunc dicturus? Quem pa-
tronum rogaturus? Cum vix justus sit
securus.

Rex tremendae majestatis, Qui salvandos
salvas gratis, Salva me, fons pietatis.

THE REQUIEM MASS
1. Requiem (Introit) and Kyrie

REH-kooee-ehm eh-TEHR-nahm DAW-nah EH-ees DAW-mee-neh:
eht looks pehr-PEH-too-ah LOO-cheh-aht EH-ees. Teh DEH-
cheht EEM-noos DEH-oos een SEE-awn, eht TEE-bee
reh-DEH-toor VAW-toom een Yeh-ROO-sah-lehm: ehgs-
AHoo-dee aw-rah-tsee-AW-nehm MEH-ahm, ahd teh AWM-nees
KAH-raw VEH-nee-eht. REH-kooee-ehm eh-TEHR-nahm
DAW-nah EH-ees DAW-mee-neh: eht looks pehr-PEH-too-ah
LOO-cheh-aht EH-ees.

KEE-ree-eh eh-LEH-ee-sawn. KREES-teh eh-LEH-ee-sawn.
KEE-ree-eh eh-LEH-ee-sawn.

2. *Dies Irae (Sequence)*

Dee-ehs EE-reh, Dee-ehs EEL-lah, SAWL-veht SEH-kloom een fah-VEEL-
lah: TEHS-teh DAH-veed koom See-BEEL-la.

KooAHN-toos TREH-mawr ehst foo-TOO-roos, Kooahn-daw
YOO-dehks ehst vehn-TOO-roos, KOONK–tah streek-teh
dees-koos-SOO-Roos!

TOO-bah MEE-room SPAHR-jehns SAW-noom Pehr seh-
POOL-krah rehjee-AW-noom, KAW-jeht AWM-nehs ahn-teh TRAW-noom.
Mawrs stoo-PEH-beet eht nah-TOO-rah, Koom reh-SOOR-jeht
kreh-ah-TOO-rah, Yoo-dee-KAHN-tee reh spawn-SOO-rah.

LEE-behr SKREEP-toos praw-feh-REH-toor, Een Kooaw TAW-
toom kawn-tee-NEH-toor, Oon-deh MOON-doos yoo-dee-CHEH-toor.

YOO-dehks ehr-gaw koom seh-DEH-beet, KooEED-kooeed LAH-
teht ah-pah-REH-beet: Neel ee-NOOL-toom reh-mah-NEH-beet.
Kooeed soom MEE-sehr toonk deek-TOO-roos? Kooehm pah-
TRAW-noom raw-gah-TOO-roos? Koom veeks YOOS-toos seet
seh-KOO-roos.

Rehks treh-MEHN-deh mah-yeh-STAH-tees, Kooee sahl-VAHN-daws
SAHL-vahs GRAH-tees, SAHL-vah meh, fawns pee-eh-TAH-tees.

Reh-kawr-DAH-reh YEH-soo PEE-eh, Kooawd soom KAHoo-sah TOO-eh VEE-eh: Neh meh PEHR-dahs EEL-lah Dee-eh.

KooEH-rehns meh, seh-DEE-stee LAHS-soos: Reh-deh-MEE-stee KROO-chehm PAHS-soos: TAHN-toos LAH-bawr nawn seet KAHS-soos.

Yoo-steh Yoo-dehks ool-tee-AW-nees, DAW-noom fahk reh-mees-see-AW-nees, Ahn-teh DEE-ehm rah-tsee-AW-ness.

Een-jeh-MEE-skaw, tahm-kooahm REH-oos: KOOL-pah ROO-beht VOOL-toos MEH-oos: Soo-plee-KAHN-tee PAHR-cheh DEH-oos.

Kooee Mah-REE-ahm ahb-sawl-VEE-stee, Eht lah-TRAW-nehm ehg-sahoo-DEE-stee, MEE-kee kooaw-kooeh spehm deh-DEE-stee.

PREH-chehs MEH-eh nawn soont DEE-nyeh: Sehd too BAW-noos fahk beh-NEE-nyeh, NEh peh-REHN-nee KREH-mehr EE-nyeh.

Een-tehr AW-vehs LAW-koom PREH-stah, Eht ahb EH-dees meh seh-kooEHS-trah, STAH-too-ehns een PAHR-teh DEHKS-trah.

Kawn-foo-TAH-tees mah-leh-DEEK-tees, FLAHM-mees AH-kree-boos ahd-DEEK-tees: VAW-kah meh koom beh-neh-DEEK-tees.

Aw-rah SOO-plehks eht ah-KLEE-nees, Kawr kawn-TREE-toom kooah-see CHEE-nees: JEH-reh KOO-rahm MEH-ee FEE-nees.

Lah-kree-MAW-sah DEE-ehs EEL-lah, Kooah reh-SOOR-jeht ehks fah-VEEL-lah Yoo-dee-KAHN-doos AW-maw REH-oos: OO-eek ehr-gaw PAHR-cheh DEH-oos.

PEE-eh YEH-soo DAW-mee-neh, DAW-nah EH-ees REH-kooee-ehm. Ah-mehn.

3. Domine Jesu Christe (Offertory)

DAW-mee-neh YEH-soo KREE-steh, Rehks GLAW-ree-eh, LEE-beh-rah AH-nee-mahs AWM-nee-oom fee-DEH-lee-oom deh-foonk-TAW-room deh PEH-nees een-FEHR-nee, eht deh praw-FOON-daw LAH-koo: LEE-beh-rah EH-ahs deh AW-reh leh-AW-nees, neh ahb-SAWR-beh-aht EH-ahs TAHR-tah-roos, neh KAH-dahnt

Recordare Jesu pie, Quod sum causa tuae viae: Ne me perdas illa die.

Quaerens me, sedisti lassus: Redemisti crucem passus: Tantus labor non sit cassus.

Juste judex ultionis, Donum fac remissionis, Ante diem rationis.

Ingemisco, tamquam resus: Culpa rubet vultus meus: Supplicanti parce Deus.

Qui mariam absolvisti, Et latronem exaudisti, Mihi quoque spem dedisti.

Preces meae non sunt dignae: Sed tu bonus fac benigne, Ne perenni cremer igne.

Inter oves locum praesta, Et ab haedis me sequestra, Statuens in parte dextra.

Confutatis maledictis, Flammis acribus addictis: Voca me cum benedictis.

Oro supplex et acclinis, Cor contritum quasi cinis: Gere curam mei finis.

Lacrimosa dies illa, Qua resurget ex favilla Judicandus homo reus: Huic ergo parce Deus.

Pie Jesu Domine, dona eis requiem. Amen.

3. Domine Jesu Christe (Offertory)

Domine Jesu Christe, Rex gloriae, libera animas omnium fidelium defunctorum de poenis inferni, et de profundo lacu: libera eas de ore leonis, ne absorbeat eas tartarus, ne cadant in obscurum: sed signifer sanctus een awb-SKOO-room: sehd SEE-nyee-fehr SAHNK-toos MEE-kah-ehl reh-preh-SEHN-teht EH-ahs een LOO-chehm SAHNK-tahm: Kooahm aw-leem AH-brah-eh praw-mee-SEES-tee, eht SEH-mee-nee EH-yoos. AW-stee-ahs eht PREH-chehs TEE-bee DAW-mee-neh LAHoo-dees awf-FEHR-ree-moos: too SOO-shee-peh praw ah-nee-MAH-boos EEL-lees, kooAH-room AW-dee-eh meh-MAW-ree-ahm FAH-chee-moos: fahk EH-ahs, DAW-mee-neh, deh MAWR-teh trahn-SEE-reh ahd VEE-tahm. Kooahm aw-leem AH-brah-eh praw-mee-SEES-tee, eht SEH-mee-nee EH-yoos.

4. Sanctus Et Benedictus

SAHNK-toos, SAHNK-toos, SAHNK-toos DAW-mee-noos DEH-oos SAH-bah-awt. PLEH-nee soont CHEH-lee eht TEHR-rah GLAW-ree-ah TOO-ah. aw-SAHN-nah een ehks-SHEHL-sees. Beh-neh-DEEK-toos kooee VEH-neet een NAW-mee-neh DAW-mee-nee. AW-SAHN-nah een ehks-SHEHL-sees.

5. Agnus Dei

AH-nyoos DEH-ee, kooee TAWL-lees peh-KAH-tah MOON-dee: DAW-nah EH-ees REH-kooee-ehm. Ah-nyoos DEH-ee, kooee TAWL-lees peh-KAH-tah MOON-dee: DAW-nah EH-ees REH-kooee-ehm. Ah-nyoos DEH-ee, kooee TAWL-lees peh-KAH-tah MOON-dee: Daw-nah EH-ees REH-kooee-ehm sehm-pee-TEHR-nahm.

6. Lux Aeterna (Communion)

Looks eh-TEHR-nah LOO-cheh-aht EH-ees, DAW-mee-neh: Koom SAHNK-tees TOO-ees een eh-TEHR-noom, kooEE-ah PEE-oos ehs. REH-kooee-ehm eh-TEHR-nahm DAW-nah EH-ees DAW-mee-neh, eht looks pehr-PEH-too-ah LOO-cheh-aht EH-ees. Koom SAHNK-tees TOO-ees een eh-TEHR-noom kooEE-ah PEE-oos ehs.

Michael repraesentet eas in lucem sanctam: Quam olim Abrahae promisisti, et semini ejus. Hostias et preces tibi Domine laudis offerimus: tu suscipe pro animabus illis, quarum hodie memoriam facimus: fac eas, Domine, de morte transire ad vitam. Quam olim Abrahae promisisti, et semini ejus.

4. Sanctus Et Benedictus

Sanctus, Sanctus, Sanctus Dominus Deus Sabaoth. Pleni sunt caeli et terra gloria tua. Hosanna in excelsis. Benedictus qui venit in nomine Domini. Hosanna in excelsis.

5. Agnus Dei

Agnus Dei, qui tollis peccata mundi: dona eis requiem. Agnus Dei, qui tollis peccata mundi: dona eis requiem. Agnus Dei, qui tollis peccata mundi: dona eis requiem sempiternam.

6. Lux Aeterna (Communion)

Lux aeterna luceat eis, Domine: Cum sanctis tuis in aeternum, quia pius es. Requiem aeternam dona eis Domine, et lux perpetua luceat eis. Cum sanctis tuis in aeternum quia pius es.

7. Libera Me, Domine (Responsorium)

Libera me, Domine, de morte aeterna, in die illa tremenda; Quando caeli movendi sunt et terra: Dum veneris judicare saeculum per ignem. Tremens factus sum ego, et timeo, dum discussio venerit, atque ventura ira. Quando caeli movendi sunt et terra. Dies illa, dies irae, calamitatis et miseriae, dies magna et amare valde. Dum veneris judicare saeculum per ignem. Requiem aeternam dona eis Domine: et lux perpetua luceat eis. Libera me, Domine, de morte aeterna, in die illa tremenda: Quando caeli movendi sunt et terra: Dum veneris judicare saeculum per ignem.

8. In Paradisum

In paradisum deducant te Angeli: in tuo adventu suscipiant te Martyres, et perducant te in civitatem sanctam Jerusalem. Chorus Angelorum te suscipiat, et cum Lazaro quondam paupere aeternam habeas requiem.

THE ORDINARY OF THE MASS
1. Kyrie

Kyrie eleison. Christe eleison. Kyrie eleison.

---

7. Libera Me, Domine (Responsorium)

LEE-beh-rah meh, DAW-mee-neh, deh MAWR-teh eh-TEHR-nah, een DEE-eh EEL-lah treh-MEHN-dah: Kooahn-daw CHEH-lee maw-VEHN-dee soont eht TEHR-rah: Doom VEH-neh-rees yoo-dee-KAH-reh SEH-koo-loom pehr EE-nyehm. TREH-mehns FAHK-toos soom EH-gaw, eht TEE-meh-aw, doom dee-SKOOS-see-aw VEH-neh-reet, aht-kooeh vehn-TOO-rah EE-rah. Kooahn-daw CHEH-lee maw-VEHN-dee soont eht TEHR-rah. DEE-ehs EEL-lah, DEE-ehs EE-reh, Kah-lah-mee-TAH-tees eht mee-SEH-ree-eh, DEE-ehs MAH-nyah eht ah-MAH-rah vahl-deh. Doom VEH-neh-rees yoo-dee-KAH-reh Seh-koo-loom pehr EE-nyehm. REH-kooee-ehm eh-TEHR-nam DAW-nah EH-ees DAW-mee-neh: eht looks pehr-PEH-too-ah LOO-cheh-aht EH-ees. Lee-beh-rah meh, DAW-mee-neh, deh MAWR-teh eh-TEHR-nah, een DEE-eh EEL-lah treh-MEHN-dah: Kooahn-daw CHEH-lee maw-VEHN-dee soont eht TEHR-rah: Doom VEH-neh-rees yoo-dee-KAH-reh SEH-koo-loom pehr EE-nyehm.

8. In Paradisum

Een pah-rah-DEE-soom deh-DOO-kahnt teh Ahn-jeh-lee: een TOO-aw ahd-VEHN-too soo-SHEE-pee-ahnt teh MAHR-tee-rehs, eht pehr-DOO-kahnt teh een chee-vee-TAH-tehm SAHNK-tahm Yeh-ROO-sah-lehm. KAW-roos Ahn-jeh-LAW-room teh soo-SHEE-pee-aht, eht koom LAH-dzah-raw kooawn-dahm PAHoo-peh-reh eh-TEHR-nahm AH-beh-ahs REH-kooee-ehm.

THE ORDINARY OF THE MASS
1. Kyrie

KEE-ree-eh eh-LEH-ee-sawn.
KREE-steh eh-LEH-ee-sawn.

Latin

2. Gloria

Gloria in excelsis Deo. Et in terra pax hominibus bonae voluntatis. Laudamus te. Benedicimus te. Adoramus te. Glorificamus te. Gratias agimus tibi propter magnam gloriam tuam. Domine Deus, Rex caelestis, Deus Pater omnipotens. Domine Fili unigenite Jesu Christe. Domine Deus, Agnus Dei, Filius Patris. Qui tollis peccata mundi, miserere nobis. Qui tollis peccata mundi suscipe deprecationem nostram. Qui sedes ad dexteram Patris, miserere nobis. Quoniam tu solus sanctus. Tu solus Dominus. Tu solus altissimus, Jesu Christe. Cum Sancto Spiritu, in gloria Dei Patris. Amen.

3. Credo

Credo in unum Deum, Patrem omnipotentem, factorem caeli et terrae, visibilium omnium et invisibilium. Et in unum Dominum Jesum Christum, Filium Dei unigenitum. Et ex patre natum ante omnia saecula. Deum de Deo, lumen de lumine, Deum verum de Deo vero. Genitum, non factum, consubstantialem Patri: per quem omnia facta sunt. Qui propter nos homines, et propter nostram salutem descendit de caelis. Et incarnatus est de Spiritu Sancto ex Maria Virgine: ET HOMO FACTUS EST. Crucifixus etiam pro nobis sub

2. Gloria

GLAW-ree-ah een ehk-SHEHL-sees DEH-aw. Eht een TEH-rah pahks aw-MEE-nee-boos BAW-neh vaw-loon-TAH-tees. Lahoo-DAH-moos teh. Beh-neh-DEE-chee-moos teh. Ah-daw-RAH-moos teh. Glaw-ree-fee-KAH-moos teh. GRAH-tsee-ahs AH-jee-moos TEE-bee prawp-tehr MAH-nyahm GLAW-ree-ahm TOO-ahm. DAW-mee-neh DEH-oos, Rehks cheh-LEHS-tees, DEH-oos PAH-tehr awm-NEE-paw-tehns. DAW-mee-neh FEE-lee oo-nee-JEH-nee-teh YEH-soo KREE-steh. DAW-mee-neh DEH-oos, ah-nyoos DEH-ee, FEE-lee-oos PAH-trees. Kooee TAW-lees peh-KAH-tah MOON-dee, mee-seh-REH-reh NAW-bees. Kooee TAW-lees peh-KAH-tah MOON-dee, SOO-shee-peh deh-preh-kah-tsee-AW-nehm NAW-strahm. Kooee SEH-dehs ahd DEHKS-teh-rahm PAH-trees, mee-seh-REH-reh NAW-bees. KooAW-nee-ahm too SAW-loos SAHNK-toos. Too SAW-loos DAW-mee-noos. Too SAW-loos ahl-TEES-see-moos, YEH-soo KREE-steh. Koom SAHNK-taw SPEE-ree-too, een GLAW-ree-ah DEH-ee PAH-trees. Ah-mehn.

3. Credo

KREH-daw een OO-noom DEH-oom, PAH-trehm awm-nee-paw TEHN-tehm, fahk-TAW-rehm CHEH-lee eht TEH-reh, vee-see-Bee-lee-oom AWM-nee-oom eht een-vee-see-Bee-lee-oom. Eht een
OO-noom DAW-mee-oom YEH-soom KREES-toom, FEE-lee-oom DEH-ee oo-nee-JEH-nee-toom. Eht ehks PAH-treh NAH-toom ahn-teh AWM-nee-ah SEH-koo-lah. DEH-oom deh DEH-aw, LOO-mehn deh LOO-mee-neh, DEH-oom VEH-room deh DEH-aw VEH-raw. JEH-nee-toom, nawn FAHK-toom, kawn-soob-STAHN-tsee-ah-lehm PAH-tree: pehr kooehm AWM-nee-ah FAHK-tah soont. Kooee prawp-tehr naws AW-mee-nehs, eht prawp-tehr NAW-strahm sah-LOO-tehm deh SHEHN-deet deh CHEH-lees. Eht een-Kahr-NAH-toos ehst deh SPEE-ree-too SAHNK-taw ehks Mah-REE-ah VEER-jee-neh: EHT AW-MAW FAHK-TOOS EHST.** Kroo-chee-FEEK-soos EH-tsee-ahm praw NAW-bees soob

146

PAWN-tsee-aw PEE-LAH-taw: PAH-soos, eht seh-POOL-toos ehst. Eht reh-soo-REHK-seet TEHR-tsee-ah DEE-eh, seh-KOON-doom Skreep-TOO-rahs. Eht ah-SHEHN-deet een CHEH-loom: SEH-deht ahd DEHKS-teh-rahm PAH-trees. Eht EE-teh-room vehn-TOO-roos ehst koom GLAW-ree-ah yoo-dee-KAH-reh VEE-vaws eht MAWR-too-aws: KOO-yoos REH-nyee nawn EH-reet FEE-nees. Eht een SPEE-ree-toom SAHNK-toom DAW-mee-noom, eht vee-vee-fee-KAHN-tehm: kooee ehks PAH-treh, Fee-lee-AW-kooee praw-CHEH-deet, Kooee koom PAH-treh, eht FEE-lee-aw SEE-mool ah-daw-RAH-toor, eht kawn-glaw-ree-fee-KAH-toor: kooee law-KOO-toos ehst pehr Praw-FEH-tahs. Eht OO-noom, SAHNK-tahm, kah-TAW-lee-kahm eht ah-paw-STAW-lee-kahm Eh-KLEH-see-ahm. Kawn-FEE-teh-awr OO-noom bahp-TEES-mah een reh-mee-see-AW-nehm peh-kah-TAW-room. Eht ehks-PEHK-taw reh-soo-rehk-tsee-AW-nehm mawr-too-AW-room. Eht VEE-tahm vehn-TOO-ree SEH-koo-lee. Ah-mehn.

4. Sanctus Et Benedictus

Sahnk-toos, sahnk-toos, sahnk-toos, DAW-mee-noos Deh-oos SAH-bah-awt. Pleh-nee soont cheh-lee eht teh-rah GLAW-ree-ah too-ah. Aw-SAHN-nah een ehks-SHEHL-sees. Beh-neh-DEEK-toos kooee VEH-neet een NAW-mee-neh DAW-mee-nee. AW-SAHN-nah een ehks-SHEHL-sees.

5. Agnus Dei

ah-nyoos DEH-ee, kooee TAWL-lees peh-KAH-tah MOON-dee:
mee-seh-REH-reh NAW-bees.
Ah-nyoos DEH-ee, kooee TAWL-lees peh-KAH-tah MOON-dee:
mee-seh-REH-reh NAW-bees.
DAW-nah Naw-bees PAH-chehm.

Pontio Pilato: passus, et sepultus est. Et resurrexit tertia die, secundum Scripturas. Et ascendit in caelum: sedet ad dexteram Patris. Et iterum venturus est cum gloria judicare vivos et mortuos: cujus regni non erit finis. Et in spiritum Sanctum Dominum et vivificantem: qui ex Patre, Filioque procedit. Qui cum Patre, et Filio simul adoratur, et conglorificatur: qui locutus est per Prophetas. Et unum, sanctam, catholicam et apostolicam Ecclesiam. Confiteor unum baptisma in remissionem peccatorum. Et exspecto resurrectionem mortuorum. Et vitam venturi saeculi. Amen.

4. Sanctus Et Benedictus

Sanctus, Sanctus, Sanctus, Dominus Deus Sabaoth. Pleni sunt caeli et terra gloria tua. Hosanna in excelsis. Benedictus qui venit in nomine Domini. Hosanna in excelsis.

5. Agnus Dei

Agnus Dei, qui tollis peccata mundi: miserere nobis.
Agnus Dei, qui tollis peccate mundi: miserere nobis.
dona nobis pacem.

Chapter Nine

Sight-Reading Techniques

One of the first ways to learn how to speak words is through mimicking parents and other family members and friends. Although a large communication language may be built up over some years, this rote process is not sufficient to participate successfully in today's society. Learning to read the symbols for word sounds at a fluent pace is prerequisite to gaining independence with the written word.

So it is with learning to read the symbols of music notation. If elementary school children's instruction consists of mere rote song experiences, their ability to participate in the making of music is severely limited. Teaching choral pieces by rote is slow, laborious, and unmusical. Students in elementary, junior high, and senior high school need instructions on how to interpret the music symbols of sound for full participation with music throughout their lives. This also helps to develop their overall understanding and appreciation of the fine art of music. Much more music may be learned and at a faster pace when music notation skills are developed. The ability to look at the music notation, hear the sound mentally, and sing it immediately is called sight singing.

Too often the choir is dependent upon those students who have studied piano or other instruments to lead the sections. The others are mostly followers. If students have not been introduced to reading rhythm and pitch symbols, this skill can be developed at any age. It is best if students are trained in some sight-singing approach starting in elementary school. This may include the Kodály method. These vocal sight-singing systems include use of either numbers, solfege, or neutral syllable such as "loo" or "lah." Various counting and rhythm reading approaches are used, including the Kodály rhythm syllables (ta, ti, ti-ri-ti-ri, etc.). Instrumental approaches, using resonator bells, Baroque recorders, and group piano instruction may complement the pure vocal approaches to sight reading. Students also need practice with various chord structures and progressions, since they will need to hear not only a linear line, but harmonically, as well, as they read their individual choral part.

The voice is so abstract an instrument that it must estimate the intervals quickly and attach the correct rhythm length to each note sung. There is no outside physical manipulation, such as fingering, to produce a specific note, as there is in instrumental music. However, some of the best sight readers are those who have studied music reading from both a vocal approach and an instrumental approach. The more practice with music notation, the quicker the voice can respond to the symbols. The eye must not center on one or two notes, but see the full sweep of the music phrase to acquire any speed. It is always frustrating when a choral singer must share music with a slow reader who does not turn the page quickly enough to keep the line moving from page to page.

This chapter will present some useful approaches to development of rhythm, melody, and harmony notation reading skills. Some reading system is better than none at all. Directors must restrict the practice of pounding out parts on the piano for singers to imitate. This rote process is childish and does not lead to any degree of independence on the part of the choral singers. Force the choir to read new material each rehearsal, whether it be hymns or chorales, folk arrangements, published or director-contrived sight-singing materials, or rhythm-melody-harmony problems extracted from current choral literature for study. Each director must feel comfortable with the system of reading utilized. The long-range results will more than justify the effort expended in the daily process of learning to read music notation with independence.

READING RHYTHM NOTATION

The question always arises as to whether the rhythm (tonal length) aspect of notation should be studied separately from the pitch aspect. The pitch problems seem more complex, and it reasons that students will be more successful with melody reading once the basic beat, meters, note and rest values have received prior attention. Many of the published sight-singing texts combine rhythm and pitch from the first lesson in notation reading. Directors will want to give stress to both aspects in rehearsal, and then add the harmonic aspect of choral singing. Reading scores should progress from reading in unison from both clefs, to reading in two parts, to full score (SATB) reading of parts simultaneously. It is important for sopranos, altos, and tenors to read from the treble staff. Tenors and basses should sight read from the bass staff. In *open score*, where each part has a separate staff, the tenor usually sings from the treble staff an octave lower than written. In *close score*, the sopranos and altos sing from one treble staff, and tenor and bass sing from one bass staff. Young singers in junior high school need help to find their parts. Tenors need to get used to seeing their part on both staves.

Dalcroze: Feeling Music Bodily

In the late nineteenth century the Swiss educator Emile Jacques-Dalcroze developed an active musicianship approach which he labeled "Ehrhythmics." The approach involves three aspects:

1. Eurhythmics—time and rhythm learned through movement.
2. Solfege—ear training, sight singing, and dictation to develop inner hearing, using "fixed do" system.
3. Improvisation—developing the capacity for free musical invention.

This approach progressed naturally from, (1) hearing and feeling music bodily (Enactive response), to (2) perceiving and organizing music sounds (Iconic response), to (3) translating music sounds into notation symbols (Symbolic response).

Choral directors have used many of the Dalcroze exercises over the years to develop concepts of beat, accent, meter, tempo, ritard, accelerando, phrasing, form, note and rest values, augmentation and diminution of note values, interrupted and pure canon, dynamics, pitch, and tonality. The stimuli for the exercises are sounds on the piano, drum, voice, recordings, as well as visual signals. Adequate floor space is needed for many of the movement exercises, and students should remove their shoes to execute them. Sometimes the choral director may schedule the use of the gym or multipurpose room for Dalcroze work. Some Dalcroze exercises may be done in place (axial); however, most require larger loco-motor movement.

Two of the most common Dalcroze signals are the "Quick Reaction" and the "Follow." The Quick Reaction demands from students a quick, accurate, predetermined response to one or more verbal, visual, or musical signals. The Follow requires students to adjust their physical reactions in a flexible manner to rapidly changing musical situations. Combining of several music elements in one exercise creates complexity and fast response. For example:

1. Quick Reaction: Walk the pulse beat, clap the pulse beat, and walk/clap the pulse beat. On the signal "hopp," change from the one movement to the next without hesitation, maintaining a steady beat.
2. Follow: Walk (♩), run (♫), or skip (♩♪) when the piano signals one of these rhythm patterns.

To help students establish pulse beat and tempo, have them walk the beat to the piano, observing any ritards or accelerandos. Have them pass a ball on the beat in a circle, or clap the beat first in unison and then individually in turn around the circle. With no beat signal, have them clap individually and build in gradual ritard or accelerando.

To understand accent and meter, have the choir members walk the beat, clapping and stamping on the first beat of two, three, four, and five meters. Change the meter by accenting beat one on the drum or piano. Add a Dalcroze two-hand conducting beat. Next, walk two beats and rest in place two beats, adjusting to three, four, and five meters on vocal signal. Singers should feel the beats of silence internally. Also, have them bounce a ball on beat one to an opposite partner in two, three, and six-eight meters, or try skipping to six-eight meter while bouncing a ball on beat one.

Have students walk quarter, half, whole, and eighth notes in a unison group, or in four individual groups on piano signal, adding a conducting beat in four meter. As students listen carefully to the piano, have them clap right-hand note values and step the left-hand note values. Then step the rhythm pattern of "Twinkle, Twinkle, Little Star." Augment the note values and also step them in diminution on signal. Verbal signals may be: 1 = regular values, 2 = augmentation, and 3 = diminution.

Use the canon exercise to supplement the singing of rounds, canons, and other polyphonic texture choral literature. Dictate a canon of two or four measures on drum or piano for students to mimic by stepping the rhythm patterns, much as they would echo an Orff pattern by clapping. Notate this "interrupted canon" on the chalkboard. Then, try a "pure canon" with students stepping the patterns a measure behind the dictated rhythms. Encourage students to improvise, clap, step, and notate their own rhythm canons.

To develop a sense of pitch, play walking, running, and skipping rhythm patterns on the piano in high, middle, and low ranges as students clap overhead, at the waist, or at the knees. For changes in major-minor tonality, have the students walk the beat, changing directions for each major and minor shift of tonality the teacher presents. Notate tonal patterns at the chalkboard, in addition to phrases and entire melodies.

Give students opportunities to improvise on pentatonic, Dorian mode, major, or minor scales at the piano. One student may play an ostinato or bourdon, while another creates a melody. Invite students to improvise phrases to a song on "lah," giving them the first phrase and pointing to different students in turn to supply successive phrases. This builds up the feeling for antecedent (question) and consequent (answer) phrases in a melody.

Kodály: Using Rhythm Syllables

To help students in elementary through senior high school learn note and rest values, the Kodály rhythm syllables may be used to advantage. This "mnemonic" system much resembles Dalcroze's use of "walk" for quarter notes and "run" for eighth notes. All directors have probably used 'Mississippi" for learning the feel of four sixteenth notes. "Merrily" works well for triplets or for three eighth notes in six-eight meter. Orff uses speech patterns to learn rhythm values and rests. Figure 9–1 illustrates a chart of conventional, simplified, and rhythm syllables used by Kodály.

Have the students chant their choral parts with Kodály rhythm syllables, and then move immediately to chanting the rhythm of the real text. Following this step, the choir is ready to attempt reading the pitches, once the key has been established and problem tonal patterns have been drilled. Try the following rhythm study in two parts in Fig. 9–2.

Conventional	Simplified	Duration syllables
♩	|	ta (tah)
♫	⌐¬	ti - ti (tee-tee)
♩	♩	ta - a (tah-ah)
𝄽	𝄽	rest
𝅝	𝅝	ta - a - a - a
♪ ♪ ♪	♪ | ♪	syn - co - pa
♫ ♫ (3)	⌐¬ (3)	trip - le - t or tri - o - la
♩.	♩.	ta - a - a
		ti - ri - ti - ri
		ti - ti - ri
		ti - ri - ti
		ti - ri or tim - ri
		ti - ri or ti - rim
♩. ♪	|. ♪ (⌐¬)	ta - i - ti
6/8 ♫ ♫	⌐¬ ⌐¬	ti - ti - ti ti - ti - ti
♩ ♪ ♩ ♪	| ♪ | ♪	ta - ti ta - ti
♪ ♩ ♪ ♩	♪ | ♪ |	ti - ta ti - ta
♩. ♩.	|. |.	ta - ta -

Figure 9–1 Kodály Simplified Notation and Rhythm Syllables

152

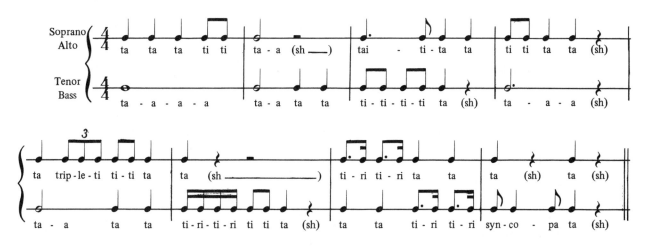

Figure 9–2 Kodály Two-Part Exercises

Other Counting Systems

Many choral directors use a counting system using numbers for the beats in a measure as in Fig. 9–3. Although this system places the beats in a measure, the voice is not always sounding the actual rhythm patterns. The system is of value to internalize the patterns while counting aloud and clapping the rhythms. The rests may be indicated by hands apart.

Edwin Gordon[1] has devised a system in which the basic beat is called the macro beat, meaning "long." The macro beat is always represented by "du." Subdivisions of the macro beat are called "micro" or small. The chanted syllables are: du-doo, de-deh, di-deh, da-dah, and ta-tah. Duple micro beats are named du-de. Triple micro beats are du da di. Practice chanting the syllables in Fig. 9–4.

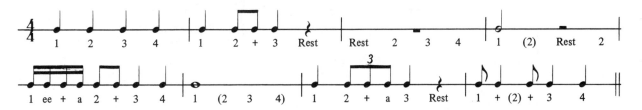

Figure 9–3 Counting Rhythm Patterns

Figure 9–4 Speaking Rhythms with Macro-Micro Syllables

4/4   Mouth-Sound Montage

Mary Val Marsh

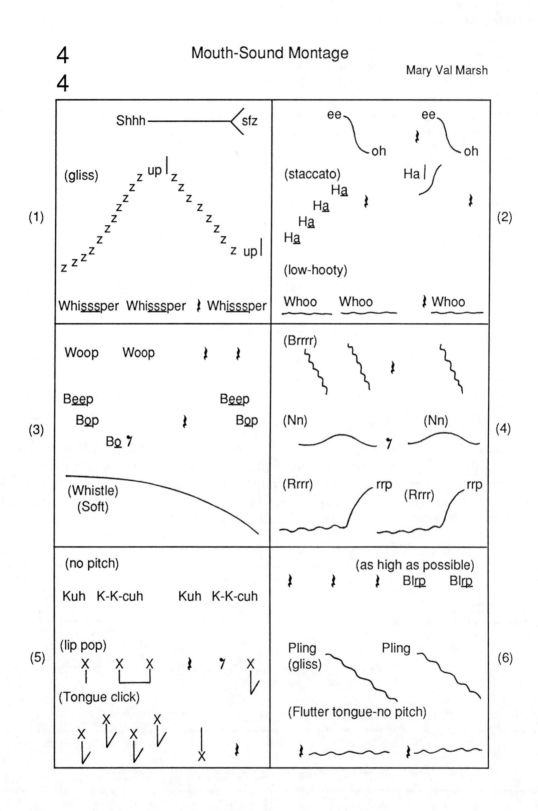

Figure 9–5 Mouth-Sound Montage

Figure 9–6 Vertical Chord Rhythm Vocalise

Many contemporary choral scores consist of indeterminate music. This aleatory, or chance music, is somewhat different each time it is performed and the conductor is given directions for performance. In Fig. 9–5, a Mouth-Sound Montage[2] is presented in traditional four meter. There are six measures, with three "choral parts" in each measure (top, middle, bottom). Divide the chorus into three parts (Soprano, Alto, Male) and assign them to the parts. You will find this exercise a valuable experience and exposure to contemporary choral notation, as well as a valuable rhythm learning piece. Work on each nontraditional sound and perform the piece at various tempi and dynamics.

Another valuable rhythm exercise in four-part harmony is illustrated in Fig. 9–6. Sing it on "tah" for clarity of attacks.

READING PITCH NOTATION

The symbols for pitch represent high and low sounds by their relative position on a music staff. In the elementary school, children often learn to play pitch instruments such as resonator bells, soprano recorders, as well as Orff mallet instruments. Some students begin study of piano or a band/orchestra instrument which continues through junior and senior high school. Much about the treble and bass staves, keys, steps and halfsteps, major and minor, chromatics, transposition, and modulation can be learned through instrument playing. Letters of staff notes are important for instrumentalists.

Using Numbers as a Pitch and Harmonic Aid

If a class vocal approach is used to sight read, usually numbers or solfege is employed. The use of numbers to read notation works well for many, since each scale tone is numbered from one to eight (octave) in both major and minor keys, and students are readily familiar with numbers. Interval work is meaningful when a second, third, or fourth is produced vocally with numbers. Numbers also help to understand chord construction (tonic = I of the scale, etc.). Chords also contain a root, third, fifth, and sometimes a seventh or ninth.

However, numbers are not too musical to sing, and there is no way to handle the singing of chromatics well. Minor scales have different whole and half step intervals from the major scale, and the number system does not provide for a consistent distance between each number. Still, some choir directors prefer to use numbers, since there are positive aspects. Some contemporary music with little or no key center must be read from note to note. The numbers may be useful with such music.

Understanding Keys and Scales

Since the days of the singing schools, various pitch reading systems, including "shape notes," have been utilized to develop skill in pitch reading. In the nineteenth century in England, John Curwen utilized the familiar solfege system along with hand-signs for each of the scale degrees, including all chromatics. In the United States, the "movable do" system, rather than the "fixed do" system has dominated. This was true of the singing school teachers who introduced music into American public schools. In the "movable do" system, "do" moves to the key center, such as C, G, F, D, A♭, etc. See the following scales in Fig. 9–7. Notice that each major scale has a related minor scale with the same key signature. "Do" is always the key name of major keys, while

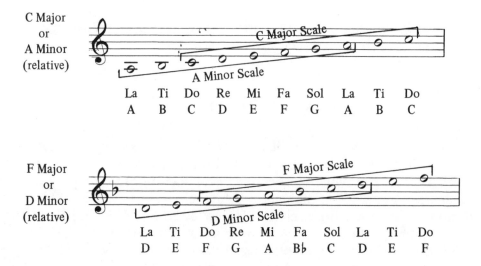

Figure 9–7 Major Scales and Relative Minor Scales

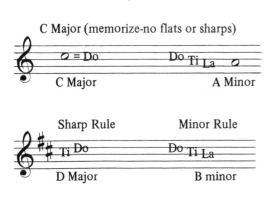

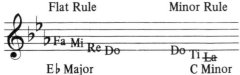

Figure 9–8 Naming Major-Minor Keys

"La" is the key name for relative minor keys. Major scales have half steps between mi-fa and ti-do and whole steps between all other scale degrees.

The rules for naming the major and minor keys are illustrated in Fig. 9–8.

In teaching keys to junior and senior high students, some rules need to be learned. To name the major key with sharps in the signature, take the last sharp on the right and call it "ti" and locate "do," the major key tone. To locate "do" when there is a flat signature, take the last flat on the right and call it "fa" and locate "do." C major never has flats or sharps. Major pieces like to end on "do."

To identify a minor key, see if the tune ends on "do." If not, the relative minor key may be in use. To find the relative minor key name, count down from "do"—"do-ti-la." Where "la" is located on the staff, is the letter name for the key. If there are flats or sharps in the signature on the letter this must be included in the key name (A♭ Major or C# Minor). Junior and senior high school students need to be taught the letters of the grand staff and how to name major and minor keys.

Choral pieces may use any of the three forms of minor scales—natural, harmonic, or melodic form. (See Fig. 9–9.) Notice that chromatics alter the whole and half steps.

Curwen and Kodály: Sol-Fa and Handsigns

The Kodály system of sight singing not only utilizes sol-fa, but the Curwen handsigns to show the various scale degrees. Following in Fig. 9–10 are the handsigns for the pentatonic (five-tone), as well as the major and minor scales. Notice the handsigns for the raised seventh (si) and sixth (fi) for harmonic and melodic minor. The flatted seventh of major scales (te or ta) is also frequently used. The handsigns create the scale ladder as a visual and manipulative aid to understanding pitch and key center. Many tonal patterns can be reinforced with the handsigns.

E Natural Minor

La   Ti   Do   Re   Mi   Fa   Sol   La

E Harmonic Minor

La   Ti   Do   Re   Mi   Fa   Si   La

E Melodic Minor

(Ascending)   (Descending)

La   Ti   Do   Fe   Mi   Fi   Si   La   La   Sol   Fa   Mi   Re   Do   Ti   La

Figure 9–9 Three Forms of Minor Scales

Singing Chromatics

The entire eighteen-tone chromatic scale, utilizing both flats and sharps is given in Fig. 9–11, with location on the piano keyboard. It may be used by choral directors for drilling intervals at the chalkboard or placed on an overhead projector transparency.

Once students have mastered the scale intervals, they are ready to read easy unison exercises and melodies. When reading a unison part, the sol-fa may be sung, and then, the actual choral text immediately following. The progression for a mixed choir (SATB) should be from unison (both treble and bass), to two-part (treble and bass), and eventually to a four-part chorale type tune. Say the rhythm with Kodály rhythm syllables or some other counting system. Drill troublesome interval leaps at the chalkboard in G major and practice the following unison, two-part, and four-part pieces. Reading four parts with solfege requires considerable concentration and independence from singers. After singing with solfege, sing the parts on neutral syllable "loo." Try singing the actual text of the Bach chorale in Fig. 9–12.

Instruments as a Pitch Reading Aid

The best vocal sight readers are also usually those who have studied an instrument privately. The more practice in reading notation, the better. Any instrument forces the player to observe notation and to move the fingers to produce the appropriate pitch. It is important that students in elementary and junior high school have experiences in recorder playing and playing melodies on resonator bells and Orff instruments, in

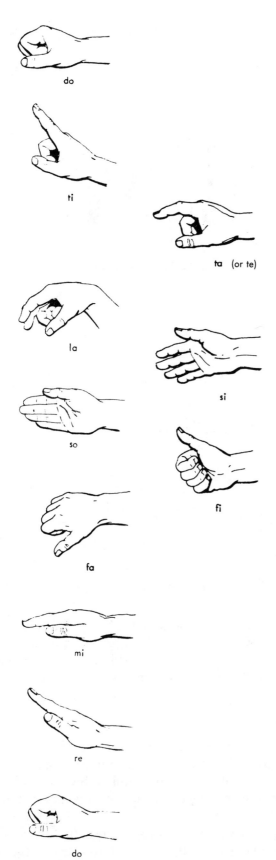

do

ti

ta (or te)

la

si

so

fi

fa

mi

re

do

Figure 9–10 Handsigns Used by Kodály

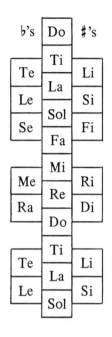

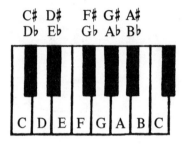

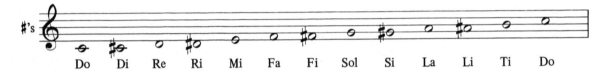

Figure 9–11 Chromatic Scale Solfege Names

addition to sight singing with sol-fa or numbers. The instruments help establish the theory and articulate performance problems. However, vocal sight singing requires mental thinking of the note before singing it. This inner hearing needs to be developed in the choral singer if any degree of independence is to be attained.

Singing on Neutral Syllables

If students have not been exposed to the number or sol-fa systems, sight reading may be attempted on "loo" or "lah" neutral syllables. This is a layman's approach to sight singing and is a more general approximation of the sound. What is lacking is the knowledge of keys, scales, intervals, and so on, which the number or sol-fa system develops.

It takes time to use any sight-reading method successfully, and it is a gradual growth process. It needs daily practice. However, it is never too late to learn to sight

Figure 9–12 Unison, Two-Part, Four-Part Sight Reading

My Inmost Heart Now Raises

Aus meines Herzens Grunde

1. My in - most heart now rais - es, In this fair
2. For Thou hast from me ward - ed All per - ils
3. My life, my soul de - fend them! My wife, child,

morn - ing hour, A song of thank - ful prais - es To
of the night; From ev - 'ry harm hast guard - ed My
goods, and home, To Thy hand I com - mend them, From

Thine al-might - y pow'r. O God, up - on Thy throne. To
soul till morn - ing light, Hum - bly to Thee I cry: O
Thee my bless - ings come; Thy boun - teous hand be - stows My

hon - or and a - dore Thee, I bring my
Sav - ior have com - pas - sion And par - don
house - hold and my treas - ures, My par - ents,

praise be - fore Thee, Through Christ, Thine on - ly Son.
my trans - gres - sion; Have mer - cy, Lord most high.
friends, and pleas - ures; My cup with good o'er - flows.

FOUR-PART
MY INMOST HEART NOW RAISES
CHORALE

J. S. Bach

read and understand the theory behind the notes on the page. Junior and senior high school is not too late to use numbers or sol-fa. The degree of proficiency will be in proportion to the amount of time spent on sight singing in rehearsals. Some directors assign sight singing to be done on a certain day by individuals.

LEARNING COMMON MAJOR AND MINOR CHORD CADENCES

Sight reading a unison melody is only one aspect of choral singing. Reading some major and minor chord progressions with numbers or sol-fa will help the choir gain harmonic independence. Fig. 9–13 shows vocal chording for a three-part treble chorus.

Some four-part (SATB) vocal cadences are illustrated in Fig. 9–14. Sing them with numbers or solfege, then "loo" or "lah" neutral syllable. Improvise a text to the chord cadences. For additional harmonic vocalises for all voicings, see Chap. 7.

Sight Singing at Contests

The best preparation for sight reading and contests is daily sight reading in rehearsals. Unless students have mastered the basic rhythm and pitch-reading skills, effective sight singing will be difficult. It is best to use progressively difficult pieces to build these skills in rehearsal. Use the tape recorder so students can critique themselves. Try sight reading a piece on a concert, where the pressure is on to produce. Let the audience know that sight singing is an important aspect of a rehearsal.

At the contest, call the singers' attention to the form of the piece, repeated patterns, meter signature, and beat. In the brief study time usually allowed, the director

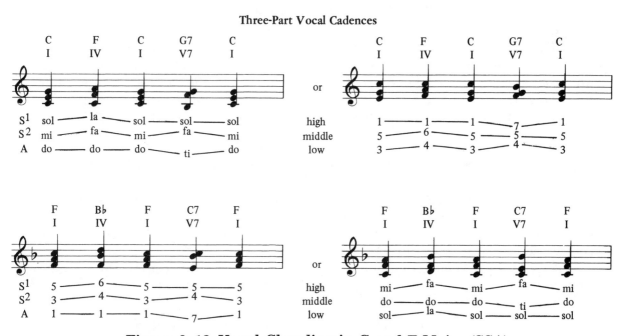

Figure 9–13 Vocal Chording in C and F Major (SSA)

Figure 9–14 Four-Part Vocal Cadences (SATB)

should point out rhythm problems, name the key, locate unison passages, scale-line, and chordal tonal patterns in parts. Identify chromatics, modulations, part entrances, and troublesome releases. Make clear in rehearsal and at the contest that the choir must sing from beginning to end without a break. If students lose their place, they must catch up and re-enter. Challenge the choir to do their best!

PUBLISHED SIGHT-READING MATERIALS FOR CHORUS

Although many directors devise their own rhythm, melody, and harmony sight-singing materials, numerous publications exist for practicing specific reading skills. Easy chorale-type and folk arrangements should be read in context, first with numbers or sol-fa, and then with the actual text.

Appendix N lists numerous published materials for choral directors. Among these are:

Bauguess, David. *The Jenson Sight Singing Course: Vol. I and II and Part Exercises*

Boyd, Jack. *Teaching Choral Sight Reading*
Cole, S. W. and Lewis, L. R. *Melodia, Vol. I and II*
Collins, Don. *The Adolescent Reading Singer* (chart and book)
Crowe, E., et al. *The Folk Song Sight Reading Series*
Edstrom, Richard. *The Independent Singer*
Ehret, Walter. *See and Sing, Vol. I, II, and III*
Hatcher, W. and Petker, A. *Choral Skills* (octavos)
Rodby, Walter. *Let's Sight-Sing* (octavos)
Steubing, Carl and Wheeler, R. *The Sol-Fa Book for Chorus and Choir*

REFERENCE NOTES

[1]Edwin Gordon, *Learning Sequences in Music.* (Chicago: G.I.A. Publications, 1984).
[2]From a handout at the 1972 MENC convention in Atlanta, Georgia.

PART
FOUR

PLANNING
REHEARSALS AND
PERFORMANCES

Chapter Ten

Organizing Successful Rehearsals

Good rehearsals do not just happen. They are a result of establishing specific goals and carrying them through efficiently and effectively. To make the most of rehearsal time with junior and senior high school choruses, directors should develop a *written plan* for each session. The rehearsal is a teaching environment, not a final performance situation. Only through careful long- and short-range planning can the year's objectives be achieved.

LONG- AND SHORT-RANGE REHEARSAL PLANNING

For each ensemble, the director must estimate the total number of rehearsal hours available over the year. Some large ensembles may be rehearsing five periods a week, where some small ensembles will meet only once or twice a week. The number of performances for each ensemble needs careful consideration. Obviously those ensembles with more rehearsal time will be able to prepare a larger repertoire to perform. Festival and contest music will also need to be prepared.

If the choral curriculum described in Chap. 1 is to receive due attention, the choral ensembles must be introduced to a variety of choral literature over the year. Exposure to Renaissance, Baroque, Classic, Romantic, and Contemporary choral styles is paramount to the choral education of the students. Folk music, spirituals, Broadway tunes, and some lighter pop music needs to be integrated into the total year's curriculum.

Much of the long-range planning may be done in late spring or summer of the preceeding school year. Music may often be purchased, ready for opening of school in September. The school calendar should contain the dates of all performances for the new year, including concert, festival, and contest dates. What is to be avoided at all costs, is the haphazard type of planning which is based on "getting ready for the next performance." Choral growth in terms of vocal skills, sight-reading skills, and literature/style understanding requires careful planning.

Only when long-range planning is effective will the individual rehearsals contribute to the long-range objectives. Each individual rehearsal must therefore have set objectives (musical stress) which are realistic and challenging for the singers. The following daily rehearsal plan format in Fig. 10–1 is useful.

This rehearsal plan format should be flexible. There will be times when the rehearsal may start with announcements. Perhaps a vocalise will be placed before a specific choral piece to help with the specific vocal problems inherent in that particular piece. It is wise to extract rhythm, pitch, harmony, phrasing, and text problems from the choral piece to drill prior to rehearsing the piece. This gives meaning and relevance to the vocalise.

Some directors like to sight read from choral sight-reading books or octavos currently published. Other directors devise their own sight-reading materials which contain various melodic and rhythmic reading problems. Frequently, the melody (interval) and rhythm-reading skills are related to the choral pieces being introduced.

The repertoire for the 45- to 50-minute rehearsal may be rehearsed for various reasons and in a specific order. It is good to have some familiar pieces to polish certain pages, as well as one or two pieces for more intensive rehearsing. It is doubtful that spending more than 12 minutes on any one choral piece will accomplish much with young singers. Interests begin to wane and the effectiveness of the rehearsal diminishes when one piece is rehearsed too long. Shorter, more frequent rehearsals of a piece achieve better long-range results. The director should have no less than five or six pieces prepared to rehearse for each rehearsal. This means making a written plan, indicating what will be rehearsed in each piece, in addition to including any specific vocalises and sight reading to be done. Specific pages and measures may be written on the plan and the objectives (rehearsal stress) to be achieved for each choral piece. The daily rehearsal plan in Fig. 10–1 is a practical rehearsal guide for the conductor.

DEVELOPING REHEARSAL TECHNIQUES

A number of factors need consideration prior to beginning a choral rehearsal.

1. The first prerequisite of a good rehearsal is to know your music to be rehearsed well ahead of the rehearsal. Do not sight read in front of the choral ensemble. Have your written plan in front of you and the materials arranged in sequential order.

Daily Rehearsal Plan Format

Choral Ensemble _____ Date _____ Time _____

Chorus Seated with Folios

Vocalises (Warmups): _____

_____

Sight Reading: _____

_____

Announcements: _____

_____

Choral Pieces to Be Rehearsed

	Title	Pages	Objectives (Rehearsal Stress)
1.	_____	_____	_____
			_____
			_____
2.	_____	_____	_____
			_____
			_____
3.	_____	_____	_____
			_____
			_____
4.	_____	_____	_____
			_____
			_____
5.	_____	_____	_____
			_____
			_____
6.	_____	_____	_____
			_____
			_____

Figure 10–1 Daily Rehearsal Plan Format

2. Expect an exciting rehearsal and be positive, even though you may not feel at your best at the moment.

3. Start the rehearsal on time. Expect performers to be in their seats with their music. Since students need to move to other classes, be sure to end the rehearsal on time.

4. Post the rehearsal order of the music on the chalkboard so the singers can arrange their music correspondingly in their folios before the rehearsal begins. Hunting for music wastes valuable rehearsal time and causes discipline problems.

5. Specify the amount of time you will spend on each aspect of the rehearsal, including vocalises, choral pieces, sight singing, announcements, and so on. This will prevent staying too long on one choral piece.

6. Set up the rehearsal room before the rehearsal. This includes chairs, piano, stands (if needed), lighting, ventilation, and music in folios in cabinet. It also implies a seating plan for each ensemble.

7. Vary the rehearsal plan. Do not use the same warm-ups each rehearsal. Avoid over-rehearsing of pieces since singers become tired of meaningless repetition.

8. Encourage the singers to listen when you are giving directions or presenting some teaching material.

9. Do not rehearse any choral part too long, but insist that the other parts listen while an individual part is rehearsing. Get back to rehearsing the entire ensemble again as soon as feasible.

10. Keep the pace of the rehearsal lively. Young singers enjoy the stimulation of a "driving" director. Move from vocalising, sight reading, and rehearsing pieces with due haste.

11. Conduct as much as possible and talk as little as possible. Long verbal discussions do not belong in a rehearsal. Sometimes a short demonstration by the director of what is desired saves many words. Sing how you want the music performed.

12. Teach the ensemble to stop when you stop to avoid wasting time. Remind the singers to place their music in such a way that you are always visible to them.

13. Do not always sing through a work from beginning to end in rehearsal. Have the spots selected for rehearsing. You may start at the ending section of the choral piece and work toward the beginning.

14. Don't count before the entrance, but teach the ensemble to follow your preparatory beat. In early rehearsals it is good to have the chorus review the conducting beats in common meters, so they know what you are conducting. Have them practice these beat patterns. Also, indicate to them what your other gestures mean. This saves much misunderstanding.

15. Give the singers a reason for repeating a section of the music. Tell them what needs to be corrected and demonstrate vocally what you desire. Then proceed to make the correction. Meaningless repetition is an insult to the chorus.

16. Don't sing with the ensemble, but listen to what you are getting from the ensemble in terms of intonation, rhythm precision, phrasing, dynamics, and so on.

17. Get the chorus accustomed to listening to your directions the first time given. Avoid repeating directions. Disciplined responses work wonders in developing the ensemble's alertness.

18. Be positive with the chorus and praise them for good work and accomplishment. This is a personal matter and style for each conductor, but the young singer needs to have his or her efforts recognized and reinforced positively. Do not praise poor work, however, but positively reinforce what was done well.

THE REHEARSAL ROOM, FOLIOS, AND SEATING

The physical environment for rehearsing needs consideration. The room should be made as attractive as possible. This can be done prior to the opening of the school year. You will probably need to arrange the chairs as you want them. The bulletin boards should be filled with not only choral announcements about concerts and musical events of interest in the community, but also with some teaching information. Record jackets of choral groups, pictures of ensembles, and information about style periods and composers make useful displays. Vocal pedagogy is another possible display utilizing pictures and diagrams of the vocal mechanism. Tempo and dynamic marks and other music symbols may be included in another bulletin board display.

The choral music is best placed in individual choral folios and stored in cabinets with numbered shelves. Students may then pick up their folios as they enter and leave them on the shelf in the cabinet when they leave rehearsal. This will also include any vocalises or sight-reading material in the folios. Larger scores may be passed out by section leaders each rehearsal.

If this is the first rehearsal of the school year, the director should have a seating plan ready when the students arrive. One way of seating the singers is to place them under signs (soprano, alto, tenor, etc.) and call off the names where they are to sit. If the folios cannot already be on the chairs, section leaders may pass these to the singers once they are seated.

The seating chart should be placed on the bulletin board near the room entrance. A listing of names and folio-number assignment should also be posted. If robes or other uniforms are used, it is helpful to have a listing for each singer, identifying the robe or uniform number to be worn. Singers can determine where they are to sit, then get their folios, and be seated. It is important that the chorus members understand that they are seated in a particular place for a purpose. Do not permit a student to sit next to a friend, but insist that the seating plan will be adhered to until you as director change it for some good reason. The sectional seating plans for junior and senior high ensembles were given in Chap. 2 and 3, respectively.

SELECTING REPERTOIRE FOR THE FIRST REHEARSAL

The criteria for selecting choral repertoire was presented in Chap. 6. This part of planning may take place in late spring or early summer. If the programs, festivals, and contests are allowed for, most music will be ordered and catalogued for the opening of the school year. There will be times when a new piece will be ordered on short notice to meet the special needs of a particular ensemble. Armed with the new choral pieces and the existing library of pieces, the director should be able to effectively select the repertoire for the school year.

Even though the students have been auditioned, hopefully prior to the first rehearsal, a variety of music from easy to difficult needs to be placed in students' folios. This will include sacred and secular, accompanied, and unaccompanied, representative master choral works, folk and spiritual arrangements, and perhaps a Broadway show or light pop tune. A patriotic piece is always useful for concerts and assemblies. Directors should estimate the capabilities of each choral ensemble when selecting the music. Attempts to force difficult pieces upon the singers to "raise the level" of the choral literature sung will cause problems. Similarly, selection of unappealing or too easy a repertoire will promote disinterest among the more dedicated singers in the group.

For the first several rehearsals, choose six to ten pieces to be placed in each singer's folio. Students like to know what they will be singing. Most of these pieces should be readily singable, but there may be one or two more challenging pieces and one or two easier ones. New choral works may be added as the director senses the capabilities and overall interest level of the group. The works chosen for the first rehearsal will help to identify both the strengths and the weaknesses of the choir and might include the following:

1. A homophonic piece, such as a Bach chorale, to determine sight reading abilities and overall balance of sections. The Mendelssohn "Cast Thy Burden Upon the Lord" from *Elijah* also makes a fine chordal piece to sight read and to develop intonation and part balance.

2. A folk or spiritual arrangement which is expressive and appealing. The tempo may be fast or slow. This is a style of singing popular with junior and senior high school singers. Smith's arrangement of *Climbin' Up the Mountain* is very workable and easily learned.

3. A unison piece, or a round, to work on a good unison tone from the choir, as well as clear articulation of the text. A piece with a unison section, such as Martin Shaw's *With a Voice of Singing* will serve the purpose well. A "fuguing tune" or round such as Billings' *When Jesus Wept* will allow the director to hear the individual parts in a polyphonic style.

4. One or two selections to be performed at the first concert, or at the Christmas concert. This allows the singers to experience the type of music they will be performing over the year. The Christmas pieces may be withdrawn from the folios and reintroduced in November closer to the performance. The Praetorius *Psallite* is a fine Christmas example.

5. One difficult piece that is unknown to the choir. It is good to have one or two difficult pieces available for the first rehearsal in case the director has underestimated the singing abilities. It also provides a challenge of the long-haul type. Dello Joio's *Jubilant Song* is just such a piece. However, tiring and tedious rehearsing should be avoided in the first rehearsal.

6. Pieces representative of several music style periods. This gives the singers a tonal variety in the first rehearsal. Moving from Hassler's *Cantate Domino* to Handel's "O Lord in Thee" from *Dettingen Te Deum* to the Berger *Five Canzonets* adds refreshment and excitement to the first choral rehearsal.

At the first rehearsal, the choir should be told that you, as director, are pleased they were selected by audition to be in the group. You should let the choir know you are looking forward to working with them in developing a fine choral ensemble. You may pass out a list of performance dates and an overview of each choir member's responsibilities. Some directors mail this singer's choral handbook to parents so they are aware of the commitment involved in choir membership. Misunderstandings about rehearsal schedules, absences from rehearsals and performances, deportment, grades in choir, award system, choir uniforms, and other matters may thus be minimized.

The director should keep the discussion to a minimum at the first rehearsal and spend the time on the main thing—singing!

WORKING WITH THE ACCOMPANIST

A good accompanist is a vital asset to the director and chorus. Although the director may play vocalises and do some occasional accompanying, it is not recommended that the director be the accompanist. The director needs to stand in front of the chorus with good eye contact to truly lead the young voices. It is difficult to hear mistakes when at the piano keyboard. In choosing student accompanists, it is advisable to identify and contact all the student accompanists from the previous year if you are new to the position. The concert programs may be checked for names of accompanists. The principal or counselor may also know some student pianists. Some may be members of the band or orchestra, in addition to the chorus, so these directors need to be contacted. The local piano teachers may be able to suggest possible accompanists. Be aware that a solo pianist may not necessarily be a good choir accompanist. Accompanying requires careful following of the director, not leading.

If sufficient pianists are available and interested in accompanying, have them audition for you. Have them play a piano solo and one or two pieces of choral music which are prepared before the audition. Sight reading a choral accompaniment and playing one, two, or three choral parts simultaneously may be checked. Direct the student in the audition to determine how well he or she follows your beat. It is useful to select two accompanists for each choral ensemble. This will allow them to take turns playing and singing with their choral part in the choir.

Once the accompanist(s) has (have) been chosen, set a time to meet for a half hour to an hour to explain the accompanist's role. All copies of the music for the early rehearsals should be given to the accompanist well in advance to practice. The tempo and dynamic levels as well as overall style of each piece should be indicated. The student should be directed to practice the accompaniment as well as each choral part. The accompanist should be ready to play the soprano and alto parts simultaneously and the tenor and bass parts simultaneously. Some student accompanists can manage all four parts with skill development.

Any vocalises should be written out for the accompanist or marked if part of a collection of vocalises. How high and low they are to go should be explained. Some students will not be able to move up or down by half steps using all the major and minor keys, and certain accompanied vocalises may need to be played by the director who understands how to add chords (I and V, especially) to the vocalise. Some directors prefer to accompany all vocalises themselves.

The accompanist should give choral part pitches from the lowest to the highest part. The root of the chord will be heard sooner, allowing the parts to build upon it. The accompanist should pay close attention to the directions of the conductor to anticipate starting points after a rehearsal stop. If the accompanist is alert, valuable time will be saved. An ineffective student accompanist can hinder the natural flow of the rehearsal. The accompanist should be at the piano immediately to start the rehearsal at the director's signal.

If the accompanist is ill, the director should be notified in advance, the night before if possible. Any conflicts, such as field trips in a class, should be worked out in advance so a substitute accompanist may be present for rehearsal. It is frustrating to plan a rehearsal requiring an accompanist's assistance and find the person absent that day. The director should make the accompanist's position important and include some accompanied choral pieces on the program. An occasional piano solo may also be included on some choral programs.

Some directors are fortunate to have hired accompanists to play for rehearsals and performances. In some cases these may be parents of choir members, other school music teachers, community piano teachers, or church organists. When no student accompanist is available, an outside accompanist is a must. The school administration will need to be convinced that this additional expenditure is necessary.

PACING THE REHEARSAL

The first rehearsal should move at a fairly rapid pace. This is true of most successful rehearsals. Every second should be filled with meaningful choral activity. This is not a time to waste on unimportant matters. It is not a social hour for visiting with friends. The singers should experience some of the rehearsal techniques from the very first rehearsal to be employed over the entire year. The singers should feel a sense of enjoyment and accomplishment in each rehearsal. Rehearsals are not "fun," but enjoyable working sessions with music. If music is not at the center of the rehearsal, the main reason for being is missing. The director needs to have a rehearsal plan and approach the task in a firm, businesslike manner. Students will soon learn that rehearsals are times for serious study of choral music and not a time to "blow off" or "clown around." Once the choir understands the limits of behavior acceptable to the director and senses the possibilities for excellence in singing, a workable relationship can be established.

Too often confusion reigns when the director stops the choir to make corrections. The director must insist upon silence when directions are being given. Young choir singers often try to take advantage of the time between selections to visit and talk with their neighbors. This tendency must be curbed by the director if the time is to be used to good advantage. Sometimes the director will allow a three-minute break to visit or let off steam, but then it must be back to serious rehearsing. Writing the titles on the chalkboard in the order to be rehearsed will lessen the tendency for talk. A flip-chart may also serve the same purpose. In most cases, students do appreciate the director's efforts to make efficient use of rehearsal time, and will often chide some of their peers who are less than cooperative. This is group dynamics functioning at its best when the motivation and self-discipline comes from within the students.

To keep the pace of the rehearsal moving, the director must know how to divide the rehearsal time efficiently. It is wise to organize each rehearsal as to time allotted for each activity. Although the following represents one type of rehearsal time allotment, be aware that there are other successful ways to organize a rehearsal. Some variety from day to day is necessary.

1. The singers enter, pick up folios, and are seated (3 min.).
2. The director or student officer takes attendance from the master seating chart (1 min.).
3. The director makes a few brief remarks (3 min.).
4. Several vocalises are studied. These may be for intonation, breath support, phrasing, diction, part balance, choral tone, and so on. These may be on the board or in folios from a collection (published or director devised) (5 min.).
5. Review a piece previously sung to polish some rhythm problems experienced. Isolate the rhythms at the chalkboard and clap or speak the text in rhythm (7 min.).
6. Sight read a portion of a new piece in homophonic style. Give the choir one minute to study their individual parts. Speak the words rhythmically for the first two pages, then give the chord and sing four parts on neutral syllable "loo" or "lah." Then go back and sing the text. Work on the other portions of the piece next rehearsal, along with a review of the first two pages (10 min.).
7. Take a three-minute break for additional announcements, if necessary (3 min.).
8. Review Mozart's *Ave Verum* singing on "loo" for good tone and part balance. Be careful to get the chromatics in tune and to achieve the crescendos and diminuendos. Play a recording of the Mozart piece, e.g., *Great Sacred Choruses—* Robert Shaw Chorale, RCA. Then teach the Latin text pronunciation for the first section, phrase by phrase in rote fashion. Sing the first section in Latin. Follow the same procedure for the second half of the piece (10 min.).
9. Close the rehearsal with a satisfying a cappella piece which is almost "finished." Stand and try Bortnianski's *Cherubim Song No. 7* from memory. This makes a psychologically sound finale to the rehearsal (5 min.).
10. Dismiss the chorus at class change signal, having the singers place their folios in the numbered storage cabinet (1 min.).

The director needs to be aware of fatigue in the rehearsal and be ready to move to the next activity or choral piece in the plan if the attention of the singers is waning.

Spending tedious rehearsing when interest level is low will produce limited or mixed results. The director should not be afraid to move away from the podium occasionally to work with a particular part. However, it is important that the director remain highly visible most of the rehearsal and that the entire chorus needs are addressed. Sometimes to keep the other sections occupied while a single section rehearses, the director may ask the other parts to hum while the one part rehearses with the text. Section rehearsals during general rehearsals must be quick and pointed to maintain overall interest.

INTRODUCING A NEW CHORAL WORK

After a choral piece has been selected for rehearsal and ultimate performance, the director must make an in-depth analysis of the piece's form, melody, rhythm, harmony, texture, dynamics, text, and the accompaniment (if accompanied). This information about the work may be noted on the director's music itself, or better, on a brief form such as that in Fig. 10–2.

This study of the work will not only note (1) the musical characteristics of the piece, some of which will be communicated to the singers, but (2) the performance considerations. Where are the difficult intervals in each part? Chromatics? Key shifts? Syncopated and dotted rhythms? Dissonant chord progressions? Text/diction problems?

If the work is a single-movement type of piece, the presentation to the chorus is easier. If a multimovement work, such as a mass or cantata, the chorus will need an overall understanding of the entire piece before rehearsing the parts. Then the individual movements may be studied and rehearsed on subsequent days over an extended time frame. It is wise to circle in red all anticipated performance problems in the score.

When a new piece is introduced, it would be well for the director to give some information about the composer or arranger, the style period and its common characteristics, possibly using a bulletin board for reference or a high school level choral text, such as *Sing!*, Hinshaw Music Co. This information need not be lengthy, but should lay the groundwork for interpreting the piece and put it in the proper time frame of history. Other bits of information may be added in subsequent rehearsals. A way to present a new choral piece follows:

1. Sing through the entire piece once if it appears easy enough to read at sight.

2. If the piece contains many difficult passages, select only an easier portion of the piece which can be mastered in this first rehearsal of it. A positive attitude among the singers toward the piece needs to be cultivated. The more difficult passages may be studied sequentially in future rehearsals.

3. The director may practice the main melodic material (such as a fugue theme) with all the sections in unison (choosing often the lower alto or bass line to read). The key rhythmic feature may be isolated at the chalkboard and clapped, chanted, and sung with text. The harmonic material may be studied through singing a major or minor chord progression from the piece.

4. If the piece is in a foreign language, the meaning and pronunciation may be

Analysis of Choral Work Form	
Title _____	
Composer/Arranger _____	
Voicing _____ Publisher _____ No. _____	
Music's Characteristics	Director's Analysis of Music
FORM (single/multi movement, binary, ternary, strophic, through-composed, aleatory, unity-variety devices)	
MELODY (type phrases, conjunct, disjunct, range, fragments, legato, marcato, staccato, common intervals, sequences, diatonic, chromatic, modal)	
RHYTHM (tempo, meter, longest and shortest note values, rests, augmentation, diminution, rit., accel., hemiola, fermata, changing meter, polymeter)	
HARMONY (major, minor, key, modulation, chromatics, suspension, unison, chord movement, pedal point, 12–tone, atonal)	
TEXTURE (monophonic, polyphonic, homophonic, organum, tape background, indeterminate)	
DYNAMICS (ppp–fff markings, cresc., dim., accent, sfz, marcato, terraced, light and heavy voice scoring)	
TEXT (English, foreign text, translation, syllabic, melismatic, strophic, semi-strophic, through composed text, text fragmentation and repetition, text painting)	
ACCOMPANIMENT (or A Cappella) piano, organ, orchestra, band, small instrument ensemble, obligatto, independence of instrumental ensemble)	

Figure 10–2 Analysis of Choral Work Form

studied and spoken. The piece may be sung on neutral syllable "loo" or "lah," and then with text on another day.

5. In the initial reading of a new choral piece, it is best to avoid using the text unless the tempo is slow and text easy to read. The eye has difficulty tracking both notes and words (a singer's dilemma, different from the instrumentalist who tracks notes, only). If the singers have utilized sol-fa system or number system in elementary and junior high school, these may be successfully employed for reading purposes. If not, a neutral syllable will suffice.

6. Do not try to "finish" the new piece in one rehearsal. Spend maybe ten to twelve minutes on it and then move to the other pieces or vocalises to be rehearsed. Since the chorus meets frequently, it is easy to review and pick up where you stopped. Rome was not built in one day!

A JUNIOR HIGH MIXED CHORUS REHEARSAL PLAN

Junior high school singers need much work on vocal production. There is also the special problem of the boy's changing voice discussed in Chap. 2. Posture, breathing, resonance, flexibility, tone quality, diction, intonation, rhythmic precision, dynamics, and part balance need attention in rehearsals. A second area for development is sight reading choral parts. Nearly every rehearsal of junior high choral ensembles should stress these two areas of vocal production and sight singing. This is a time for musical growth and the pressure of performances is not as great as in the senior high school. It is hoped that a good mix of choral literature will be studied in the rehearsal. One rehearsal plan for junior high mixed chorus follows:

1. Chorus members enter, pick up folios of music from numbered cabinets, and take assigned seats.

2. Director (section leader or chorus president) takes attendance, checking any absentee singer's names with the daily office list.

3. Have the chorus stand, with each singer's hands joined behind the back. This lifts the rib cage so the lungs and diaphragm can function. Try panting to feel the action of the breath hitting the vocal chords. Chant the alphabet on one pitch in one breath.

4. For developing resonance, vocalise on a hum moving to a vowel, moving up and down by half steps, see Fig. 10–3.

5. Next, try some staccato and legato articulation exercises illustrated in Fig. 10–4. Directors may also use Ex. 1, 2, and 3 in *Sing Legato* (Vocalises by Kenneth Jennings, Kjos Music Co.).

6. Rehearse *Praise the Lord, Alleluia!* (Boyce-Wagner, 3-Part Mixed, Coronet CP326). Sight read the canon in unison with sol-fa or numbers, after drilling rhythm problems and pitch intervals from the piece at the chalkboard. Add the text, then practice in polyphonic harmony.

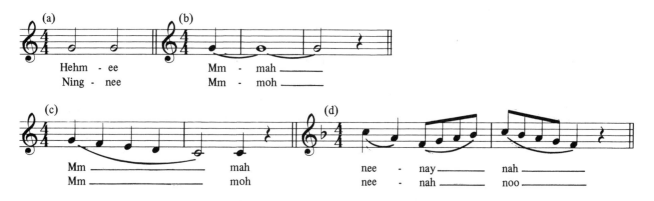

Figure 10–3 Resonance Vocalises

Figure 10–4 Staccato and Legato Articulation Vocalises

7. Rehearse *Ride the Chariot* (Spiritual, arr Wm Melton, SACB, Cambiata Press S117450). This four-part setting is in the polishing stage. Work on rhythmic articulation of the text by chanting it clearly to the conductor's beat. Practice the following chord progression in C major, see Fig. 10–5, the key of the arrangement to improve the choir's intonation.

8. Make announcements about upcoming performances, times, dress, warm-up, and so on.

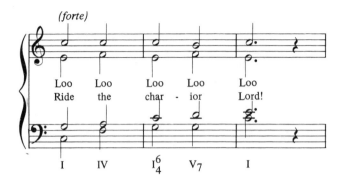

Figure 10–5 C Major Chord Progression

9. Rehearse the two-part piece, *Come, Jesus, Holy Son of God* (Handel-Hopson, 2-Part Mixed Voices, Flammer). Drill the 6/8 meter rhythm patterns in both parts at the chalkboard. Sing them in the piece. Ask the chorus to tell you if the piece is monophonic, polyphonic, or homophonic texture (polyphonic, imitation style). What kind of texture was *Ride the Chariot*, previously rehearsed? (homophonic, chordal).

10. Rehearse *Alleluia! Sing Praise* (Bach-Hirt, SATB, from Cantata 142, C. Fischer CM7140). This chorale tune is nothing more than a hymn with an elaborate accompaniment of introduction, interludes, and coda in typical Baroque style. Have the choir read this minor piece for the first time on "lah" neutral syllable. Note values are easy and harmony straight forward. Drop the accompaniment and play only the four-voice parts, connecting the hymn phrases. Next rehearsal, sing text and add the "dressed up" accompaniment.

11. Close the rehearsal with *It's a Grand Night for Singing* (Rodgers-Hammerstein-Ehret, SACB, Williamson W830750-363). Work on the dynamics and phrasing of this popular show tune. Rehearse any individual parts needing assistance, then stand and try the piece from memory. Eyes on the conductor for precision!

12. Have singers return folios to storage cabinet by rows, and file out of the rehearsal room to next class.

A SENIOR HIGH MIXED CHORUS REHEARSAL PLAN

Senior high school singers display a greater maturity overall in the rehearsal than their junior high counterparts. The male voice has undergone the voice change and is settling into its adult range and quality. Although these voices are still developing, much of the standard choral repertoire may be performed in senior high. A word of caution seems appropriate, however. Directors should avoid over-rehearsing of pieces with extreme ranges which make excessive demands upon young voices. The human voice is a delicate instrument that can be permanently damaged through improper use. Directors should select repertoire wisely and plan rehearsals and performances with this in mind. A variety is required in the senior high chorus rehearsal. One plan follows:

1. Chorus members enter, pick up individual folios from numbered cabinet, and are seated in assigned seats.

2. Director (section leaders or chorus president) takes attendance, checking any absentee singers' names with the daily office list.

3. Have the chorus stand and raise their hands high over their heads, reaching skyward five or six times. Push up from the toes to the finger tips. Then bend forward, with heads and arms hanging down. The head, neck, and arms should feel loose and heavy. Gradually come up from the lower back, keeping head down and arms loose.

4. Then have the chorus sit up in the chairs, with backs away from the chair, and feet slightly apart, on the floor. Keep the head back and avoid the jutting jaw. Inhale through the nose and mouth, and exhale on an unvoiced "f" over six, ten, fifteen, or twenty counts. Try to exhale evenly, without giving out all the breath at once. Each section may practice their long opening phrases in Mendelssohn's "He Watching Over Israel" from *Elijah*, with attention to extending the breath through the phrase. Then work on only the more difficult middle section, "Should'st Thou walking in grief languish, He will quicken Thee."

5. Drill the chorus in G major at the chalkboard (or from a sight-reading book) in treble and bass clef in unison and chords. Use sol-fa, numbers, or "loo." See Fig. 10–6.

6. Read the Bach chorale, *Grant Me True Courage, Lord* (SATB, E. C. Schirmer 313 or from a Bach chorale collection) in G major, 4/4 meter. Use sol-fa, numbers, or "loo," reading all four parts simultaneously with no piano reinforcement.

Figure 10–6 G Major Interval-Chorded Exercise

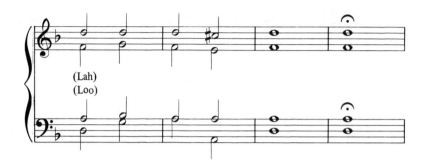

(Lah)
(Loo)

Figure 10–7 D Minor Chordal/Dynamics Vocalise

Then add the text. This will build sight-singing growth and independence in the singers. It is also an excellent piece to "tune up" the intonation of the chorus.

7. Begin work on Pinkham's *In the Beginning of Creation* (SATB, E. C. Schirmer 2902, with Electronic Tape). Discuss indeterminate aleatory music with the chorus, other contemporary modes of composition. Text is Biblical. Explain the time frame is expressed in minutes and seconds, i.e., 00:00−3:45 = beginning to 3 minutes and 45 seconds into the piece. Certain vocal and tape sounds must occur at specific times as indicated in the score. Play a recording of the piece if available. Then work on only the "traditional" vocal parts this first day. Later rehearsals will introduce the speaking, nontraditional singing in aleatory style. The tape accompaniment will be introduced, also.

8. Polish the "Lacrymosa" movement from Mozart's *Requiem* (SATB, G. Schirmer 11564). Sing a d minor choral vocalise at varied dynamic levels at a lento tempo. See Fig. 10–7. Be careful singing the eighth notes/eighth rest figure. The eighth note needs full length for the chords to sound. They are not staccato notes.

9. Close the rehearsal with Noble Cain's setting of the English folksong, *Early One Morning* (SATB, Presser 322-15147). Keep the tempo brisk and bouncy and work on improving diction, especially consonants, since there are many words in a short space of time. If possible, stand and sing the piece from memory.

10. Chorus returns folios to storage cabinet and files out of the rehearsal room.

REHEARSING CHORAL PIECES WITH INSTRUMENT PARTS

The addition of repertoire with instruments such as guitar, flute, trumpet, oboe, brass choir, string quartet, handbells, and percussion provides both variety and excitement to the concert program. It is important for the director to meet several times with the instrumentalist(s) before rehearsing with the choir. If the players come from the high school band or orchestra, several practices may be arranged fairly easily. The director must determine the difficulty of the instrument parts and the skills of the players. Sometimes adult players in community bands and orchestras are available.

When instrumentalists are placed with the choir for the first time, neither group should have to endure prolonged rehearsing of one or the other. This type of rehearsing should have occurred prior to the combined rehearsal. When utilizing numerous instruments, directors must maintain a balance between vocal and instrumental forces. When instruments double voice parts, the voices and text are often lost in the sound. Sometimes the director will need to scale down the number of instrumentalists, the dynamic level of playing, or both, to achieve a satisfying sound. Large festival chorus pieces frequently utilize orchestra or band accompaniments (See Appendix G). Many extended works, such as cantatas, masses, and oratorios utilize orchestra.

Start and end these combined rehearsals on time. If several groups are brought together, plan to rehearse the largest group first, and release singers and instrumentalists as you progress to smaller ensembles. Be careful not to rehearse solo singers at length while the large choir stands waiting to sing. Combined rehearsals of vocal and instrumental forces require care in planning and execution.

PREPARING EXTENDED CHORAL WORKS

There is a need for senior high school choral groups to prepare an extended multi-movement work on a yearly basis. There are many choral masterworks singable by senior high school choruses. These include (1) choral suites, (2) cantatas, (3) masses, and (4) oratorios. Students enjoy tackling such a work and there is a built in motivator to continue rehearsing until the entire piece is completed. Appendix I lists some multimovement works for SSA, SAB/SSCB and SATB voicings. The bulk falls in the SATB mixed chorus category. These works often contain solos, duets, trios, quartets, in addition to choruses. A few works require speaking parts, such as a narrator. Some works, such as Handel's *Messiah* or Mendelssohn's *Elijah* may be presented in part, not in their entirety. The director will need to secure the instrumentalists well in advance to accompany such works.

Many high school choruses have successfully sung the Bach cantatas, *For Us a Child Is Born* and *Now Thank We All Our God*. The Britten *Ceremony of Carols* (Treble or Mixed Voice Settings) and Praetorius *In Dulci Jubilo*, Rutter *Gloria* and *Requiem* are popular. Pinkham's *Christmas Cantata*, Durufle's *Requiem*, and Dubois' *Seven Last Words of Christ* are possible. The Irving Fine *Alice in Wonderland Suite* and the Hindemith *Six Chansons* make exciting choral suites. The Brahms *Six Folk Songs* is an easy group to prepare. The Hammerschmidt *O Beloved Shepherds* may be accompanied by two violins or two trumpets in Baroque fashion. Other works include Poulenc *Gloria*, Schubert *Mass in G*, R. Thompson *Testament of Freedom* and *Frostiana*, Vivaldi *Gloria*, Saint-Saens *Christmas Oratorio*, Vaughan Williams *Fantasia on Christmas Carols*, and Pachelbel *Nun Danket Alle Gott*.

Sometimes directors can "invent" their own extended work using individual octavos within a unified, narrative framework. This works well for Christmas concerts. This type of program offers more opportunities for variety in the music sung and the possible inclusion of several choirs in the program, with less rehearsal time required of each.

ORGANIZING SPECIAL REHEARSALS

As performance dates approach, the director may need to schedule rehearsals that include all the ensembles, soloists, and instrumentalists. Choral directors should be cognizant of the demands that extra rehearsals make upon the students, other teachers, and parents. This rehearsal will often be the final rehearsal prior to the concert in the school auditorium.

If at all possible, the director should have rehearsed each ensemble in the auditorium at the regular rehearsal hour of each group. In some cases, the auditorium and gymnasium are combined, and it is impossible to rehearse when gym classes are scheduled. If so, the final rehearsal may be the only time when all singers and instrumentalists may be able to meet collectively. If an evening rehearsal just prior to the concert is not possible, perhaps a Saturday or Sunday afternoon time will work. Senior high students frequently work on weekends, and will need lead time to rearrange their work schedules.

Sometimes a principal will permit a 90-minute dress rehearsal on a school day afternoon. This requires upsetting all school classes, something which does not endear the director with other faculty. If done, teachers need two weeks notice to avoid class teaching and testing problems.

Occasionally, special rehearsals of small ensembles, soloists, duets, octets, and so on, need to be called prior to contest dates. Most of this rehearsing should be done during the student's free study halls, and before and after school. Students should not be taken from scheduled classes for this type of rehearsing.

FINAL REHEARSALS

The final or dress rehearsal should include all ensembles, instrumentalists, and soloists (if needed). It is good if the pieces can be rehearsed nonstop as the concert will be performed. All major rehearsing should have been accomplished prior to the final rehearsal.

The director must be careful of what comments are made at the final rehearsal. This is not a time to be fussy and ill-tempered, but a time to demonstrate your finest organizational and diplomacy skills. The bond between singers and conductor is closest in the final rehearsal and concert itself. At the last rehearsal the conductor should bolster the confidence of the choir. Point out strengths and indicate places in the performance where the chorus must be very alert to succeed. The singers must watch the conductor closely for precision. Keep the final rehearsal moving and before stopping, give the choruses last minute instructions, and preconcert warm-up times. Insist that they get sufficient rest and conserve energy and voices on the concert day to ensure maximum performance at the concert. You look forward to a fine performance.

Chapter Eleven

Performing at Concerts, Festivals, Contests, and Other Events

The performances of junior and senior high school students may take several educational directions, and may include school concerts, assemblies, festivals, contests, exchange concerts, clinics, Broadway musicals, and other performances. Commissioning a choral work to perform and sing at professional meetings of choral directors-educators provides stimulation and motivation to singers and director alike. Special tours and appearances on television or radio broadcasts provide additional performance avenues. The chorus is usually expected to sing at special school events such as baccalaureate and commencement, in addition to the usual Christmas and spring concerts.

Out of school performances need special consideration and full discussion by the director and administrator prior to making commitments. The group size, effect on the school program, travel involved, and financing the performance (paid by the school or by students/parents) need attention. It is necessary to obtain administrative permission for student absences from school classes and study halls. The invitation to perform needs discussion with the ensemble concerned to see that all can make the commitment. Directors need to make sure that homework and class assignments are arranged beforehand. These outside performances may often be at the invitation of PTAs, service clubs, women's clubs, churches, and other organizations. Community organizations sometimes take advantage of school music groups, and often call at short notice for a performance. The director should consider if a group is ready to perform at short notice and the importance of the inviting group to the school program. The director can always decline the invitation this year, but express a willingness to perform next year if given sufficient advance invitation. These community-type performances should be limited to twenty to thirty minutes in length. Some follow banquets or are part of a business meeting.

A small ensemble, such as a chamber group, madrigal group, jazz/show choir, or soloists may sing for these organizations easier than a large choral ensemble. Accepting out-of-school performance invitations for large ensembles will require the expense of busing, whereas the small group may travel in several automobiles. Sometimes the small ensembles, in order to gain experience in performing before an audience, may sing in a rehearsal period of a larger choral ensemble. This will help build rapport for small ensembles and soloists.

All concerts, festivals, and contests must be placed on the official school calendar as far in advance as possible, preferably late spring or summer of the preceding year. Any additional performances, such as service clubs, may be discussed with the school principal and added to the calendar when the commitment to perform is made. Directors should be aware of conflicts with sports events on weekends and certain evenings and avoid these dates. Also, churches do not like to have school concerts appearing in holy week just before Easter, due to the various church services and church singing groups involved. Setting the concert schedule for the year requires careful thought. Being overcommitted to large numbers of performances can bring on exhaustion and tends to exploit the singers. On the other hand, too few performances over the year may not provide sufficient motivation for the ensembles. The director and choral groups will "hit their stride" over several years of working together. Junior high school choral ensembles will perform less frequently than their senior high counterparts.

PROGRAM BUILDING

Program building really begins in the selection of music for the year's work for each choir. If the long-range planning has been careful, the individual programs will fall into place easier. Some concert considerations include:

1. the educational and aesthetic value of the music
2. the needs of the particular school and community
3. the abilities of each ensemble with regard to music selected
4. a balance of accompanied and unaccompanied music
5. use of assisting instruments such as flute, drum, brass choir, etc.
6. solos within the choral pieces selected
7. placement of the piano so the choir can hear it and the accompanist can see the director
8. the possible use of microphones for soloists
9. the audiences' endurance and span of attention. Most programs should not ex-

ceed one hour and fifteen minutes to one hour and a half. It is best to stop when psychologically ahead.

10. the need to allow for quick changing from one choral ensemble to the next
11. the need to allow for applause, acknowledgments, or other brief announcements in the total concert time
12. allowing for both unity and variety in the entire program.

There is a need to consider which ensembles (large and small) will perform in a given concert. A concert may have a theme underlying the total concert or may be more general in nature. A Christmas concert will put limits on music chosen to sing. Such themes as "Music of the Americas" or "Our Singing World" are frequently used. Directors should be aware that the more specific the theme chosen, the more limited will be the choice of music. While "theme" concerts can be successful, they are often lacking musically. A general concert provides greater diversity and interest in repertoire selections.

The order of the choral ensembles on the concert is an important factor. Opening the concert with a small ensemble does not seem psychologically sound. If a jazz/show choir is to perform, its order of placement on the program needs careful consideration. This is usually an appealing ensemble, both visually and aurally to the average audience, and will make it difficult for the next ensemble following it to recapture audience interest. The use of more serious versus lighter music needs some degree of balance in school concert planning. A mix of standard choral literature from Renaissance through Contemporary, in addition to folk and spiritual arrangements, Broadway and lighter pop tunes needs to be considered.

Deciding the Order of Groups to Perform

Junior and senior high school concerts usually involve more than one ensemble. It is difficult for one ensemble to learn sufficient repertoire to present an entire hour and fifteen-minute concert. The logistical problem of putting several ensembles on the same concert is workable if the ensembles never have to perform together *en masse*. If the concert is given on stage with curtain, the curtain may be drawn after each ensemble while the ensembles change on the stage. In some cases, a small ensemble may perform in front of the stage on the apron and in front of the curtain. The larger ensemble can quietly take its place on risers on the stage behind the curtain and be ready to sing once the small ensemble has concluded its selections. The concert needs to be kept moving. However, an audience often prefers to have a few moments between groups to adjust to the next type of repertoire.

If the performance must take place in a gymnasium or multipurpose room, and there is no convenient room to use as an off stage room, the students can be seated in the gym in the front seats reserved for them. Risers may be placed in the center of the floor, with choirs seated on both sides. One choir can move to the risers as the other leaves.

Sometimes, choral directors desire to combine various ensembles into one large chorus to perform one or two final selections on the concert. The individual groups should be well rehearsed and several rehearsals of the large group will need to take place outside of school time. These large groups will often sing a festival-type piece, frequently, with instrumental accompaniment such as brass choir. The piece(s) should not over-challenge the less select ensemble(s). The large massed choirs can provide a thrilling finish to a spring concert. Additional risers may be required, or some groups may stand in rows on the gym floor in horseshoe effect on either side of the group on risers. For very large massed choruses, some singers may be on stage and other groups placed on risers in front of the stage. The ensembles must be prepared carefully to take their assigned positions as quickly and efficiently as possible and also shown how to exit the auditorium at the close of the concert. A large massed bow by all singers needs to be practiced following the conductor's signal.

For a junior high school concert, the order of choral groups might be:

1. Mixed Chorus
2. Girls' Chorus
3. Small Ensemble (mixed, girls', boys')
4. Boys' Chorus
5. Mixed Chorus (and possibly massed choirs for final numbers)

Some junior high/middle schools may include choruses organized by grade level (sixth, seventh, eighth and/or ninth). These may be placed in acceptable order for best effect in the program.

An order for groups at the senior high school level might include:

1. Concert Choir
2. Girls' Chorus
3. Mixed Chorus (less select, often ninth and tenth grades)
4. Madrigal Singers
5. Boys' Chorus
6. Mix Octet (Quartet, Trio, etc.)
7. Concert Choir (and possibly massed choirs for final numbers)

Some directors prefer to place a jazz/show choir on the concert, also. Other directors prefer to present separate concert programs for this high-appeal ensemble. Jazz/show choir frequently sings at many out-of-school community programs.

The repertoire of the ensembles will also determine order. A madrigal or chamber group will sing a specific type of literature different from the concert choir. Also, the girls' and boys' chorus repertoire tends to be unique to those groups. There is also a different choral sonority among these various groups which lends variety. A treble sound or a male sound is refreshing following the mixed voice ensemble. Addition of instrument accompaniments adds even more color possibilities to a concert. A Christmas concert is improved by the singing of chorus and audience of carols to a brass choir accompaniment.

It is sometimes difficult to maintain unity and variety and a natural progression in a program involving many ensembles. The following programming suggestions should help:

1. Keep the total time of the concert to one hour and fifteen minutes to no more than one hour and a half.

2. Build a unity and variety within the entire program for the various ensembles utilized. Select a wise order for the various groups to perform.

3. Achieve a variety within the pieces for each ensemble in terms of tempi, keys, and meters of individual pieces. An ensemble singing all pieces in 4/4 meter in G major key at a constant andante tempo soon becomes boring.

4. Select outstanding opening and closing numbers for the entire program. The audience remembers best the initial and finale pieces. These should have strong psychological impact and be performed at their best. These pieces may be fast or slow, loud or soft, serious literature, or lighter literature. Some directors like to begin concerts with a patriotic tune and close with the same type or perhaps a pleasing Broadway show tune. Others would prefer to close the concert with the concert choir singing "Hallelujah" from Beethoven's *Mount of Olives*. This is a matter of taste and estimating the audience's reaction.

5. Select outstanding opening and closing number for each group, using the same criteria in number 4 previous.

An ensemble should probably sing no less than three selections and no more than five or six. Most pieces are three minutes in length and a single ensemble may be on stage anywhere from ten to fifteen or eighteen minutes. Again, the larger ensembles, because of more rehearsal time, will have prepared the larger amount of repertoire.

Types of Choral Concerts

There are several formats widely used for choral concert programming. These include (1) the Christmas concert, (2) the general concert, (3) the program of short works (suites and movements), and (4) single multimovement extended work with choruses, solos, and possible instrumental accompaniment.

Almost every choral department presents a Christmas concert and a spring concert. Some schools present a Thanksgiving or patriotic concert in November. Since Christmas occurs late in the first semester, it allows adequate time to develop a concert repertoire with several ensembles.

Following is an example of a junior high school Christmas choral concert. It contains a mixture of composed choral literature from several style periods, as well as folk and spiritual arrangements.

I

Come, Redeemer, Come (SAB, C. Fisher CM8199)	Cherubini-Hopson
Veni, Veni Emmanuel (SAB, Boosey & Hawkes 5564)	Kodály
Psallite (SATB, Bourne ES 21)	Praetorius
Carol of the Bells (SATB, C. Fischer CM7989)	Leontovich-Wilhousky

Mixed Chorus

II

Caroling, Caroling (SA, Insts., Shawnee E-74)	Burt-Ades
Glad Tidings Bringing (SA, Skidmore SK-4019)	Arr. Kirk
This Little Babe (Ceremony of Carols) (SSA, Boosey & Hawkes 5138)	Britten
Now It Is Christmas Time (SSA, Augsburg TC17)	Arr. Pooler

Girls' Chorus

III

The Holy and the Ivy (CCB, Cambiata Press L97688)	Arr. Collins
Medley for Christmas (CBB, Cambiata Press U978115)	Arr. Stiltman
Christmas Hymn (TTBB, G. Schirmer 1414)	Arr. Jungst

Boys' Chorus

IV

What You Gonna' Call Yo' Pretty Little Baby (SSA, Schott 334)	Arr. Ehret
Love Came Down at Christmas (SSA, Kjos 6184)	Arr. Duson
Still, Still, Still (SSA, Hal Leonard 08547300)	Arr. Eilers

Treble Folksingers

V

Sing We All Noel! (Flute, SATB, Flammer A-6122)	Besig
Mary Had a Baby (SACB, Cambiata Press S117210)	Penninger
The Friendly Beasts (SATB, G. Schirmer 8714)	Arr. Downing
Carol of the Drum (SATB, B. F. Wood 568)	K. Davis

Mixed Chorus

Following is an example of a general concert for senior high school level. It is not tied to a specific season or theme and permits a wide selection of repertoire. Included is a group of Renaissance music of sacred text, as well as music from the Baroque, Classic, and Contemporary periods. Some folk and spiritual settings are included.

I

Cantate Domino (SATB, Bourne 2737-6)	Hassler
Call to Remembrance (SATB, Gray GCME 1751)	Farrant
Adoramus Te (SATB, E. C. Schirmer 2985)	Palestrina
Almighty and Everlasting God (SATB, Oxford 36)	Gibbons

Concert Choir

II

He is Good and Handsome (SSAA, Bourne ES9A)	Passereau
Now Is the Month of Maying (SSA, Bourne B237008-353)	Morley
Laudamus Te (Gloria) (SA, Walton W5014)	Vivaldi
Alleluia (SSA, Flammer B-5002)	Mozart
How Excellent Is Thy Name (SSA, Bourne 205765-354)	Butler

Girls' Chorus

III

Early One Morning (SATB, Presser 332-15147)	Arr. Cain
Charlottown (SATB, J. Fischer 8136)	Arr. Bryan

I Bought Me A Cat (SATB, Boosey & Hawkes 5024)	Arr. Copland-Fine
Plenty Good Room (SATB, Kjos 1003)	Arr. Smith

Mixed Chorus

IV

I Thought That Love Had Been a Boy (SSATB, E. C. Schirmer 653)	Byrd
Come Again, Sweet Love (SATB, E. C. Schirmer 420)	Dowland
Madrigals Three (SATB, C. Fischer CM7799)	Diemer
My Heart Doth Beg You'll Not Forget (SATB, E.C. Schirmer 1145)	Di Lasso

Madrigal Singers

V

Good Fellows Be Merry (TTBB, Boston 12065)	J. S. Bach
My Lord, What a Morning (TTBB, Colombo NY 1713)	Arr. Burleigh
Sing for Joy (TTBB, Hinshaw HMC-517)	Pote
Brothers, Sing On! (TTBB, J. Fischer 6927)	Grieg

Boys' Chorus

VI

Soon I Will Be Done	Arr. Dawson
Nun Danket Alle Gott (SATB, Brass, R. King 604)	Pachelbel

Concert Choir

The following concert program example uses fewer, but longer works for a senior high school concert choir of mixed voices. These short works may include complete works, choral suites, or choral excerpts from larger works.

Part I

Three Choruses from Elijah (G. Schirmer)	Mendelssohn

He, Watching Over Israel

Cast Thy Burden Upon the Lord (Quartet sung by chorus)
Be Not Afraid

Part II

Six Chansons (SATB unaccompanied, Schott   Hindemith
A504-A509)

The Doe
A Swan
Since All Is Passing
Springtime
In Winter
The Orchard

Part III

Gloria (SATB Chorus, Brass, Percussion,   Rutter
Organ, Oxford Press)

Allegro vivace
Andante (with Soprano Solo)
Vivace e ritmico

The fourth type of concert program is that of singing a single multimovement extended work which may include soloists and instrumental accompaniment. The following extended works are useful for high school singers to expand interests and endurance. Style features may be stressed with each work.

Schubert. *Mass in G* (G. Schirmer)
Britten. *Ceremony of Carols* (SATB or SSA, Oxford)
Bach. *For Us A Child Is Born* (Galaxy)
F. J. Haydn. *Missa St. Nicolai* (Faber Music Co.)
R. Thompson. *Testament of Freedom* (SATB or TTBB, E. C. Schirmer)
R. V. Williams. *Fantasia on Christmas Carols* (Galaxy)

See Appendix I for additional extended choral works.

PREPARING CHORUSES FOR CONCERTS

If a choral concert is to be effective, a certain amount of preconcert planning is necessary.

Preconcert Planning

Once the groups and individual pieces have been chosen and sequentially ordered for a concert, the director needs to attend to (1) performance date finalization, (2) reserving the auditorium for concert and final rehearsals, (3) printing the programs, (4) printing tickets if admission is charged, (5) planning the publicity, (6) sending complimentary tickets and letters of invitation to selected people, (7) staging the performance, and (8) securing ushers.

The performance date, in most cases, will have been set the preceeding spring or summer. The director must be sure that the date is relatively free of any conflicting school or community events. Attendance should be maximized. It is always good to recheck the date in the school office to see that no other problems have arisen since the initial securing of the date. This holds true for all performance dates over the school year. The auditorium should be reserved for the performance, as well as for final rehearsals. If the gym is used for the concert, the custodians must set up chairs, risers, and piano. They will need a diagram for this purpose and the total number of folding chairs required. If a microphone is required, its location should be specified on the diagram. The director or stage crew can supply any stands or chairs needed by performers. If a portion of the front chairs needs to be reserved to seat choral ensembles, they should be so marked and ushers informed.

Printed programs make a lasting impression on the audience. Sometimes a zeroxed copy of a typed original will suffice, or perhaps mimeographed programs. The school vocal budget will need to allow for the printing of programs. The director must be careful to include names of superintendent, school principal, soloists, accompanists, assisting faculty, and choir names on the program with correct spelling. Proofread to be sure the copy is correct before printing. Tickets may be required if admission is to be charged. Each school has a policy with regard to charging admission. Be careful to follow these guidelines.

For a concert to be successful, it needs to be advertised. The school newspaper is one source of value in informing other students about the choir concert. The director may send two or more news articles to the local newspaper two weeks, one week, and two days before the concert. Including a picture of one or two choral ensembles will catch the attention of townspeople. Posters may be placed in local shops and on school bulletin boards. The local radio stations or television stations may also present newscasts or interviews with the director for airing prior to performance.

Complimentary tickets and letters of invitation may be mailed to the superintendent, principal, other teachers, community music teachers, directors in nearby schools, church choir directors and organists, and civic club presidents. Each contact will help advertise the event and indicate thoughtfulness on the part of the director.

Staging the performance requires the help of a stage crew to handle lighting, sound, curtain, ventilation, scenery changes, riser set-up, piano, stands, and chairs. If several students will be seen by the audience while stage changes are made, the director should specify the dress. Dark trousers and light sport shirts, and dark socks and shoes will create a uniformity and dignity to these student-helper appearances. Laughter can result if this detail is not handled properly. The crew needs to meet with the director and mark on the programs when specific stage events are to occur. Curtain pulling needs to be practiced. Changes between choral groups must be done quickly and quietly.

Frequently, the school has an usher's club which handles all programs or concerts at the school. If not, the director can select several singers. The ushers will hand out programs, greet the audience, and seat them. Any reserved seating areas intended for choral groups or special guests should be clearly marked or roped off. The ushers should be dressed uniformly and present a positive image of greeter as the audience arrives. They should return all unused programs to a box in the choral rehearsal room after the concert.

Concert Manners: Chorus and Audience

School audiences, although appreciative of the student's work, are frequently not the most polite. Similarly, choral singers need to know how to act when in front of an audience.

Strongly enforced rules need to be laid down for the choral members of each ensemble. Proper stage deportment includes moving on and off stage quietly and quickly. Students must know the order of rows to move onto risers. Usually, the front row enters first, followed by the fourth, third, and second rows. The first row thus helps hide the other rows climbing into position on choral risers. This is important if no curtain is used. The singers must focus always on the conductor throughout the concert. If something unusual occurs, the chorus should not acknowledge this to the audience, but continue the performance as usual. Making faces, chewing gum, waving to friends or parents is "out." If choir robes and stoles are worn, they must be neatly pressed and properly worn. The chorus must learn how to group "bow" at the conductor's signal. Soloists and accompanists must come forward to bow upon the conductor's indication. Any distractions by chorus members during a performance must be eliminated to hold the proper mood and audience's attention.

Often school assemblies are noisy and students must be informed of what is expected of the audience. The principal or director can do this with a few well chosen words from the microphone prior to beginning the assembly program. Students can be quite rude with their own peers at times. "Whistling and cat calls," rather than applause, must not be permitted. The director should stop the performance until the audience is quiet and respectful.

Parents can also cause confusion and noise at evening concerts. Although the program may contain four or five choral ensembles, some parents will attempt to leave when their son or daughter's group has completed singing. This practice should be stopped by an announcement in the program and enforced by the director and ushers. Information about applaud points may be announced. Parents often bring children who are too young to appreciate the choral concert, and who tend to become rowdy. The director can hold up the performance until the proper concert atmosphere is attained for singing. Music is meant to be heard and requires a formal atmosphere to appreciate the fine points of performance.

A Concert Checklist

A basic concert preparation checklist as shown in Fig. 11–1 will help the director ascertain that all tasks are completed at specific times.

CHORAL FESTIVALS

Typically, festivals refer to singer get-togethers where numerous singers meet together and rehearse for a day or two under a guest conductor. The festival climaxes in a public performance. They are held at children's level, junior high level, and senior high level. Some of these are statewide or district in nature, where others may be city-wide events. If the singers are well prepared with the music beforehand, they can benefit from working under an outstanding conductor. Instead of learning notes of parts, they can be challenged to interpret each piece of music well.

Types of Festivals

There are two basic types of choral festivals. One type involves the entire choir from several schools in rehearsal and performance. These are usually held at local or district level. Each choir prepares two or three selections to perform individually, and several pieces to be rehearsed under a guest conductor in a massed choir situation. Six to seven choirs make a splendid festival. These festivals work best when the level of performance of all participating choirs is similar. The large chorus repertoire should offer a challenge, but should be within each ensemble's individual performance abilities. This festival is of value especially to the average singer in the ensembles, the singer who would probably not be chosen to participate in an auditioned festival.

A second type of festival rewarding for the best singers is popular from local to state level. The All-State Festivals held in most states are examples of this type of festival. Students must be selected from individual ensembles.

Selected Chorus Participants

Selection of choral students for festivals varies from area to area. Sometimes each local director recommends his best singers, and a panel of directors select the festival chorus on the basis of these recommendations and achieving a balance of choral parts. Each school is represented, therefore. The director must be very professional in recommending only qualified students or the quality of the festival will deteriorate.

The most widely used method of selecting festival singers is the audition method. Students are given music to rehearse, and on a specified day and time, attend area auditions at some central location. The students may be auditioned as mixed quartets or on an individual basis. Auditions seem to best guarantee the best singers will be chosen. After the students are selected, it is important that they learn their choral parts well. Each individual director must schedule out-of-school rehearsals with the singers selected.

A CONCERT CHECKLIST FORM

Place _____   Ensembles: _____

Date _____   _____

Time _____   _____

Accompanists: _____   _____

_____   _____

Assistant Conductors: _____ _____

Pre-concert Plans:

   Printed Programs Date: _____

   News Releases: Newspaper _____   Printed _____

               Radio _____   Reviewed _____

               TV _____   Viewed _____

   Posters: Students _____ _____ Date _____

   School Newspaper: _____ Date _____

   Ticket Printing: _____ Date _____

   Piano Tuning: _____ Date _____

Concert Needs:

   Piano _____   Ticket Takers _____

   Risers _____   Programs _____

   Chairs _____   Curtains _____

   Music Stands _____   Lighting _____

   Microphone System _____   Taping _____

   Conductor's Stand _____   Platforms _____

Diagram of Stage Set-Up: Apparel _____

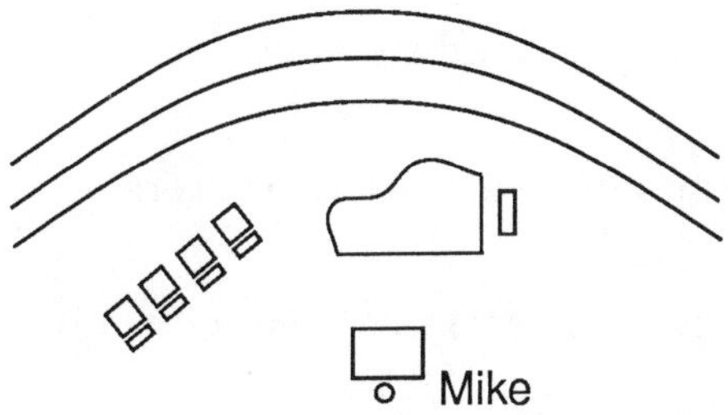

Seating (if folding chairs):

_____

_____

_____

_____

Mike

Figure 11–1 A Concert Checklist Form

Very often music of greater complexity is selected for this select type of festival, because of the higher caliber of singers, and because the size permits singing some grandiose works. Even though the best singers are involved, they have never sung together and will have a limited amount of rehearsal time. There is little time for "maturation" and parts must be well learned ahead of the festival. Some groups call this select group of singers an Honors Choir. Selection for the privilege and honor of singing in it can be a goal toward which each singer can aim.

CHORAL CONTESTS

Contests are musical experiences where either large choral ensembles, small vocal ensembles, or soloists compete against each other, or against a standard of excellence for a rating. Most often judges rate the ensembles or soloists against an unwritten standard, which means that more than one ensemble may receive a superior rating. Each state has area or district contests, then a regional, and finally a state contest. Some have only regional and state contests, while others have only a state contest. Very often choirs are categorized by the size of school, in order to make the competition more equal. The rating the choir received in its own state association contest is also used for contests involving several states. Choirs receiving Division I ratings in state association contests would compete against each other, and the outstanding choir selected from this group. Sometimes prize money is offered to winning choirs; however, not all states permit accepting money. It is best to know your own state's governing association's rules before entering the contest.

Strengths and Weaknesses of Contests

Contests have been a controversial subject for some time in music education. Directors need not participate in contests, and probably should not until the ensembles have achieved a musical level sufficient to compete. A continuous string of unsuccessful contest results has a demoralizing effect upon the singers and conductor. As for all performances, the choir should be prepared to sing its best.

Some contest strengths include the following:

1. motivation to perform at a higher level
2. opportunity to hear similar ensembles and compare how they rank
3. opportunity to be critiqued constructively by an expert
4. establishment of an *esprit de corps* or winning tradition
5. preparation for competition in life
6. evaluation of the success of the choral program by administrators.

On the other hand, there are some negative factors associated with music contests which some espouse.

1. Teachers, not contests, are the real motivators.
2. Clinics allow for constructive criticism better. Contests pit directors against each other.
3. Very often contest schedules do not permit students to hear each other.
4. A school tradition of excellence creates the same spirit as a contest.
5. Fine arts competition is undesirable and better left to sports where distinct winners and losers can be determined.
6. Contests do not measure teaching. Even though the music and level of the choir have improved over several years, it may not receive a superior rating.

In spite of these positive and negative feelings about contests, they do exist and are sponsored by leading music and educational associations. If you decide to compete in contests, compete to win.

Selecting and Preparing the Literature

Before selecting music and beginning serious rehearsal for a contest, examine the rules governing the contest and be sure you understand them. After satisfying yourself with the rules, you will need to select the repertoire that your ensemble will sing. Some contests will utilize a "required" number and a selected number. Sometimes pieces must be chosen from published lists of the organization. Most contests give the conductor the freedom to choose one or two pieces to perform.

There is a difference between selecting music for your school concerts and for contests. You may have a great diversity of type and difficulty level on your school concerts. Some pieces will have been selected for an educational reason. Some of these pieces are not "sure things."

When selecting music for a contest, the director should try to present the ensemble in the best light. It may be possible to pick pieces from those chosen for the spring concert if the director is careful. Usually a director will choose several works for the spring concert with contest performance in mind. This will relax the choir some and permit a public performance of the contest pieces before the contest itself. The following considerations apply:

1. Select music that the judges will respect as being worthy of performance. Avoid popular tunes or Broadway show tunes.
2. Do not overchallenge the ensembles for the contest performance. Avoid experimentation and stay fairly close to the style of music with which your students are familiar. Students are under much pressure in a contest and need to feel comfortable with the music to be performed.
3. Select music that shows off your group to best advantage. Maximize the strength of your group and minimize the weaknesses. If the tenors are weak, choose music with an easier tenor line. Avoid exposing weak sections.
4. If there are range problems in any part, the piece is best avoided.

5. Avoid transposing the piece up or down, without indicating this on the judge's copy of the music. Voice ranges may not be improved.

6. Avoid divided parts. Difficulty is not the standard in the contest, but quality is.

7. The work should not be too long. Perform two pieces of contrasting styles (sometimes required). There could be one sacred and one secular work, or two works in contrasting tempi. One could be in a foreign language and the other in English. Be sure any foreign language pronunciation is correct.

8. Avoid too much repetition of the contest pieces in rehearsal. Overrehearsing can take the spontaneity out of the contest rendition.

For small ensembles, the students are frequently chosen from the concert choir. This may be made a rule for any participation in small ensembles; it is a requirement in some states. The director can encourage students to audition for the small ensembles. This is good for morale and often exposes hidden talent within the choir.

Some voices will blend well in a large ensemble, but not a small one. Directors should enter only those small ensembles that can represent the school well. Enter only those groups you can personally rehearse. The first type of small ensemble to enter in contests would probably by the mixed octet, girls' sextet, boys' octet, and madrigal group. With two voices on a part there is greater confidence. Mixed quartet, girls' trio, girls' quartet, and boys' quartet should be entered in contests only when there is sufficient talent to justify these groups.

In selecting music for small ensembles, music usable with a large ensemble may not be suitable. A highly dramatic and vocally demanding piece does not fit the small ensemble. Divisi repertoire should be avoided. Basically, the director needs to be more conservative in choosing music for small ensembles. There is greater pressure in small groups.

Contest rehearsals should start at least five or six weeks prior to the contest. Two half-hour rehearsals on contest music per week is ideal. Check the students' schedules and select those who are free to prepare for the contest. A fine singer who is unable to attend all rehearsals will hurt the ensemble. Many students will be in several ensembles, as well as solo events.

There is a need to secure fine student or adult accompanists for all the ensembles and solos. More than one ensemble has had its rating suffer at the hands of a weak accompanist. Often the director may accompany some small ensembles and solos. All pieces should be memorized for choral and solo contests, in most cases. Sometimes memorization is required. It is important to instill confidence in each small ensemble and soloist. Some soloists are studying privately with a voice teacher and will be coached by their teacher for the contest. The director, however, should make the decision as to which soloists will compete, since they represent the school and the director.

Be sure all participants know the time and place of their particular contest events and where the warm-up area is. Advise them to rest the night before and not to tire themselves on the contest day. Instruct the participants of school departure time, how they will travel, and what they are to wear. The director or representative of each ensemble should provide the judge with a copy of the music to be sung by each ensemble and soloist. Sometimes, there are conflicts between instrumentalists and singers, but these can be resolved beforehand with some cooperative vocal and instrumental teachers.

OTHER MOTIVATING EXPERIENCES

In addition to concerts, festivals, and contests, there are other choral activities appropriate to junior and senior high school students.

Exchange Concerts and Tours

With exchange concerts, the director takes a choral group(s) to a nearby school to perform, often at an assembly during the school day. That school's chorus group(s) then visits your school in reciprocal fashion to present a concert. If it is possible to sing for the entire student body of a school, this is desirable. If not, the chorus may perform only for the other choir(s) at the school. It may be possible for both directors to prepare several pieces to perform jointly at both schools. This doubles the size of the group and allows for a bigger choral sound. It is also good to have the senior high school ensembles perform at the junior high school in the same district, since the future choir members are in the junior high. Junior high choirs should perform for elementary schools to demonstrate good choral singing to prospective choir members and the school population at large. These are good recruiting endeavors.

Although choir tours are difficult to arrange, these may be organized by a director to provide additional motivation and experiences for the students. Decisions will have to be made as to the length of the tour, absences from school classes, the stopover route, financial support, and supervision. Adult chaperones, both male and female, should be recruited to assist the director with the trip.

Tours may be as short as three days or extended into several states. The overseas tour to European countries is popular presently and is frequently done in the summer months. Professional tour companies exist to help the director arrange such a tour to one or several countries.

For a three- to five-day tour, planners should get out a map and try to arrange concerts no farther than two hundred miles apart. Too much travel will fatigue the singers. Personal contacts with other choir directors in these communities will be helpful in setting up a schedule of concerts. The host schools, churches, or community groups which sponsor the concert should be asked to feed and house choir members, director, accompanist, and chaperones in individual homes. Staying at motels is very expensive. Young people enjoy the companionship afforded by host families, and a warm breakfast to start the day is invigorating. Singers should leave personally-signed thank you notes with each host family.

The host for each concert along the tour route should advertise the concert. The director of the touring ensemble should provide a newspaper release, pictures, and posters for the use of the host. Each concert should be advertised for several weeks in advance.

Chartering a bus with air-conditioning, storage space, and an experienced driver is the major expense for the tour. If funds are not available through the school, various fund raising activities may be conducted. These include a car wash, talent show, card sale, fruit or candy sale, and a paid concert at school. If monies appear short, it may be necessary to assess each singer a specified amount. Certain service clubs in the community will often lend financial support to such a tour.

Choir parents should understand the requirements of the tour and sign a letter of support for the tour. Parents should also agree to provide transportation home if any singer acts irresponsibly and has to leave the tour. The letter should also empower the director to act in the parents' behalf in case a singer should require hospital care during the tour.

In addition to chaperone assistance, choir section leaders or officers should be given responsibiliy for checking the role, moving equipment, making en route decisions, and giving guidance to the group. Peer pressure can be positive, and youth will provide leadership when trusted to be part of the decision-making process.

Commissioning a Choral Work

Performing a new choral work commissioned by the choir and composed by a notable choral composer can be very stimulating to a well-established choir program. Sometimes the singers will know a particular composer through the singing of some of their published works. Some composer may live nearby. This person may be asked to write a piece for four-part mixed voices (accompanied by piano or unaccompanied) for a set fee, to be ready by a specific date. This type of project is not undertaken yearly, but is often done to mark an anniversary of the school or for singing at a convention appearance of the choir. The composer must have a good understanding of the choir's singing abilities so as not to undershoot or exceed the capacities of the singers. The composer may be invited to direct the performance of the piece if this seems practical or desirable.

Singing at Professional Meetings

When a choir has achieved a significant performance level and performed an extensive literature of quality music, it is frequently invited to sing at state, division, and national conventions, such as those of the American Choral Directors Association and Music Educators National Conference. This is a distinct honor and responsibility not to be taken lightly. The choir must uphold the highest standards of literature chosen and highest performance level possible. The audience is a very elite group of musicians-directors. Also, the junior or senior high school's reputation as a whole is "on the line" to say nothing of the director's reputation among his colleagues.

Such appearances at conventions require wise selection of music for a twenty to thirty-minute concert. Sometimes the director will be asked to present a choral interest session, using the choir as the demonstration vehicle. Such sessions must be carefully planned.

Sponsoring a Choral Clinic

A choral clinic can be valuable to junior and senior high school choral ensembles. A clinician with an outstanding choral conducting record may be invited to your school to rehearse one or several of your choral ensembles. Clinics allow this person to work with your singers and to critique their work and level of accomplishment.

One of the better types of clinics is one that permits the clinic to be held on a school day, with students released from classes, when necessary, to attend the clinic sessions. This requires the cooperation of principal and teachers who must understand the value of such an experience. The schedule for the day should be held as closely as possible to the normal school schedule. Hopefully, this clinician would work with your concert choir for two hours and one hour each with your girls' chorus, mixed chorus, and boys' chorus.

If the previous schedule cannot be arranged, a half day clinic, or a clinic on Saturday might work. A clinic could begin after classes are dismissed for the school day. This after school rehearsal would consist of a one hour and a half clinic, an evening meal for participants at school, and a two-hour rehearsal in the evening. Only one or two ensembles should be utilized for this type of schedule.

A Saturday clinic may involve one choir or several choirs. Students often work on Saturdays, however, and would need much advance notice. Then too, students tend to take events held during in-school time with more seriousness. For a Saturday clinic, several choirs may be involved, or perhaps, just the concert choir for a Saturday morning clinic. This select group can benefit most by the clinician's suggestions.

Whatever time is chosen, a clinician should not be invited to the school until the students know the notes of their parts well. However, the clinic should not be held too close to a concert date or contest date. The students should feel free to respond to the clinician's suggestions. While the clinician rehearses the ensembles, the school director should observe and jot down all items of interest and questions to ask the clinician. It is also beneficial to record the sessions for later playback and evaluation. Following the clinic, the director and clinician go to lunch or dinner and discuss the performance suggestions or problems encountered during the clinic.

The clinician should be able to expand the musical understanding of the choirs, should have experience with junior and senior high school choirs, and be able to analyze their performance, and suggest corrections or improvements. The director must prepare his students to accept changes, such as tempi and dynamics, diction alterations, and style interpretation. Following the clinic, the director can pursue the suggestions of the clinician with the choirs.

Sometimes a choral director may work with the choir of a neighboring school district in exchange for a visit of that school's director to work with the host choir. It is always desirable to observe other directors rehearsing. At festivals and conventions it is valuable to observe a director in an "open rehearsal." This is one way we all can continue to grow professionally.

Presenting a Broadway Musical

Some directors and senior high schools wish to give the choral students an opportunity to perform an opera, operetta, or Broadway musical. If this has been a tradition at the school, the director should be prepared to direct such a performance. Some directors will prefer to present only choral concerts of higher quality literature than a musical show. There is a philosophical problem here as to whether music is an art or an entertainment. Students are usually enthusiastic about this type of vocal production and it can serve to motivate the entire choral program. Some schools present a musical every two or three years so that there may be time to prepare some larger choral works. Several high school departments, including music, drama or speech, art, and dance may need to assist in preparing a musical.

The first step is selection of a show which fits the facilities and the talents of the high school. Four major agents who handle booking of shows and rental of scores are: (1) Tams-Witmark Music Library, Inc., 560 Lexington Avenue, New York, N. Y. 10022, (2) The Rodgers and Hammerstein Theatre Library, 598 Madison Ave., New York, N. Y. 10022, (3) Music Theatre International, 810 Seventh Ave., New York, N. Y. 10019, and (4) Samuel French, Inc., 45 West 25th St. These companies will forward catalogues and on-approval scores upon request.

After studying the music, the director and selection committee must examine it for the following production difficulties:

1. stage size and space in the wings needed
2. elaborateness of the scenery
3. number of scenery changes
4. costumes and properties called for in the production
5. lighting and special effects required
6. number of scene and costume changes
7. subject matter and language used in the libretto (appropriateness for students and community)
8. possibilities for cutting and editing
9. number of principal acting/singing parts, male, female, children roles
10. worthwhile music and plot
11. cost, including materials furnished, score rental, and royalties to be paid. The music and dialogue is contained in the piano conductor score. Complete orchestra scores are usually not available.

Music and dialogue are shipped, often three months prior to the performance. If more time is needed an additional rental charge is made. One prompt book is supplied, with additional ones for rent. A stage manager's guide can be obtained. It contains prompt book, vocal score containing plots, stage directions, diagrams of scenes, groupings, and other details. A book of choreography plots is not always available, but it may be rented for certain musicals for a fee. Usually, twenty-five chorus books are provided for soprano, alto, tenor, and bass. Additional choir books may be rented. Sometimes vocal scores are provided for the singing characters; however, these are usually purchased.

Dialogue parts for speaking characters are provided. Orchestra parts include one stand of each of the wind parts, two stands of first violin, and one stand of second violin, viola, cello, and bass. Orchestra parts are shipped one month prior to the performance date. Extra parts may be rented for a fee. The rentee pays all mail and express charges on packages both ways. The royalty cost depends upon the size of the auditorium, price of tickets, number of performances, and the dates selected. Rights to radio broadcast or telecast are not included in the royalty fee. To determine total costs of producing the musical, the director must add up the royalty cost, rental of orchestrations, cost of scores, lights, costumes, property, scenery, advertising costs, and printing of tickets and programs. A budget must be approved by the school administration before ordering any materials.

Tryouts must be held to select the singing/speaking roles. It is wise to teach selected solos from the show to the whole chorus to develop enthusiasm and to discover talent. Announce the tryout times and make the music and speaking parts available to those interested. A selection committee, composed of a dramatics teacher, an English teacher, home economics teacher, dance instructor, and another interested teacher needs to be formed. During tryouts the committee should consider each candidate on the basis of singing and speaking voice, dramatic flair, suitability for the part, dependability, and cooperation. Some understudys may also be selected. The cast should then be announced and placed on the bulletin board. The chorus will often have a significant part in certain chorus scenes. Some of these involve choreography.

The vocal music teacher is usually the overall general director. This person is in charge of chorus, soloists, accompanists, and orchestra. A stage manager will handle details of carpentry work (school shop), scenery crew, costumes (with home economics teacher), and properties. A drama or speech teacher will handle speaking roles. Sometimes a physical education teacher has a dance background and can work with choreography. A dance teacher from the community may assist. It is best to select a faculty business manager to handle finances, advertising, publicity, tickets, programs, and ushers.

The principal singers may be rehearsed separately, and the chorus rehearsed during regular school rehearsal hour. Availability of the stage and other rehearsal areas must be determined and these rehearsal areas scheduled. To have a well-polished musical may require forty to seventy hours of rehearsal. At least ten weeks before the performance, call the complete cast and production crew together and pass out a complete rehearsal schedule. Call for the student to memorize immediately and set deadlines for completing specific portions of dialogue and music.

The staging of the musical is best left to a drama coach who understands placement of properties, solo characters, and choral and dance groups on stage. The vocal teacher should not attempt to manage the many details of staging. Movement on the stage must be carefully planned. Two or three weeks before the performance, rehearsals should be conducted with the scenery in place. Allow for all persons not on stage at a given time to have an area or room available. Prior to the final rehearsal, time the production, including all scene and costume changes.

By the final dress rehearsal, all tickets and money should be turned in by the students, programs should be available, and ushers ready for the actual performance. At the final rehearsal, the students should become accustomed to acoustics, lights, costumes, and moving of properties and scenery. Performers must know exact order of performance. A balance between singers, piano, or orchestra must be sought. The accompaniment must be clearly heard by the soloist and chorus. The orchestra will be in the pit in front of the stage.

For the performance of the musical, the director must arrive an hour before the performance to check that everything is still in place, lights are turned on and ventilation adequate. Ticket sellers and takers must be in place, printed programs and ushers ready. Check to see if the stage crew is ready with lights, sound, and curtain. Test on stage spotlights and public address system. Instruments must be tuned to the piano. Chorus, leads, and dancers are properly costumed and made-up. Faculty assistants backstage must be at their posts in rehearsal rooms and make-up rooms. Prompters should be in place. The director should carefully check if all music is in sequential order on the conductor's stand. Ushers will close the auditorium doors when the musical begins and allow no one to enter during a number until it has ended. Students will not talk backstage or make other noises. When on stage, soloists and choir will keep an eye on the conductor for all signals and direction.

The conductor should acknowledge applause in a gracious manner. Give the soloists and choir credit. Have the entire cast come forward at the end of the musical in order of importance with the important leads acknowledged last. After the performance, a clean-up committee may straighten up the stage and rehearsal rooms. The director should promptly return all rented materials. Congratulate the students for making the show a success, and send thank-you notes to every person who assisted in any way. Deposit the money and pay all bills, preparing a report for the school administration. Appendix O lists books on music theater and gives addresses of companies for costumes, scenery, and make-up.

The Madrigal Dinner

The Madrigal Dinner has become a popular event for both high school and university chorus singers. Sometimes called a Christmas Madrigal Dinner or a Renaissance Dinner, it is popular with both the audience and performers. People will attend this event who may never attend a formal choral concert. The madrigal dinner provides an opportunity to perform madrigals in an old Renaissance setting around a table during or after a pleasant dinner. The repertoire can be varied to fit the ensemble and can include quality literature. This event permits a variety of performing combinations, such as, the madrigal group of 12-20 mixed voices, quartets, duets, solos, brass ensembles, recorder consorts, harpsichord, dancers, gymnasts, jugglers, and fencers.

This type of event will require costumes, makeup, and some degree of well rehearsed staging to be effective. There is not only the problem of singing and playing music, but the additional problem of coordinating the music with the serving of the meal. One simple approach might have the madrigal enter, sing several pieces, have the meal served, and then have the madrigal sing another group of pieces and exit. This basic format probably needs to be elaborated upon to provide more interest and variety as the meal progresses. Directors should strive to keep the event as authentic as possible and not add music or dances outside the Renaissance period. Scripts are available commercially which outline the major events of a madrigal dinner. One such plan follows:

Brass ensemble or recorder consort play (perhaps alternating as guests are seated)
Brass fanfare
Madrigal enters
Lord and lady of the manor enter

Welcome and wassail toast

Group of madrigals sung (from center stage around table or at front of hall
with singers facing audience behind long table)

Recorder consort plays (or other group)

First course of dinner served

Group of madrigals sung

A dance (or several) of the period is performed

Second course of dinner served

Solos or duets (vocal or instrumental)

Brass fanfare and boar's head procession

Main course of dinner served

Dance (or jugglers, gymnasts, fencers) is performed from the period

Group of madrigals sung

Brass fanfare and serving of flaming plum pudding

Final group of madrigals sung

Madrigals, other performers exit to singing of *Silent Night* (audience joining
in singing the carol)

Brass ensemble plays as audience leaves the hall

Directors may write their own scripts and intersperse welcomes, toasts, and
introduction of events. Other pleasing touches include use of a jester, who announces
many events and visits each table during the meal; wandering minstrel singers who
accompany themselves on lute or guitar as they move from table to table; herald
trumpeters for fanfares; English style hall banners; costumed servers; appropriately
designed program; spreading of flower petals as the ladies of the madrigal enter; and
other such additions. Directors will find the following sources invaluable in presenting a madrigal dinner:

Arbeau, Thoinot. *Orchesography* (16th century dances). New York: Dover,
1966.

Adams, Douglas. *Dancing Christmas Carols*. Resource Pub., 1978.

Brandvik, Paul. *The Complete Madrigal Dinner Booke*. San Diego, CA: Curtis
Music Press, 1984. (Kit of scrips and music)

Catalog of Music for a Madrigal Dinner. Belwin-Mills Pub. Corp.

Cosman, Madelaine P. *Medieval Holidays and Festivals: A Calendar of Celebrations*. New York: Charles Scribner's Sons, 1981.

Dolmetsch, Mabel. *Dances of England and France: 1450-1600*. New York: Da
Capo Press, 1975.

Fissinger, Edwin. *The Madrigal Concert: Choral Music for the Madrigal Dinner, Renaissance Feast, and Madrigal Concert*. Milwaukee: Jensen Publications, Inc., 1981.

Haberlen, John and Stephen Rosolack. *Elizabethan Madrigal Dinners*. Champaign, IL: Mark Foster Music Co., 1978.

McKelvy, James, ed. *A Christmas Madrigal Dinner at the Home of Charles
Wesley*. Champaign, IL: Mark Foster Music Company, 1980. (Rental
Production)

Munrow, David. *Instruments of the Middle Ages and Renaissance*. New York: Oxford University Press, 1976.

Morley, Thomas. *Plain and Easy Introduction to Practical Music*. New York: W. W. Norton and Company, 1973.

Scott, K. Lee, ed. *Madrigals for Christmas*. New York: Carl Fischer, Inc., 1987. (Includes choral music, accompanying instrument parts for trumpets, trombones, violin, viola, cello, and soprano-alto-tenor recorders)

Appendixes

A. TWO-PART OCTAVOS (SA or TB)

Sacred

Atwood, Thomas. *Teach Me, O Lord.* E. C. Schirmer 1576

Bach, J. S.-Kjelson. *Alleluia! Sing Praise to the Lord.* Belwin 2020

Bach, J. S. *Der Herr Segne Euch* (Cantata #196). C. F. Peters 6079

Bach, J. S.-Fargo, M. *Jesu, Be Thou Here Beside Us.* Kendor 4319

Bach, J. S. *Ten Tod* (Cantata #4). Belwin 2131

Bach, J. S.-Lefebvre. *Jesu, Joy of Man's Desiring.* Galaxy 1.223.1

Bach, J. S.-Bambton. *My Heart Ever Faithful* (Cantata #68). Presser 312-40474

Bach, J. S.-Holler, John. *Now Thank We All Our God.* Gray 1206

Bach, J. S.-Davis, K. *Sheep May Safely Graze.* Galaxy 1280

Bach, J. S. *Wie Will Ich Mich Freuen.* E. C. Schirmer 2507

Beethoven, Ludwig van-Glaser. *The Heavens Are Telling.* E. C. Schirmer 1980

Beethoven, Ludwig Van-Davis, K. *O God, Thy Goodness Reacheth Far.* E. C. Schirmer 1569

Bortniansky, D.-Ehret. *Cherubim Song No 7.* Pro Art 1537

Bouman. *Behold the Lamb of God.* Concordia 98-1088

Boyce, William-Kirk, T. *Alleluia.* Pro Art 2381

Braz. *Three Hebrew Psalms* (No 3). Belwin 2284

Butler, Eugene. *Praise the Lord of Heaven.* Sacred Music Press S-5711

Buxtehude, D. *Zion Hort Die Wachter Singen.* E. C. Schirmer 538

Carter, John. *The Shepherd Psalm.* Hope A555

Casals, Pablo. *Hymn to the Virgin.* Tetra/A. Broude 138-4

Couperin, F.-Jewell. *Be Joyful in the Lord.* Concordia 98-1734

Crotch, William. *Comfort, O Lord, the Soul of Thy Servant.* E. C. Schirmer 1005

Davis, Katherine K., arr. *Ye Watchers and Ye Holy Ones.* E. C. Schirmer 1581

Decius-Davis. *To God on High Be Thanks and Praise.* E. C. Schirmer 1577

Dvorak, Antonin-Jewell. *I Will Sing New Songs of Gladness.* World Lib. ESA-1718-2

Elgar, Edward. *Aspiration.* Boston 721

Farrant, Richard. *Lord, For Thy Tender Mercies' Sake.* E. C. Schirmer 1013

Faure, Gabriel. *Ave Verum.* E. C. Schirmer 860

Faure, Gabriel. *Holy, Holy, Holy* (Requiem). H. T. FitzSimons 5017

Franck, Cesar. *O Lord Most Holy* (Panis Angelicus). Belwin 1971

Goemanne, N. *I Have Touched the Face of God.* Kjos 107

Gregor, Christian-Latrobe. *O Shepherd of Israel.* Brodt Music 1005

Handel, G. F.-Koppitz. *Angels Ever Bright and Fair* (Theodora). E. C. Schirmer 1038

Handel, G. F.-Hopson. *Come, Jesus, Holy Son of God.* Flammer A-5623

Handel, G. F.-Warren. *Daughter of Zion Now Rejoice.* E. C. Schirmer 1956

Handel, G. F.-Hopson. *O Lord, In Thee We Put Our Trust.* Flammer A-5703

Handel, G. F.-McKinney. *Thanks Be to Thee.* J. Fischer 8827

Haydn, F. J.-Davies. *Achieved Is the Glorious Work.* Oxford E-111

Haydn, F. J.-Davis, K. *The Spacious Firmament* (Creation). E. C. Schirmer 1829

Hopson, Hal. *The Gift of Love.* Hope CF148

Horman, John. *Come, Play Upon Thy Harp.* Choristers Guild A-221

Jacob, Gordon, arr. *Brother Jamse's Air.* Oxford OCS 166

Jothen, Michael. *Joyful, Joyful Jubilate* (Flute, Bells). Coronet CP284

Kocher, Conrad-Howorth, W. *For the Beauty of the Earth.* Belwin 1531

Laland. *I Will Praise Thee, O Lord.* Elkan-Vogel 1238

Marcello, B.-Weinhorst. *Oh Hold Thou Me Up.* Concordia 98-1046

Mendelssohn, Felix-Glaxer. *He, Watching Over Israel* (Elijah). E. C. Schirmer 1979

Mendelssohn, Felix-Riegger. *How Lovely Are the Messengers.* Flammer 86068

Mendelssohn, Felix. *Lift Thine Eyes.* Oxford OM14

Mozart, W. A.-Riegger. *Alleluia* (Exsultate, Jubilate). Flammer 86046

Mozart, W. A. *Ave Verum.* E. C. Schirmer 484

Mozart, W. A.-Heinrich. *Today with Loud Rejoicing.* Boston 3117

Mueller, arr. *Sing Hallelujah, Praise the Lord.* G. Schirmer 10754

Paulus, Stephen. *Hear My Words.* Hinshaw HMC-201

Pergolesi, G. *Stabat Mater.* Belwin 6375

Peeters. *The Lord's Prayer.* C. F. Peters 6202

Pfautsch, Lloyd. *The Lord Is My Shepherd.* Summy Birchard 5025

Powell, Robert J. *We Give Thee Thanks Today.* Augsburg 11-2028

Purcell, Henry-Moffat. *Sound the Trumpet.* E. C. Schirmer 487

Rutter, John. *For the Beauty of the Earth* (Small Orch.) Hinshaw HMC-469

Saint-Saens-Fargo, M. *Praise Ye the Lord of Hosts* (Christmas Oratorio). Kendor 4317

Schein, H. *Ein Feste Burg Ist Unser Gott.* Abingdon 401-5

Schubert, Franz-Ehret. *Holy, Holy, Holy.* Marks MC-4127

Schutz, Heinrich. *Give Ear, O Lord.* E. C. Schirmer 2789

Sleeth, Natalie. *Amen, So Be It!* C. Fischer CM7807

Teschner-Wainrow. *All Glory, Laud, and Honor.* Choral Art R-128

Thiman, Eric. *A Hymn of Freedom.* Gray 1885

Thomson, Virgil. *My Shepherd Will Supply My Need.* Gray CMR2562

Vivaldi, A. *Laudamus Te* (Gloria). Walton 5014

Secular

Bach, J. S.-Campbell-Watson. *Three Excerpts from the Peasant Cantata.* Warner W3427

Barthelson, arr. *I Love Little Willie.* Belwin 1748

Bartok, Bela. *Don't Leave Me.* Boosey & Hawkes 1668

Berger, Jean. *A Child's Book of Beasts, Set I and II.* J. Fischer 9562, 9796

Brahms, Johannes. *Am Strande.* National WHC-99

Brahms, Johannes. *Die Schwestern.* Kjos 6166

Brahms, Johannes. *Three Love Songs.* E. C. Schirmer 1055

Britten, Benjamin. *The Ride-by-Nights.* Oxford 54.124

Britten, Benjamin. *The Ship of Rio.* Oxford OCS-170

Copland, Aaron. *What Do We Plant?* Boosey & Hawkes 1639

Copland-Swift, *Younger Generation.* Boosey & Hawkes 5506

Duson, Dede. *And You Are Not Alone.* Kjos 6170

Floyd, Carlisle. *Who Has Seen the Wind?* Boosey & Hawkes 5628

Foster, Stephen. *Some Folks.* Kjos 4207

Frackenpohl, A. *Be Like the Bird.* Kjos 6118

Frackenpohl, A. *Roll Call.* Plymouth PCS-528

Frackenpohl, A. *Three Limericks in Canon Form.* Marks 90

Hagemann. *The Mysterious Pineapple.* Presser 312-41020

Hennagin, Michael. *Three Emily Dickinson Songs.* Walton M-139

Humperdinck-Davis. *Sandman's Song and Children's Prayer* (Hansel and Gretel). E. C. Schirmer 1833

Kabalevsky-Heiberg. *One Fine Morning.* MCA Music UC-26

Persichetti, Vincent. *Dominic Has a Doll.* Elkan-Vogel 1222

Persichetti, Vincent. *Maggy and Milly and Molly and May.* Elkan-Vogel 1224

Persichetti, Vincent. *Sam Was a Man.* G. Schirmer 9791

Pinkham, Daniel. *Five Canzonets.* Associated A-329

Schumann, Robert. *Herbstlied.* National WHC-54

Schumann, Robert. *Schon Blumelein.* National WHC-61

Thompson, Randall. *Velvet Shoes.* E. C. Schirmer 2526

Folk/Spiritual

Artman, Ruth, arr. *Ready, Lord.* Hope AM6694

Bacon, arr. *Buttermilk Hill.* Boosey & Hawkes 5944

Barthelson, arr. *The Elephant and the Flea.* Belwin 1747

Barthelson, arr. *I Love Little Willie.* Belwin 1748

Catelinet, P., arr. *Down in Demarara.* Shawnee E-34

Churchill, arr. *Lolly Tu Dum.* Belwin 1630

Coates, John, arr. *Amazing Grace.* Shawnee E-102

Coates, John-Lowry, arr. *Shall We Gather at the River.* Glory Sound

Copland, Aaron. *Simple Gifts.* Boosey & Hawkes 1903

Davis, Katherine, arr. *The Deaf Old Woman.* Galaxy. 1645

Davis, Katherine, arr. *Let All Things Now Living.* E. C. Schirmer 11017

Dawson, Mark, arr. *Prayer of Thanksgiving.* Pro Art 1802

Ehret, Walter, arr. *Hava Nagila.* Frank F-2034

Ehret, Walter, arr. *Dry Bones.* Alfred

Ehret, Walter, arr. *Hol-Di-Ri-Di-A.* Spratt 190

Ehret, Walter, arr. *There's a Little Wheel A-Turnin'.* Frank Music F2032

Ehret, Walter, arr. *Spin, Spin, My Darling Daughter.* Spratt 188

Gardner, Maurice, arr. *Good News!* Staff 948

Gardner, Maurice, arr. *I'm Gonna Sing.* Staff 571

Giebel-Churchill. *Kentucky Babe*. Belwin 1836

Grier, Gene. *Gonna Get to Heaven on That Judgment Day*. Heritage H5726

Gillies, D., arr. *All Night, All Day* (Recorder, Orff Insts.). Oxford U155

Hadley, arr. *Charlie Is My Darlin'*. Pro Art 1401

Hardwick, Arthur, arr. *Great Day*. Alfred 6133

Hopson, Hal, arr. *Fill Us with Your Love* (Ghana). Agape HH3923

Howard, Ron, arr. *Oh, Won't You Sit Down?* Alfred

Howorth, Wayne, arr. *Come All Ye Lads and Lassies*. Belwin 1874

Howorth, Wayne, arr. *He's Goin' Away*. Belwin 1848

Howorth, Wayne, arr. *He's Got the Whole World in His Hands*. Belwin 1777

Howorth, Wayne, arr. *Joshua Fit De Battle Ob Jericho*. Belwin 934

Howorth, Wayne, arr. *Let Us Cheer the Weary Traveller*. Belwin 1846

Johnson, Stuart, arr. *The Gospel Train* (Recorders). Oxford T108

Kingsbury, John, arr. *Climb Up, Ye Children, Climb*. Plymouth PCS-532

Kirk, Theron, arr. *Little Wheel A-Turnin'*. Pro Art 1775

Kirk, Theron, arr. *Loch Lomond*. Belwin 1605

Kjelson, Lee, arr. *Ah Lovely Meadows*. Belwin 1901

Kjelson, Lee, arr. *At the Gates of Heaven*. Belwin 1903

Kjelson, Lee, arr. *I Walk the Unfrequented Road*. Belwin 2207

Kjelson, Lee, arr. *Jesus Walked This Lonesome Valley*. Belwin 1970

Kjelson, Lee, arr. *Standin' in the Need of Prayer*. Belwin 1902

Miller, arr. *Barbara Allen*. Chappell 0063289-351

Miller, arr. *On Top of Old Smoky*. Chappell 0063222-351

Newbury, Kent, arr. *Jesus Walked This Lonesome Valley*. Coronet CP287

Norman, Robert, arr. *Little Wheel A-Turnin'*. Staff 975

Ortlip, Stephen J., arr. *Little David*. Classic Artists CAP-10

Petker, Allan, arr. *He's Got the Whole World in His Hands*. Bock B-60384

Pitcher, G., arr. *I'm Goin' To Leave Old Texas Now*. Belwin 1835

Richardson, John, arr. *Gonna Ride Up in the Chariot*. Presser 312-41188

Ridenour, Joe, arr. *Sometimes I Feel Like a Motherless Child*. Somerset SP744

Rodby, Walter, arr. *Movin'*. Somerset Press WR 1021

Stone, Peter, arr. *Shenandoah*. Belwin 2141

Swift, F., arr. *Sweet Betsy from Pike*. Belwin 1622

Tate. *Cielito Lindo*. Oxford T72

Taylor, Deems, arr. *May Day Carol*. Belwin 54.221

Thygerson, Robert, arr. *Ev'ry Time I Feel the Spirit*. Heritage H5702

Thygerson, Robert, arr. *Sing and Shout* (Drums, Guitar). Heritage H5723

Thygerson, Robert, arr. *Walk on the Water, Peter*. Richmond TEV-73

Vance, M., arr. *There's a Little Wheel A-Turnin'*. Belwin 1898

Vance, M., arr. *Tum Balalayka*. Belwin 2055

Vaughan Williams, Ralph, arr. *Greensleeves*. Oxford T4

Verrall, John, arr. *Deep River*. Boston 11168

Willet, Pat, arr. *Joshua Fit the Battle of Jericho*. Heritage H5724

Zaninelli, Luigi, arr. *The Water Is Wide*. Shawnee E-83

Christmas

Bach, J. S.-Warren. *Beside Thy Cradle Here I Stand*. E. C. Schirmer 1938

Bach, J. S.-Davis, K. *O Jesu, So Sweet*. E. C. Schirmer 1570

Barthelson, arr. *Go Tell It on the Mountain*. Belwin 1833

Brahms-Suchoff. *A Jubilant Carol*. Fox PS-173

Binkherd, Gordon. *The Christ Child*. Boosey & Hawkes 5987

Boda. *Before the Paling of the Stars*. Concordia 98-1566

Britten, Benjamin. *The Oxen*. G. Schirmer 11637

Burt, A.-Ades. *Caroling, Caroling* (Insts.). Shawnee E-74

Burt, Alfred. *We'll Dress the House*. Shawnee E-72

Carrie, arr. *The Coventry Carol* (Oboe). T. Presser BP1007

Chass, arr. *Hanerot Halelu* (Hanukah). Mark Foster 877

Coates, John, arr. *How Far Is It to Bethlehem?* Shawnee E-160

Couperin-Jewell. *A Star Carol*. Concordia 98-1711

Davis, Katherine. *Carol of the Drum*. Belwin 64228

Davis, Katherine, arr. *The Coventry Carol*. E. C. Schirmer 1037

Davis, Katherine, arr. *Shepherds, Awake!* Warner Bros. R3488

Davis, Katherine. *Sing Gloria*. Warner R-3416

Debussy, C. *Noel Des Enfants Qui N'ant Plus De Maisons*. Durant 9418

Ehret, Walter, arr. *Although You Are So Tiny*. Lawson-Gould 51230

Ehret, Walter, arr. *Bright Star*. E. B. Marks 4407

Ehret, Walter, arr. *Carol, Sweetly Carol*. Boosey & Hawkes 5426

Ehret, Walter, arr. *Christ Is Born to You Today*. E. B. Marks 4408

Ehret, Walter, arr. *The Friendly Beasts*. G.I.A. 1889

Ehret, Walter, arr. *O Little Jesus Child*. Frank F-619

Ehret, Walter, arr. *On Bethlehem's Hill*. Frank F-615

Ehret, Walter, arr. *On Christmas Night*. Volkwein/Columbia

Ehret, Walter, arr. *On the Very First Christmas Morning*. Marks 4410

Ehret, Walter, arr. *Therefore Be Merry*. Shawnee E-147

Gordon, arr. *Jesus Christ Our Savior Is Born*. Belwin 1844

Gordon, arr. *O Come, All Ye Children*. Belwin 1720

Grieg, Edward. *A Song of Christmas.* Galleon GCS 1002

Grundman, arr. *Three Noels.* Boosey & Hawkes 5734

Hruby, Doris, arr. *Shepherds! Shake Off Your Drowsy Sleep.* Plymouth JR-506

Jacques, arr. *Patapan.* Oxford T86

Kirk, Theron, arr. *Glad Tidings Bringing.* Skidmore SK-4019

Kirk, Theron, arr. *Kling Glockchen.* Belwin PRO CH2993

Kirk, Theron, arr. *Three Carols in New Settings.* G. Schirmer 12299

Kodály, Zoltan. *Christmas Dance of the Shepherds.* T. Presser 312-40573

Kountz, Richard. *Hasten Swiftly, Hasten Softly.* Galaxy 1776-7

Kountz, Richard. *Rise Up Early.* Galaxy 1.1701.1

Krapf, arr. *While By My Sheep and Lo, How a Rose E'er Blooming.* Concordia 98-2105

Lewis, Aden, arr. *African Noel.* Plymouth PCS-501

McKelvy, James, arr. *Masters in This Hall.* Mark Foster 852

Nelson, Ronald, arr. *Lullaby, Jesus Child.* Augsburg 1316

Niles, John J., arr. *I Wonder As I Wander.* G. Schirmer 9787

Pfautsch, Lloyd. *Balulalow.* Wynn Music Pub. 2202

Pfautsch, Lloyd. *What Child Is This?* Wynn Music Pub. 2203

Pfautsch, Lloyd. *When Christ Was Born.* Wynn Music Pub. 2201

Pooler, Marie, arr. *A Child Is Born in Bethlehem.* Augsburg TC15

Pooler, Marie, arr. *O How Beautiful the Sky.* Augsburg 0918

Sleeth, Natalie. *Long Time Ago.* Sacred Music Press S-5396

Sowerby, Leo, arr. *Manger Carol.* Gray GCMR2419

Stevens, arr. *Ding-dong, Merrily on High.* Pro Art 1923

Stocker, arr. *As Lately We Watched* (Insts.). Kjos 6144

Track, G., arr. *Dear Nightingale, Awake.* Schmitt 224

Walker, W., arr. *The Little Cradle Rocks Tonight in Glory.* Concordia 98-2139

Walters, arr. *The Cuckoo Carol.* Boosey & Hawkes 5721

Wilson, arr. *Fum, Fum, Fum.* Bourne 6

B. THREE-PART OCTAVOS (SSA, SSAA)

Sacred

Anerio. *O Jesu Mi Dulcissimi.* Belwin NY2183

Arcadelt. *Ave Maria.* Bourne ES-3

Bach, J. S.-Treharne. *Jesu, Joy of Man's Desiring.* G. Schirmer 8388

Bach, J. S.-Trusler. *Praise Ye the Lord.* Plymouth TR-103

Bach, J. S. *Suscepit Israel* (Magnificat). E. C. Schirmer 813

Balakirev. *Send Out Thy Light*. Boosey & Hawkes 1924

Berlioz, Hector. *Veni Creator Spiritus*. Marks 13

Binkerd, G. *Song of Innonence*. Boosey & Hawkes 6988

Bortnianski, D. *Lo, A Voice to Heaven Sounding*. E. C. Schirmer 1079

Brahms, J. *Ave Maria* (SSAA). G. Schirmer 4

Brahms, J. *Three Sacred Choruses*. Broude Bros. 136-1

Cherubini, Luigi. *Like As a Father*. Summy Birchard

Casals, Pablo. *Nigra Sum*. A. Broude 120-8

Des Pres, J. *Ave Verum*. Bourne ES 88A

Di Lasso, Orlando. *Blest Is the Man*. Augsburg PS603

Diemer, E. L. *Alleluia*. C. Fischer CM7289

Duson, Dede. *Psalm Twenty-Three* (SSAA). Kjos 6182

Farrant, Richard-Whitford. *Lord, For Thy Tender Mercies' Sake*. E. C. Schirmer 1890

Faure, Gabriel. *Tantum Ergo*. E. C. Schirmer 861

Handel, G. F.-Whitford. *Hallelujah, Amen* (Judas Macabbeus). E. C. Schirmer 1915

Ippolitov-Ivanoff. *Bless Ye the Lord*. C. Fischer 639

James, W. *Hear My Prayer*. G. Schirmer 8943

Kodály, Zoltan. *Ave Maria*. Universal 312-40592

Kodály, Zoltan. *Psalm 150*. Oxford W-72

Kremser, arr. *Prayer of Thanksgiving*. G. Schirmer 6812

Krenek. *In Paradisium*. Rongwen Bros. SRM 3510

Lassus, Orlando. *Adoremus Te, Christe* (SSSAA). E. C. Schirmer 890

Lassus, Orlando. *Hodie Apparuit in Israel*. E. C. Schirmer 1285

Lotti-Hunter. *Surely He Hath Borne Our Griefs*. Marks 4457

Mendelssohn, Felix. *Laudate Pueri*. Marks AJ81

Mendelssohn, Felix. *Lift Thine Eyes* (Elijah). T. Presser 332-00820

Mendelssohn, Felix. *Veni Domini*. A. Broude 166-10

Mozart, W. A. *Lacrymosa* (Requiem). C. Fischer CM 6325

Palestrina-Glaser. *Adoramus Te, Christe*. E. C. Schirmer 2510

Palestrina, G. *Pars Mea Dominus*. Belwin NY 2186

Pitoni. *Cantate Domino*. Flammer 89181

Poulenc, Francis. *Ave Maria* (Dialogues of the Carmelites). Ricordi

Poulenc, Francis. *Ave Verum Corpus*. Salabert RL 12532

Purcell, Henry-Davis. *Rejoice in the Lord Always*. E. C. Schirmer 1875

Roberton, H. *All in the April Evening*. G. Schirmer 9564

Saint-Saen, Camille. *Praises Ye the Lord of Hosts*. Belwin 698

Schubert, F.-Ehret. *Agnus Dei.* Marks 4598

Schubert, F. *Sanctus.* Plymouth DC-201

Tallis, T-Harris. *All Praise to Thee, My God, This Night.* Plymouth PCS-222

Thompson, Randall. *Now I Lay Me Down to Sleep.* E. C. Schirmer 1985

Victoria. *Benedictus.* Belwin NY 2040

Secular

Bach, J. S. *Three Excerpts from the Peasant Cantata.* Witmark W-3445

Bartok, Bela. *Only Tell Me.* Boosey & Hawkes 1670

Berger, Jean. *Facts.* T. Presser 312-40632

Berger, Jean. *Minnie and Winnie.* J. Fischer 9169

Berger, Jean. *The Mock Turtle's Song.* T. Presser. 312-40633

Berger, Jean. *Three Choral Pieces.* Kjos 6081

Brahms, Johannes. *Four Songs*, Op. 17. C. F. Peters

Brahms, Johannes. *Twelve Songs of Romance: Set I* (Three songs). Marks 105

Britten, Benjamin. *A New Year Carol* (Friday Afternoons). Boosey & Hawkes 5848

Diamond, David. *All in Green My Love Came Riding.* Peer-Southern Org.

Diemer, Emma Lou. *Come Hither, You That Love.* Marks MC4614

Diemer, Emma Lou. *The Shepherd to His Love.* Marks 97

Duson, Dete. *Something Beyond.* R. Dean HCB 809

Duson, Dete. *To Those Who See* (SSAA). R. Dean HCB-807

Duson, Dede. *Wild, Beautiful, and Free.* Kjos G179

Este. *How Merrily We Live.* Sam Fox EA6

Faure, Gabriel. *Apres Un Reve.* Lawson-Gould 52162

Fine, Irving. *Father William* (SSAA). Warner Bros. 2-W3204

Fine, Irving. *The Lobster Quadrille.* Warner Bros. 2-W3205

Fine, Irving. *Lullaby of the Duchess.* Warner Bros. 2-W3206

Hassler, H. L. *Come, Let Us Start a Joyful Song.* Bourne ES 74A

Hilton. *Now Is the Summer Springing.* Belwin

Hilton, T. *You Lovers That Have Loves Astray.* Marks 4333

Holst, Gustav. *Pastoral.* Stainer & Bell. Part Songs 62

Jordahl. *Sweet Day* (SSAA) Belwin 2420

Kodály, Zoltan. *Ladybird.* Boosey & Hawkes 5674

Kubik, Gail. *O Dear! What Can the Matter Be?* G. Schirmer 9995

Luboff, N. *Oh, My Love* (SSAA). Walton 5001

McCray, James. *Rise Up, My Love, My Fair One.* National WHC-44

McKelvy, James, arr. *Gute Nacht.* Mark Foster

Mennin, P. *Bought Locks*. C. Fischer CM6484

Monteverdi, C. *Ahi, Che Si Parti*. R. Dean CA-109

Morley, T. *Fire, Fire My Heart*. Bourne 9S65A

Morley, T. *Love Learns by Laughing*. Stainer & Bell MIB-23

Morley, T. *Now Is the Month of Maying*. Oxford SHM54.927

Morley, T. *O Sleep, Fond Fancy*. Marks 4216

Morley, T. *Though Philomela Lost Her Love*. SB 23

Mozart, W. A. *Mi Lagerno Tacendo*. G. Schirmer 11850

Mozart, W. A. *Five Canons* (SSSS). G. Schirmer 2620

Nelson, Ron. *He's Gone Away* (Three Mountain Ballads). Elkan-Vogel 362-03075

Passereau. *Il Est Bel et Bon* (SSAA). Bourne ES9A

Persichetti, Vincent. *This Is the Garden*. C. Fischer CM6652

Phillips. *The Hag* (SSAA). C. Fischer CM6486

Pierce, Brent. *Travelog*. Walton 2974

Poulenc, Francis. *Petite Voix*. Salabert 7

Purcell, Henry. *My Dearest, My Fairest*. Gentry G-236

Reed. *The Willow Song*. Marks MC4666

Schubert, Franz. *Two and Three-Part Choruses for Women's Voices*. C. F. Peters 4639

Schein, Heinrich. *Juchholla! Freut Euch Mit Mir!* Belwin 2465

Schumann, Robert. *Tambourinschlagerin* (SSAA). Leeds Music L-428

Smetana, Bedrich. *Three Choruses for Female Voices*. R. Dean HRD 110

Thompson, Randall. *A Girl's Garden*. E. C. Schirmer 2540-5

Vaughan Williams, Ralph. *Sigh No More, Ladies*. Oxford 54.143

Vecchi, O. *Sing, Sing a Song for Me*. Bourne ES53A

Washburn. *Scherzo for Spring*. Oxford 95P400

Weelkes, Thomas. *The Nightingale*. Bourne ES 66

Weelkes, Thomas. *Though My Carriage Be But Careless*. Sam Fox EA2

Wilbye, John. *As Fair as Morn*. Stainer & Bell. M 7-5

Wolf, Hugo. *Songs from the Morike Lieder: Er Ist's and Jagerlied*. National WHC-19

Folk/Spiritual

Allen, arr. *At the Gate of Heaven*. Summy Birchard 1570

Barthelson. *Spin, Spin*. Marks MC-4012

Bartok-Suchoff. *Three Hungarian Folk Songs*. Boosey & Hawkes 5488

Best. *Three Highland Airs*. Shawnee B-158

Boberg. *Shy Love*. Kjos 6088

Britten-Holst. *O Can Ye Sew Cushions?* Boosey & Hawkes 5213

Bryan. *Charlottown.* J. Fischer 7993

Burleigh. *Swing Low, Sweet Chariot.* Ricordi 116469

Cain. *Little David, Play on Your Harp.* Flammer 83178

Cain. *I Got Shoes.* Flammer 83206

Coates. *Parsley, Sage, Rosemary and Thyme.* Shawnee B-332

Churchill. *Johnny Has Gone for a Soldier.* Plymouth CH-200

Copland. *At the River.* Boosey & Hawkes 5512

Davis. *I Gave My Love a Pretty Little Ring.* Summy Birchard B-140

Davis. *The Soldier.* Galaxy 1.1698

Donovan. *Down By the Sally Gardens.* Galaxy 555

Duson, D. *Danny Boy* (SSAA). Kjos 6171

Frackenpohl. *Three Irish Songs.* Shawnee B-200

Gardner. *I'm Gonna Sing.* Staff 569

Grant. *Little Bird.* Belwin 1723

Guthrie-Ehret. *This Land Is Your Land.* Ludlow S-9003

Hairston. *Elijah Rock.* Bourne S1025

Hallstrom. *Three Songs from Sweden.* Shawnee B-215

Harley and Aschenbrenner. *Ifca's Castle.* C. Fischer 5223

Hays-Seeger-Leyden. *If I Had a Hammer.* Ludlow S-9011

Kodály. *Dancing Song.* Oxford 54.942

Lester. *Vreneli.* Belwin 1830

Marlowe. *Chiapanecas.* Huntzinger 2039

Niles. *The Lass from the Low Countree.* G. Schirmer 11206

Owen. *All the Pretty Little Horses.* Presser 312-40518

Palmer. *Kum Ba Yah.* Alfred 6214

Palmer. *Scarborough Fair.* Alfred 6222

Parker. *I Am in Love, I Dare Not Own It.* Hinshaw HMC457

Pfautsch. *Beautiful Yet Truthful.* G. Schirmer LG549

Row. *Czechoslovakian Dance Song.* R. D. Row 234

Scott. *Early One Morning.* Shawnee

Smith. *The Ash-Grove.* G. Schirmer 11203

Taylor. *May Day Carol.* J. Fischer 4872

Taylor. *Waters Ripple and Flow.* J. Fischer 5065

Trinkans. *When Love Is Kind.* C. Fischer 6139

Vaughan Williams. *Lindea Lea.* Boosey & Hawkes MFS219

Zaninelli. *The Water Is Wide.* Shawnee B-222

Christmas

Billings, W. *Shepherd's Carol*. H. W. Gray 3024

Boberg. *Christ Is Born*. C. Fischer 7455

Bohn, arr. *O Tannenbaum*. Kjos 6177

Burt, A. *The Alfred Burt Carols: Set I and II*. Shawnee

Britten, B. *Sweet Was the Song* (SSAA). G. Schirmer 11639

Britten, B. *This Little Babe* (Ceremony of Carols). Boosey & Hawkes 5138

Britten, B. *Wolcom Yole!* (Ceremony of Carols). Boosey & Hawkes 1755B

Butler, Eugene. *On the Nativity of Christ*. Somerset. SP727

Collins, arr. *Susanni*. C. Fischer R-6118

Costeley-Cramer. *Come, Ye Gay Shepherds*. Ed. Marks 4482

Davis, arr. *Wassail Song*. E. C. Schirmer 1066

Dello Joio, N. *A Christmas Carol* (SSAA). Marks 4323

Dello Joio, N. *The Holy Infant's Lullaby*. Ed. B. Marks 4392

Di Lasso. *Hodie Apparuit*. G. Schirmer 11783

Duson, Dede, arr. *Love Came Down at Christmas*. Kjos 6184

Ehret, arr. *He Is Born, the Child Divine*. Sam Fox CC-17

Ehret, arr. *What You Gonna Call Yo' Pretty Little Baby*. Schmitt 334

Eilers, arr. *Still, Still, Still*. Hal Leonard 08547300

Gevaert-Davis. *Slumber of the Infant Jesus*. E. C. Schirmer 1088

Hallstrom, arr. *Shepherds Awake*. Shawnee

Jungst, H. *Christmas Hymn*. G. Schirmer 9890

Kodály, Zoltan. *Angels and the Shepherds*. Universal 312-40593

Krone, arr. *Pat-a-Pan*. Kjos 1236

Lee, arr. *Japanese Christmas Carol*. H. W. Gray GCMR-2948

Malin, Don, arr. *The Call of the Shepherds*. B. F. Wood 826

Malin, Don. *Rejoice, Holy Mary*. Belwin 693

Monteverdi, C. *Angelus ad Pastores Ait and Hodie Christus Natus Est*. Mercury 352-000-24

Nunn, arr. *Bring a Torch, Jeannette, Isabella*. E. C. Schirmer 496

Pergolesi, G. *Glory to God in the Highest*. Flammer 89041

Pooler, arr. *Now It Is Christmas Time*. Augsburg TC17

Shearer, arr. *Rocking Carol*. Schmitt

Terri, Salli. *Away in a Manger*. Lawson-Gould 666

Thompson, Randall. *The Carol of the Rose*. E. C. Schirmer 2800

Vaughan Williams, R. *Lullaby*. Oxford 44.603

Zgodava, arr. *Carol of the Italian Pipers*. Shawnee B-321

C. JUNIOR HIGH MIXED CHORUS (Changing Voice Octavos)

Two-Part Mixed (SC, SB)

Artman, Ruth. *Tomorrow* (SC). Hal Leonard 08598202

Collins, Don L., arr. *Pray Tell Me* (SC). Cambiata 4117696

Collins, Don L., arr. *Wondrous Love.* Cambiata Press S97685

Cooper, Irvin, arr. *Watchman, Tell Us* (SC). Cambiata Press I979131

Ehret, Walter, arr. *It's Good Bye Liza Jane* (SC). Cambiata T981160

Ferris, William. *Gentle Mary* (SB). H. W. Gray. GCMR3311

Finzi, Gerald. *Let Us Now Praise Famous Men* (SB). Boosey & Hawkes 1919

Goodman, Joseph, arr. *Praise to the Lord* (SB) Presser 312-41220

Grancini, M. *Lord of Life, King of Glory* (SB). G.I.A. Pub. G-2357

Gelineau, Joseph. *Psalm 148* (SB). G.I.A. Pub. G-2245

Handel, G. F.-Hopson. *Blest Are They Whose Spirits Long* (SB). Choristers Guild CGA183

Handel, G. F.-Edwards. *Come, Lord, Quickly Come* (SB). Coronet CP277

Handel, G. F.-Proulx. *Keep Me Faithfully in Thy Paths* (SB). G.I.A. Pub G-2355

Handel, G. F.-Causey. *O Worship the Lord* (SB). Beckenhorst BP1235

Hughes, Miki. *Listen with an Open Mind* (SB). Lorenz 5768

Hutson, Wihla. *Not Every One* (SB). Plymouth JR-501

Hopson, Hal. *Lord of All Most Holy* (SB). Flammer EA5002

Joncas, Michael-Causey. *The Lord Is Near* (SB). Coronet CP300

Ker, Ann. *Hear This* (SB). General Words/Kjos GC55

Kirby, Charles. *Rise Up, O Youth of God* (SB). Pro Art 2570

Lovelace, Austin C. *Roundelay* (SB). Hope A478

Mendelssohn, Felix-Hopson. *The Lord Is a Mighty God* (SB). Hope A540

Moore, J. Chris. *Clap Your Hands* (SC or SB). Heritage HS700

Pergolesi, G-Hopson. *O, My God, Bestow Thy Tender Mercy* (SB). C. Fischer CM7974

Young, Carlton, arr. *Ye Servants of God* (SB). Kjos 5277

Tallis, Thomas-Cooper. *The Spacious Firmament on High* (SC). Cambiata I979132

Three-Part Mixed (SSC, SAT, SAC)

Sacred

Ashton, Bob. *Kyrie Eleison* (SSC). Cambiata Press C979125

Butler, Eugene. *Sanctus* (SAT). C. Fischer CM8156

Byrd, William-Weck. *Non Nobis Domine* (SAT). Somerset SP749

Cherubini, Luigi-Weck. *Veni Jesu* (SAT). Somerset SP754

Carter, John. *Praise the Lord* (SAT). Hope JC285

Cooper, Gwyneth, arr. *Simple Gifts* (SC, opt. B). Cambiata Press T978116

Constantini, A-Kirk. *Confitemini* (SAT). Pro Art CH3002

Davis, Katherine K. *Thanksgiving Song* (SAT). Warner W7-1009

Handel, G. F.-Taylor. *Hallelujah, Amen* (Judas Maccabeus) (SSC). Cambiata Press M17312

Hopson, Hal. *Praise the Lord with Joyful Song.* Jenson 433-16010

Kirby, Charles. *A Prayer for Right Now* (SC, opt. B). Cambiata Press L17673

Mozart, M. A.-Ehret. *Alleluia* (SSC). Cambiata Press M979124

Schubert, Franz-Weck. *Sanctus* (German Mass in F) (SAT). Somerset SP767

Thugerson, Robert, arr. *Sing and Shout* (SAT). Heritage Press HV103

Secular

Arlen-Koehler. *I've Got the World on a String* (Three Part). Belwin 6433

Artman, Ruth, arr. *O Freedom* (Three Part). Hal Leonard 08595500

Ashton, Bob. *Evening Time Melody* (SSC). Cambiata Press U483173

Avalos, A. *Sing a Happy Song* (Three Part). Pro Art 2776

Besig, Don. *Just a Little Sunshine* (Three Part). Jenson 418-10010

Butler, Eugene. *Hitch Your Dream to the Morning Star* (Three Part). Hal Leonard

Butler, Eugene. *The Best Day of My Life* (Three Part). Hal Leonard

Butler, Eugene. *River, Sing Your Song* (Three Part). Richmond TEV-54

Collins, Don L. *There Is a Ladye* (SC, opt. B). Cambiata Press ARS980152

Chapin, Harry. *Hand* (SAT, Opt. B). Silver Burdett

Eddleman, David. *Bell Toll* (SAT, Opt. B). Silver Burdett

Eilers, Joyce. *Goodbye* (Three Part). Hal Leonard 08543500

Eilers, Joyce. *Just a Bit of Sunshine* (Three Part, Guitar). Hal Leonard 085443000

Eilers, Joyce. *Risin Out of My Soul* (Three Part). Jenson 402-18010

Eilers, Joyce. *Send Down the Rain* (Three Part). Jenson 402-19030

Eilers, Joyce. *You Must Fly* (Three Part). Jenson 402-25010

Emerson, Roger. *Let Your Love Fly Free* (Three Part). Jenson 402-12030

Freed, Arnold. *Those Good Old Days* (SA, SSA, or SAB). C. Hansen C833

Gallina, Jill. *I'm A-Headin' Home* (Three Part). Jenson 415-09040

Granito, Raymond. *Sing a Happy Song* (SAT). Alfred 7037

Hoem, Jean. *We Like to Sing!* (SAT). C. Fischer CM7782

Kirkman, Terry. *Cherish* (SA, SSA, or SAB). C. Hansen C-505

Kirk, Theron. *Bring a Little Joy* (SSC). Cambiata Press A979128

Kirk, Theron. *From Scotland with Love* (Three Part). Pro Art CH3003

Mallow-Steffy. *A Smile Can Make a Difference* (SAC). Coronet CP324

Norred, Larry, arr. *I'm Comin' Back* (Three Part). Jenson 412-09020

Olson, Lynn. *Love Is the Way* (SAC). C. Fischer CM8060

Poorman, Sonja. *Footlights and Fame* (Three Part). Hal Leonard 08602855

Ramseth, Betty Ann. *Wake Up to the World of Rhythm* (Two or Three Part). Coronet CP216

Robertson, Ed. *Sing!* (Three or Four Part). Jenson 404-19010

Thygerson, Robert. *The Marching Saints* (SAT). Heritage H6504

Thygerson, Robert, arr. *Wait for Love* (Three Part). Hal Leonard 08603800

Tsuruoka, Linda. *Tomorrow's Here* (SAC). Belwin OCT2454

Van Wyatt, arr. *Ching-A Ring Chaw* (Three Part). Pro Art 2850

Willet, Pat. *Bile Them Cabbage Down* (Three Part). Heritage HV131

Wilson, Mark. *Sing Me a Song of the Land I Love* (Three Part). Jenson 409-19020

Wilson, Mark. *Welcome the Day* (Three Part). Jenson 409-23010

Folk/Spiritual

Dodds, Lindy, arr. *Stan' Still Jordan* (SC, opt. B). Cambiata Press T180138

Ehret, Walter, arr. *The Old Ark's A-Moverin'* (SSC). Cambiata Press S97205

Eilers, Joyce. *Brighten My Soul with Sunshine* (Three Part). Hal Leonard 08541000

Eilers, Joyce, arr. *My Lord* (Three Part). Hal Leonard 08545500

Eilers, Joyce, arr. *Old Joe Clark* (Three Part). Jenson 423-15030

Eilers, Joyce, arr. *The Power and the Glory* (Three Part). Jenson 402-16010

Emerson, Roger, arr. *Wade in the Water* (SAT). Jenson 403-23050

Freed, Arnold, arr. *Brennan on the Moor* (Three Part). McAfee DMC 8120

Freed, Arnold, arr. *Drill, Ye Tarriers, Drill!* (Three Part). McAfee DMC8124

Freed, Arnold, arr. *Michie Banjo* (Three Part). McAfee DMC8121

Freed, Arnold, arr. *The Riddle Song* (Three Part). McAfee DMC8122

Freed, Arnold, arr. *Simple Gifts* (Three Part). McAfee DMC 8126

Freed, Arnold, arr. *The Wabash Cannonball* (Three Part). McAfee DMC8118

Harlow, Barbara, arr. *Liza Jane* (SAT, opt. B). Heritage H6508

Harris, Kent, arr. *In That Great Gettin' Up Morning* (Three Part). Pro Art 2773

Kalbach, Don, arr. *New River Train* (SAT, opt. B). Silver Burdett

Kalbach, Don, arr. *Nine Hundred Miles* (SAT, Opt B). Silver Burdett

Kirk, Theron, arr. *Green Grow the Rushes-O* (SAC). Pro Art 2775

Roach, Donald, arr. *Kum Ba Yah* (SSC). Cambiata Press U180136

Rowen, R. and Simon, B., arr. *Whoa, Mule, Whoa!* (Three Part). C. Fischer CM6973

Thygerson, Robert, arr. *Three Novelty Choruses* (SAT). Heritage H6500

Thygerson, Robert, arr. *Sing and Shout!* (Three Part). Heritage HV103

Willet, Pat, arr. *Joshua Fit the Battle of Jericho* (Three Part). Heritage HV108

Christmas

Avalos, A. arr. *O Shepherds, Come Running* (SAC). Pro Art CH2995

Bach, J. S.-Weck, D. *Two Chorales from Christmas Oratorio* (SAT). Somerset SP774

Brenclley, Douglas. *Alleluia* (SAT). Shawnee D-260

Covert, Mary Ann, arr. *Good Christian Men Rejoice* (SSC). Cambiata Press U97561

Davenport, David. *Joy in Judea* (Three Part). Richmond Press TEV61

Eilers, Joyce. *Alleluia!* (SAT, opt. B). Hal Leonard 08540200

Kalbach, Donald, arr. *O Mary, Where Is Your Baby?* (Sat, opt. B). Silver Burdett

Kirk, Theron, arr. *The Walloon Carol* (Three Part) Pro Art CH3008

Saint-Saens-Eilers, J. *Praise Ye the Lord of Hosts* (Christmas Oratorio) (SAT). Jenson 40216020

Schroeder, Herman, arr. *Up, O Shepherds* (Tyrolean, SAT). Concordia 98-2066

Thygerson, Robert, and Iams, V. *Holiday Time* (SAT). Heritage H6501

Vance, Margaret. *It's Time for Christmas* (SAC). Schmitt 7652

Wasner, Franz, arr. *Bring Your Torches* (SAT, Insts.). G. Schirmer 8791

Three-Part Mixed (SCB, SAB)

Sacred

Bach, J. S.-Ehret. *Blessing, Glory and Wisdom.* Elkan-Vogel 362-03118

Bach, J. S.-Hopson. *Jesu, Joy of Our Desiring.* Jenson 433-10010

Bach, J. S.-Coggin. *Jesus, Source of My Salvation.* Flammer D5226

Boyce, William-Wagner, D. *Praise the Lord, Alleluia.* Coronet CP326

Burroughs, Bob. *If You Will Only Let God Guide You.* Coronet CP200

Busorow, Donald. *My Song is Love Unknown.* Concordia 98-2336

Butler, Eugene. *Sing Aloud to God, Our Strength.* Galaxy 1.2373.1

Butler, Eugene. *Sing to Our God* (Opt. Tpt.). Beacon Hill/Belwin

Caldara, A.-Hines, R. *Lord, Have Mercy on Me.* Lawson-Gould 51981

Cherubini, Luigi-Wagner, D. *Alleluia, Praise!* Hope MW1223

Coates, John, arr. *Amazing Grace.* Shawnee D-143

Cooper, Irvin, arr. *Praise to the Lord* (SCB). Cambiata Press 1978105

Cruger, Johann-Burroughs, Bob. *Now Thank We All Our God* (Brass). Coronet CP 182

Des Prez, J.-Coggin, E. *Thou Lord, the Refuge of the Meek.* J. Fischer FEC10085

Elvey, George-Cooper E. *Come, Ye Thankful People, Come* (SCB). Cambiata Press 1978106

Ford, Thomas-Proulx. *Almighty God Who Hast Me Brought.* G.I.A. G-2353

Franck, J. W.-Ehret. *Great God of Nations.* Flammer D5220

Friend, Jerry. *Sing Alleluia for Your Soul* (Bass and Guitar). Warner WB 132

Handel, G. F.-Kirby, L. *Deck Thyself, My Soul, with Gladness.* Flammer D5234

Handel, G. F.-Hines, R. *Let the Whole Earth Stand in Awe.* Concordia 98-2473

Handel, G. F.-Kirby, L. *Now Let Us Sing the Christian Joy.* Flammer D5235

Hassler, Hans L.-Hopson. *O Sing Unto the Lord.* C. Fischer CM8200

Haydn, F. J.-Wagner, D. *The Heavens Are Telling* (Creation). Coronet CP 318

Haydn-Brahms-Hopson. *Sound the Trumpet! Praise Him* (Brass). Coronet CP 242

Hopson, Hal, arr. *Dona Nobis Pacem.* Agape HH3903

Hopson, Hal. *Praise the Lord, His Glories Show.* Beckenhorst BP1122

Johnson, David N. *God of Grace and God of Glory* (Tpt.). Augsburg 11-1757

Kauffman, Ronald. *Lift Up Your Hearts.* Coronet CP 198

Lovelace, Austin. *The Tree Springs to Life.* Hope A440

Lotti, Antonio. *Might Lord, Thy Faithfulness Abideth Ever.* E. C. Schirmer 1716

McGlohon, L.-Coates. *Teach Me, Lord.* Shawnee D204

Mendelssohn, F. *Lift Thine Eyes* (Elijah). Kjos 5710

Montanus, Lee A. *Sing a New Song* (Three Equal Voices). Richmond TEV-67

Morley, Thomas-Proulx, R. *Sound Forth the Trumpet in Zion.* G.I.A. G1867

Mozart, W. A.-Wagner, D. *Bless Us with Your Love.* Hope MW 1224

Mozart, W. A.-Martin, F. *Jesu, Son of God* (Ave Verum). Schmitt 5502

Mozart, W. A.-Hopson, A. *Praise the Lord* (Canon). Mark Foster MF257

Pachelbel, J.-Hopson, H. *Canon of Praise.* Somerset MW1226

Palestrina, G. P.-Ehret. *O Jesus Christ, Lord Most Holy.* Skidmore 5026

Powell, Robert. *Sing All the Earth.* C. Fischer CM7822

Quiett, Connie. *White Wings.* Studio PR V8113

Sleeth, Natalie. *A Canon of Praise.* Choristers Guild A-79

Sleeth, Natalie. *Gaudeamus Hodie* (Perc.). C. Fischer CM7776

Sleeth, Natalie. *Go Into the World.* Choristers Guild 209

Telemann, G.-Haegland, B. *Amen, Praise and Honor.* Mark Foster 180

Thomson, Virgil, arr. *My Shepherd Will Supply My Need.* Gray CMR2571

Vaughan Williams, R.-Elrich. *Festival Piece on Sine Nomine* (Brass). Flammer D5323

Wagner, Douglass. *And No Bird Sang*. Flammer D-5360

Williams, Aaron-von Camp, L. *I Love Thy Kingdom, Lord* (Brass). Presser 312-41218

Wilson, Mark. *Sing and Be Joyful*. Studio PR SV7832

Young, Gordon. *God Is My Shepherd*. Flammer D5240

Zabel, Albert. Rejoice and Sing (Perc.). Hope F951

Secular

Althouse, Jay. *We're the Men*. Shawnee D-303

Avalos, A. *Have a Nice Day*. Pro Art 2778

Bach, J. S.-Gordon. *To Spring*. Skidmore SK5009

Beebe, Hank. *This Is the Tune*. Hinshaw HPC-7003

Besig, Don. *Bright, Sunshiny Morning*. Studio PR V7803-2

Burke, Larry. *Faces on the Mountain*. Coronet CP258

Burton, Daniel. *A Red, Red Rose*. Kjos 5755

Burton, Daniel. *Come Live with Me and Be My Love*. Shawnee D-295

Certon, Pierre-Haberlen. *The Joy of Dancing*. Elkan-Vogel 362-03261

Choate, R. and Isaac, M. *Early California* (SAB and Narrator). C. Fischer CM6810

Clarkson-Hale-Plank. *An A^b Cricket and a B^b Frog*. Kendor 4031

Coates, John. *My Song*. Shawnee D-241

Coleman, Larry-Cassey. *Tennessee Wig-Walk*. Belwin HMC 371

Compere, Loyset. *Le Renvoy*. Music Press DC5-42

Cox, Ronald B. *October* (SCB). Cambiata Press C485194

Este, Michael-Razey. *How Merrily We Live*. Plymouth PCS-409

Harris, Ed. *How Beautiful Life Can Be*. Hinshaw HMC-328

Harris, Ed. *The Music Makers*. Coronet CP235

Hassler, Hans L. *Come Let Us Start a Joyful Song*. Bourne B236992-356

Hassler, Hans L.-Greyson. *Dancing and Springing*. Bourne ES8

Hoggard, Lara, arr. *Lucky Little Cricket*. Shawnee D-121

Horman, John, arr. *Follow the Drinking Gourd*. Somerset SP782

Kirk, Theron. *I Sing*. Somerset SP771

McKinney, H., arr. *Madrigals, Set I and II*. J. Fischer 9455, 9612

MacLellan, Gene. *Put Your Hand in the Hand*. C. Hansen C575

Mason, L-Wyatt. *O Music*. Pro Art RROCH3016

Matheny, Gary. *If I Were a Bird*. Somerset SP781

Matheny, Gary. *Listen to the Wind A-Blowin'*. Somerset SP794

Murray, Carol. *Except for You and Me*. Curtis 8318

Ornadel, C.-Smith. *If I Ruled the World*. Chappell 260000-356

Perry, David. *Feel Like a Million*. Coronet CP362

Rodgers, Richard. *Getting to Know You* (King and I). Williamson 104

Russell, H. and Knight, V. *The Halls of Ivy*. Chappell IV-105

Sleeth, Natalie. *Love Is a Song*. Hinshaw HMC-186

Simpson, Betty. *Under the Umbrella of the Red, White and Blue*. Shawnee D-161

Snyder, Audrey. *The Wind*. Studio PR SV8323

Thygerson, Robert. *Music Always Makes Me Feel So Good*. Heritage H7014

Wagner, Douglass. *For As the Rains Come Down*. Coronet CP193

Weelkes, Thomas. *Since Robin Hood*. National NMP 100

Folk/Spiritual

Cain, Noble, arr. *Ezekiel Saw the Wheel*. Belwin 1131

Collins, Don L., arr. *Come All Ye Fair and Tender Ladies* (SCB). Cambiata ARS980152

Cooper, Gwyneth, arr. *All My Trials* (SCB). Cambiata Press S980145

Cooper, Gwyneth, arr. *He's Got the Whole World* (SCB). Cambiata Press S117695

Cooper, Gwyneth, arr. *Waltzing Matilda* (SCB). Cambiata Press U117451

Cooper, Irvin, arr. *Balm in Gilead* (SCB). Cambiata Press 1978102

Davis, Katherine, arr. *Cider through a Straw*. Boston 13798

Davis, Katherine, arr. *Goin' to Boston*. Summy Birchard. B-1556

Dett, Nathaniel. *Listen to the Lambs*. G. Schirmer 7337

Dylan, Bob-Fortune. *Blowin' in the Wind*. Warner Bros. W3765

Ehret, Walter, arr. *Ev'ry Night When the Sun Goes In*. A. Broude AB 408

Ehret, Walter, arr. *Tum Balalaika*. Shawnee D-102

Ehret, Walter, arr. *Water Come a Me Eye*. Skidmore SK5022

Emerson, Roger, arr. *Sinner Man*. Jenson 403-19010

Emerson, Roger arr. *Wade in the Water*. Jenson 403-23050

Gray, Michael, arr. *This Old Hammer*. G. Schirmer 12473

Hatch, Winnagene. *There Is a Balm in Giliad*. Studio PR V-7947

Haufrecht, H., arr. *Missy Mouse and Mister Frog*. Belwin FC2997

Hayward, Lou, arr. *Guantanamera*. Shawnee

House, L. M., arr. *Jamaica, Farewell*. Sam Fox PS120

Howorth, Wayne, arr. *Soon-a Will Be Done*. Belwin 1418

Johnson, Maggie, arr. *Johnson's Old Gray Mule*. A. Broude AB871

Kirk, Theron, arr. *Great Day!* Pro Art 3004

Larson, L. *Stephen Foster Medley*. Somerset SP776

Larson, LeRoy, arr. *The Linden Tree*. Schmitt 5017

Lewis, Aden, arr. *The Crawdad Song*. Plymouth PCS-406

Martin, Gilbert, arr. *Lonesome Valley*. Hinshaw HMC 476

Oliver, Richard, arr. *There's a Little Wheel A-Turnin'*. Hal Leonard R5-11

Quiett, Connie, arr. *Steal Away to Jesus* (SCB). Cambiata Press S982168

Rodgers, Thomas, arr. *Sky Boat Song*. Shawnee D-281

Stanton, Royal, arr. *King Jesus Is A-Listening*. J. Fischer FE9807

Suerte, Buen, arr. *Poor Man Laz'rus* (SCB). Cambiata Press S17675

Thomas, C. E., arr. *It's Me*. Curtis 8124

Trusler, Ivan, arr. *Chumbara*. Warner Bros. W7-1058

(Walton). *I Want to Be Ready*. Walton W4002

Wyatt, Van, arr. *Raise a Ruckus*. Pro Art 2780

Wyatt, Van, arr. *Ride On, Moses*. Pro Art 2996

Zaninelli, Luigi, arr. *Go 'Way from My Window*. Shawnee D-93

Christmas

Bach, J. S. *Four Songs from the Schemelli Gesangbuch*. Concordia 98-2621

Bach, J. S.-Wagner, D. *Prepare Thyself, Zion* (Christmas Oratorio). Flammer D-5252

Brandon, George, arr. *Go, Tell It on the Mountain*. Schmitt 5523

Brockway, Howard, arr. *Pat-a-pan*. H. W. Gray 1260

Burt, Alfred-Ades. *Alfred Burt Carols, Set I, II, III*. Shawnee D113, D114, D115

Butler, Eugene. *Advent Song*. Coronet CP285

Carter, John. *How Far Is It to Bethlehem?* Hinshaw HMC563

Cherubini, Luigi-Hopson, H. *Come, Redeemer, Come*. C. Fischer CM8199

Cooper, Irvin, arr. *Angels We Have Heard on High* (SCB). Cambiata Press I97678

Cooper, Irvin, arr. *When Jesus Christ Was Born* (SCB). Cambiata Press 197679

Cox, Ronald, arr. *Jesus, Jesus, Rest Your Head* (SCB). Cambiata Press 4982169

Davidson, Charles. *Freedom's Flame* (Hanukkah). McAfee M7028

Delmonte, Pauline. *One Shining Night*. Choristers Guild CGA-259

Eddleman, David. *Festival of Lights* (Hanukkah). Coronet CP222

Eddleman, David. *There's A Holy Baby*. Coronet CP223

Ehret, Walter, arr. *Gifts We Shall Bring*. G.I.A. Pub. G-1848

Ehret, Walter, arr. *Shepherds, Rejoice, Lift Up Your Eyes*. Flammer D5223

Ehret, Walter, arr. *Sweet Mary, Guard Thy Precious Child*. Flammer D-5214

Ehret, Walter, arr. *Therefore Be Merry*. Shawnee D-196

Ehret, Walter, arr. *'Twas in the Moon of Wintertime* (Oboe, Perc.). G.I.A. G-1849

Ehret, Walter, arr. *What You Gonna Call Your Pretty Little Baby?* Schmitt 5525

Harris, Ed. One Star. *Hinshaw* HMC 317

Hatch, W. *Child Jesus Came to Earth This Day*. Hal Leonard. 08602501

Kauffman, Ronald. *Follow the Star!* Coronet CP278

Kirby, Lewis. *Gentle Mary.* Flammer D-5221

Kodály, Zoltan, arr. *Veni, Veni Emmanuel.* Boosey & Hawkes 5564

Krone, Beatrice, arr. *Christmas Star.* Kjos 5733

Laster, James, arr. *The Infant King.* Hinshaw HMC484

Lovelace, Austin C. *Christmas Gloria.* Hope F159

Noble, Tim-Ades. *Ring, Christmas Bells.* Glory Sound D-5318

Praetorius, M-Carter. *Lo, How a Rose E'er Blooming.* Somerset AD 2017

Praetorius, M.-Greyson. *Psallite.* Bourne ES21B

Preston, Robert, arr. *On That Earliest Christmas Night.* Shawnee D180

Riegger W., arr. *Masters in This Hall.* Flammer 88592

Rocherolle, Eugene. *See the Pretty Baby.* Warner WB 111

Springfield, J. G., arr. *Joy That Knows No Bounds.* Cambiata L97438

Thygerson, Robert, arr. *O Come, O Come, Emmanuel.* Heritage HV133

Thygerson, Robert, arr. *The Holly Bears a Berry* (Handbells). Beckenhorst BP1144

Wagner, Douglas. *Sing Nowell.* Beckenhorst BP1129

Young, Gordon. *Three Wise Men Traveling.* Flammer D5239

Four-Part Mixed (SSCB, SSAB, SACB)

Sacred

Bach, J. S.-Collins. *Jesu Priceless Treasure.* Cambiata Press M982170

Bach, J. S.-Collins. *Now Let All the Heavens Adore Thee.* Cambiata Press D938122

Bach, J. S.-Coggin. *Praise to Thee, Thou Great Creator.* Pro Art 3012

Bortniansky, D-Collins. *Cherubim Song No. 7.* Cambiata Press. D978119

Byrd, W.-Collins. *Ave Verum Corpus.* Cambiata Press D978121

Butler, Eugene. *Blessed Is the Man.* Cambiata Press C97203

Butler, Eugene. *Sing to His Name for He Is Gracious.* Cambiata Press C17429

Collins, Don, arr. *I Heard the Voice of Jesus Say.* Cambiata Press L17798

Collins, Don. *Praise Thee, Lord.* Cambiata Press L117553

Cox, Ronald. *How Firm a Foundation.* Cambiata Press U48193

Cruger-Bach-Collins. *Jesu, Priceless Treasure.* Cambiata Press M982170

Davis, Katherine K. *Stand Up and Sing* (Tpt.). Cambiata Press C97319

Dubois, T.-Richison. *Adoramus Te Christe* (Seven Last Words). Cambiata Press 17797

Eddleman, David. *Amazing Grace.* Silver Burdett

Farrell, Michael. *Send Out Thy Light*. Cambiata Press C980149

Franck, Merchoir-Purdue. *Da Pacem Domine*. Cambiata Press M979126

Gabrieli, A.-McCray. *Agnus Dei*. Cambiata Press M97682

Gluck, C.-Taylor. *O Saviour, Hear Me*. Cambiata Press M17672

Handel, G. F.-Beal. *Behold the Lamb of God* (Messiah). Cambiata Press M97317

Handel, G. F.-Richison. *Hallelujah* (Messiah). Cambiata Press M97317

Handel, G. F.-Beal. *Surely, He Hath Borne Our Griefs* (Messiah). Cambiata Press M97201

Hooper, William. *Glory to God*. Cambiata Press C97437

Ingegner, A-Collins. *Tenebrae Factae Sunt*. Cambiata Press D981155

Kirby, Charles. *May the Road Rise to Meet You*. Cambiata Press C982165

Kirk, Theron. *Praise the Lord All Ye Nations* (Brass). Cambiata Press C117694

Kirk, Theron. *Sing a Song to the Lord* (Perc.). Cambiata Press C978107

Lotti, A.-Farrell. *Joy Fills the Morning*. Cambiata Press M983177

Luther-Vick. *Mark Well, My Heart*. Cambiata Press. C117209

Mendelssohn, Felix-Farrell. *Cast Thy Burden Upon the Lord*. Cambiata Press M980143

Mendelssohn, Felix-Collins. *He Watching Over Israel* (Elijah). Cambiata M97557

Mozart, W. A.-Lyle. *Ave Verum*. Cambiata Press M17552

Mozart, W. A.-Collins. *Gloria in Excelsis Deo* (Twelfth Mass). Cambiata Press M97437

Newbury, Kent A. *Clap Your Hands*. Kjos GC68

Peninger, David, arr. *I Love the Lord, His Strength Is Mine*. Cambiata Press C17314

Roff, Joseph. *Sing to the Lord of Love*. Cambiata Press L117568

Snyder, Wesley. *Lord, Thou Hast Been Our Dwelling Place*. Cambiata Press C978108

Taylor, Noxie. *The Twenty-Third Psalm*. Cambiata Press U17556

Vivaldi, A.-Collins. *Gloria*. Cambiata Press M117207

Secular

Ashton, Bob. *Where Are the Flowers?* Cambiata Press AH85186

Besig, Don. *It's a Wonderful Thing to Be Me!* Shawnee D-170

Boyd, Jack. *Moonscape*. General Words/Kjos GC74

Brahms, J.-Hokanson. *She Walks in Beauty*. Cambiata Press M117447

Burger, Dave. *Good Health, All Gathered Here!* Heritage H7022

Burroughs, Bob. *Life Is . . .* Cambiata Press L97318

Burroughs, Bob. *This Is Our Land*. General Words/Kjos GC71

Butler, Eugene. *A Lincoln Log*. Hal Leonard 08041950

Crocker, Brin, arr. *How Lovely Is the Rose* (Medley). Cambiata Press U485189

Casey-Jacobs-Winston. *Those Magic Changes*. Silver Burdett

Collins, Don L. *Give Me Liberty, or Give Me Death*. Cambiata Press P47434

Denver, John-Curtright. *Take Me Home, Country Roads*. Cherry Lane 8159

Denver, John-Curtright. *How Can I Leave You Again*. Cherry Lane 8153

Eddleman, David. *I'm Gonna Walk*. Silver Burdett

Drake-Carlyle. *I Believe*. Tro SCC-2015

Eilers, Joyce. *Spread Your Wings and Fly*. Jenson 402-19124

Fain-Wyatt. *Let a Smile Be Your Umbrella*. Belwin 64434

Gershwin-Ehret. *Summertime* (Porgy and Bess). Chappell 5565023-36309

Gustafson, Don. *Campfire Blues*. C. Fischer CM6863

Joyner-Carter-Simeone. *Young Love*. Shawnee D-171

Kirby, Charles. *What Do All of These Things Mean?* Cambiata Press L117208

Kirk, Theron. *I Climbed the Mountain*. Cambiata Press A983178

Kirk, Theron. *Sing a Song of Happiness*. General Words/Kjos GC77

Kirk, Theron. *There Is Something to Sing About*. Pro Art 2998

Kirk, Theron. *When It's Love*. Cambiata Press A981159

Leigh-Riley-Schwartz. *The Impossible Dream*. Cherry Lane 3799

Lerner-Loewe-Ehret. *They Call the Wind Maria*. Chappell 5930003-36309

McCray, James. *Appalachian Lament*. European American B-355

Middlemas, Nancy. *Passing By*. Cambiata Press A1800142

Nelson, Jerry. *Love's the Reason Why*. Cambiata Press L117448

Peninger, David. *The Pirate Don Durk of Dowdee*. Cambiata Press C17674

Pfautsch, Lloyd. *Lovers Love the Spring*. General Words/Kjos GC69

Riley-Wilson. *The Good Time Singers*. Cherry Lane 8169

Rodgers-Hammerstein-Ehret. *It's a Grand Night for Singing*. Williamson W830750-363

Roberton, Ed. *Let Love Come Near*. C. Fischer CM7916

Roff, Joseph. *Sail On, O Ship of State*. Cambiata Press P978112

Rowen, R. and Simon, B. *Somebody Cares for Me*. C. Fischer. CM7078

Smith-Collins. *The Star Spangled Banner*. Cambiata Press D978123

Spencer, Linda. *Teacher, Help Me*. Cambiata Press ARS980154

Terri, Salli. *Oh, Freedom*. General Words/Kjos GC73

Wiley, Marcus. *Climbin' Up Those Golden Stairs*. Pro Art 2997

Wink, Irma and Sue. *Lovely Guitar*. Kjos GC78

Folk/Spiritual

Collins, Don L., arr. *Hallelujah!* Cambiata Press S485192

Collins, Don L., arr. *Nobody Knows the Trouble I've Seen.* Cambiata Press S97320

Davis, Bruce, arr. *Good News!* Cambiata Press 980144

Ehret, Walter, arr. *Dunderbeck.* Sgudio PR

Ehret, Walter, arr. *O It's Good Bye Liza Jane.* Cambiata Press U97321

Eisman, L. and Winston, G. *Goin' Down the Road.* Silver Burdett

Foster-Stephen-Ashton. *Foster Mania.* Cambiata Press U485184

Foster, Stephen-Cooper. *Nelly Bly.* Cambiata Press U117571

Grant, Louise, arr. *Git on Board, Little Chillen'.* Belwin 1688-6

Kicklighter, Hampton, arr. *English Street Crys.* Cambiata Press U978110

Kirby, Charles, arr. *Swing Low, Sweet Chariot.* Cambiata Press S17555

Knight, Calirice, arr. *Charlie Is My Darlin'.* Cambiata Press U17431

Knight, Clarice, arr. *My Lord, What a Morning.* Cambiata Press S485185

Knight, Clarice, arr. *Battle of Jericho.* Cambiata Press S97440

Knight, Clarice, arr. *Hold On!* Cambiata Press S177100

Lyle, J. B., arr. *The Colorado Trail.* Cambiata Press U17316

Lyle, J. B., arr. *Wade in the Water.* Cambiata Press S117570

Melton, William, arr. *Plenty Good Room.* Cambiata Press S983179

Melton, William, arr. *Ride the Chariot.* Cambiata Press S117450

Nightingale, Mae, arr. *Sakura.* C. Fischer CM6694

North, Jack. *Lonesome Valley.* Alfred. 7087

Riley, David, arr. *Bingo.* Cambiata Press U17676

Suerete, Buen, arr. *Green Grow the Rushes, Oh.* Cambiata Press U97206

Suerete, Buen, arr. *O Sinner Man.* Cambiata Press S17430

Suerte, Buen, arr. *Saints Bound for Heaven.* Cambiata Press S97560

Welch, John, arr. *Blow, Ye Winds.* Studio PR

Welch, John, arr. *No Lov'lier Countryside.* Studio PR

Welch, John, arr. *Over the River.* Studio PR

Welch, John, arr. *Were You There?* Studio PR

Christmas

Beal, Loy, arr. *Little Chilun.* Cambiata Press S17315

Collins, Don L., arr. *Three Sacred Christmas Songs.* Cambiata Press MP983171

Ehret, Walter, arr. *Hail the King of Heaven* (2 Tpts). Cambiata Press U97441

Ehret, Walter, arr. *Joseph Dearest, Joseph Mine.* Cambiata Press U117326

Ehret, Walter, arr. *On This Blessed Merry Season.* Cambiata Press U97686

Gilbreath-Brown. *The True Gift of Christmas*. Cambiata Press L97683

Gordon, Philip, arr. *A Tribute of Carols*. Warner W7-1014

Hooper, William. *Glory to God*. Cambiata Press. C97439

Kirk, Theron, arr. *Follow, Follow*. Kjos GC84

Knighton, Merrill. *Gloria*. Flammer 88678

Kochanek, Susan, arr. *Three English Carols*. Heritage HV184

Krone, Beatrice, arr. *God's Gift of Love*. Kjos 5741

Leontovich, M.-Wilhousky, P. *Carol of the Bells*. C. Fischer CM7989

Lovelace, A., arr. *God Rest Ye Merry Gentlemen*. Cambiata Press C117324

Middlemas, Nancy. *One Small Boy*. Cambiata Press C485188

Newbury, Kent. *Clap Your Hands*. Kjos GC68

Niles, John J., arr. *O Come, Emmanuel*. C. Fischer CM6751

Nightingale, Mae, arr. *Fum, Fum, Fum*. C. Fischer CM7105

Nightingale, Mae, arr. *Two Christmas Carols, Set I*. C. Fischer CM7987

Penninger, David, arr. *Mary Had a Baby*. Cambiata Press S117210

Springfield, J. G. *Go Tell It on the Mountain*. Cambiata Press S117210

Vance, Margaret. *We Come to the Manger Again*. Cambiata Press C978109

Vick, Beryl. *Long Years Ago O'er Bethlehem's Hills*. Cambiata Press C97684

Welch, John. *Christmas Morning*. Studio PR

D. SENIOR HIGH MIXED CHORUS OCTAVOS (SATB AND DIVISI)

Sacred

Ahlen, Waldemar-Jennings. *The Earth Adorned*. Walton WH-126

Aichinger-Martens. *Confirma Hoc, Deus*. Walton 6016

Anerio, G.-Stephens. *Cantate Domino*. G. Schirmer 11273

Antes, John. *All Praises Be to the Lord*. Boosey & Hawkes 5938

Archangelsky, A.-Krone. *Hear My Supplication*. Witmark 5-W2727

Archangelsky, A.-Walker. *Light Divine*. Hal Leonard 08681500

Archangelsky, A.-Tellep. *To Thee We Sing*. Schmitt 857

Arensky, A.-Davison. *O God, We Pray*. E. C. Schirmer 1126

Bach, J. S.-Ramsey. *Alleluia*. Kjos 5381

Bach, J. S.-Hirt. *Alleluia! Sing Praise* (Cantata 142). C. Fischer CM7140

Bach, J. S.-Kemmer. *Be Calm and Peaceful*. Gray 1934

Bach, J. S.-Tkach. *Blessing, Glory and Wisdom*. Kjos 5140

Bach, J. S.-Ehret. *Glory and Worship* (SSAATTBB). Presser 312-40729

Bach, J. S.-Davison. *Grant Me True Courage, Lord*. E. C. Schirmer 313

Bach, J. S.-Heller. *In Steadfast Faith I Stand*. Schmitt 1696

Bach, J. S.-Riegger. *Jesu, Joy of Man's Desiring*. Flammer 84137

Bach, J. S.-Clough-Leighter. *O Rejoice, Ye Christians, Loudly*. E. C. Schirmer 367

Bach, J. S.-Dickinson. *O Saviour Sweet* (Alto Solo). Gray GSC 82

Bach, J. S.-Malin. *We Pledge You Forever* (Cantata 208). Belwin Mills OCT 2406

Beck, John Ness. *Canticle of Praise* (Band/Orch Accomp). Presser 312-40588

Beck, John Ness. *Every Valley*. Beckenhorst Press BP1040

Beck, John Ness. *Upon This Rock* (Brass Sextet). G. Schirmer 11467

Beethoven, Ludwig van. *Hallelujah Chorus* (Mount of Olives). Presser 312-20978

Beethoven, Ludwig van. *The Heavens Declare the Glory of God*. Flammer 84802

Berger, Jean. *The Eyes of All Wait Upon Thee*. Augsburg 11-1264

Berger, Jean. *I to the Hills Lift Up Mine Eyes*. Augsburg 11-0678

Berger, Jean. *A Rose Touched by the Sun's Warm Rays*. Augsburg 11-0953

Billings, William. *David's Lamentation*. C. Fischer CM6572

Billings, William. *Kittery*. G. Schirmer 10309

Billings, William. *When Jesus Wept* (fuguing tune). A. Broude 995

Bizet, Georges-Ryder. *Lamb of God* (Agnus Dei). Oliver Ditson 12246

Bortniansky, Dimitri. *Lo, A Voice to Heaven Sounding*. E. C. Schirmer 151

Brahms, Johannes-Fettke. *All Sing Loudly*. Flammer A-5715

Brahms, Johannes-Williamson. *Create in Me, O God*. G. Schirmer 7504

Brahms, Johannes. *How Lovely Is Thy Dwelling Place* (German Requiem). C. Fischer CM632

Brahms, Johannes-Buszin-Soldan. *Let Nothing Ever Grieve Thee*. C. F. Peters 6093

Brahms, Johannes-Dickinson. *Lord, Lead Us Still*. Gray GSC 60

Bruckner, Anton. *Christus Factus Est*. Summy Birchard 5249

Bruckner, Anton. *Let Us Celebrate God's Name*. Augsburg PS 626

Bruckner, Anton. *O How Blessed*. Choral Art R154

Butler, Eugene. *Go Ye into All the World*. C. Fischer CM7880

Butler, Eugene. *How Excellent Is Thy Name*. Bourne 837

Butler, Eugene. *Sing to the Lord a Marvelous Song*. Hope A-451

Buxtehude, D.-Hunter. *Blessed Lord Jesus* (SSATB). Marks MC4508

Buxtehude, D.-Granville. *Hark Ye! The Lord Comes with His Thousands*. Sam Fox CM23

Byrd, William-Greenburg. *Ave Verum Corpus*. Assoc. Music Pub.

Cadman, Charles W. *Sons of Men*. Flammer 4038

Cain, Noble. *The Lord Is My Shepherd*. Flammer 84221

Caldara, A.-Pauly. *Lord, From Thee Comes Our Strength*. E. C. Schirmer 3075

Candlyn, T. Frederick. *Thee We Adore*. C. Fischer CM492

Casals, P. *O Vos Omnes* (Divisi). Tetra AB128

Charpentier, Marc Antoine-Lovelace. *Out of the Depths.* Concordia 98-1521

Cherubini, Luigi-Hall. *Pie Jesu* (Requiem in C Minor). National WHC-46

Christiansen, F. Melius. *Beautiful Savior.* Augsburg 11-0051

Christiansen, Paul, arr. *Wondrous Love.* Augsburg 1140

Clokey, Joseph W. *Let Hearts Awaken* (Plainsong, Orch.). Gray 1597

Clokey, Joseph W. *O Make Our Hearts to Blossom* (SSAATTBB). Summy Birchard B-2065

Copland, Aaron. *Sing Ye Praises to Our King* (Four Motets). Boosey & Hawkes 6021

Costeley, G.-Mochnick. *I Love the Word of God the Father.* Broude Bros. CR 28

Croce, Giovanni-Kjelson. *O Vos Omnes.* Belwin 2149

Croce, Giovanni-McCray. *Two Motets.* Shawnee A-1731

Des Pres, Josquin. *Ave Vera Virginitas.* G. I. A. Pub. G-565

Des Pres, Josquin. *Tu Solus.* E. C. Schirmer 2253

Di Lasso, Orlando-Cramer. *O Lord of Heav'n.* Marks 4062

Durante, F.-Durand. *Misericordias Domini* (Double Chorus). Walton 2193

Durufle, Maurice. *Notre Pere.* Durand 14075

Durufle, Maurice. *Ubi Caritas.* Durand 312-41253

Dvorak, Antonin. *Blessed Jesu, Fount of Mercy* (Stabat Mater). G. Schirmer 4490

Farrant, Richard-Shaw. *Call to Remembrance, O Lord.* Gray GCME 1751

Farrant, Richard-Hallagan. *Hide Not Thy Face.* Presser 312-40445

Farrant, Richard-Davies. *We Sing Our Praises Now to Thee.* Flammer 84411

Faure, Gabriel. *Cantique De Jean Racine.* Broude Bros. 801

Faure, Gabriel. *Holy, Holy, Holy* (Requiem). FitzSimons 2119

Franck, Cesar-Gillette. *O Lamb of God.* Birchard 1370

Franck, Cesar. *O Lord Most Holy* (Panis Angelicus). Summy Birchard 396

Franck, Cesar. *Psalm 150* (Praise Ye the Lord). Oliver Ditson 332-14082

Franck, Melchior. *Jesu, Thy Blessings Give to Me.* C. Fischer CM7505

Frackenpohl, Arthur. *Alleluia, Amen.* Shawnee A-1524 (Canon)

Gabrieli, Giovanni-Nordin. *Come, Let Us Sing A Song of Joy* (Double Chorus). Shawnee A-1243

Gallus, J.-Thomas. *This Is the Day* (Double Chorus). Concordia 98-1702

Gaul, Harvey. *All Praise to God Eternal* (Russian Tune). J. Fischer/Belwin 6500

Gibbons, Orlando. *Almighty and Everlasting God.* Oxford TCM 36

Goemanne, Noel. *Praise the Lord* (Brass, Timp.). Summy Birchard M-5949

Gounod, Charles. *Praise Ye the Father.* G. Schirmer 3325

Gounod, Charles. *Sanctus and Benedictus* (St. Cecelia Mass). Presser 332-00114

Gounod, Charles. *Send Out Thy Light*. Presser 332-00068

Graun, Carl H.-Craig. *Sing and Be Joyful*. Plymouth FS-101

Green, Maurice-Martens. *Sing We Merrily*. Walton W2300

Gretchaninoff, A.-Matterling. *The Cherubic Hymn* (SSAATTBB). Kjos 7015

Grieg, Edward-Dickinson. *Jesus, Blest Redeemer* (Ave Maris Stella SSAATTBB). Gray

Haazen, Guido. *Kyrie* (Missa Luba). Lawson-Gould 51803 (Tenor solo, Perc.)

Hammerschmidt, Andreas-Malin. *How Lovely Is Thine Own Dwelling Place* (SSATB). Belwin 2436

Handel, G. G.-Craig. *And I Will Exalt Him* (Israel in Egypt). Plymouth FS-103

Handel, G. F.-Barrie. *Day By Day We Magnify Thee* (SSATB). Lawson-Gould 797

Handel, G.F.-Malin. *Glory and Worship Are Before Him* (Chandos #8). Belwin 2435

Handel, G. F.-Carlton. *Great Lord God! Thy Kingdom Shall Endure*. Presser 312-41125

Handel, G. F.-Williams. *Hallelujah, Amen* (Judas Maccabaeus; 3 Tpts., Timp.). A. Broude 1042

Handel, G. F.-Ehret. *In Thee, O Lord, Have I Trusted*. Mercury MC361

Handel, G. F.-Bunjes. *Jesus, Sun of Life, My Splendor*. Concordia 98-1445

Handel, G. F. *Let Their Celestial Concerts All Unite* (Samson). E. C. Schirmer 312

Handel, G. F.-Lefebvre. *Thanks Be To Thee* (Cantata Con Stromenti). Galaxy 1228-6

Handel, G. F.-Klein. *Thou Art the King of Glory* (Utrecht Te Deum). Kjos 5481A

Handel, G. F.-Cain. *Verdant Meadows* (Alcina). Schmitt 1061

Hassler, Hans L.-Greyson. *Cantate Domino*. Bourne 2737-6

Hassler, Hans L. *Come, Let Us Start a Joyful Song*. Bourne ES74

Hassler, Hans L. *Gloria from Mass II*. G. Schirmer 9410

Hauptmann, Moritz-Young. *Gebet* (Prayer). Broude Bros. MGC 37

Haydn, Franz J.-Neuen. *Awake the Harp* (Creation). Lawson-Gould 51982

Haydn, Franz J.-Suchoff. *Gloria* (Heiligmesse). Walton 5025

Haydn, Franz J. *The Heavens Are Telling* (Creation). G. Schirmer 3521

Haydn, Franz J.-Hines. *Kyrie* (Missa Brevis Sancti Joannis de Deo). G. Schirmer 11442

Haydn, Michael-Walker. *Sanctus*. Hal Leonard 08681753

Haydn, Michael-Strickling. *Tenebrae in E Flat*. Schmitt 1536

Holst, Gustav. *Let All Mortal Flesh Keep Silence* (Band or Orch.). Galaxy 3.2309.1

Holst, Gustav. *Turn Back O Man* (Band or Orch.). Galaxy 1.5001.1

Hovaness, Alan. *Behold, God Is My Help*. C. F. Peters 66190

Hovhaness, Alan. *Psalm 61*. C. F. Peters 6255

Ingegneri-Decker. *Tenebrae Factae Sunt.* National NMP-140

Ippolitoff-Ivanoff/Clough-Leighter. *Bless the Lord.* Presser 332-13770

Ivanoff, P.-Douglas. *Praise Ye the Lord.* Pro Art 1591

Ives, Charles E. *Sixty-Seventh Psalm* (Divisi). Assoc. Music Pub. A-274

Ives, Charles E. *Three Harvest Home Chorales* (Orch.). Mercury 352-00361

Jacobs, Gordon, arr. *Brother James's Air* (Marosa). Oxford 763

Jothen, Michael. *The Lord Is a Mighty God.* Coronet CP 210

Kallinikof, B.-Ryg. *Agnus Dei.* Belwin 848

Kauffmann, Ronald. *A Festival Psalm* (Brass Quintet). Elkan-Vogel 362--3266

Kirk, Theron. *Lift Your Hearts and Sing.* C. Fischer CM8195

Kodály, Zoltan. *Psalm 121.* Boosey & Hawkes 5330

Kopyloff, A.-Clough-Leighter. *Hear My Cry, O God.* Presser 332-13804

Kubik, Gail. *How Lovely Thy Place.* Gray CCS 16-(4)

Lotti, A. *Agnus Dei.* Mercury 352-00475

Macfarlane, Will C. *Open Our Eyes* (SSAATTBB). G. Schirmer 7273

Marcello, Benedetto-Hopson. *Psalm Nineteen.* Agape HH 3912

Mendelssohn, Felix. *All Ye That Cried Unto the Lord.* National NMP-102

Mendelssohn, Felix. *Cast Thy Burden Upon the Lord* (Elijah). G. Schirmer 10015

Mendelssohn, Felix-McKelvy. *For the Lord Is a Mighty God.* Mark Foster 233

Mendelssohn, Felix. *He, Watching Over Israel* (Elijah). G. Schirmer 2498

Mendelssohn, Felix. *How Lovely Are the Messengers* (St. Paul). G. Schirmer 3741

Mendelssohn, Felix. *Let Me, God, Your Help Be Finding.* Presser 312-41192

Miles, Russell H. *Rise Up, O Men of God!* (SSAATTBB). FitzSimons 2074

Moe, Daniel. *Let Your Eye Be to the Lord.* Augsburg 11-0544

Monteverdi, Claudio. *Lasciatemi Morire.* Recordi NY841

Morley, Thomas-Greyson. *Agnus Dei.* Bourne

Mozart, W. A. *Dies Irae* (Requiem). G. Schirmer 10016

Mozart, W. A.-Cramer. *Gloria in Excelsis* (Missa Brevis in C). Marks 4553

Mozart, W. A. *Gloria in Excelsis* (Twelfth Mass). G. Schirmer 3515

Mozart, W. A. *Lacrymosa* (Requiem). G. Schirmer 11564

Mozart, W. A. *Sanctus* (Missa Brevis in C). Marks 4555

Mozart, W. A. *Ave Verum Corpus.* G. Schirmer 5471

Nelson, Ron. *O Lord, How Can We Know Thee?* Boosey & Hawkes 5439

Nystedt, Knut. *I Will Greatly Rejoice.* Hinshaw HMC-226

Nystedt, Knut. *The Path of the Just.* Augsburg 11-9333

Pachelbel, Johann-Goemanne. *Canon in D.* Flammer A-5833

Pachelbel, Johann. *Magnificat* (Double Chorus). C. F. Peters 6087

Palestrina, Giovanni P. *Adoramus Te.* E. C. Schirmer 2985

Palestrina, Giovanni P. *Adoramus Te Christe*. E. C. Schirmer 1760

Palestrina, Giovanni P. *O Bone Jesu*. G. Schirmer 10022

Pasquet, Jean. *Blessed Is the Nation*. Elka

Peninger, David. *Sing to the Lord of Harvest*. Hinshaw HMC-364

Pergolesi, G.-Howorth. *Amen* (Stabat Mater). Belwin 1259

Pergolesi, G.-McEwen. *Glory to the Father*. Hinshaw HMC 685

Persichetti, Vincent. *Agnus Dei*. Elkan-Vogel 362-001173

Pfautsch, Lloyd. *Go and Tell John*. Hope CY 3334

Pfautsch, Lloyd. *In Music God Is Glorified*. Hinshaw HMC-403

Pfautsch, Lloyd. *O Be Joyful in the Lord* (Brass). Hinshaw HMC-445

Pinkham, Daniel. *Festival Magnificat* (Organ and Brass). C. F. Peters 6555

Pinkham, Daniel. *In the Beginning of Creation* (Electronic Tape). E. C. Schirmer 2902

Pitoni, G.-Greyson. *Cantate Domino*. Bourne ES5

Pitoni, G. *Christus Factus Est*. Tetra AB757

Pitoni, G.-Gray. *Praise Ye the Lord of Heaven*. A. Broude 1044

Pooler, Frank, and Pierce, Brent. *The Rising Sun* (Aleatory). Somerset CE 4328

Pote, Allen. *A Jubilant Song* (Brass and Handbells). Hope F 979

Poulenc, Francis. *Exultate Deo*. Salabert

Poulenc, Francis. *Salve Regina*. Salabert

Praetorius, M. *Sing We All Now with One Accord*. G. Schirmer 7543

Praetorius, M. *We Turn Our Eyes to Thee* (Double Chorus). Belwin 2268

Purvis, Richard. *Benedictus Es, Domine*. Gray 2043

Purcell, Henry-Morse. *Thou Knowest, Lord, the Secrets of Our Hearts*. Presser 14713

Purcell, Henry-Hilton. *O Worship the Lord*. Mercury MC 396

Purcell, Henry-Davison. *O Sing Unto the Lord*. E. C. Schirmer 1103

Roberton, Hugh S. *Let All the World in Every Corner Sing*. G. Schirmer 8721

Rorem, Ned. *O Magnum Mysterium*. Boosey & Hawkes 6006

Rorem, Ned. *Praise the Lord, O My Soul*. Boosey & Hawkes 6105

Rossini, G.-Fitzhugh. *I Will Give Thanks Unto Thee, O Lord*. Flammer 4058

Rutter, John. *For the Beauty of the Earth* (Orch.). Hinshaw HMC-550

Rutter, John. *Lord, Make Me an Instrument of Thy Peace*. Hinshaw HMC-470

Rutter, John. *O Clap Your Hands*. Oxford A 307

Saint-Saens, Camille-Jurey. *Praise Ye the Lord of Hosts* (Christmas Oratorio). Belwin 60597

Scarlatti, A. *Exultate Deo*. G. Schirmer 11001

Scarlatti, A.-Ehret. *O Thou Most High*. Lawson-Gould 52105

Schein-Porter. *Die Mit Tranen Saen.* Assoc Music Pub. A-870

Schubert, Franz-Rodby. *God of Wisdom, God of Mercy.* Marks 4161

Schubert, Franz-Spicker. *The Omnipotence.* G. Schirmer 4346

Schubert, Franz-Sisson. *Salve Regina.* A. Broude 969

Schubert, Franz-Craig. *Sanctus* (German Mass in F). Plymouth DC-109

Schuetky, F. J.-Hilton. *Send Forth Thy Spirit* (SSATTBB). Mercury 352-00280

Schumann, Robert-Hines. *Kyrie* (Mass in C Minor). Chor Pub. 30049

Schutz, Henrich. *Also Hat Godt Die Welt Geliebt.* Hanssler-Verlag 20.380/5

Schutz, H.-Shaw-Speer. *Blessed Are the Faithful.* G. Schirmer 10114

Schutz, H.-Ehret. *Be Thou Exalted, Lord My God.* Flammer A-5632

Schutz, Heinrich-Hilton. *Christ, To Thee Be Glory* (St. Matthew Passion). Mercury MC375

Schutz, Heinrich-Williamson. *The Pharisee and the Publican.* G. Schirmer 7473

Shaw, Martin. *With a Voice of Singing* (Orch.). G. Schirmer 8103

Sibelius, Jean. *Onward, Ye Peoples.* Galaxy GM 938-10

Sjolund, Paul. *Go Forth into the World in Peace* (Flute). Hinshaw HMC-511

Stevens, Halsey. *Praise the Lord Who Reigns Above* (Canon). Mark Foster EH9

Stevens, Halsey. *Psalm 148 Praise Ye the Lord.* Mark Foster EH2

Stravinsky, Igor. *Ave Maria.* Boosey & Hawkes 1832

Sweelinck-Klein. *O Sing Unto the Lord* (SSATB). G. Schirmer 12102

Sweelinck-Aks. *We Have Heard the Words* (Psalm 44). Marks 86

Tallis, Thomas-Simkins. *O Lord, Give Thy Holy Spirit.* Concordia 98-2249

Telemann, Georg P. *Psalm Settings* (Violin I, II, Cello). Concordia 97-4838

Thiman, Eric H. *Jesu, the Very Thought of Thee.* Gray 1845

Thompson, Randall. *Alleluia.* E. C. Schirmer 1786

Thompson, Randall. *The Last Words of David.* E. C. Schirmer 2294

Thompson, Randall. *The Lord Shall Be Unto Thee.* E. C. Schirmer 2641

Thomson, Virgil, arr. *My Shepherd Will Supply My Need.* Gray 2046

Tschesnokoff, P.-Tkach. *Come Thou, Holy Spirit.* Kjos 6521

Tschesnokoff, P.-Ehret. *Salvation Is Created.* Bourne WE 8

Tye, Christopher. *As Pants the Heart.* Concordia 98-2297

Vecchi, Orazio. *Fa Una Canzona.* G. Schirmer 556

Vaughan Williams, Ralph, arr. *All Hail the Power.* Oxford

Vaughan Williams, Ralph-Barthelson. *For All the Saints* (Brass). Plymouth HA 9

Vaughan Williams, Ralph. *O Clap Your Hands* (Organ and Brass). Galaxy 1.5000.1

Vaughan Williams, Ralph. *O Taste and See.* Oxford 43

Vaughan Williams, Ralph, arr. *The Old Hundredth Psalm Tune* (Orch.). Oxford 42P953

Vaughan Williams, Ralph. *Sine Nomine.* C. Fischer CM 6637

Verdi, Giuseppe-Howorth. *Grant Them Rest Eternal* (Requiem). Belwin 1348

Victoria, Thomas L.-Wilhousky. *Ave Maria* (Orch). C. Fischer CM6581

Victoria, Thomas L.-Klein. *O Vos Omnes.* G. I. A. G-1525

Vivaldi, Antonio-Martens. *Et in Terra Pax* (Gloria). Walton 2044

Vivaldi, Antonio-Kjelson. *Et Misericordia.* Belwin 2236

Vivaldi, Antonio-McEwen. *In Memoria Aeterna.* Hinshaw HMC-179

Von Lvov-Wilhousky. *Hospodi Pomilui.* C. Fischer CM 6580

Walton, William. *Jubilate Deo* (SSAATTBB). Oxford 42-373

Wetzler, Robert. *Lord, Give New Tunes* (Harp, Tpts, Trbns, Timp). C. Fischer CM 7772

Willan, Healey. *Lift Up Your Heads, Ye Mighty Gates.* Concordia HA 2003

Willan, Healey. *Rise Up, My Love, My Fair One.* Hinshaw HMC 218

Willan, Healey. *Te Deum Laudamus.* Gray 224

Wood, Dale. *Arise, My Soul, Arise!* Sacred Music S-181

Young, Gordon. *Laudate Dominum.* Coronet CP 321

Secular

Ahlen-Jennings. *The Earth Adorned* (SSATB). Walton WH-126

Ahrold, arr. *Es Steht Ein Lind.* Witmark W3616

Alfven, Hugo. *Aftonen* (Evening). Walton W2705

Alfven, Hugo. *A Maiden Is in a Ring* (SATBB). Walton

Barber, Samuel. *Reincarnations: Mary Hymes.* G. Schirmer 8908
                                       Anthony O'Daley. G. Schirmer 8909
                                       The Coolin. G. Schirmer 8910

Berger, Jean. *It Is Good to Be Merry.* Kjos 5293

Brahms, Johannes. *All Meine Herzgedanken* (SSATBB). Walton W700a

Brahms, Johannes. *Der Abend.* G. Schirmer 10134

Brahms, Johannes-Robinson. *Four German Folk Songs.* Hinshaw HMC 353

Brahms, Johannes. *Nachtens.* G. Schirmer 11799

Brahms, Johannes. *O Lovely May* (O Susser Mai). Presser 332-14456

Brahms, Johannes. *Six Folk Songs.* Marks 9

Brahms, Johannes. *Woodland Cool, Thou Woodland Quiet.* G. Schirmer

Brahms, Johannes. *Let Nothing Ever Grieve Thee.* Peters 6093

Brahms, Johannes. *Create in Me, O God.* G. Schirmer 7504

Bright, H. *Never Tell Thy Love.* Assoc. Music Pub. A-171

Bright, H. *Rainsong.* Assoc. Music Pub. A-269

Bright, H. *Reflection.* Shawnee A-609

Britten, Benjamin. *Five Flower Songs.* Boosey & Hawkes 1873

Britten, Benjamin. *The Evening Primrose.* Boosey & Hawkes 1874

Britten, Benjamin. *Old Abram Brown.* Boosey & Hawkes 1786

Cain, Noble, arr. *Early One Morning.* Presser 332-15147

Certon-Hirt. *I'll Say It Anyway.* Hinshaw HMC 519

Clemens Non Papa. *The Lusty Month of May.* Tetra AB 847

Clements. *Flower of Beauty.* Galaxy 1.5024.1

Copland, Aaron. *Flower of Beauty.* Boosey & Hawkes 5020

Copland, Aaron-Fine. *I Bought Me a Cat.* Boosey & Hawkes 5024

Copland, Aaron. *Stomp Your Foot* (Four Hand Piano). Boosey & Hawkes 5019

Copland, Aaron-Swift. *Younger Generation.* Boosey & Hawkes 1723

Costeley-Greyson. *Go Now My First Love.* Bourne ES127

Debussy, Claude. *Three Chansons: Dieu Au'l La Fait Bon Regarder.* Durant 7191-1
Quant J'ae Ouy Le Tabourin. Durant 7191-2
Yver, Vous N'Estes Qu'un Villain. Durant 7191-3

Dello Joio, N. *A Fable.* C. Fischer CM5299

Dello Joio, N. *Come to Me, My Love.* Marks MC4609

Dello Joio, N. *Jubilant Song.* G. Schirmer 9580

Des Pres, J.-Unruh. *Scarabella.* Mark Foster 352

Diemer, Emma Lou. *Three Madrigals.* G. Schirmer 5417

Di Lasso, Orlando. *Es Jagt Rin Jager Vor Dem Holz* (SSATB). Schott AP510

Di Lasso, Orlando. *Io Ti Verila.* G. Schirmer 11339

Di Lasso, Orlando. *Matona, Lovely Maiden.* C. Fischer 4637

Di Lasso, Orlando. *My Heart Is Offered Still to You.* Lawson-Gould 563

De Lasso, Orlando. *O Bella Fusa.* E. C. Schirmer 11338

Dowland, John. *Come Again, Sweet Love.* E. C. Schirmer

Dowland-McCray. *Fine Knacks for Ladies.* Lawson-Gould 52121

Dowland-Contino. *Say, Love If Ever Thou Didst Find.* Dean HCA-108

Duson, Dede. *The Air Is Moving.* Kjos

Duson, Dede. *Of Love* (Divisi). Walton W2722

Dvorak-Suchoff. *The Wedding Ring.* Plymouth PXW100

Eberlin-Hilton. *People Know Thee.* Mercury 352-00471

Eccard-Richter. *Hort Ich Ein Kuckuck Singen* (SSATB). Schott AP508

Effinger, Cecil. *Basket of Wood* (Four Pastorales). G. Schirmer 11061

Elgar, Edward. *As Torrents in Summer* (King Olaf). Flammer 81068

Faure, G. *Madrigal*. Broude Bros.

Fine, Irving. *Father William* (Alice in Wonderland). Witmark 5-W3182

Gastoldi-Greyson. *This Sweet and Lovely Siren*. Bourne ES-103

Gombert-Malin. *Votre Beaute Plainsante Et Lie*. Belwin 2327

Gilbert & Sullivan. *Finale from The Gondoliers*. E. C. Schirmer 356

Handel, G. F.-Cramer. *Music Spread Thy Voice* (Solomon). Marks MC4132

Hassler, Hans L. *Come, Let Us Start a Joyful Song*. Bourne ES-74

Hassler-Knight. *Im Kuhlen Maien* (Double Chorus). C. Fischer CM7554

Haydn F. J.-Shaw. *Come, Lovely Spring* (Seasons). Lawson-Gould 52078

Hennagin, Michael. *Walking on the Green Grass* (SATTBB). Boosey & Hawkes 5443

Hindemith, Paul. *The Harp That Once Through Tara's Halls*. Assoc. Music Pub.

Isaac-Howerton. *Innsbruck, I Now Must Leave Thee*. C. Fischer CM4704

Ives, Charles. *Three Harvest Home Chorales*. Mercury MC446

Janequin-Contino. *Ce Moys De May*. R. Dean CA-106

Janequin-Klein. *Petite Nymphy Folastre*. G. Schirmer 11725

Kirk, Theron. *It Was a Lover and His Lass*. Shawnee

Lefevre-Knight. *Love Me Truly*. C. Fischer CM7561

Mechem, K. *The Tune*. E. C. Schirmer 2647

McCray, James. *Rise Up, My Love My Fair One*. National WHC-77

Mendelssohn-Richter. *Andenken*. Tetra AB-162-8

Mendelssohn-Robinson. *Die Nachtigall*. Hinshaw HMC 407

Mendelssohn, Felix. *In Praise of Spring*. Assoc. Music Pub. WHC 95

Mozart, W. A.-Malin. *Pleasure Awaits Us*. Belwin 2403

Mozart, W. A.-Wagner. *Placido Eil Mar*. Lawson-Gould 841

Nelson, Ron. *Fanfare for a Festival*. Boosey & Hawkes 5383

Nelson, Ron. *Spring Canticle*. Boosey & Hawkes 6073

Offenbach, J. *Beggar's Canon*. Broude Bros.

Palestrina-Greyson. *Ah, May the Sun*. Bourne AP 513

Pfautsch, Lloyd. *Musick's Empire*. G. Schirmer 51418

Pfautsch, Lloyd. *Who Hath a Right to Sing* (Divisi). Lawson-Gould 52048

Praetorius, Michael. *Nach Gruner Farb Meine Herz Verlangt*. Schott AP 513

Purcell, Henry. *In These Delightful Pleasant Groves*. Witmark 5-W2641

Ravel, Maurice. *Pavane Pour Une Infant Defunte*. Broude Bros. 100

Ravel, Maurice. *Three Chansons*, Durant

Rutter, John. *Blow, Blow, Thou Winter Wind*. Oxford 52024

Rutter, John. *Monday's Child*. Oxford

Rutter, John. *The Riddle Song.* Oxford X230

Schein, J. H. *Five Secular Songs.* Broude Bros.

Schubert, Franz. *Der Tanz.* Hinshaw HMC 247

Schubert, Franz-Gordon. *Lebenslust.* Tetra AB258-6

Shaw-Parker. *Apres De Ma Blonde.* Lawson-Gould 644

Schumann, Robert. *So Wahr Die Sonne Scheinet.* National WHC 117

Schumann, Robert-Kaplan. *Zigeunerleben* (Solo). Lawson-Gould W2708

Staden-Howerton. *A Galliard.* C. Fischer CM4705

Stevens, Halsey. *Go Lovely Rose.* Mark Foster

Thompson, Randall. *The Road Not Taken.* E. C. Schirmer 2485

Vaughan Williams, Ralph. *Fain Would I Change That Note.* Gray Mod 587

Vaughan Williams, Ralph. *The Lover's Ghost.* Galaxy 1.5177.1

Vaughan Williams, Ralph. *Rest.* Galaxy 1.2478.1

Vaughan Williams, Ralph. *Sweet Day.* Galaxy 1.50.11

Vecchi-Greyson. *Come Now Let Us Be Joyful.* Bourne ES 64

Weelkes-Porter. *In Pride of May* (SSATB). Assoc. Music Pub. A-817

Wilder, T. *I Lost My Love in Scarlet Town.* G. Schirmer 11158

Willbye, John. *Adieu, Sweet Amarillas.* Lawson-Gould 51865

Folksongs

Ahrold, Frank, arr. *Gold Fever.* Lawson-Gould 51999

Bardos, Lajos. *Tambur.* Boosey & Hawkes 6055

Bartok, Bela. *Four Slovak Folk Songs.* Boosey & Hawkes 17658

Bartok-Suchoff. *Three Hungarian Folk Songs.* Boosey & Hawkes 5326

Binkerd, Gordon. *Minnedienst.* Boosey & Hawkes 5980

Bock, Fred. *Scarborough Fair.* Gentry J6104

Boyd, J. *Coffee Grows on White Oak Trees.* Shawnee A-1003

Brandon, George. *The Keeper.* Greenwood Press CE-1940-8

Bratt, C. Griffith. *I Am a Poor Wayfaring Stranger.* Spire ED. ESE 978-8

Bryan, Charles F. *Charlottown.* J. Fischer 8136

Bryan, Charles F. *Skip to My Lou.* Peabody College

Carter, John. *She'll Be Comin' Round the Mountain.* Somerset SP785

Christiansen, Paul. *Wondrous Love.* Augsburg 11-1140

Coates, John. *Parsley, Sage, Rosmary and Thyme.* Shawnee A-1063

Copland, Aaron-Fine. *Ching-a Ring Chaw.* Boosey & Hawkes 5024

De Cormier, Robert. *Ahrirang.* Lawson-Gould 51540

De Cormier, Robert. *Bella Bimba.* Lawson-Gould 51256

De Cormier, Robert. *Deep Blue Sea.* Lawson-Gould 51754

De Cormier, Robert. *Tumbalalaika*. Lawson-Gould 51225

Donovan. *Down By the Sally Gardens*. Galaxy 555

Dooley, James. *Johnny Has Gone for a Soldier*. Franco Colombo FC2798

Ehret, Walter. *Nine Hundred Miles* (SSATB). Frank Music F671

Enders, Harvey. *Russian Picnic*. G. Schirmer 9544

Erb, Robert. *My Lagan Love*. Lawson-Gould 52134

Erb, Robert. *Shenandoah*. Lawson-Gould 51846

Frackenpohl, Arthur. *Annie Laurie*. Mark Foster 347

Frackenpohl, Arthur. *Londonderry Air*. Mark Foster 354

Frackenpohl, Arthur. *Three Irish Songs*. Shawnee B-200

Goldman, Maurice. *Hava Nageela*. Lawson-Gould 51270

Goldman, Maurice. *Zum Gali Gali*. Lawson-Gould 52026

Harley-Aschenbrenner. *Ifca's Castle*. C. Fischer CM4708

Harris, Roy. *Birds' Courting Song*. Belwin 64432

Hendrickson, Paul. *The Gypsy*. Mark Foster 3010

Hendrickson, Paul. *Mary Ann*. Mark Foster 3002

Holst, Gustav. *I Love My Love*. J. Curwen 8117

House, L. M. *Jamaica Farewell*. Sam Fox PS106

Jennings, Carolyn. *Dance and Turn*. Curtis 8327

Kodály, Zoltan. *Birthday Greeting*. Boosey & Hawkes 312-40579

Kubik, Gail. *Polly Wolly Doodle*. G. Schirmer 9854

Koepke, Allen. *Kum Bah Ya*. Belwin OCT02524

Lojeski, Ed. *American Folk Trilogy*. Hal Leonard 08200555

Luboff, Norman. *Alouette*. Walton 3057

Makil-Gomez. *Idden-Dem Mallida*. Lawson-Gould 52216

Miller, John D. *O, No John*. Presser 312-40506

Parker, Alice. *Johnny, I Hardly Know Ye*. Lawson-Gould 51452

Parker, Alice. *My Gentle Harp*. Lawson-Gould S-1409

Pierce. *Afton Water*. Plymouth BP-113

Pierce. *Ye Banks and Braes O' Bonnie Doon*. Plymouth BP115

Puerling, Gene. *Cockles and Mussels*. Hal Leonard 07359067

Rutter, John. *Fiddler Man* (Three American Lyrics). Hinshaw HMC815

Rutter, John. *O Waly, Waly*. Oxford 52.026

Rutter, John. *Two American Folk Songs*. Plymouth BPX247

Seals, Karen. *Don't Be Weary, Traveler*. Roger Dean/Heritage HRD 133

Seeger, Pete-Joyce. *The Bells of Rhymney*. Aberdeen 1036

Seiber, M. *Three Hungarian Folk Songs*. G. Schirmer 10715

Simeone, Harry. *Country Style*. Shawnee

Shaw-Parker. *Beautiful Dreamer* (S. Foster). Lawson-Gould 853

Shaw-Parker. *Johnny Has Gone for a Soldier.* Lawson-Gould 502

Smith, Gregg. *Shenandoah.* G. Schirmer 11055

Somers, Harry. *Feller from Fortune.* Gordon Thompson WEI-1008

Taylor, Deems. *Mayday Carol.* J. Fischer 4838

Taylor, Deems. *Waters Ripple and Flow.* J. Fischer 5676

Terri, Salli. *Streets of Laredo.* Lawson-Gould 694

Valerio-Buchner. *Amazing Grace.* Continuo AB 943

Vance, Margaret. *Every Night.* G. Schirmer 12556

Vance, Margaret. *Pretty Saro.* Belwin 2336

Vaughan Williams, Ralph. *Linden Lea.* Boosey & Hawkes 1401

Wagner, Douglass. *All Through the Night.* Lawson-Gould 659

Willcocks, David. *Barbara Allen.* Oxford 53.097

Williams, Wendy. *Every Night When the Sun Goes In.* G. Schirmer 52193

Zaninelli, Luigi. *Americana* (Folk Suite). Shawnee A-935

Zaninelli, Luigi. *Come All You Fair and Tender Ladies.* Shawnee A-935

Zaninelli, Luigi. *The Water Is Wide.* Shawnee A-616

Spirituals

Beck, John Ness, arr. *Let Us Break Bread Together.* Hope A447

Bright, Houston. *I Hear a Voice a'Prayin'.* Shawnee A-335

Brunner, David L. *All My Trials.* Somerset SP778

Burleigh, Harry T. *Sometimes I Feel Like a Motherless Child.* Ricordi NY1707

Burleigh, Harry T. *Were You There?* Belwin FCC592

Cain, Noble. *Go Down, Moses.* G. Schirmer 7575

Cain, Noble. *Keep A Inchin Along.* Boosey & Hawkes 1605

Christiansen, Larry. *My Lord, What a Morning.* Choral Art

Christiansen, Paul. *Mary and Martha.* Schmitt 664

Clark, Edgar. *Wade in the Water.* Marks 830

Cram, James. *I Want Jesus to Walk with Me.* Fine Arts Music Press S1261B

Curtis, Marvin. *By An' By.* Mark Foster 249

Dawson, William L. *Ain'-a That Good News.* Kjos T103-A

Dawson, William L. *Ev'ry Time I Feel the Spirit.* Kjos T117

Dawson, William L. *Ezekiel Saw de Wheel.* Kjos T110

Dawson, William L. *In His Care-O.* Kjos T122

Dawson, William L. *King Jesus Is A-Listening.* Fitzsimons 4025

Dawson, William L. *Soon-Ah Will Be Done.* Kjos T102-A

Dawson, William L. *Steal Away.* Kjos T108

Dawson, William L. *There Is a Balm in Gilead.* Kjos T105

De Cormier, Robert. *Hallelujah.* Lawson-Gould 51272

De Cormier, Robert. *Pick a Bale of Cotton.* Lawson-Gould 51375

De Cormier, Robert. *Stars Shinin' By 'n By.* Lawson-Gould 51751

De Cormier, Robert. *Study War No More.* Lawson-Gould 51477

Dett, R. Nathaniel. *I'll Never Turn Back No More.* J. Fischer FE 4435

Dett, R. Nathaniel. *Listen' to the Lambs.* G. Schirmer

Dressler, John. *Josua Fit the Battle of Jericho.* Agape 7128

Gardner, Maurice. *I'm Gonna Sing.* Staff 499

Gardner, Maurice. *Pick a Bale of Cotton.* Staff 1063

Gillum R. H. *Roll Jordan Roll.* J. Fischer 8390

Hairston, R. *Elijah Rock.* Bourne S1017

Hairston, R. *Hold On'.* Bourne

Hairston, R. *I Can Tell the World.* Bourne

Hairston, R. *Poor Man Lazrus.* Schumann S-1001

Hall, Frederick. *Steal Away.* Rodheaver 1945

Hayden, Philip. *Wade in the Water.* Shawnee A-1490

Heath, Fenno. *In That Great Gettin' Up Mornin'.* G. Schirmer 11867

Heath, Fenno. *Guide My Head.* G. Schirmer 11868

Johnson, Hall. *Ain't Got Time to Die.* G. Schirmer 10301

Johnson, Hall. *Hol' de Light.* C. Fischer CM7104

Kirk, Theron. *Wade in the Water.* C. Fischer CM8022

Kjelson, Lee. *I'm Goin' to Sing!* Belwin 2061

Krone, Max. *Jesus Walked This Lonesome Valley.* Kjos 1032

Kubik, Gail. *Oh Rock-a-Mah-Soul.* Lawson-Gould 52013

Laster, James H. *Lord, I Want to Be a Christian.* Augsburg 11-1739

Lewis, Aden. *Keep in the Middle of the Road.* Plymouth PCS-152

Lee, Orrie. *Shadrack.* C. Fischer CM4670

Lynn, George. *Lonesome Valley.* Presser 312-40062

Luboff, Norman. *All My Trials.* Walton 3065

Luboff, Norman. *Steal Away.* Walton 3061

Montgomery, Bruce. *Set It Down.* Plymouth JR106

Moore, Undine. *We Shall Walk Through the Valley.* Augsburg 11-0565

North, Jack. *Somebody's Knockin' at Your Door.* Coronet CP120

Parks, James. *Sometimes I Feel Like a Motherless Child.* Hal Leonard 08603701

Parks, James. *Were You There?* Hal Leonard 08603818

Pfautsch, Lloyd. *Little Wheel A-Turnin.* Lawson-Gould 547

Rhea, Raymond. *He Knows*. Belwin 1352

Rhea, Raymond. *A Little Talk with Jesus*. Bourne RSS1

Rhea, Raymond. *My Soul Is a Witness for My Lord*. Choral Art R142

Richardson, Michael. *The Morning Trumpet*. Mark Foster 245

Richardson, Michael. *Poor Wafarin' Stranger*. Mark Foster 251

Richardson, Michael. *Promised Land*. Mark Foster 255

Ringwald, Roy. *Deep River*. Shawnee A-90

Ringwald, Roy. *Join Hands*. Shawnee A-1257

Rodby, Walter. *I Got the Spirit*. WR1008

Rodby, Walter. *Written in De Holy Book*. Schmitt 1876

Rumery, L. R. *Steal Away*. Thomas House C28-8419

Shaw-Parker. *Dere's No Hidin Place*. Lawson-Gould 51110

Shaw-Parker. *I Got a Key*. Lawson-Gould 1105

Shaw-Parker. *I Got Shoes*. Lawson-Gould 51116

Shaw-Parker. *John Saw Duh Number*. Lawson-Gould 51109

Shaw, Robert. *Set Down Servant*. Shawnee 7

Simeone, Harry. *Dry Bones*. C. Hansen 1977-260

Simeone, Harry. *Ezekiel Saw the Wheel*. Shawnee A-130

Smith, Don. *There Is a Balm in Gilead*. Plymouth LC101

Smith, Wm. Henry. *Children Don't Get Weary*. Kjos 1007

Smith, Wm. Henry. *Didn't My Lord Deliver Daniel*. Kjos 1014

Smith, Wm. Henry. *Every Time I Feel the Spirit*. Kjos 1006

Smith, Wm. Henry. *Plenty Good Room*. Kjos 1003

Smith, Wm. Henry. *Sometimes I Feel Like a Motherless Child*. Kjos 1013

Smith, Richard H. *Lawd I Wanna Go Home*. AMSI 305

Thomas, Andre. *When the Trumpet Sounds*. Mark Foster 261

Terri, Salli. *Let Us Break Bread Together*. Lawson-Gould 896

Thygerson, Robert. *This Little Light of Mine*. Coronet CP 266

Thygerson, Robert. *Witness*. Heritage H315-3

Watson, Russell. *Listen to the Lambs*. Belwin 1263

Wilson, John F. *I Got a Shoe*. Somerset JW7771

Worley, Ray B. *Roll De Chariot Along*. Belwin 1381

Christmas

Alwes, Chester L., arr. *Ding Dong Merrily on High* (SSAATBB). Roger Dean/Heritage HRD 130

Arkhangelsky, A.-Norden. *O Gladsome Light*. J. Fischer/Belwin 4332

Averre, Richard E. *Did Mary Know?* Presser 312-40289

Bach, J. S. *Break Forth, O Beauteous, Heavenly Light* (Christmas Oratorio). Kjos 5002

Bach, J. S. *Rejoice and Sing* (Christmas Oratorio). Kjos 20

Barlow, Michael. *A Boy Was Born in Bethlehem.* Novello 644

Beck, John Ness. *And in That Day.* Kjos GC 31

Beck, John Ness. *Every Valley.* Beckenhorst BP 1040

Berlioz, Hector. *Thou Must Leave Thy Lowly Dwelling* (Childhood of Christ). Gray CMR 1898

Besig, Don. *Sing We All Noel!* (Flute) Flammer A-6122

Billings, William-Dickinson. *A Virgin Unspotted.* Music Press MP-64

Binkerd, Gordon. *The Christ-Child.* Boosey & Hawkes 5982

Black, Charles, arr. *As Lately We Watched.* Gray CMR 1358

Black, Charles, arr. *Masters in This Hall.* Gray 2710

Bodenschatz, Ehr. *A Christmas Cradle Song of the 14th Century.* C. Fischer CM 173

Bortniansky, D. S. *Cherubim Song No. 7.* G. Schirmer 2560

Brahms, J.-Fettke. *All Sing Loudly.* Flammer A-5715

Brahms, J.-Suchoff. *A Christmas Lullaby.* Sam Fox XPS 191

Brahms, J.-Granville. *The Hunter.* Choral Art

Britten, Benjamin, arr. *As Dew in Aprille* (Ceremony of Carols). Boosey & Hawkes 1829

Britten, Benjamin, arr. *A Boy Was Born.* Oxford X92

Britten, Benjamin, arr. *This Little Babe* (Ceremony of Carols). Boosey & Hawkes 1830

Brubeck, Dave. *Gloria* (La Fiesta de la Posada). Shawnee A-1365

Brubeck, Dave. *Run, Run, Run to Bethlehem* (La Fiesta de la Posada). Shawnee A-1534

Brubeck, Dave. *Sleep, Holy Infant, Sleep* (La Fiesta de la Posada). Shawnee A-1360

Burt, Alfred. *The Alfred Burt Carols.* Shawnee Set I A-449, Set II A-450, Set III A-451

Butler, Eugene. *Glory to the Son* (2 Tpts, Timp.). Hope A 520

Butler, Eugene. *Rejoice and Be Merry.* Beacon Hill/Belwin AN-6015

Byrd, William. *An Earthly Tree a Heavenly Fruit.* Stainer & Bell 2631

Cain, Noble. *On This Good Christmas Morn.* Flammer 84177

Charpentier, Marc-Antoine-Ehret. *Noel Benedictus.* Shawnee A-1430

Christiansen, F. M., arr. *Lost in the Night* (Finnish). Augsburg 11-0119

Christiansen, F. M., arr. *Beautiful Savior.* Augsburg 51

Christiansen, F. M. *Lullaby on Christmas Eve.* Augsburg 136

Christiansen, O. C. *We've Been a While A'Wandring* (Yorkshire). Kjos 5105

Christiansen, Paul. *How Far Is It to Bethlehem?* Kjos 42

Clark, Rogie, arr. *Six Afro-American Carols.* Piedmont/Marks/Belwin 15595-6

Clausen, Rene, arr. *Cold December Flies Away.* Mark Foster 543

Clausen, Rene, arr. *Sweet Was the Song.* Mark Foster 550

Cobb, Nancy H. *Gloria in Excelsis Deo* (Brass). Gentry JG-502

Coggin, Elwood, arr. *Willie, Take Your Little Drum* (Patapan). Kjos 5944

Davenport, David N. *Mary, Did You Know?* Richmond MI-174

Davis, Katherine K. *Carol of the Drum.* B. F. Wood 568 (Czech)

Davis, Katherine K. *Glory in the Highest.* Galaxy 1092

Davis, Katherine K. *Sing Gloria.* Remick 5-R3158

Davison, Archibald T. *Ye Watchers and Ye Holy Ones.* E. C. Schirmer 1780

Dawson, William L., arr. *Mary Had a Baby.* Tuskegee 118

Dello Joio, Norman. *Bright Star* (Light of the World). Marks 4567

Dello Joio, Norman. *A Christmas Carol.* Marks

Dering, Richard-Terry. *Quem Vidistis Pastores?* (SSATTB). Gray 1594

Dickinson, Clarence, arr. *Is This the Way to Bethlehem?* Gray 178

Dickinson, Clarence, arr. *Shepherds' Christmas Song.* Gray 7

Diemer, Emma Lou. *A Babe Is Born.* Sacred Music Press S61

Downing, Kenneth, arr. *The Friendly Beasts.* G. Schirmer 8714

Edmundson, Garth. *Let All Mortal Flesh Keep Silence.* J. Fischer/Belwin 8749

Ehret, Walter, arr. *That's My Jesus.* McAfee M1233

Ehret, Walter, arr. *What You Gonna Call Yo' Pretty Little Baby.* Schmitt 884

Fissinger, Edwin, arr. *Holly Carol.* Jenson 411-08024

Fissinger, Edwin, arr. *O Shepherds, Go Quickly.* Jenson 411-15014

Franck, M.-Haufrecht. *'Twas Here a King Was Born.* Sam Fox PS 158

Gabrielli, G.-Proulx. *Gloria in Excelsis.* G.I.A. Pub. G-2412

Gaul, Harvey B., arr. *Carol of the Russian Children.* G. Schirmer 6770

Gaul, Harvey B., arr. *Five Traditional French Christmas Carols.* Oliver Ditson 12377

Gevaert, Francois A. *A Joyous Christmas Song.* Gray GSC 11

Gevaert, Francois A. *Slumber Song of the Infant Jesus.* Gray 14

Greenburg, Noah, arr. *E la don don, Verges Maria.* Associated NYPMA 8

Greenburg, Noah, arr. *Dadme albricias, hijos d'Eva.* Associated NYPMA 9

Grundman, Clare, arr. *Pat-a-Pan* (Burgundian). Boosey & Hawkes 6038

Halter, Carl, arr. *A Virgin Most Pure* (English). Concordia 98-1237

Handel, G. F. *And the Glory of the Lord* (Messiah). G. Schirmer 3829

Handel, G. F. *For Unto Us a Child Is Born* (Messiah). G. Schirmer 3580

Handel, G. F. *Glory to God* (Messiah). G. Schirmer 7217

Handel, G. F. *Hallelujah Chorus* (Messiah). G. Schirmer 7217

Harris, Ed., arr. *I Saw Three Ships*. Somerset AD 2015

Harris, Roy, arr. *Red Bird in a Green Tree*. Belwin 64428

Holden, Oliver. *Christmas*. Broude Bros. WW 18

Holst, Gustav. *Christmas Day* (Solos, Orch. Parts). Novello 29012903

Holst, Gustav. *Let All Mortal Flesh Keep Silence*. Galaxy 1.5019.1

Hutson, Wihla-Raymond. *The Creche Carol*. Plymouth JR 100

Jennings, Carolyn, arr. *Here We Come A-Caroling*. Curtis/Kjos C8421

Jennings, Carolyn, arr. *I Saw Three Ships*. Curtis 8323

Jungst, Hugo, arr. *While Shepherds Watched Their Sheep* (Echo Carol). Gray 103

Kauffmann, Ronald. *African Noel* (SSATBB). Elkan-Vogel 362-03288

Kirk, Theron. *Noel, Noel* (Finger Cymbals, Tamb.). Somerset AD 2005

Kodály, Zoltan, arr. *A Christmas Carol*. Oxford 84.091

Kountz, Richard. *Carol of the Sheep Bells*. Galaxy 1080

Kountz, Richard. *Rise Up Early*. Galaxy 1665

Kuhnau, J. (Bach)-McKelvy. *Alleluia* (Cantata 142). Mark Foster MF 544H

Leontovich, M.-Wilhousky. *Carol of the Bells*. C. Fischer CM 4604

Lewis, Aden, arr. *African Noel* (Liberian). Plymouth PCS 38

Luboff, Norman, arr. *Still, Still, Still* (Austrian). Walton 3003

Lundquist, Matthew, arr. *Gentle Mary and Her Child* (Finnish). Elkan-Vogel 1152

Luvaas, Morten, arr. *Hark, Now, O Shepherds* (SSAATTBB). Birchard 840

Luvaas, Morten, arr. *On Christmas Night* (SSATBB). Kjos 2038

Luvaas, Morten, arr. *When Christmas Morn Is Dawning* (German). Augsburg TC9

McGlohon, Loonis-Ringwald. *Love Came Down at Christmas*. Glorysound/ Shawnee A-5858

McGlohon, Loonis, arr. *Rise Up, Shepherd, and Follow*. A. Broude 1026

Mendelssohn, F. *Then Shall a Star Come Out of Jacob* (Christus). Schmitt 1903

Moe, Daniel. *Hosanna to the Son of David*. Mercury/Presser 352-00212

Niles, John J.-Warrell. *Jesus, Jesus, Rest Your Head* (Appalachian). G. Schirmer 8302

Niles, John J-Horton. *I Wonder As I Wander* (Appalachian). G. Schirmer 8708

Paulus, Stephen. *A Savior from on High*. AMSI 339

Peninger, David. *Sleep Now, King Jesus Child*. Hinshaw HMC-365

Pergolesi, G. B.-Manney. *Glory to God in the Highest* (Stabat Mater). Belwin 64046

Pfautsch, Lloyd. *Christmas in the Straw* (Violin). Lawson-Gould 51587

Pfautsch, Lloyd. *Fanfare for Christmas* (2 Tpts, 2 Trbns.). Flammer 84758

Pooler, Marie, arr. *Now It Is Christmas Time* (Swedish). Augsburg TC13

Pote, Allen. *Love Came Down at Christmas* (Handbells, C Inst.). Hinshaw HMC-404

Poulenc, Francis. *Hodie Christus Natus Est.* Salabert

Praetorius, M.-Clough-Leighter. *En Natus Est Emanuel.* E. C. Schirmer 2298

Praetorius, M.-Luvaas. *In Natali Domini.* Kjos 2007

Praetorius, M.-Baker. *Lo, How a Rose E'er Blooming.* G. Schirmer 2484

Praetorius, M.-Greyson. *Psallite.* Bourne ES 21

Praetorius, M.-Baker. *To Us Is Born Immanuel.* G. Schirmer 2482

Purvis, Richard, arr. *What Strangers Are These?* (Scottish). Birchard 1447

Roberton, Hugh S. *For Tonight a King Is Born in Bethlehem* (SSATB). Presser 312-41238

Rodby, Walter, and Roff, J. *Noel, Noel, Let Us Sing Merry Christmas.* Schmitt 8039

Rorem, Ned. *O Magnum Mysterium.* Boosey & Hawkes 6006

Routley, Erik, arr. *Remember* (English). G.I.A. Pub. G-2317

Rutter, John, arr. *Christmas Bells* (Norwegian). Hinshaw HMC-348

Rutter, John, arr. *Mary's Lullaby.* Oxford X-272

Saint Saens-Walker. *Praise Ye the Lord of Hosts* (Christmas Oratorio). Hal Leonard 08681662

Scarlatti, A.-Brandvik. *O Magnum Mysterium.* Schmitt 1439

Scheidt-Granville. *Ah, My Beloved Jesus Child* (SSATB). Sam Fox FXCM

Schein, Hermann-Boepple. *Christmas Chorale.* Mercury DCS 7

Schein, Hermann-Pinkham. *Vom Himmel Hoch da Komm Ich Her.* E. C. Schirmer 2722

Schreck, Gustav-Christiansen, O. C. *Advent Motet* (SSAATTBB). Kjos 5083

Schroth, Gerhard, arr. *De Glory Manger* (SATB Divisi). Kjos 5214

Schroth, Gerhard, arr. *Keeping Holy Vigil.* Kjos 5185

Schulz, J. P. A.-Fritschel. *O Come, Little Children.* Hinshaw HMC-148

Shaw, Martin. *Fanfare for Christmas Day.* G. Schirmer 8745

Shaw, Robert-Parker, A. *O Sanctissima.* G. Schirmer 10194

Shaw, Robert-Parker, A. *Saboly: Touro-louro-louro!.* G. Schirmer 10167

Shaw, Robert-Parker, A. *What Child Is This.* G. Schirmer 10199

Sjolund, Paul, arr. *Away in a Manger.* Walton WW1023

Sojlund, Paul. *Little Jesus Came to Town*. Hinshaw HMC-734

Sleeth, Natalie. *Calypso Christmas*. Hope A-508

Sowerby, Leo. *Love Came Down at Christmas*. Fitzsimons 2054

Sweelinck, Jan P. *Hodie Christus Natus Est* (SSATB). Presser 312-40155

Thompson, Randall. *Glory to God in the Highest*. E. C. Schirmer 2470

Vance, Margaret, arr. *Jesus, Jesus, Rest Your Head*. New Music NMA143

Victoria, Tomas L.-Beebe, E. *O Magnum Mysterium*. Broude Bros. CR 30

Victoria, Tomas L.-Banner. *Magi Viderunt Stellam*. Shawnee A-1355

Victoria, Tomas L.-Klein. *Quem Vidistis, Pastores* (SSATBB). G. Schirmer 11974

Vree, Marion, arr. *Fum, Fum, Fum*. Presser 312-40281

Wagner, Douglas. *Born, Born in Bethlehem*. Somerset AD 2020

Walther, Johann-Ehret. *Joseph Dearest, Joseph Mine*. Flammer A-5763

Walton, William. *What Cheer*. Oxford 84.090

Weelkes, Thomas-Haberlen. *We Shepherds Sing*. Kjos 5997

Weiss, Donn, arr. *The Happy Christmas Comes Once More* (Danish). Shawnee A-1351

Wesley, Samuel-Stevens, D. *Hodie Christus Natus Est*. A. Broude 1022

Wetzler, Robert. *Wondrous News!* Curtis/Kjos C8419

Willan, Healy. *The Three Kings*. Oxford 43P214

Wilson, John F., arr. *Gloria in Excelsis Deo* (French). Hope JW 7782

Wood, Dale, arr. *Love Came Down at Christmas* (Irish). AMSI 346

Young, Gordon. *Joseph Came Walking to Bethlehem*. Flammer A-5860

Young, Gordon. *Sing We All Noel*. Somerset AD 1999

Zaninelli, Luigi, arr. *Carols Three: A Christmas Overture*. Shawnee A-1270

Zaninelli, Luigi. *Christmas Collage*. Shawnee A-1345

E. JUNIOR AND SENIOR HIGH MALE CHORUS OCTAVOS

Junior High Male Chorus

Bach, J. S.-Siltman. *Jesu, Joy of Man's Desiring* (CBB). Cambiata Press M97687

Baker, Margaret. *Who Came to See?* (CBB). Cambiata Press C485181

Beal, Loy. *Brother, Show Us the Way* (CCBB). Cambiata Press C97444

Beal, Loy. *Together We'll Make the Journey* (CCBB). Cambiata Press L97563

Burney, Charles. *Round for 20 Voices*. Belwin 2458

Butler, E.-Rich. *Blessed Is the Man* (CCBB). Cambiata Press C97564

Buxtehude, Dietrich. *Zion Hears the Watchman Singing* (TB). E. C. Schirmer 538

Collins, Don L. *Be Strong and Wise in the Lord* (CBB). Cambiata Press C97689

Collins, Don L., arr. *The Holly and the Ivy* (CC, opt. B). Cambiata Press L97688

Cram, James. *Where'er You Walk* (CCBB). Cambiata Press C978113

Driggers, Samuel, arr. *Sometimes I Feel Like a Motherless Child* (CBB). Cambiata S97690

Flemming-Johnstone. *Integer Vitae* (CCBB). Cambiata Press M97562

Gadie, The. (Scottish, TB). E. C. Schirmer 586

Gilbert-Sullivan-Artman. *We Sail the Ocean Blue.* Hinshaw HMC572

Giles, Lee, arr. *Poor Lonesome Cowboy* (CCBB). Cambiata Press U97446

Johnson, Neil, arr. *Poor Wayfaring Stranger* (TTB). Jenson 446-16011

Kahn-Artman. *Toot, Toot, Tootsie* (TB). Hal Leonard 08598205

Kirby-Rich. *What Do All of These Things Mean* (CCBB). Cambiata Press L97443

Lawrence, R., arr. *Drink to Me Only with Thine Eyes* (CBB). Cambiata Press U485181

Lucas, Michael-Houston, Jim. *Girls!* (TTB). Studio PR V-7939

Siltman, Bobby, arr. *Emmanuel's Birth* (CBB). Cambiata Press U982161

Siltman, Bobby, arr. *Medley for Christmas* (CBB). Cambiata U978115

Siltman, Bobby, arr. *Salty Dog* (CBB). Cambiata Press U485183

Siltman, Bobby, arr. *Spiritual Trilogy* (CBB). Cambiata Press S980148

Siltman, Bobby, arr. *This Train* (CBB). Cambiata Press U978114

Swanson, Frederick, arr. *Sing Out Young Voices; Vol 1: Four Songs* (TB). G. Schirmer 12328

Swenson, Harry, arr. *Christmas Medley* (CBB). Cambiata Press U97566

Swenson, Harry, arr. *Li'l Liza Jane* (CCB). Cambiata Press U979134

Swenson, Harry, arr. *Scarborough Fair* (CCB). Cambiata Press U97691

Swenson, Harry, arr. *Three Christmas Carols* (CBB). Cambiata Press U979133

Van Wormer, Gorden. *The Captain* (TBB). General Works/Kjos GC44

Willis-Lawrence. *Fairest Lord Jesus* (CBB). Cambiata Press U983180

Senior High Male Chorus

Sacred

Appling-William. *We Shall Walk through the Valley in Peace* (TTBB). World Library CE-2328

Arcadelt-Greyson. *Ave Maria* (TTBB). Bourne ES4

Bach, J. S. *Come Sweet Death* (TTBB). G. Schirmer 8956

Bach, J. S. *Good Fellows Be Merry* (Peasant Cantata)(TTBB). Boston 12065

Bach, J. S. *The Lord Bless You* (TB). Concordia 98-1474

Bach, J. S. *May God Smile on You* (TB) C. F. Peters

Bach, J. S. *My Spirit, Be Joyful* (Cantata 146)(TB with four-hand piano). E. C. Schirmer 938

Beck, John N. *A New Heart I Will Give You* (TTBB). G. Schirmer 11781

Beethoven, L. van. *Hallelujah* (Mount of Olives). G. Schirmer 10774

Berlioz, Hector. *Thou Must Leave Thy Lowly Dwelling* (TTBB). Galaxy 2065

Binkerd, Gordon. *Alleluia for St. Francis* (TB). Boosey & Hawkes 5686

Blakley. *If with All Your Heart* (TTBB). Hinshaw HMC-342

Brahms, Johannes. *Let Nothing Ever Grieve Thee* (TTBB). C. F. Peters 6009

Bruckner, Anton. *Inveni David* (TTBB, four trombones). C. F. Peters 6318

Burnham. *A Thanksgiving to God for His House* (TTBB). Heritage 2874

Butler, Eugene. *Come Peace of God* (TTBB). Sacred Music Press 2859

Casals, P. *O Vos Omnes* (TTBB). Abingdon 242

Christiansen-Wycisk, arr. *Beautiful Savior* (TTBB). Augsburg 263

Copland, Aaron. *Zion's Walls* (TTBB). Boosey & Hawkes 6072

Corsi-Cain. *Adoramus Te* (TTBB). Choral Art R180

Cruger-Mendelssohn. *Now Thank We All Our God* (TTBB). Boston 471

Des Pres, J. *Gloria* (Missa Mater Patris)(TTBB). G. Schirmer 11012

Diemer, Emma Lou. *O Come, Let Us Sing unto the Lord* (TTBB). C. Fischer CM8014

Gevaert-Grayson. *Noel, Noel* (TTBB). Kjos 5513

Gevaert-Lefebvre. *Sleep of the Child Jesus* (TTBB). Franco Colombo NY773

Goemanne, Noel. *Jubilate Deo* (3 pt.). McLaughlin & Reilly 2366

Gerike. *Jerusalem, My Happy Home* (TTBB). Mark Foster 1002

Gretchaninoff. *Glory to God* (TTBB). Marks 53

Grieg-Pitcher. *Ave, Maris Stella* (TTBB). Summy Birchard 881

Handel, G. F. *Swell the Full Chorus* (Solomon)(TTBB). Plymouth FO-300

Hassler, Hans Leo-Beveridge. *Cantate Domino* (TTBB). E. C. Schirmer

Hassler, Hans Leo. *Gratias Agimus Tibi* (TTBB). Lawson-Gould 782

Heath. *Thy Word Is a'Lantern* (TTBB). G. Schirmer 11217

Handel-Dawe. *Alleluia* (TTBB). G. Schirmer 9412

Handel, G. F. *Then Round About the Starry Throne* (Samson)(TTBB). E. C. Schirmer 907

Hunter, arr. *Be Thou My Vision* (TBB). Hinshaw HMC-375

Janacek. *Veni Sancte Spiritus* (TTBB). Universal 1678NJ

Jungst, Hugo, arr. *Christmas Hymn* (TTBB). G. Schirmer 1414

Kopylov-Wilhousky. *Heavenly Light!* C. Fischer CM611

Krone, Max. *God Rest You Merry, Gentleman* (TTBB). Kjos 1117

Lotti, A. *Surely He Hath Borne Our Griefs* (TTB). Marks 15311-4

Malin, Don, arr. *All Glory Be to God on High* (TTBB). Summy Birchard 1538

Mead. *Beati Mortui* (Blessed Are the Dead)(TTBB). G. Schirmer 51707

Mead. *Once to Every Man and Nation* (TTBB). Galaxy 1.2264.1

Moe, Daniel. *I Will Extol Thee* (TTBB). Augsburg PS623

Mauton, arr. *A Babe So Tender* (TTBB). E. C. Schirmer 543

Palestrina, G. *Adoramus Te* (TTBB). Bourne ES16

Palestrina, G. *O Bone Jesu* (TTBB). Bourne ES45

Persichetti, Vincent. *Song of Peace* (TTBB). Elkan-Vogel 130

Pfautsch, Lloyd. *Brothers, Lift Your Voices* (TTBB). H. W. Gray CMR2556

Pote, Alan. *Sing for Joy* (TTBB). Hinshaw HMC-517

Quilter, Roger. *Non Nobis, Domine* (TTBB). Boosey & Hawkes MFS348

Rossini, G. *Chant Funebre* (Dirge)(TTBB and Tenor Drum). Joseph Boonin 103

Rutter, John. *Lord, Make Me an Instrument of Thy Peace* (TTBB). Hinshaw

Schuetky-Treharne. *May Now Thy Spirit* (TTBB). Willis 5641

Shaw, Martin. *With a Voice of Singing* (TTBB). G. Schirmer 10454

Sleeth, Natalie. *Seek and You will Find* (2 Part) Hinshaw HMC589

Sjolund, Paul. *The Light of the World* (TTBB). Walton 9002

Sowerby, Leo. *Psalm 133* (TTBB). H. W. Gray CMR 2982-4

Thompson, Randall. *The Last Words of David* (TTBB). E. C. Schirmer 2154

Tschesnokov-Ehret. *Let Thy Holy Presence* (TTBB). Boosey & Hawkes 5022

Vene. *Ave Maria* (TTBB). E. C. Schirmer 2137

Viadana. *O Sacrum Convivium* (TTBB). E. C. Schirmer 78

Victoria, Thomas L. *Ave Maria* (TTBB). E. C. Schirmer 2515

Victoria, Thomas L. *O Sacrum Convivium* (TTBB). Oxford A232

Secular

Beethoven, Ludwig van. *Oh, What Delight* (Fidelio)(TTBB). C. Fischer CM2245

Beveridge. *Drop, Drop, Slow Tears* (TTBB). E. C. Schirmer 2174

Bouchieri. *The Match Sellers* (TTB). Marks 4387

Butler, Eugene. *As Beautiful As She* (3 Part). Warner Bros. W3771

Butler, Eugene. *Come Peace of God* (TTBB). Sacred Music Press S-5017

Butler, Eugene. *Give Me the Love* (2 Part). Schmitt 255

Butler, Eugene. *If Ye Would Drink Delight* (TTBB). Heritage Music 2871

Butler, Eugene. *Laura* (2 Part). C. Fischer CM7905

Butler, Eugene. *Why So Pale, Fond Lover* (TTBB). Hal Leonard 08071575

Chenoweth, W. *Vocalise with Sop, Solo* (Male Voices). G. Schirmer 51041

Copland, Aaron. *Song of the Guerrillas* (North Star)(TBB). Boosey & Hawkes 1729

Copland, Aaron. *Stomp Your Foot* (Tender Land)(TTBB). Boosey & Hawkes 6136

De Paur. *Marry a Woman Uglier Than You* (TTBB). Lawson-Gould 543

Dowland, John. *Sweet Love Doth Now Invite* (TTBB). Bourne ES7

Dunstable, John. *The Agincourt Song* (TTBB). Boston 12633

Durien, E. *Land-Sighting* (TTBB). G. Schirmer 1013

Este, M. *How Merrily We Live* (TTB). E. C. Schirmer 540

Finzi. *Thou Didst Delight My Eyes* (TBB). Boosey & Hawkes 5456

Gounod, Charles. *Soldier's Chorus* (Faust)(TTBB). G. Schirmer 4283

Grieg-McKinney. *Brothers, Sing On* (TTBB). J. Fischer 6927

Heath. *Beat! Beat! Drums!* (TTBB). G. Schirmer 10344

Heath. *Grass* (TTBB). G. Schirmer 10118

Holst, Gustav. *Good Friday.* (TTBB). Boosey & Hawkes

Holst, G. *I Love My Love* (TTBB). G. Schirmer 10967

Johnson. *Honor! Honor!* (TTBB). C. Fischer CM2182

Kodály, Zoltan. *The Bachelor* (3 Part). Boosey & Hawkes 1893

Kodály, Zoltan. *Evening Song* (3 Part). Boosey & Hawkes 5798

Kodály, Zoltan. *The Ruins* (TTBB). T. Presser 312-40595

Kodály, Zoltan. *Soldier's Song* (3 Part, Tpt, Drum). Boosey & Hawkes 1892

Korte. *Jenny Kissed Me* (2 Part). E. C. Schirmer 2311

Lully, J. *Woods So Dense.* G. Schirmer 8568

Mead. *No Man Is an Island* (TTBB). G. Schirmer 52043

Mechem, Kurt. *Jenny Kissed Me* (3 Part). Boosey & Hawkes 5856

Mendelssohn, Felix. *Drinking Song* (TTBB). G. Schirmer 12034

Mendelssohn, Felix. *Hunting Song* (TTBB). G. Schirmer 12074

Mendelssohn, Felix. *Love and Wine* (TTBB). G. Schirmer 12033

Merrifield. *Now Look Away* (TTBB). Boston 12774

Morley, Thomas. *Round Around About a Wood* (TTBB). G. Schirmer 10745

Nelson, Ron. *Behold Man* (TTBB). Boosey & Hawkes 5403

Pearsall, R. *When Allen-A-Dale Went A-Hunting* (TTBB). Modern Music Press 4152

Pelz. *Love Is Here to Stay* (TTBB). New Music Co. 3001

Persichetti, Vincent. *Jimmie's Got a Goil* (2 Part). G. Schirmer 9860

Peterson. *Poly Von* (TTBB). Jenson 413-16011

Purcell, Henry. *Passing By* (TTBB). Lawson-Gould 967

Ravenscroft. *We Be Three Poor Mariners* (TTBB). Bourne 2587-5

Romberg, S.-Scotson. *Stouthearted Men* (TTBB). Harms 9-H1184

Schubert, Franz. *By the Sea* (TTBB). Belwin 1145

Schubert, Franz. *La Pastorella* (The Shepherdess)(TTBB). Lawson-Gould 512

Schubert, Franz. *Liebe* (Love)(TTBB). Mark Foster 1059

Schubert, Franz. *The Night* (TTBB). Brodt DC5

Schubert, Franz. *Standchen* (Serenade)(TTBB). Lawson-Gould

Schubert, Franz. *Widerspruch* (Contradiction)(TTBB). Lawson-Gould 513

Schuman, Robert. *Die Rose Stand im Tau* (5 Part). Broude 241

Thiman, Eric. *She Is My Slender Small Love* (TTBB). G. Schirmer 10671

Thompson, Randall. *The Pasture* (3 Part). E. C. Schirmer 2181

Thompson, Randall. *Stopping by Woods on a Snowy Evening* (3 Part). E. C. Schirmer 2182

Thompson, Randall. *Tarantella* (TTBB). E. C. Schirmer 560

Vaughan Williams, Ralph. *Down Among the Dead Men* (TTBB). Galaxy 1.5025.1

Vaughan Williams, Ralph. *Drinking Song* (2 & 3 Part). Oxford

Vaughan Williams, Ralph. *The Farmer's Boy* (TTBB). Stainer & Bell 2078

Vaughan Williams, Ralph. *The Vagabond* (TTBB). Boosey & Hawkes 5454

Wagner, R.-Dawson. *Pilgrims' Chorus* (Tannhauser). Kjos 5490

Weber, C. M. *Hunter's Chorus* (Der Freischutz)(TTBB). G. Schirmer 11689

Folk/Spiritual

Andrews, arr. *John Peel* (TTBB). H. W. Gray 31

Bartholomew, M. *Amo, Amas, I Love a Lass* (TBB). Mercury 352-001338914

Barthomomew, M., arr. *De Animals a-Comin'* (TTBB). G. Schirmer 8046

Bartholomew, M., arr. *Erie Canal* (TTBB). G. Schirmer 9222

Bartholomew, M., arr. *I Couldn't Hear Nobody Pray* (TTBB). G. Schirmer

Bartholowmew, M., arr. *I Got Shoes* (TTBB). G. Schirmer 7144

Bartholomew, M., arr. *Little Innocent Lamb* (TTBB). G. Schirmer 9907

Bartholomew, M., arr. *Standin' in the Need of Prayer* (TTBB). G. Schirmer 8050

Bartholomew, M. *Two Old English Airs: Shall I, Wasting in Despair and Drink to Me Only with Thine Eyes* (TTBB). G. Schirmer 7413

Bartholomew, M. *Two Spirituals: Old Ark's a-Moverin' and Steal Away* (TTBB). G. Schirmer 7756

Bartholomew, M. *What Shall We Do with a Drunken Sailor?* G. Schirmer

Bock, F. *Scarborough Fair* (TTBB). Gentry HM G-110

Brown-Gary. *Good News* (TTB). Studio PR V7707

Burleigh, arr. *My Lord, What a Mornin'* (TTBB). Franco Colombo NY1713

Churchill. *Black Is the Color of My True Love's Hair* (TTBB). Shawnee C-51

Copland, A. *At the River* (TTBB). Boosey & Hawkes 5514

Copland, A. *Simple Gifts* (TB). Boosey & Hawkes 1903

Dawson, William. *Ain't-a That Good News* (TTBB). Tuskegee 104

Dawson, William. *Ev'ry Time I Feel the Spirit* (TTBB). Tuskegee 125

Dawson, William. *Soon-ah Will Be Done* (TTBB) Tuskegee T101-A

Dawson, William. *There Is a Balm in Gilead* (TTBB). Tuskegee 106

Dawson, William. *Two Spirituals: Jesus Walked This Lonesome Valley and You Got to Reap Just What You Sow* (TTBB). Warner Bros. C10783

De Cormier, Robert, arr. *The Erie Canal* (2 Part). Lawson-Gould 52073

Duey, arr. *Ain't Got Time to Die* (TTBB). Boston 13010

Duey, arr. *The Minstrel Boy* (TTBB). Boston 2947

Duson, Dede. *Loch Lomond* (TTBB). Kjos 5564

Foster, M. *Three Old American Songs* (TTBB). G. Schirmer 3233

Hairston, arr. *Poor Man Lazrus* (TTBB). Bourne 2653-7

Heath, arr. *Didn't My Lord Deliver Daniel* (TTBB). G. Schirmer 11058

Heath, arr. *Guide My Head* (TTBB). G. Schirmer 11868

Heath, arr. *He's Got the Whole World in His Hands* (TTBB). G. Schirmer 10854

Heath, arr. *Sometimes I Feel Like a Motherless Child* (TTBB). G. Schirmer 10567

Heath, arr. *This Train* (TTBB). G. Schirmer 11244

Heath, arr. *When Johnny Comes Marching Home* (TTBB). G. Schirmer 10873

Holst, Gustav. *Swansea Town* (TTBB). Curwen 50615

Kubik, Gail. *Polly-Wolly-Doodle* (TTBB). G. Schirmer 9997

Leontovich-Wilhousky. *Carol of the Bells*. C. Fischer CM2270

Luboff, Norman. *The Ash Grove* (TTBB). Walton 1014

Luboff, Norman. *Colorado Trail* (TTBB). Walton 1005

Luboff, Norman. *Poor Lonesome Cowboy* (TTBB). Walton 1007

Parker-Shaw, arr. *Blow the Man Down*. Lawson-Gould 51055

Parker-Shaw, arr. *The Boar's Head Carol* (TTBB). G. Schirmer 10179

Poulton-Hauter. *Aura Lee* (TTBB). Lawson-Gould 527

Quilter, Roger. *Drink to Me Only with Thine Eyes* (TTBB). Boosey & Hawkes 18078

Richardson, arr. *Blow the Candles Out* (TTBB). Mark Foster 1061

Ringwald, arr. *All Through the Night* (TTBB). Shawnee C-21

Roberton, H., arr. *Green Grow the Rushes O!* (TTBB). R. D. Row 519

Scott, arr. *Gloucestershire Wassail* (TTBB). Words and Music/Kjos

Shaw, Robert, arr. *Set Down Servant* (TTBB). Shawnee C-26

Shaw, Robert, arr. *Shanandoah* (TTBB). Lawson-Gould 51062

Shaw, Robert, arr. *Vive L'Amour* (TTBB). G. Schirmer 51026

Smith, Wm. Henry, arr. *Climbin' Up the Mountain* (TTBB). Kjos 1101

Smith, Wm. Henry, arr. *Ride the Chariot* (TTBB). Kjos 1102

Steffe-Ringwald. *Battle Hymn of the Republic* (TTBB, four-hand piano). Shawnee

Vaughan Williams, Ralph. *Lindea Lea* (TTBB). Boosey & Hawkes 1991

Vaughan Williams, Ralph. *Loch Lomond* (TTBB). Galaxy 1.5215

Vaughan-Williams. *The Turtle Dove* (TTBB). Curwen 50570

Wagner, arr. *A-Roving* (TTBB). Lawson-Gould 791

Wagner, arr. *Shenandoah* (TTBB). Lawson-Gould 848

Washburn, arr. *Sigh No More, Ladies* (TTBB). Oxford 95.109

Whalum, arr. *Been in the Storm* (TTBB). Lawson-Gould 52246

Whalum, arr. *My Lord, What a Morning* (TTBB). Lawson-Gould 51917

Whalum, arr. *Somebody's Calling My Name* (TTBB). G. Schirmer 51932

Whalum, arr. *You'd Better Run* (TTBB). Lawson-Gould 51749

Note: Some of the Limited Range Senior High Male Chorus listings may be utilized in a Junior High Male Chorus.

F. JAZZ AND SHOW CHOIR OCTAVOS (VARIED VOICINGS) (ALPHABETICAL BY TITLE)

Ain't Gonna Grieve. Artman (2 Part). Hal Leonard

Ain't Misbehavin'. Cassey (SATB). Belwin

Ain't Nobody. Fredrickson (SATB). Scott Music

Alexander's Ragtime Band. Berlin (SATB). Shawnee

All of Me. Shaw (SATB). Hal Leonard

All the Things You Are. Puerling (SATB). Studio PR

Anything Goes. Porter, arr. Rizzo (SATB). Warner Bros.

Anywhere the Heart Goes. Kerr (SAB, SATB). Jenson

Aura Lee. Shaw (SATB). Hal Leonard

Beautiful City (Godspell). Schwartz-Lojeski (SATB). Hal Leonard

Big Band Sing. Shaw. (SAB, SATB). Hal Leonard.

Blues Down to My Shoes. Shaw (SATB). Hal Leonard

Bluer Than Blue. Kraintz (SATB). Alfred

Body and Soul. Mattson (SATB). Hal Leonard

Brandy. Lurie,-Lojeski (SATB). Hal Leonard

Brothers and Sisters. Shaw (SAB, SATB). Hal Leonard

Button Up Your Overcoat. Puerling (SATB). Studio PR

Can't Help Lovin' Dat Man. Mattson (SATB). Studio PR

Christmas Song. Azleton (SATB). Jenson

Christmas Wishes. Shaw (SAB, SATB). Hal Leonard

Circles. Chapin-Lojeski (SATB). Hal Leonard

Come Go with Me. Quick, arr. Shaw (SATB). Hal Leonard

Come Rain or Come Shine. Puerling (SATB). Hal Leonard

Corner of the Sky (Pippin). Schwartz-Cacavas (SATB). Belwin

Crazy Rhythm. Meyer and Kahn-Bretton (SATB). Warner Bros.

Da Lovely. Fredrickson (SATB). Scott Music

Daybreak. Manilow-Metis (SATB). Kamakazi Music

Deck the Halls. Puerling (SATB). Shawnee

Don't Get Around Much Anymore. Kunz (SATB). Jenson

Doctor Jazz. Shaw (SATB). Hal Leonard

Don't Take Away the Music. Tawney-Lojeski (SATB). Hal Leonard

Dream Your Dream. Hannison (SATB). Jenson

Ease on Down the Road (Wiz). Small-Beard (SATB). Shawnee

Embraceable You. Gershwin-Chinn (SATB). Jenson

Entertainer, The. Joplin-Lojeski (SATB). Hal Leonard

Everybody Rejoice (Wiz). Vandross-Ades (SATB). Shawnee

Fifty-Second Street. Allen-Shaw (SATB). Hal Leonard

Five Foot Two, Eyes of Blue. Artman (2 Part, SAB, SATB). Hal Leonard

For Once in My Life. Shaw (SATB). Columbia

Forrest Shadows. Perry (SATB). Jenson

Georgia on My Mind. Puerling (SATB). Studio PR

God Bless the Child. Herzog and Holiday-Kerr (SATB). E. B. Marks

Goodbye, Love. Kraintz (SATB). Scott Music

Got to Get You into My Life. Lennon and McCartney-Lojeski (SATB). Hal Leonard

Great Feelin'. Fredrickson (2 Part, SSA, SATB). Hal Leonard

He Gave Us a Love Song. Drummond (SATB). Glory Sound

Here's That Rainy Day. Shaw, arr. (SATB). Hal Leonard

Hold Tight. Brandow, Miller and Spotswood-Rutherford (SATB). Belwin

How Long Has This Been Going On? Mattson (SATB). Jenson

I Can't Give You Anythiing But Love. Fields and McHugh, arr. Rutherford

I Can't Stop Loving You. Gibson-Shaw (SATB). Hal Leonard

I Got A Shoes. Artman (2 Part). Hal Leonard

I Had a Dream. Shaw (SATB). Scott Music

I Hear Music. Lane-Lapin (SATB). Warner Bros.

I Left My Heart in San Francisco. Puerling (SATB). Studio PR

I'll Never Smile Again. Lowe-Kerr (SATB). MCA Music

I'm Feeling Right. Kraintz (SATB). Scott Music

I'm a-Headin' Home. Gallina (SAB). Jenson

I've Got the World on a String. Arlen-Rutherford (SATB). Belwin

I've Got Rhythm. Kunz (SATB). Jenson

I've Got You under My Skin. Mattson (SAB, SATB). Hal Leonard

Jubilation. Arr. Shaw (2 Part, SAB, SATB). Hal Leonard

Laughter in the Rain. Sedaka-Cassey (SATB). Warner Bros.

Let Me Be the One. Nichols-Lojeski (SATB). Hal Leonard

Let the Sunshine In. Arr. Shaw (SATB). Jenson

Let There Be Love. Rand-Shaw (SATB). Hal Leonard

Life Is Just a Bowl of Cherries. Puerling (SATB). Hal Leonard

Lonesome Road. Arr. Shaw (SATB). Hal Leonard

Lookin' For the Right Words. De Miero (SATB). Scott Music

Love Is the Answer. Hannison (SATB). Shawnee

Loving You. Kunz (SATB). Scott Music

Long Ago and Far Away. Gershwin-Kern-Mattson (SATB). Studio PR

Magic to Do (Pippin). Schwartz-Fisher (SATB). Belwin

Michelle. Lennon and McCartney-Puerling (SATB). Shawnee

Mighty Clouds of Joy. Arr. Shaw (SATB). Hal Leonard

Mood Indigo. Ellington-Rutherford (SATB). Belwin

Mountain Dew. Willet (SAB). Heritage Press

My Funny Valentine. Arr. Shaw (SATB). Hal Leonard

My Sweet Lady. Denver-Lojeski (SATB). Hal Leonard

Noah, Bring Your Children. Olson (SAB). Aberdeen

Night and Day. Porter-Evans (SATB). Warner Bros.

Once Upon a Rainbow. Carter (SATB). Somerset

People Need Love. Anderson and Ulvaeus (SATB). Hal Leonard

Pippin Choral Medley. Schwartz-Cassey (SATB). Belwin

Place Where Lovers Dream. DeMiero (SATB). Somerset

Raise a Ruckus Tonight. Willet (SAB). Heritage

Reach for the Stars. G. Fry (SATB). Belwin

Risin' Out of My Soul. Eilers (SAB). Jenson

Salvation Train. Schwartz (SATB). Heritage

Seems Like Old Times. Arr. Puerling (SATB). Hal Leonard

Side by Side. Woods-Coates (SATB). Shawnee

Spread Your Wings and Fly. Eilers (SATB). Jenson

Stayin' Alive. Arr. Lojeski (2 Part, SSA, SAB, SATB). Hal Leonard

String of Pearls. Arr. Kerr (SAB, SATB). Hal Leonard

Summer Nights (Grease). Casey and Jacobs-Lojeski (SATB). Hal Leonard

Summer's Eyes Are Blue. Kraintz (SSAA, SATB). Alfred

Summertime. Gershwin-Shaw (SATB). Hal Leonard

Swing Into Spring. Schwartz (2 Part). Heritage

'S Wonderful. Arr. Mattson (SATB). Jenson

Tangerine. Arr. Mattson (SATB). Hal Leonard

That Old Black Magic. Arr. Shaw (SATB). Hal Leonard

Theme from Ice Castles. Arr. Besig (SATB). Studio PR

This Is It! David and Livingston-Lapin (SATB). Warner Bros.

This Old Hammer. Willet (SAB). Heritage

Through the Years. Arr. Lojeski (2 Part, SAB, SATB). Hal Leonard

To Be in Love. Kunz (SATB). Hal Leonard

Tuxedo Junction. Arr. Nowak (SAB, SATB). Hal Leonard

You Are So Beautiful. Preston and Fischer-Lojeski (SATB). Hal Leonard

Way You Look Tonight, The. Arr. Knowles (SATB). Jenson

When I Fall in Love. Young, arr. Azelton (SATB). Hal Leonard

When Will I Find Love. Kraintz (SATB). Jenson

Wonderful Day Like Today, A. Bricusse and Newley-Leyden (SATB). Musical Comedy Prod.

Yesterday. Arr. Puerling (SATB). Shawnee

G. PUBLICATIONS WITH BAND OR ORCHESTRA ACCOMPANIMENT

Bach, J. S. *Break Forth, O Beauteous Heavenly Light* (SATB and Orch.). G. Schirmer

Bencriscutto, F. *Sing a New Song* (SATB and Band). Kjos B-407

Berlioz, Hector. *Glory and Triumph* (SATB, Band or Orch.). Mercury

Berlin-Ringwald. *God Bless America* (SA, SSA, SAB, TTBB, SATB, Band or Orch). Shawnee

Berlin-Ringwald. *Give Me Your Tired, Your Poor* (SA, SSA, SAB, TTBB, SATB, Orch.). Shawnee

Brahms, J. *How Lovely Is Thy Dwelling Place* (Requiem) (SATB, Orch.). G. Schirmer

Butler, Eugene. *And Thou America* (SATB and Band).

Carey-Bennett. *America* (SATB, Small Orch.). G. Schirmer 51770

Christensen, James. *Sing Praise to Him Our Lord* (Brass Quartet or Band, SATB). Hal Leonard

Handel, G. F. *Hallelujah Chorus* (Messiah) (SATB and Orch. or Band). C. Fischer

Handel-Houseknecht. *Thanks Be to Thee* (SATB and Band). Kjos

Haydn, F. J. *The Heavens Are Telling* (Creation) (SATB and Orch.). C. Fischer

Holst, Gustave. *Christmas Day* (SATB, Small Orch.). Gray

Holst, Gustave. *Let All Mortal Flesh Keep Silence* (SATB, Orch.). Boosey & Hawkes

Holst, Gustave. *Turn Back, O Man* (SATB, Orch.). Boosey & Hawkes

Kinyon, John. *For the Beauty of the Earth* (SA and Band). Alfred

Kinyon, John. *Let the Trumpets Ring* (SA and Strings). Alfred 1635

Kinyon, John. *Salute to America* (SA and Band). Alfred 1205

Lang. *Yuletide Overture* (SATB and Band). Belwin

Loewe-Leidzen. *Brigadoon Choral Selections* (SATB, Band or Orch.). Sam Fox

Luther-Caillet. *A Mighty Fortress is Our God* (SATB, TTBB, Band or Orch.). Boosey & Hawkes

Mendelssohn, Felix. *Come Let Us Sing* (95th Psalm for SATB and Orch). G. Schirmer

Mendelssohn-Wilson-Harris. *Festival Song of Praise* (SATB, Orch.). Bourne

Miller-Jackson-Ades. *Let There Be Peace on Earth* (SA, SSA, SAB, TTBB, SATB, Band or Orch.). Shawnee

Mozart, W. A. *Gloria in Excelsis* (Twelfth Mass) (SATB and Orch.). Presser

Pergolesi-Houseknect. *Glory to God in the Highest* (SATB and Band). Kjos

Rimsky-Korsakov. *Glory* (SSAATTBB and Orch). Witmark

Ringwald, arr. *This Is My Country* (SA, SSA, SAB, TTBB, SATB and Band). Shawnee

Ringwald, arr. *We Shall Overcome* (SA, TTBB, SATB Band or Orch.). Shawnee

Schubert, F.-Wilson. *To Music* (SSA, SAB, SATB and Orch.). Schmitt

Schubert, F. *The Omnipotence* (SSA, TTBB, SSAATTBB and Orch.). G. Schirmer

Shaw, Martin. *With a Voice of Singing* (SATB and Orch.). G. Schirmer

Sibelius-Lefebvre. *Onward, Ye Peoples* (SSA, TTBB, SATB and Orch.). Galaxy

Steele-Ades. *America, Our Heritage.* (SA, SSA, SAB, SATB and Band). Shawnee

Steffe-Ringwald. *Battle Hymn of the Republic* (SA, SSA, SAB, TTBB, SATB, Band or Orch.). Shawnee

Steffe-Wilhousky. *Battle Hymn of the Republic.* C. Fischer (SSATTBB and Orch.). C. Fischer

Teschner-Cain. *All Glory Laud and Honor* (SATB, Band or Orch.). Flammer

Vaughan-Williams, Ralph. *Fantasy on Christmas Carols* (SATB, Bar. Solo, Orch.). Galaxy

Vaughan-Williams, Ralph. *O Clap Your Hands* (SATB, Brass, Percussion). Boosey & Hawkes

Wagner, R.-Duelzman. *Elsa Entering the Cathedral* (Lohengrin) (SSAATTBB, Orch.). C. Fischer

Ward-Bennett. *America, the Beautiful* (SATB, Small Orch.). G. Schirmer 51771

H. PUBLICATIONS WITH ELECTRONIC TAPE OR NONCONVENTIONAL NOTATION

Electronic Tape (Usually a separate order number for the tape)

Bassett, Leslie. *Collect* (SATB). World Lib. Sacred Music CA2000-8

Felciano, Richard. *Hymn of the Universe* (SAB). E. C. Schirmer 2944

Felciano, Richard. *Out of Sight* (SATB). E. C. Schirmer 2909

Felciano, Richard. *Pentecost Sunday* (Unison Male, Organ). World Lib. Pub. EMP1532-1

Felciano, Richard. *Sic Transit* (SSA, Organ, Light). E. C. Schirmer 2807

Felciano, Richard. *Signs* (SATB). E. C. Schirmer 2927

Felciano, Richard. *Two Public Pieces: Cosmic Festival.* E. C. Schirmer 2938

Felciano, Richard. *Two Public Pieces: The Not-Yet Flower* (Unison). E. C. Schirmer 2937

Felciano, Richard. *Words of St. Peter* (SATB, Organ). World Lib. Pub. CA2093-8

Erb, Donald. *Kyrie.* (SATB, Piano, Perc.). Merion 342-40026

Pinkham, Daniel. *Alleluia, Acclamation and Carol* (SATB, Timp.). E. C. Schirmer 2954

Pinkham, Daniel. *Amens* (SATB). E. C. Schirmer 3016

Pinkham, Daniel. *Evergreen* (Unison, Opt. Insts.). E. C. Schirmer 2962

Pinkham, Daniel. *I Saw an Angel* (SATB). E. C. Schirmer 2973

Pinkham, Daniel. *In the Beginning of Creation* (Mixed Chorus). E. C. Schirmer 2902

Pinkham, Daniel. *The Call of Isaiah* (SATB, Organ). E. C. Schirmer 2911

Trythall, Gilbert. *In the Presence* (SATB). Ed. B. Marks 4495

Trythall, Gilbert. *A Time to Every Purpose* (SATB). Ed. B. Marks 4586

Nonconventional Notation

Butler, Eugene. *How Excellent Is Thy Name* (SATB, Speaking Chorus). Bourne 837

Browne, Richmond. *Chortos I* (Speech Choir). Flammer A-5629

Erb, Donald. *God Love You Now* (SATB) Merion 342-40099

Gaburo, Kenneth. *Ave Maria* (SATB A Cappella). World Lib. Pub. MO-985-8

Goemanne, Noel. *Song of Hope* (Insts. Speech Choir). G.I.A. G-1713

Hennagin, Michael. *The Unknown* (SSA, Speech Choir). Walton 2802

Homberg, Eskil. *Signposts* (SATB A Cappella). G. Schirmer 11842

Hopson, Hal. *Chant and Jubilation* (SATB, Organ, Drum, Speaking Chorus). Flammer

Kam, Dennis. *Two Moves and the Slow Cat* (SATB). Belwin 2282

Karlen, Robert. *Psalm 27, Part III* (SATB). AMSI 160

Lamb, Gordon. *Aleatory Psalm* (SATB). World Lib. Pub. CA-4003-8

Ludlow, Ben. *Let the Floods Clap Their Hands* (3 Part Speech and Perc.). Flammer A-5673

McElheran, Brock. *A Bilogy* (4 Part Chorus). C. Fischer CM7802

McElheran, Brock. *Etude and Pattern*. (SSAATBB). Oxford

McElheran, Brock. *Etude and Scherzo* (SSAATBB). Oxford

Mason, Vito. *Burst of Applause* (4 Part Chorus). Presser G-201

Nystedt, Knut. *All the Ways of a Man*. Augsburg 11-9004

Nystedt, Knut. *Praise to God* (Mixed, A Cappella). Associated A-597

Oliveros, Pauline. *Sound Patterns* (SATB, Speech Choir). J. Boonin B-111

Pfautsch, Lloyd. *Prelude and Dance for Voices and Hands* (SATB). C. Fischer CM7803

Pierce, Brent. *Down a Different Road* (SATB, Piano). Walton 2915

Pooler, Frank and Pierce, Brent. *The Rising Sun* (SATB). Somerset CE4328

Read, Gardner. *Praise Ye the Lord* (SATB). Lawson-Gould 51871

Reynolds, Roger. *The Emperor of Ice Cream* (Piano, Perc. Bass, Multi-Media). C. F. Peters

Schramm, Harold. *Canticle* (SATB). Capella Music, Inc.

Slogedal, Barne. *Antiphona De Morte* (Speech Choir). Walton 2903

Toch, E. *Valse* (SATB, Speaking Chorus). Belwin A-112

Weinland, J. D. *Anabathmos I* (Strings, Woodchimes). Walton M-116

I. EXTENDED CHORAL WORKS

Compiler's Note: Directors should exercise care in selecting large choral works for junior and senior high school voices. Many were written for adult voices and therefore ranges, phrasing, and overall vocal demands should be carefully considered.

SSA Extended Works

Britten, Benjamin. *Ceremony of Carols* (SSA). Boosey & Hawkes

Britten, Benjamin. *Missa Brevis in D* (SSA). Boosey & Hawkes

Britten, Benjamin. *Psalm 150* (SA). Boosey & Hawkes

Debussy, Claude. *The Blessed Damoiselle* (SSA, A). G. Schirmer

Faure, Gabriel. *Messe Basse* (Low Mass) (SSA). A. Broude

Pergolesi, G. *Stabat Matar* (SA, SA). G. Schirmer

Persichetti, Vincent. *Spring Cantata* (SSA). Elkan-Vogel

Persichetti, Vincent. *Winter Cantata* (SSA). Elkan-Vogel

Pinkham, Daniel. *An Emily Dickinson Mosaic* (SSA). C. F. Peters

Stainer, John. *The Crucifixion* (SSA). Novello

Thompson, Randall. *The Place of the Blest* (SSAA). E. C. Schirmer

Vaughan Williams, Ralph. *Folk Songs of the Four Seasons* (SSA). Oxford

Vaughan Williams, Ralph. *Magnificat* (SA, A). Oxford

Villa Lobos. *Mass in Honor of St. Sebastian* (SSA). Assoc. Music Pub.

Vivaldi, T. L. *Gloria* (SSA). Novello

SAB/SSCB Extended Works

Buxtehude, Dietrich. *In Dulci Jubilo* (SAB). Concordia

Distler, Hugo. *A Little Advent Music* (SAB). Concordia

Hamill, Paul. *A Candlelight Carol Service* (SAB). Flammer

Petzold, Johannes. *The Christmas Story* (SAB, Insts.). Concordia

Schubert, Franz-Kicklighter. *Mass in F* (SSCB). Cambiata Press

SATB Extended Works

Bach, J. S. *Christ Lay in Death's Dark Prison* (Cantata #4). G. Schirmer

Bach, J. S. *For Us a Child Is Born* (Cantata #142). Galaxy

Bach, J. S. *Jesu, Meine Freude*. C. F. Peters

Bach, J. S. *I Know That My Redeemer Lives* (Cantata #160). Galleon

Bach, J. S. *Now Thank We All Our God* (Cantata #192). G. Schirmer

Bach, J. S. *The Peasant Cantata*. Pattersons Pub. Ltd

Bach, J. S. *Sleepers, Wake* (Cantata #140). H. W. Gray

Bach, J. S. *A Stronghold Sure* (Cantata #80). G. Schirmer

Beethoven, Ludwig van. *Mass in C*, Op. 86. Broude Bros.

Bennett, Robert Russell. *Carol Cantata I, II, III, IV*. G. Schirmer

Bennett, Robert Russell. *The Many Moods of Christmas I, II, III, IV*. G. Schirmer

Berger, Jean. *Brazilian Psalm*. G. Schirmer

Berlioz, Hector. *Childhood of Christ*. G. Schirmer (H. W. Gray Abridged Ed.)

Bernstein, Leonard. *Chichester Psalms*. G. Schirmer

Bobrowitz, David and Porter, Steven. *The Creation* (Rock Cantata). Walton

Brahms, Johannes. *A German Requiem*. G. Schirmer

Brahms, Johannes-Shaw. *Liebeslieder Walzer* (Four-Hand Piano). G. Schirmer

Brahms, Johannes. *Nanie*. G. Schirmer

Britten, Benjamin. *Ceremony of Carols*. Boosey & Hawkes

Britten, Benjamin. *Choruses from Gloriana*. Boosey & Hawkes

Britten, Benjamin. *Festival Te Deum*. Boosey & Hawkes

Britten, Benjamin. *Rejoice in the Lamb*. Boosey & Hawkes

Brubeck, Dave. *La Fiesta de la Posada: Christmas Carol Pageant*. Shawnee Press

Buxtehude, D. *Good Christian Men, with Joy Draw Near*. Concordia

Buxtehude, D. *Rejoice, Earth and Heaven*. C. F. Peters

Buxtehude, D. *Sing to God the Lord*. Concordia

Burt, Alfred-Merman. *Star of Love*. (Burt Carol Cantata). Flammer

Carissimi, G. *Jephte*. Ricordi

Charpentier, Marc-Antoine. *Christmas Cantata*. E. C. Schirmer

Charpentier, Marc-Antoine. *Midnight Mass for Christmas*. Elkan-Vogel

Cherubini, Luigi. *Requiem Mass in C. Minor*. G. Schirmer

Clokey, Joseph and Kirk, H. *Childe Jesus*. Summy Birchard/Fred Bock

Copland, Aaron. *In the Beginning*. Boosey & Hawkes

De Cormier, Robert. *Shout for Joy* (Suite of Christmas Spirituals). Lawson-Gould

Dello-Joio. *The Mystic Trumpeter*. G. Schirmer

Dubois, Theodore. *The Seven Last Words of Christ*. G. Schirmer

Durufle, Maurice. *Requiem*. Durand

Faure, Gabriel. *Requiem*. H. T. Fitzsimons

Fine, Irving. *Alice in Wonderland Suite*. Witmark

Gregor, Christian-Kroeger. *The Prince of Peace is Come* (Moravian Christmas Cantata). C. Fischer

Haazen, Guido. *Missa Luba* (Mass in Congolese Style). G. Schirmer

Hammerschmidt, A. *O Beloved Shepherds*. Concordia

Handel, G. F. *Messiah*. G. Schirmer

Handel, G. F. *O Sing Unto the Lord*. G. Schirmer

Hanson, Howard. *The Cherubic Hymn*. C. Fischer

Hanson, Howard. *Song of Democracy*. C. Fischer

Haydn, Franz J. *Te Deum*. Assoc. Music Pub.

Hindemith, Paul. *Six Chansons*. Schott

Ives, Charles. *Psalm 90*. Theodore Presser

Mendelssohn, F. *Christus*. G. Schirmer

Mendelssohn, F. *Elijah*. G. Schirmer

Mendelssohn, F. *Hear My Prayer*. G. Schirmer

Mendelssohn, F. *St. Paul*. G. Schirmer

Mozart, W. A. *Missa Brevis in F*. G. Schirmer

Mozart, W. A. *Missa Brevis in D*. Arista

Mozart, W. A. *Requiem Mass*. G. Schirmer

Nystedt, Knut. *The Seven Words from the Cross*. Augsburg

Orff, Carl. *Carmina Burana*. Schott

Pachelbel, J. *Nun Danket Alle Gott* (Brass). Robert King Music

Pfautsch, Lloyd. *Gloria*. G. Schirmer

Pfautsch, Lloyd. *God With Us: Christmas Cantata*. Lawson-Gould

Pinkham, Daniel. *Christmas Cantata* (Brass). Robert King Music

Poulenc, F. *Gloria*. Salabert

Rutter, John. *Gloria*. Oxford

Rutter, John. *Requiem*. Oxford/Hinshaw

Rutter, John. *Fancies*. Oxford

Saint-Saens, Camille. *Christmas Oratorio*. G. Schirmer

Schubert, Franz. *Mass in F Major*. G. Schirmer

Schubert, Franz. *Mass in G Major*. G. Schirmer

Schutz, Heinrich. *The Christmas Story*. G. Schirmer

Stainer, John. *The Crucifixion*. G. Schirmer

Telemann, G.-Conlon. *Jesu, Joyous Treasure*. Augsburg

Thompson, Randall. *Frostiana*. E. C. Schirmer

Thompson, Randall. *The Peaceable Kingdom*. E. C. Schirmer

Thompson, Randall. *Testament of Freedom*. E. C. Schirmer

Vaughan Williams, Ralph. *Fantasia on Christmas Carols*. Galaxy

Vaughan Williams, Ralph. *Three Choruses from Shakespeare*. Oxford

Vivaldi, T. L. *Gloria*. Ricordi

TTBB Extended Works

Barker, S. *A Stopwatch and an Ordinance Map* (TTBB, 3 Timp., Brass). Schott 8799

Berlioz, Hector. *Choruses from The Damnation of Faust* (TTB/TB, Orch./Piano). Schott 567

Bernstein, Leonard. *If You Can't Eat You Got To* (TTBBBB, Tenor Solo, Bass, Perc.). Boosey & Hawkes 565

Brahms, Johannes. *Alto Rhapsody* (TTBB, Alto Solo, Orch./Piano). J. Fischer 8559

Britten, Benjamin. *The Ballad of Little Musgrave and Lady Barnard* (TBB, Piano). Boosey & Hawkes 8559

Cherubini, Luigi. *Requiem in D Minor* (TTBB, Orch./Piano). Peters S1

Des Pres, Josquin. *Missa Mater Patris* (TTBB). Schott 2642

Hanson, Howard. *Song of Democracy* (TTBB, Orch./Piano). C. Fischer

Hindemith, Paul. *The Demon of the Gibbett* (TTBB). Schott

Hoddinet, Alun. *Four Welsh Songs* (TTBB, Orch./Piano). Oxford Press 56.133

Holst, Gustave. *A Dirge for Two Veterans* (TTBB, Brass, Drums, Piano/Organ). G. Schirmer

Nelson, Ron. *Thy Will Be Done* (TTBB), Brass, Perc., or Piano). Boosey & Hawkes 557

Piston, Walter. *Carnival Song* (TBB, Brass or Four-hand Piano). Assoc. Music A-296

Pitfield. *A Sketchbook for Men* (TBB, B Solo, Strings, Perc., Piano). C. F. Peters H-268

Schubert, Franz. *Nachtgesang im Walde* (Night Song in the Forest.) (TTBB, Four Horns). Broude Bros.

Thompson, Randall. *The Testament of Freedom* (TTBB, Orch., Band, or Piano). E. C. Schirmer 2118

Villa-Lobos, Heitor. *Mass in Honor of St. Sebastian* (TTB) Assoc. Music Pub.

J. JUNIOR HIGH MIXED CHORAL COLLECTIONS

Ades, Hawley, and Hoggard, Lara. *Three to Make Music* (SAB). Shawnee Press

Ades, Hawley. *I Have Traveled with the Angels* (SCB). Shawnee Press

Beckman, Frederick. *More Partner Songs* (Two equal voices). Ginn

Beckman, Frederick. *Partner Songs* (Two equal voices). Ginn

Christiansen, F. Melius. *The Junior A Cappella Chorus* (SA, SSA, SATB).

Collins, Walter. *Christmas Medley* (Unison, SA, or SAB). Pro Art

Cooper, Gwendolyn. *Young Folk Sing* (SSCB). Bourne

Cooper, Irvin. *Accent on Singing* (SSCB). Charles Hensen

Cooper, Irvin. *Choral Music for Changing Voices* (SSCB). C. Fischer

Cooper, Irvin. *Descants for Jr. High Singing* (SCB). C. Fischer

Cooper, Irvin. *Junior High Choral Concert* (SSCB). C. Fischer

Cooper, Irvin. *Sing One, Sing All* (SSCB). Bourne

Cooper, Irvin. *Songs for Pre-Teen Time* (SA, SSC, SCB). C. Fischer

Cooper, Irvin. *Tunetime for Teen Time* (SSCB). C. Fischer

Cooper, Irvin. *Yultime for Teentime* (Unison, SC, SSCB). C. Fischer

Dart, Thurston. *Introduction to Madrigals*, Vol. I (SAB). Galaxy

Ehret-Gardner. *Hi-Lo* (2 Part). Staff

Gardner, Maurice. *Four in Harmony* (SACB). Staff

Gardner, Maurice. *Four-Way Chorister* (SA, SAT, SAB, SATB). Staff

Gardner, Maurice. *Tunes for Three or Four* (SAT, SATB). Staff

Glarum, L. Stanley, et al. *SSAB Choruses*. Schmitt

Hardin, Donna. *Familiar Christmas Carols for Changing Voices* (SA-CB). Cambiata Press

Hausmann, Charles, et al. *World of Choral Music*. Morristown, N. J.: Silver Burdett & Ginn

Hopson, Hal. *Christmas Classics* (SAB). Jenson

Jenkins, David and Visocchi, Mark. *Mix 'n Match: Instant Part Singing for Juniors*. Universal

Johnson, David N. *Easy Anthems for Mixed Voices, Books 1 and 2* (SATB). Augsburg

Kirk, Theron. *Cambiata Contempora* (SSCB). General Words & Music/Kjos

Kjelson, Lee. *I'd Like to Teach the World to Sing* (U, SA, SAT). Charles Hansen

Krone, Max, and Krone, Beatrice. *Descants and Easy Basses* (SAB). Kjos

Krone, Max, and Krone, Beatrice. *Songs from the Four Corners* (SSACB). Kjos

Perinchief, Robert. *Honor Your Partner*. Perry Pub., Whitewater, Wisconsin

Rhea, Lois. *Junior-Senior Hi in Song* (SAT, Opt. Bar.). Bourne

Riggs. *The Junior Hi Chorister* (SAB). Bourne

Rorke, Genevieve. *Sing by Fours* (SATB). T. Presser

Simeone, Harry. *Teach the World to Sing* (SAT). Shawnee Press

Simeone, Harry. *Youth Sings* (SB, SAB). Shawnee Press

Simeone, Harry. *Youth Sings at Christmas* (SAB). Shawnee Press

(Schirmer, G.) *Something to Sing About* (Selected Octavos from Texas ACDA lists for Junior High Mixed, Treble, and Male Chorus). G. Schirmer/Glencoe Pub. Co., Mission Hills, CA

Thomas, Dick. *Basic Repertoire for the Developing Choir* (Mostly SAB). J. W. Pepper

Thomas, Paul. *The SAB Chorale Book* (SAB). Concordia

Thygerson, Robert. *Comin' and Goin'* (SAT). Heritage Press

Thygerson, Robert. *Going, Going, Gone* (SAT). Heritage Press

Thygerson, Robert. *Here We Go Again* (SAT). Heritage Press

Tkach, Peter. *Junior Teen Age Singer* (SAC). Kjos

Tkach, Peter. *Teenage Singer* (SACB). Kjos

Trusler, Ivan. *SAB Chorister*. Warner Bros.

Wilson, Harry R. *Choral Program Series, Book 4* (SAB). Silver Burdett

K. SENIOR HIGH MIXED CHORUS COLLECTIONS

(American Book Co.). *ABC Choral Art Series, Vols. 1, 2, 3, 4.* (Mixed, Treble, and Male Voices). American Book Co.

(Associated Music). *Madrigals and Motets of Four Centuries* (SATB). Associated Music

Bach, J. S.-Goetschius, Percy. *Sixty Chorales* (SATB). Oliver Ditson/Presser

Buszin, Walter E. *Choral Music Through the Centuries* (SATB). Schmitt, Hall, McCreary

Buszin, Walter E. *101 Chorales Harmonized by Johann S. Bach*. Schmitt, Hall, McCreary

Cain, Noble. *Madrigals and A Cappella Choruses*. Schmitt, Hall, McCreary

Christiansen, F. Melius. *Choral Program Book, Vols. 1 and 2*. Augsburg Pub. House

Clough-Leighter. *The A Cappella Singer* (SATB). E. C. Schirmer

Dart, Thurston. *Invitation to Madrigals, Vol-2* (SATB). Galaxy

Davison, Archibald T., and Foote, Henry W. *The Concord Anthem Book* (SATB). E. C. Schirmer

Davison, Archibald T. and Foote, Henry W. *The Second Concord Anthem Book* (SATB). E. C. Schirmer

Dearmer, Percy; Vaughan Williams, R.; and Shaw, M. *The Oxford Book of Carols.* Oxford

Engel, Lehman, *Renaissance to Baroque, Vol. I: French-Netherlands Music.* Flammer

Engel, Lehman, *Renaissance to Baroque, Vol. II: Italian Music.* Flammer

Engel, Lehman. *Renaissance to Baroque, Vol. III: English Music.* Flammer

Engel, Lehman. *Renaissance to Baroque, Vol. IV: German Music.* Flammer

Engel, Lehman. *Renaissance to Baroque, Vol. V: Spanish Music.* Flammer

Einstein, Alfred. *The Golden Age of the Madrigal* (SATB). G. Schirmer

Harmon. *Oxford Book of Italian Madrigals* (SATB). Oxford

Hartshorn, William, et al. *Five Centuries of Choral Music.* G. Schirmer 2529

Jacques, R.; Willcocks, D.; and Rutter, J. *Carols for Choirs, Vols. I, II, III* (SATB).

Kirk, Theron. *Choral Art for Mixed Voices* (SATB). General Words & Music/Kjos

Kraus, Egon. *European Madrigals* (Mixed Voices). G. Schirmer 2601

Kraus, Egon. *More European Madrigals* (Mixed Voices). G. Schirmer 2837

(Lawson-Gould). *Selected Choruses for SATB.* Lawson-Gould/G. Schirmer

Ledger. *Oxford Book of English Madrigals* (SATB). Oxford Press

Lundquist, Matthew. *Chorales and Motets* (SATB). Summy Birchard

McKelvy, James. *Bach Chorales* (SATB). Mark Foster

Malin, Don. *Choral Perspective* (SATB). Marks Music Corp.

Malin, Don. *Rediscovered Madrigals* (SATB). Marks Music Corp.

Malin, Don. *Renaissance Choral Music* (SATB). Ed. B. Marks

Red, Buryl. *Choral Sounds, Vol. I, II, III, IV.* (Mixed, Treble, Male Choruses). Holt Rinehart Winston Co.

Rutter, John. *Joy to the World: Fifteen Sacred Carols and Christmas Hymns* (SATB). Hinshaw

Rutter, John. *O Holy Night: Thirteen Sacred Carols and Christmas Hymns* (SATB). Hinshaw

(G. Schirmer). *Christmas Chorales and Motets* (SATB). G. Schirmer

(G. Schirmer). *Something To Sing About, Vols. 1, 2, 3* (Selected Octavos from Texas ACDA Lists for Sr. High Mixed, Treble, and Male Chorus). G. Schirmer

Schott, Sally, et al. *Sing* (Text and Literature for Treble, Male, and Mixed Chorus). Hinshaw

Scott. *Invitation to Madrigals, Vol. 6* (SATB). Galaxy

Scott. *Invitation to Madrigals, Vol. 7* (SATB). Galaxy

Thomas, Paul. *A First Motet Book* (SATB). Concordia

Tischler, Hans. *A Medieval Motet Book* (Mixed Voices). Associated Music Pub.

Victoria, T. *Album of Hymns and Motets* (SATB). Belwin 6495

Willcocks, David, and Rutter, John. *100 Carols for Choirs* (SATB). Oxford Press

Wilson, Harry. *Choral Program Series*, Books 5 and 6 (SATB). Silver Burdett

L. TREBLE CHORUS COLLECTIONS

Ades, Hawley. *Sugar and Spice* (SSA). Shawnee Press

Appleby-Fowler. *First and Seconds* (SA). Oxford

Appleby-Fowler. *More First and Seconds* (SA). Oxford

Appleby-Fowler. *Seconds and Thirds* (SA, SSA). Oxford

Bell. *The Festival Song Book, Vol. 1* (Unison, SA, SSA). Mills

Bradley. *Schirmer's SSA Program Collection.* G. Schirmer

Brahms, Johannes. *Duets, Op. 20, 61, 66, 75* (SA). C. F. Peters 3909

Brahms, Johannes. *Twelve Songs and Romances, Op. 44, Set I.* Marks 105

Britten, Benjamin. *Friday Afternoon* (SA). Boosey & Hawkes

Dart, Thurston. *Invitation to Madrigals, Vol. 3* (SSA). Galaxy

Dart, Thurston. *Invitation to Madrigals, Vol. 4* (SA). Galaxy

Davis, Katherine K. *The A Cappella Singer* (SSA). E. C. Schirmer

Davis, Katherine K. *The Galaxy Junior Chorus Book* (SA). Galaxy

Davis, Katherine K. *Green Hill Junior Choir and Duet Book* (SA). E. C. Schirmer

Davis, Katherine K. *The Green Hill Three-Part Sacred Music for Women's Voices* (SSA). E. C. Schirmer

Di Lasso, Orlando, *Twelve Motets* (SA). Mercury Music

Ehret, Walter. *We Sing in Harmony* (SA). Belwin

Ehret, Walter. *The Youthful Chorister* (SA). Marks Music

Gearhart, L. and Ades, H. *A Christmas Singing Bee* (SA). Shawnee Press

Geer. *Fifteen Two-Part Christmas Carols* (SA). Shawnee Press

(G.I.A. Pub.). *Anthology of Polyphonic Masters, Book 2* (SA/SSA). G. I. A. Pub. 640

Hancock, J. *Thirteen Spirituals* (SA). H. W. Gray

Hartshorn, William. *Presser Choral Collection, Vol. 2.* Theodore Presser

Hood, Marguerite. *Art Songs for Treble Voices* (Unison, SA, SSA). Mills

Hood, Marguerite. *The Girls Book* (SSA). Ginn

Kraus, Egon. *European Madrigals* (Equal Voices). G. Schirmer

Marsh, Mary Val. *Choruses and Carols* (SA). Summy Birchard

Martin, Florence. *Christmas Carols for Treble Choirs* (SA, SSA). Schmitt

Matteson. *American Folksongs for Young Singers* (Unison, SA, SSA). G. Schirmer

Mendelssohn, Felix. *Duets for Two Parts* (SA). C. F. Peters 4747

Morley, Thomas. *Two-Part Cànzonets* (SA). C. F. Peters H-1998

Pooler, Marie. *Concert Time for Treble Voices* (SSA).

Pooler, Marie. *Descants on Sixteen Traditional Songs* (SA). G. Schirmer

(T. Presser). *Christmas Carols for Treble Voices* (SA). Theodore Presser

Rorke, Genevieve. *Sing by Threes* (SSA). Theodore Presser

Rossi, Nick. *Musical Masterpieces for Young Voices* (Unison, SA, SSA). MCA Music

(G. Schirmer). *Concert Choral Collection* (SSA). G. Schirmer

Schubert, Franz. *Two and Three Part Choruses for Women's Voices.* C. F. Peters 2639

Schumann, Robert. *Duets* (SA). C. F. Peters 2392

Stevens, Georgia. *Medieval and Renaissance Choral Music* (Equal Voices). McLaughlin & Reilly Co.

Strickling, George F. *SSA Carols for Christmas* (Opt. Handbells). Abingdon Press

Thomas, Paul. *The SSA Chorale Book.* Concordia

Willcocks, David, and Rutter, John. *Carols for Choirs, IV.* (SSA, SSAA). Oxford

Wilson, Harry R. *Choral Program Series, Bk. 1* (SA, SSA, SSAA). Silver Burdett

M. MALE CHORUS COLLECTIONS

Ades, Hawley. *Music, Men* (TTBB). Shawnee Press

Cain, Noble. *Songs for Boys* (TBB). Harold Flammer

Cassler, G. W. *Hymns for Men* (48 hymns for TTBB). Augsburg

Christiansen-Wycisk. *Selected Songs for Men* (57 sacred and secular male pieces).

Dart, Thurston. *Invitation to Madrigals, Vol. 4* (TB). Galaxy

Davison, Archibald. *Harvard Glee Club Collection* (Many separate male chorus octavos). E. C. Schirmer

Follett. *Library of Song for Male Voices* (Book 1-5). Pro Art/Belwin

Gearhart, L. and Hoggard, Lara. *Gentlemen Songsters* (TB, TTB, TTBB). Shawnee Press

Hansen. *Hymn Anthems for Male Voices* (TTBB). Kjos

Holler, John. *The Chapel Choir Anthem Book* (TTBB). H. W. Gray

Johnson, David N. *Eight Folksongs and Spirituals* (TTB). Augsburg

Johnson, David N. *Four Folksongs and Spirituals* (TTBB). Augsburg

Johnson. *Rise Up, O Men of God!, Vols. 1 & 2* (TTBB). Sacred Music Press

Krone, Max, and Krone, Beatrice. *Songs from Many Lands for Jr. High Boys* (TTBB). Kjos

(Lorenz). *Men's Get-Together Songs* (TTBB). Lorenz

Luboff, Norman. *Caroling, Caroling* (12 Carols for Male Chorus).

Morgan, Hayden. *Songs for Young Gleeman* (TB, TBB, TTBB). Schmitt Hal & McCreary

(Oxford). *Anthems for Men's Voices, Vols. 1 & 2* (TTBB). Oxford Press

(G. Schirmer). *Schirmer's Favorite Two Part Choruses for Boy's Voices* (TB). G. Schirmer

(SPEBSQSA). *Strictly Barbershop* (20 songs for barbershop chorus). SPEBSQSA

Strickling, George F. *Christmas Carols for Male Voices* (TTBB). Schmitt

Vandevere, J. Lillian, and Hopkin, Stuart B. *Birchard Choral Collection No. 1* (TTBB). Birchard

Weil, Kurt. *First Steps in Part-Singing* (TB, TTB, TBB). G. Schirmer

Wheeler-Wadsworth. *For Boys Only*. Associated Music Pub.

Wheeler-Wadsworth. *Jr. Hi Collection for Male Voices*. Assoc. Music Pub.

Wilson, Harry R. *Choral Program Series, Book 3* (TB, TTB, TTBB). Silver Burdett

Wilson-Ehret. *Salute to Music* (Unison, TB, TTB, TTBB). Boosey & Hawkes

N. VOCAL TECHNIQUE AND SIGHT-SINGING MATERIALS

Vocal Technique

Christiansen, Olaf C. *Voice Builder*. Kjos Music Co.

Craig, Don. *Twenty Choral Warmups*. Plymouth IC-101 (Octavo).

Emerson, Roger. *Choral Concepts*. Jenson 403-03414

Haaseman/Ehmann. *Voice Building for Choirs*. Hinshaw Music, Inc.

Haywood, Frederick H. *Universal Song*, Vol. I. G. Schirmer.

Heifetz, Josefa. *Preposterous Vocalises*. Kjos Music Co. V-80

Herman, Sally. *Building a Pyramid of Musicianship* (Kit). Curtis/Kjos Music Co. C8829

Jennings, Kenneth. *Sing Legato*. Kjos Music Co. V-74

McKinney, James C. *The Diagnosis and Correction of Vocal Faults*. Broadman 4268-11

Rinehart, Marilyn and Rinehart, Carroll. *Patterns to Part-Singing*. Kjos V-53

Tjernlund, Gordon and Eilers, Joyce. *Quickstarts, Vol. 1 Choral Warm-ups*. Jenson 402-17014.

Tkach, Peter. *Vocal Artistry: A Guide to Artistic Solo and Ensemble Singing*. Kjos V-21T

Tkach, Peter. *Vocal Technique*. Kjos V-17T.

Van Camp, Leonard. *Warmups for Minds, Ears, and Voice*. Lawson-Gould.

Sight Singing and Theory

Arkis, Stanley; and Schuckman, Herman. *An Introduction to Sight Singing*. C. Fischer.

Arkis, Stanley; and Schuckman, Herman. *The Choral Sight Singer*. C. Fischer.

Bauguess, David. *The Jenson Sight Singing Course: Vol. I; Vol. II; Part Exercises*. (in unison, two-part, and three-part using treble and bass clef). Jenson.

Boyd, Jack. *Teaching Choral Sight Reading*. Parker Pub. Available Mark Foster Music.

Carter, John; and Beall, Mary Kay. *Sol Fa, So Good!* (12 songs for children or junior high level utilizing Curwen hand signs, solfege). Somerset Press.

Cole, Samuel W.; and Lewis, Leo R. *Melodia—A Comprehensive Course in Sight Singing, Vols. I and II*. Oliver Ditson.

Collins, Don. *The Adolescent Reading Singer: The Kodály-Cooper-Collins Sight Singing Method* (Charts and accompanying booklet of graded arrangements and compositions for changing voice choirs). Cambiata Press.

Crowe, Edgar; Lawton, Annie; and Whittaker; W. Gillies. *The Folk Song Sight Singing Series* (earliest volumes useful). Oxford Press.

Edstrom, Richard. *The Independent Singer* (for junior–senior high level). Curtis/Kjos Music.

Ehret, Walter. *See and Sing*, Vols. I, II, III. Pro Art.

Hatcher, W.; and Petker, A. *Choral Skills #1/2, #1, #2*. Fred Bock B-G0511, 0276, 0510.

Nelson, Russell C. *Visual Solfege*. Kjos Music V-40.

Olvera, John/Schroth. *The Ups and Downs of Music*. Kjos Music V-36.

Rodby, Walter. *Let's Sight-Sing, Series A:* #1 Key of C Major (WR1031), #2 Key of G Major (WR1032), #3 Key of F Major (WR 1033), #4 Key of B^b and D Major (WR 1034). #5 Key of E$_b$ and A Major (WR1035), Somerset Press.

Steubing, Carl; and Wheeler, Rufus. *The Sol-Fa Book for Chorus and Choir* (Unison and Two-Part Sol/Fa Sight Singing). Dickson-Wheeler, Inc., Scotia, NY

Stone, Leonard. *Belwin Chorus Builder, Parts I and II*. Belwin-Mills.

Thompson, William; and McClard, LeRoy. *Developing Sightsinging Ability*. Broadman Press.

Whitlock, Ruth. *Choral Insights* (series on style periods, theory, vocabulary for choral singers). Kjos Music Co.

O. MUSIC THEATER SOURCES AND MATERIALS

Books

Hawthorne, Grace. *There's More to Musicals Than Music*. Carol Stream, IL: Somerset, 1980.

Novak, Elaine. *Performing in Musicals*. Schirmer-Macmillan Co., 1988.

Stahura, Raymond. *All About Musical Theater*. Portland, ME: J. Weston Walch, Pub., 1977.

Wright, Gene, and Lambson, Arthur. *The Staged Choral Concert*. Delaware Water Gap, PA: Shawnee Press, Inc., 1967.

Rental Scores, Costumes, and Makeup

Music Theatre International, MII Enterprises, Inc., 810 Seventh Ave., New York, NY 10022 (212) 975-6841

Northwestern Theatre Associates, 501 Ogden Avenue, Downers Grove, IL 60515 (312) 964-2528.

Pioneer Drama Service, 2172 S. Colorado Blvd., P. O. Box 22555, Denver, CO 80222.

The Rodgers and Hammerstein Theatre Library, 598 Madison Avenue, New York, NY 10022 (212) 486-0643.

Samuel French, Inc., 45 West 25th Street, New York, NY 10010 (212) 206-8990

Tams-Witmark Music Library, Inc., 560 Lexington Avenue, New York, NY 10022 (300) 221-7196.

Theatre House, Inc., 400 West Third Street, Covington, KY 41011 (606) 431-2414.

P.   EQUIPMENT AND INSTRUMENT SOURCES

Choir Apparel

Academic Choir Apparel, 6867 Farmdale Avenue, N. Hollywood, CA 91605

C. M. Almy & Son, Inc., 37 Purchase Street, Rye, NY 10580

Collegiate Cap & Gown Co., 1000 N. Market St., Champaign, IL 61820

DeMoulin/Monticello Gown Co., 1809 W. Bernice Ave., Chicago, IL 60613

Formal Fashions, Inc., 1500 W. Drake, Tempe, AZ 85283

Lyric Choir Gown Co., P. O. Box 16954, Jacksonville, FL 32216

E. R. Moore Co., 7230 N. Caldwell, Niles (Chicago), IL 60648

Southeastern Career Apparel, 58 Porter Square, Dothan, AL 36302

C. E. Ward, Inc., New London, OH 44851

Music Risers, Stands, Chairs, Music Cabinets

Gamble Music Co., 312 S. Wabash Ave., Chicago, IL 60604

Humes and Berg Mfg. Co., 4801 Railroad Ave., E. Chicago, IN 10003

Karnes Music Co., 2399 Devon Ave., Elk Grove Village, IL 60007

The Monroe Co., 316 N. Walnut St., Colfax, IA 50054

Peery Products Co., Box 8156, Portland, OR 97207

Wenger Corp., 555 Park Dr., Owatonna, MN 55060

Choral Music Folios and Filing Supplies

Carl Fischer Music Stores: 156 Boylston St., Boston, MA 02116
312 S. Wabash Ave., Chicago, IL 60604
54 Cooper Square, New York, NY 10003

Gamble Music Co., 312 S. Wabash Ave., Chicago, IL 60604

G.I.A. Publications, Inc., 7404 S. Mason Ave., Chicago, IL 60638

Kjos Music Company, P. O. Box 178270, San Diego, CA 92117

Mark Foster Music Company, Box 4012, Champaign, IL 61820

Malecki Music, Inc., 3404 S. Eleventh St., P. O. Box 411, Council Bluffs, IA 51502

J. W. Pepper: P. O. Box 850, Valley Forge, PA 19482
P. O. Box 3520, 552 Robbins Drive, Troy, MI 48084
P. O. Box 43186, 4273 Wendell Dr. S. W., Atlanta, GA 30336
P. O. Box 11736, Cor. 56th & Chelsea, Tampa, FL 33680

Shattinger Music Co., 1810 S. Broadway, St. Louis, MO 63104

Southern Music Co., 1100 Broadway, P. O. Box 329, San Antonio, TX 78292

Wingert–Jones Music, Inc., 2026 Broadway, Box 1878, Kansas City, MO 64141

Handbell Manufacturers

Bells of David, David Workman, 7037 Indiana Ave., Kansas City, MO

Malmark, Inc., 21 Bell Lane, New Britain, PA 18901

Petit & Fritsen Bell Foundry, Bellfounderstreet, Aarle-Rixel, Holland. USA Agent: G.I.A., 7404 S. Mason Ave., Chicago, IL 60638

Schulmerich Carillons, Inc., Carillon Hill, Sellersville, PA 18960

Trusonic Bells, Box 31-111, Los Angeles, CA

I. T. Verdin Company, 2021 Eastern Avenue, Cincinnati, OH 45202

Whitechapel Bell Foundry, 32 & 34 Whitechapel Road, London E1, 1DY, England

Orff Instruments

Augsburg Pub. House, Box 1209, Minneapolis, MN 55440

Gamble Music Co., 312 S. Wabash Ave., Chicago, IL 60604

Wm. Lewis & Son, 3000 Marcus Ave., Suite 2W7, Lake Success, NY 11042

MMB Music, Inc., 10370 Page Industrial Blvd., St. Louis, MO 63132

Music Education Group, 1415 Waukegan Rd., Northbrook, IL 60062

Suzuki Corporation, P. O. Box 261030, San Diego, CA 92126

Recorders, Guitars, Autoharps, Percussion Instruments

Gamble Music Co., 312 S. Wabash Ave., Chicago, IL 60604

Karnes Music Co., 2399 Devon Ave., Elk Grove Village, IL 60007

Lyons, 530 Riverview Ave., Elkhart, IN 46514

Oscar Schmidt-International, 1415 Waukegan Rd., Northbrook, IL 60062

Music Education Group, 1415 Waukegan Rd., Northbrook, IL 60062

Peripole. Browns Mills, NJ 08015

Rhythm Band, Inc., P. O. Box 126, Fort Worth, TX 76101

Suzuki Corp., P. O. Box 261030, San Diego, CA 92126

Choir Pins and Certificates, Safety Candles, Posters, Other Aids:

Augsburg Publishing House, Box 1209, Minneapolis, MN 55440

Award Company, P. O. Box 2029, Tuscaloosa, AL 35401

Bale Company, Dept. 1-2A, 222 Public St., P. O. Box 6400, Providence, RI 02940

Choristers Guild, 2834 W. Kingsley Road, Garland, Texas 75041

Dinn Brothers, Inc., P. O. Box 111, Dept. CD1, Holyoke, MA 01041

Gamble Music Co., 312 S. Wabash Ave., Chicago, IL 60604

Hanson House, 1722 W. Chanute Road, Peoria, IL 61615

Kjos Music Company, 4382 Jutland Drive, San Diego, CA 92117

Music in Motion, 122 Spanish Village, Suite 645, Dallas, TX 75248

Malecki Music, Inc., 3404 S. Eleventh St., P. O. Box 411, Council Bluffs, IA 51502

Q.   PROFESSIONAL ORGANIZATIONS AND JOURNALS

American Choral Directors Association
P. O. Box 6310
Lawton, OK 73506
Journal: *The Choral Journal*

American Choral Foundation
130 West 56th Street
New York, NY 10019
Journal: *American Choral Review*

American Guild of English Handbell Ringers, Inc.
601 West Riverview Drive
Dayton, OH 45406
Journal: *Overtones*

American Guild of Organists
815 Second Ave.
Suite 318

New York, NY 10017
Journal: *The American Organist*

American Orff-Schulwerk Association
Dept. of Music, Cleveland State University
Cleveland, OH 44115
Journal: *The Orff Echo*

Choristers Guild
2834 W. Kingsley Road
Garland, TX 75041
Journal: *Choristers Guild Letters*

Dalcroze Society of America
Ithaca College—School of Music
Ithaca, NY 14850
Journal: *American Dalcroze Journal*

Music Educators National Conference
1902 Association Drive
Reston, VA 22091
Journal: *Music Educators Journal*

Music Teachers National Association
2113 Carew Tower
Cincinnati, OH 45202
Journal: *American Music Teacher*

National Association of Teachers of Singing
c/o New York University
35 W. Fourth St. Room 778
New York, NY 10003
Journal: *The Bulletin*

Organization of American Kodály Educators
Music Department
Nicholls State University
Thibodaux, LA 70810
Journal: *Kodaly Envoy*

R. DIRECTORY OF PUBLISHERS

Aberdeen Music, Inc. (order from Plymouth Music Co.)
Abingdon Press, 201 Eighth Ave. South, Nashville, TN 37202
Addington Press (order from Hinshaw Music, Inc.)
Agape (order from Hope Publishing Co.)
Alexandria House, P. O. Box 300, Alexandria, IN 46001
Alfred Publishing Co., P. O. Box 5964, Sherman Oaks, CA 91413
Almo Publications (order from Columbia Pictures Pub.)

American Composers Alliance, 170 W. 74th St., New York, NY 10023

AMSI, 2614 Nicollet Ave., Minneapolis, MN 55408

Arista Music Co., 8370 Wilkshire Blvd., Beverly Hills, CA 90211

Associated Music Publishers, Inc., 866 Third Ave., New York, NY 10022

Augsburg Publishing House, 426 S. Fifth St., Minneapolis, MN 55415

Bärenreiter Music Publishers (order from European American Music Distributors Corp.)

Barry E. C. I., Argentina (order from Boosey & Hawkes, Inc.)

Beckenhorst Press, P. O. Box 14273, Columbus, OH 43214

Belmont Music Publishers, Box 231, Pacific Palisades, CA 90272

Belwin-Mills Publishing Corp. (order from Columbia Pictures Pub.)

Irving Berlin Music Corp., 1290 Avenue of the Americas, New York, NY 10019

Big 3 Music Corporation (order from Columbia Pictures Pub.)

Birch Tree Group, Ltd., 180 Alexander St., Princeton, NJ 08540

Blixt Publications, 413 Rutland Ave., San Jose, CA 95128

Fred Bock Music Co., P. O. Box 333, Tarzana, CA 91356

Boelke-Bomart, Inc., and Mobart Publications, Hillsdale, NY 12529

Joseph Boonin, Inc. (order from European American Music Distributors Corp.)

Boosey & Hawkes, Inc., 24 West 57th St., New York, NY 10019

Boston Music Company (order from Frank Music Affiliates)

Bourne Company, 5 West Thirty-seventh St., Sixth Floor, New York, NY 10018

Breitkopf & Härtel (order from Alexander Broude, Inc. or Associated Music)

Broadman Press, 127 Ninth Ave. North, Nashville, TN 37203

Alexander Broude, Inc., 225 W. 57th St., New York, NY 10019

Broude Brothers, Ltd., 141 White Oaks Rd., Williamstown, MA 01267

Byron-Douglas (order from Belwin-Mills Publishing Corp.)

Cambiata Press, P. O. Box 1151, Conway, AR 72032 (order from Birch Tree Group, Ltd.)

Chantry Music Press, 32 N. Center St., P. O. Box 1101, Springfield, OH 45501

Chappell Music (order from Theodore Presser Co. or Hal Leonard Pub. Corp.)

Charter Publications, Valley Forge Corp. Center, Valley Forge, PA 19487

Cherry Lane Music Co., Inc., P. O. Box 430, Port Chester, NY 10573

Chor Publications, Box 4037, Wichita, KA

Choral Art (order from Plymouth Music Co., Inc.)

Choristers Guild, 2834 W. Kingsley Road, Garland, TX 75041

John Church Company (order from Theodore Presser Co.)

Classic Artists Pub., 2904 Central St., Evanston, IL 60201

Franco Colombo Publications (order from Belwin-Mills Publishing Corp.)

Columbia Pictures Publications, 16333 N. W. 54th Ave., P. O. Box 4340, Hialeah, FL 33014

Concordia Publishing House, 3558 S. Jefferson Ave., St. Louis, MO 63118

Consolidated Music Publishers, Inc. (order from Music Sales Corp.)

Continuo Music Press, Inc. (order from Alexander Broude, Inc.)

Cooperative Recreation Service, Delaware, OH

Coronet (order from Theodore Presser Co.)

J. B. Cramer, London (order from Alexander Broude, Inc.)

Creative Jazz Composers, P. O. Box T, Bowie, MD 20715

Creative World Music Publications (order from Warner Bros. Publications, Inc.)

Criterion Music Corp., Joe Goldfeder, P. O. 666, Lynbrook, NY 11563

Curtis Music Press (order from Neil A. Kjos Music Co.)

J. Curwen & Sons (order from G. Schirmer, Inc.)

Dartmouth Collegium Musicum (order from Shawnee Press, Inc.)

Roger Dean Publishing Company (order from Lorenz Industries)

Oliver Ditson (order from Theodore Presser Co.)

Editio Musica, Budapest, Hungary (order from Boosey & Hawkes, Inc.)

Edition Musicus, 198 Selleck St., P. O. Box 1341, Stamford, CT 06904

Editions Salabert, Inc. (order from G. Schirmer, Inc.)

Edizione Suvini Zerboni, Milan, Italy (order from Boosey & Hawkes, Inc.)

Elkan-Vogel, Inc. (order from Theodore Presser Co.)

European American Music Distributors Corp., 2480 Industrial Blvd. Paoli, PA 19301

Fine Arts Music Press, P. O. Box 220128, Dallas, TX 75222

Carl Fischer, Inc., 62 Cooper Sq., New York, NY 10003

J. Fischer & Bros. (order from Belwin-Mills Publishing Corp.)

H. T. Fitzsimons Co., Inc., 357 W. Erie, Chicago, IL 60610

Harold Flammer, Inc. (order from Shawnee Press, Inc.)

Fortress Press, 2900 Queen Lane, Philadelphia, PA 19129

Mark Foster Music Company, Box 4012, Champaign, IL 61820

Sam Fox Publishing Company (order from Plymouth Music Co.)

Frangipani Press, P. O. Box 669, Bloomington, IN 47402

Frank Music Affiliates, 116 Boylston St., Boston, MA 02116

Galaxy Music Corporation (order from E. C. Schirmer Music Co.)

Gamut Co. (order from Southern Music Co.)

Genesis III Music Corp. (order from Plymouth Music Co., Inc.)

Gentry Publications (order from Alexandria House)

GlorySound (order from Shawnee Press, Inc.)

G. I. A. (Gregorian Institute of America), 7404 S. Mason Ave., Chicago, IL 60638

H. W. Gray Company, Inc. (order from Belwin-Mills Publishing Corp.)

Hansen Publications, Inc., 1870 West Ave., Miami Beach, FL 33139 or 1860 Broadway, New York, NY 10023

Harms, Inc. (order from Warner Bros. Publications, Inc.)

T. B. Harms Co. (order from Cherry Lane Music Co., Inc.)

The Frederick Harris Music Co., Ltd., 529 Speers Blvd., Oakville, Ontario, Canada L6K 2G4

Heritage Music Press (order from Lorenz Industries)

Heugel and Cie (order from Theodore Presser Co.)

Highgate Press (order from E. C. Schirmer Music Co.)

Hinrichsen & Peters (order from C. F. Peters Corp.)

Hinshaw Music, Inc., P. O. Box 470, Chapel Hill, NC 27514

Charles W. Homeyer & Co. (order from Carl Fischer, Inc.)

Hope Publishing Company, 380 S. Main Place, Carol Stream, IL 60187

InterVarsity Press, Downers Grove, IL 60515

Ione Press (order from E. C. Schirmer Music Co.)

Jenson Publications, Inc., P. O. Box 248, New Berlin, WI 53151

Edwin F. Kalmus & Co., Inc., Box 1007, Opa Locka, FL 33054

Kendor Music, Inc., P. O. Box 278, Delevan, NY 14042

E. C. Kerby, Ltd., 198 Davenport Rd., Toronto, Ontario, Canada M54 1J2

Neil A. Kjos Music Company, 4382 Jutland Dr., San Diego, CA 92117

Michael Kysar, Publisher (order from Alfred Publishing Co.)

Laudamus, 1810 S. Broadway, St. Louis, MO 63104

Lawson-Gould Music Publishers, Inc., 866 Third Ave., New York, NY 10022

Leeds Music (order from Belwin-Mills Publishing Corp.)

Hal Leonard Publishing Corp., 8112 W. Bluemound Rd., Milwaukee, WI 53213

Lorenz Industries, 501 E. Third St., Dayton, OH 45401

Manna Music, Inc. (order from Alexandria House)

Margun Music, 168 Dudley Rd., Newton Centre, MA 01259

Edward B. Marks Publishing Corp. (order from Hal Leonard Pub. Corp.)

McAfee Music Corporation (order from Belwin-Mills Publishing Corp.)

MCA Music (order from Belwin-Mills Publishing Corp.)

McLaughlin & Reilly Company (order from Summy Birchard Co.)

Mercury Music Corporation (order from Theodore Presser Co.)

Merion Music, Inc. (order from Theodore Presser Co.)

Miller Music Corporation (order from Big 3 Music Corp.)

Edwin H. Morris & Co., Inc. (order from Hal Leonard Music Co.)

Music Press, Tuskegee Institute (order from Neil A. Kjos Music Co.)

Music Sales Corporation, 33 W. 60th St., New York, NY 10023

Music 70 (order from Plymouth Music Co.)

National Music Publishers, P. O. Box 868, Tustin, CA 92680

North American Liturgy Resources, 10802 N. 23rd., Phoenix, AZ 85029

Novello Publications (order from Theodore Pressor Co.)

Oxford University Press, 200 Madison Ave., New York, NY 10016

Patterson's Pub., Ltd. (order from Carl Fischer, Inc.)

Paull Pioneer Publications (order from Shawnee Press, Inc.)

Pembrook Music Co., Inc. (order from Carl Fischer, Inc.)

C. F. Peters Corp., 373 Park Ave. South, New York, NY 10016

Plymouth Music Co., Inc., 170 Northeast 33rd St., Ft. Lauderdale, FL 33334

Theodore Presser Company, Presser Place, Bryn Mawr, PA 19010

Proclamation Productions, Inc., Orange Sq., Port Jervis, NY 12771

Pro-Art Publications (order from Belwin-Mills Publishing Corp.)

Psaltery Pub., P. O. Box 11325, Dallas, TX 75223

Remick Music Corporation (order from Warner Bros. Publications, Inc.)

Richler Publications, Inc., 2580 Thomasson Rd., P. O. Box 28218, Dallas, TX 75228

Richmond Music Press, Inc., P. O. Box 465, Richmond, IN 47374

G. Ricordi & Company (order from Associated Music Pub.)

Robbins Music Corporation (order from Big 3 Music Corp.)

Rongwen Music (order from Broude Brothers, Ltd.)

R. D. Row Music Co. (order from Carl Fischer, Inc.)

Sacred Music Press (order from Lorenz Industries)

E. C. Schirmer Music Company, 138 Ipswich St., Boston, MA 02215

G. Schirmer, Inc., 866 Third Ave., New York, NY 10022

Arthur P. Schmidt (no current address)

Schmitt Publications (order from Belwin-Mills Publishing Corp.)

Schott & Company, Ltd. (order from European American Music Distributors Corp.)

Scott Music Publications (order from Alfred Publishing Co.)

Shawnee Press, Inc., Delaware Water Gap, PA 18327

John Sheppard Music Press (order from European American Music Distributors Corp.)

Silver Burdett Co., 250 James St., Morristown, NJ 07960

Somerset Press (order from Hope Publishing Co.)

Southern Music Company, 1100 Broadway, P. O. Box 329, San Antonio, TX 78206

Spratt Music Publishers (order from Plymouth Music Co.)

Staff Music Publishing Co., Inc., 170 NE 33rd St., Ft. Lauderdale, FL 33334

Stainer & Bell (order from E. C. Schirmer Music Co.)

Studio P/R, Inc. (order from Columbia Pictures Pub.)

Summa Publications (order from AMSI)

Summy Birchard Co., 180 Alexander St., Princeton, NJ 08540 (order from Birch Tree Group, Ltd.)

Tetra Music Corp. (order from Alexander Broude, Inc.)

Thomas House Publications, P. O. Box 1423, San Carlos, CA 94070

Gordon Thompson, Ltd., 29 Birch Ave., Toronto, Ontario, Canada

Transcontinental Music Publications, 838 Fifth Ave., New York, NY 10021

Triune Music, Inc. (order from Lorenz Industries)

United Artist Music Co., Inc. (order from Big 3 Music Corp.)

Universal Editions (order from European American Music Distributors Corp.)

Volkwein Bros. Publications, Inc. (order from Columbia Pictures Pub.)

Walton Music Corp. (order from Hinshaw Music Co.)

Warner Bros. Publications, Inc., 265 Secacus Rd., Secacus, NJ 07094

Josef Weinberger, Ltd., London (order from Boosey & Hawkes)

Weintraub Music Co., 39 W. 60th St., New York, NY 10023

Westminster Press, 925 Chestnut St., Philadelphia, PA 19107

Willis Music Co., 7380 Industrial Rd., Florence, KY 41042

M. Witmark & Sons (order from Warner Bros. Publications, Inc.)

Word, Inc., P. O. Box 1790, Waco, TX 76703

World Library Publications, 2145 Central Parkway, Cincinnati, OH 45214

The Zondervan Corporation, 1415 Lake Drive SE, Grand Rapids, MI 49506

Bibliography

A. CHOIR ORGANIZATION AND ADMINISTRATION

Althouse, Jay, ed. *The School Choral Program* (Conversations with Besig, Nygard, Albrecht). E. Stroudsburg, PA: Music in Action, 1987.

Bessom, Malcolm F.; Tatarunis, Alphonse; and Forcucci, Samuel L. *Teaching Music in Today's Secondary Schools.* 2d ed. New York: Holt, Rinehart & Winston, Inc., 1980.

Collins, Don L. *The Cambiata Concept: A Comprehensive Philosophy and Methodology of Teaching Music to Adolescents.* Conway, AR: Cambiata Press, 1981.

Ehret, Walter. *The Choral Conductor's Handbook.* New York: Edward B. Marks Corp., 1959.

Hammar, Russell A. *Pragmatic Choral Procedures.* Metuchen, NJ: Scarecrow Press, 1984.

Holst, Imogen. *Conducting a Choir: A Guide for Amateurs.* New York: Oxford University Press, 1973

Hoffer, Charles. *Teaching Music in the Secondary Schools.* 3d ed. Belmont, CA: Wadsworth Pub. Co., 1983.

Lamb, Gordon. *Choral Techniques.* 3d ed. Dubuque, IA: William C. Brown Pub., 1988.

Roach, Donald W. *Handbook for Children's and Youth Choir Directors.* Garland, TX: Choristers Guild, 1987.

Roe, Paul F. *Choral Music Education.* 2d ed. Englewood Cliffs, NJ: Prentice-Hall, Inc., 1983.

Swears, Linda. *Teaching the Elementary School Chorus.* W. Nyack, NY: Parker Pub. Co., 1985.

The United States Copyright Law: A Practical Outline. Pamphlet published by Music Publishers Association, 130 W. 57th Street, New York, NY 10019.

B. VOCAL TRAINING AND CHORAL TEACHING

Armstrong, Kerchal; and Hustad, Donald. *Choral Musicianship and Voice Training.* Carol Stream, IL: Somerset Press, 1986.

Bartle, Jean Ashworth. *Lifeline for Children's Choir Directors.* Toronto, Canada: Gordon V. Thompson, 1988. (Available Oxford Press)

Bessom, Marcolm F.; Tatarunis, Alphonse; and Forcucci, Samuel L. *Teaching Music in Today's Secondary Schools.* 2d ed. New York: Holt, Rinehart & Winston, Inc., 1980. (See Chaps. 8 and 10.)

Christy, Van A. *Foundations in Singing.* 4th ed. Dubuque, IA: William C. Brown Pub., 1979.

Cox, Richard. *The Singer's Manual of German and French Diction.* New York: Schirmer Books, 1970.

Decker, Harold; and Herford, Julius. *Choral Conducting: A Symposium.* 2d ed. Englewood Cliffs, NJ: Prentice-Hall, Inc., 1988.

Decker, Harold; and Kirk, Colleen. *Choral Conducting: A Focus on Communication.* Englewood Cliffs, NJ: Prentice-Hall, Inc., 1988.

Eilers, Joyce. *Dealing with "Uncertain Singer" Problems through Careful Selection of Music.* New Berlin, WI: Jenson, 1979.

Hall, William D. *Latin Pronunciation According to Roman Usage.* Tustin, CA: National Music Pub., Inc., 1971.

Hassemann, Frauke; and Ehman, Wilhelm. *Voice Building for Choirs.* Chapel Hill, NC: Hinshaw Music, 1982.

Heffernan, Charles W. *Choral Music: Technique and Artistry.* Englewood Cliffs, NJ: Prentice-Hall, Inc., 1982.

Hoffer, Charles. *Teaching Music in the Secondary Schools.* 3d ed. Belmont, CA: Wadsworth Pub. Co., 1983. (See Chap. 11)

Kenney, James. *Becoming a Singing Performer: A Text for Voice Class.* Dubuque, IA: William C. Brown Pub., 1987.

Lamb, Gordon H. *Choral Techniques*. 3d ed. Dubuque, IA: William C. Brown Pub., 1988.

Lindsley, Charles E. *Fundamentals of Singing for Voice Classes*. Belmont, CA: Wadsworth Pub. Co., 1985.

Marshall, Madeleine. *The Singer's Manual of English Diction*. New York: G. Schirmer, 1953.

May, William, and Tolin, Craig. *Pronunciation Guide for Choral Literature*. Reston, VA: Music Educators National Conference, 1987.

Miller, Kenneth E. *Vocal Music Education*. Englewood Cliffs, NJ: Prentice-Hall, Inc., 1988.

Moe, Daniel. *Basic Choral Concepts*. Minneapolis, MN: Augsburg Pub. House, 1972.

Moriarty, John. *Diction: Italian, Latin, French, German*. Boston: E. C. Schirmer, 1975.

Pfautsch, Lloyd. *English Diction for the Singer*. New York: Lawson-Gould, 1971.

Roe, Paul F. Choral Music Education. 2d ed. Englewood Cliffs, NJ: Prentice-Hall, Inc., 1983. (See Chaps. 4, 5, 6, and 9)

Rao, Doreen. *Choral Music Experience* (Twelve Volumes on Children's Choral Singing). Farmingdale, NY: Boosey & Hawkes, 1987–.

Schmidt, Jan. *Basics of Singing*. New York: Schirmer-Macmillan, 1984.

Stanton, Royal. *Steps to Singing*. 2d ed. Belmont, CA: Wadsworth Pub., 1976.

Swan, Howard. *Conscience of a Profession*. Chapel Hill, NC: Hinshaw Music, 1988.

Trusler, Ivan; and Ehret, Walter. *Functional Lessons in Singing*. 2d ed. Englewood Cliffs, NJ: Prentice-Hall, Inc., 1986.

Trusler, Ivan. *The Choral Conductor's Latin*. Lanham, MD: University Press of America, 1987.

Vennard, William. *Singing: The Mechanism and the Technique*. Rev. ed. New York: Carl Fischer, Inc., 1967.

C. BOYS' CHANGING VOICES

Books

Collins, Don L. *The Cambiata Concept: A Comprehensive Philosophy and Methodology of Teaching Music to Adolescents*. Conway, AR: Cambiata Press, 1981.

Cooper, Irvin. *Letters to Pat*. New York: Carl Fischer, Inc., 1953.

Cooper, Irvin; and Kuersteiner, Karl O. *Teaching Junior High School Music*. 2d ed. Boston: Allyn and Bacon, Inc., 1970. (Reprinted by Cambiata Press)

McKenzie, Duncan. *Training the Boy's Changing Voice*. New Brunswick, NJ: Rutgers University Press, 1956.

Monsour, Sally; and Perry, Margaret. 2d ed. *A Junior High School Music Handbook*. Englewood Cliffs, NJ: Prentice-Hall, Inc., 1970. (See Chap. 2)

Swanson, Frederick J. *The Male Voice Ages Eight to Eighteen*. Cedar Rapids, IA: Laurance Press, 1977.

Articles

Adcock, Eva. "The Changing Voice—The Middle/Junior High Challenge." *The Choral Journal*. 23 (October 1987): 9–12.

Bragg, George. "The Adolescent Voice." *The Choral Journal* 11 (May 1971): 10–11.

Busch, Stephen E. "Some Voice Classifications and Developments in Young Adolescent Choirs." *The Choral Journal* 14 (September 1973): 22–24.

Coffman, Wesley S. "The Changing Voice—The Elementary Challenge." *The Choral Journal* 28 (October 1987): 5–8.

Collins, Don L. "The Changing Voice—A Future Challenge." *The Choral Journal* 28 (October 1987): 19–20.

Collins, Don L. "The Changing Voice—The High School Challenge." *The Choral Journal* 28 (October 1987): 13–18.

Conrad, Robert M. "Developing the Boy's Changing Voice." *Music Educators Journal* 60 (April–May 1964): 68–70.

Cooksey, John M. "The Development of a Contemporary, Eclectic Theory for the Training and Cultivation of the Junior High School Male Changing Voice, Part I, II, III, IV." *The Choral Journal* 18 (October 1977): 5–14; (November 1977): 5–16; (December 1977): 5–15; (January 1978): 5–18.

Diercks, Louis H. "The Detection, Care and Preservation of the Young Tenor." *Music Educators Journal* 51 (February–March 1965): 35–38.

Rice, William C. "Young Singers: Handle with Care." *Music Educators Journal* 49 (June–July 1963): 75–76.

Slaughter, C. H. "Those Dissonant Boys." *Music Educators Journal* 46 (February–March 1966): 110–112.

Swanson, Frederick J. "The Changing Voice: An Adventure, Not a Hazzard." *The Choral Journal* 16 (March 1976): 5–14.

Swanson, Frederick J. "Changing Voices: Don't Leave Out the Boys." *Music Educators Journal* 70 (January 1984): 47–50.

D.   CONDUCTING TECHNIQUES

Busch, Brian R. *The Complete Choral Conductor*. New York: Schirmer Books, 1984.

Decker, Harold; and Herford, Julius. *Choral Conducting: A Symposium.* 2d ed. Englewood Cliffs, NJ: Prentice-Hall, Inc., 1988.

Decker, Harold; and Kirk, Colleen. *Choral Conducting: A Focus on Communication.* Englewood Cliffs, NJ: Prentice-Hall, Inc., 1988.

Garretson, Robert. *Conducting Choral Music.* 6th ed. Englewood Cliffs, NJ: Prentice-Hall, Inc., 1988. (See Chap. 1.)

Lamb, Gordon. *Choral Techniques.* 3d ed. Dubuque, IA: William C. Brown Co., Pub., 1988. (See Chap. 1.)

McElheran, Brock. *Conducting Technique.* New York: Oxford University Press, 1966.

Moe, Daniel. *Problems in Conducting.* Minneapolis, MN: Augsburg Pub. House, 1973.

Roe, Paul F. *Choral Music Education.* 2d ed. Englewood Cliffs, NJ: Prentice-Hall, Inc., 1983. (See Chap. 8.)

Simons, Harriet. *Choral Conducting: A Leadership Teaching Approach.* Champaign, IL: Mark Foster Music Co., 1983.

E.   CHORAL MUSIC REPERTOIRE AND INTERPRETATION

Adler, Samuel. *Choral Conducting: An Anthology.* 2d ed. New York: Holt, Rinehart, and Winston, 1985.

Dart, Thurston. *Interpretation of Music.* Rev. ed. London: Hutchinson University Library, 1960.

Drotleff, John E. "Renaissance Music for Junior High School Singers." *The Choral Journal* 16 (January 1976): 5–6.

Garretson, Robert L. *Conducting Choral Music.* 6th ed. Englewood Cliffs, NJ: Prentice-Hall, Inc., 1988. (See Chap. 3.)

Hawkins, Margaret B. (ed.). *An Annotated Inventory of Distinctive Choral Literature for Performance at the High School Level.* Monograph No. 2. Lawton, OK: American Choral Directors Association, 1976.

Kjelson, Lee; and McCray, James. *The Conductor's Manual of Choral Music Literature.* Melville, NY: Belwin-Mills Pub. Corp., 1973.

Lamb, Gordon. *Choral Techniques.* 3d ed. Dubuque, IA: William C. Brown Co., Pub., 1988. (See Chaps. 2, 3, 7, 11, and App. A.)

Laster, James. *Catalogue of Choral Music Arrranged in Biblical Order.* Metuchen, NJ: Scarecrow Press, 1983.

Pooler, Frank; and Pierce, Brent. *New Choral Notation.* New York: Walton Music Corp., 1971.

Robinson, Ray; and Winold, Allen. *The Choral Experience.* New York: Harper and Row, 1976.

Robinson, Ray. *Choral Music: An Anthology*. New York: W. W. Norton and Co., 1978.

Selective Music Lists: *Vocal Solos and Vocal Ensembles*. Reston, VA: Music Educators National Conference, 1985.

Ulrich, Homer. *A Survey of Choral Music*. New York: Harcourt Brace Jovanovich, Inc., 1973.

White, J. Perry. *Twentieth Century Choral Music: An Annotated Bibliography of Music Suitable for Use by High School Choirs*. Metuchen, NJ: Scarecrow Press, 1982.

Young, Allen (ed.). *Choral Educators Resource Handbook*. San Francisco, CA: Choral Resource Seminars, 1985.

F.   JAZZ AND SHOW CHOIR

Books

Albrecht, Sally K. *Choral Music in Motion*. Delaware Water Gap, PA: Shawnee Press, 1984.

Anderson, Doug. *Jazz and Show Choir Handbook*. Chapel Hill, NC: Hinshaw Music, Inc., 1978.

Garretson, Robert L. *Conducting Choral Music*. 6th ed. Englewood Cliffs, NJ: Prentice-Hall, Inc., 1988. (See Chap. 5, The Jazz/Show Choir)

Jacobson, John. *Dance Warm-Ups and Workouts for the Show Choir* (Booklet and one LP Recording). New Berlin, WI: Jenson Pub., 1984.

Shaw, Kirby. *Vocal Jazz Style*. Milwaukee, WI: Hal Leonard, 1976. (Manual, Books, Tape)

Spolin, Viola. *Improvisation for the Theatre*. Evanston, IL: Northwestern University Press, 1963.

Strommen, Carl. *The Contemporary Choir: Jazz, Pop, and Rock*. Sherman Oaks, CA: Alfred Publishing Co., 1980.

Articles

Aitken, Gene. "Individual Miking." *Jazz Educators Journal* 17 (February–March 1985), 47–59.

_____. "Individual Miking the Set-Up and Rehearsal." *Jazz Educators Journal* 18 (October–November 1985), 17–18, 53.

_____. "Rehearsal Techniques." *Jazz Educators Journal* 16 (February–March 1984), 56–59.

_____. "Rehearsal Techniques." *Jazz Educators Journal* 16 (April–May 1984), 68–70.

_____. "Vocal Jazz Techniques." *Jazz Educators Journal* 17 (October–November 1984), 22–23.

_____. "Vocal Jazz Vibrato." *Jazz Educators Journal* 17 (October–November 1984), 16–17.

Albrecht, Sally K. "Choral Music in Motion." *Pop, Jazz & Show Choir Magazine* 3 (Fall 1985), 21–27.

Anderson, Doug. "A Conversation with Jack Kunz." *Pop, Jazz & Choir Magazine* 1 (Fall 1984), 12–14.

_____. "The Phil Mattson School." *Pop, Jazz & Show Choir Magazine* 2 (Spring 1985), 14–16.

Borla, Janice. "Key Selection for the Solo Vocalist." *Jazz Educators Journal* 18 (October–November 1985), 14–16.

Cryder, John. "Getting the Most from a Sound System." *Pop, Jazz & Show Choir Magazine* 2 (Spring 1985), 10–13.

Dwiggins, Rose R. "One Step at a Time for Show Choirs." *Music Educators Journal* 70 (February 1984), 41–45.

Edwards, Jim. "How to Mike Jazz, Swing and Show Choirs." *Pop, Jazz & Show Choir Magazine* 1 (Fall 1984), 26–29.

Fredrickson, Scott. "Gene Puerling: An Exclusive Interview." *Pop, Jazz & Show Choir Magazine* 2 (Spring 1985), 5–9.

_____. "Vocal Improvisation: A Practical Approach." *Pop, Jazz & Show Choir Magazine* 1 (Fall 1984), 22–24.

Grier, Audrey. "Choreography for a Large Ensemble: A Checklist." *Pop, Jazz & Show Choir Magazine* 2 (Spring 1985), 21–22.

_____. "Choreography Guidelines for the Swing and Show Choir Director." *Pop, Jazz & Show Choir Magazine* 1 (Fall 1984), 8–11.

_____. "How to Choreograph a Picture." *Pop, Jazz & Show Choir Magazine* 3 (Fall 1985), 10.

Grier, Gene. "Adjudication: A View from the Other Side." *Pop, Jazz & Show Choir Magazine* 1 (Fall 1984), 19–21.

_____ and Grier, Audrey. "Adjudication: Some Things to Think About." *Choral Journal* 26 (March 1986), 40–41.

_____. "Female Show Choirs." *Pop, Jazz & Show Choir Magazine* 3 (Fall 1985), 11–13.

Moriarty, Kevin. "A New Look at Show Choir Choreography." *Pop, Jazz & Show Choir Magazine* 3 (Fall 1985), 11–13.

Rinzler, Paul. "Does Vocal Jazz Really Hurt the Voice?" *Jazz Educators Journal* 18 (October–November 1985), 12–13, 75.

Schwartz, Dan. "Resources for the Jazz and Show Choir Through November, 1983." *Choral Journal* 24 (February 1984), 25–26.

_____. "A Selected Listing of SATB Gospel or Gospel Oriented Choral Arrangements." *Choral Journal* 24 (March 1984), 27.

_____. "Supplement #3 to A Comprehensive List of Medleys Published for SATB, SAB, SSA, and Two-Part Choirs." *Choral Journal* 24 (March 1984), 28.

_____. "Supplement #18 to A Selected List of Choral Arrangements." *Choral Journal* 26 (September 1985), 35, 37, 39.

Schwartz, Dan, et al. "Will Movement or Choreography Improve Your Group's Performances?" *Choral Journal* 25 (October 1984), 21–24.

Thoms, Paul. "Show Choir Research: An Important Study." *Choral Journal* 25 (March 1985), 22–23.

Index